AF539622

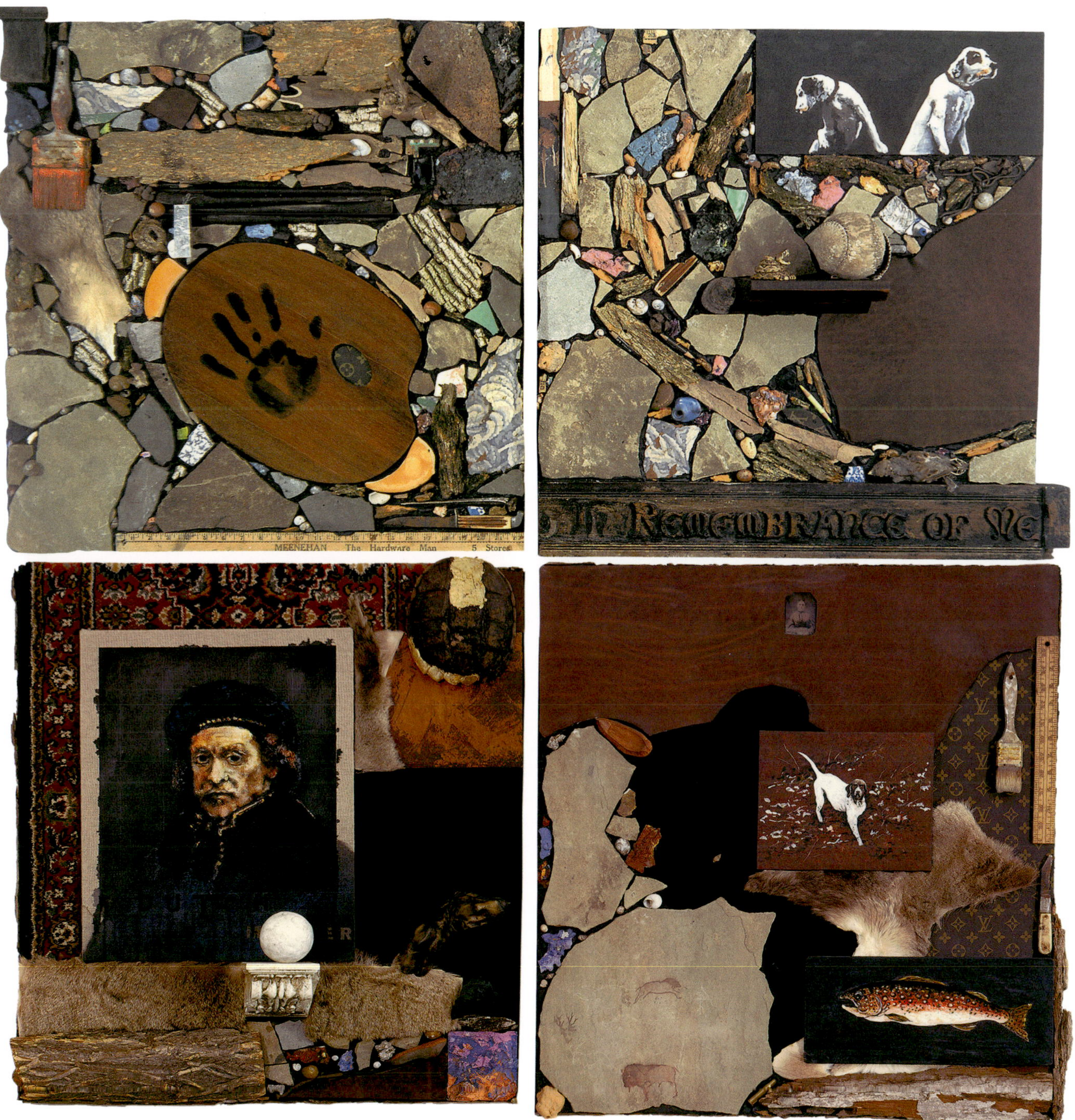
MEENEHAN The Hardware Man 5 Stores
In Remembrance of Me

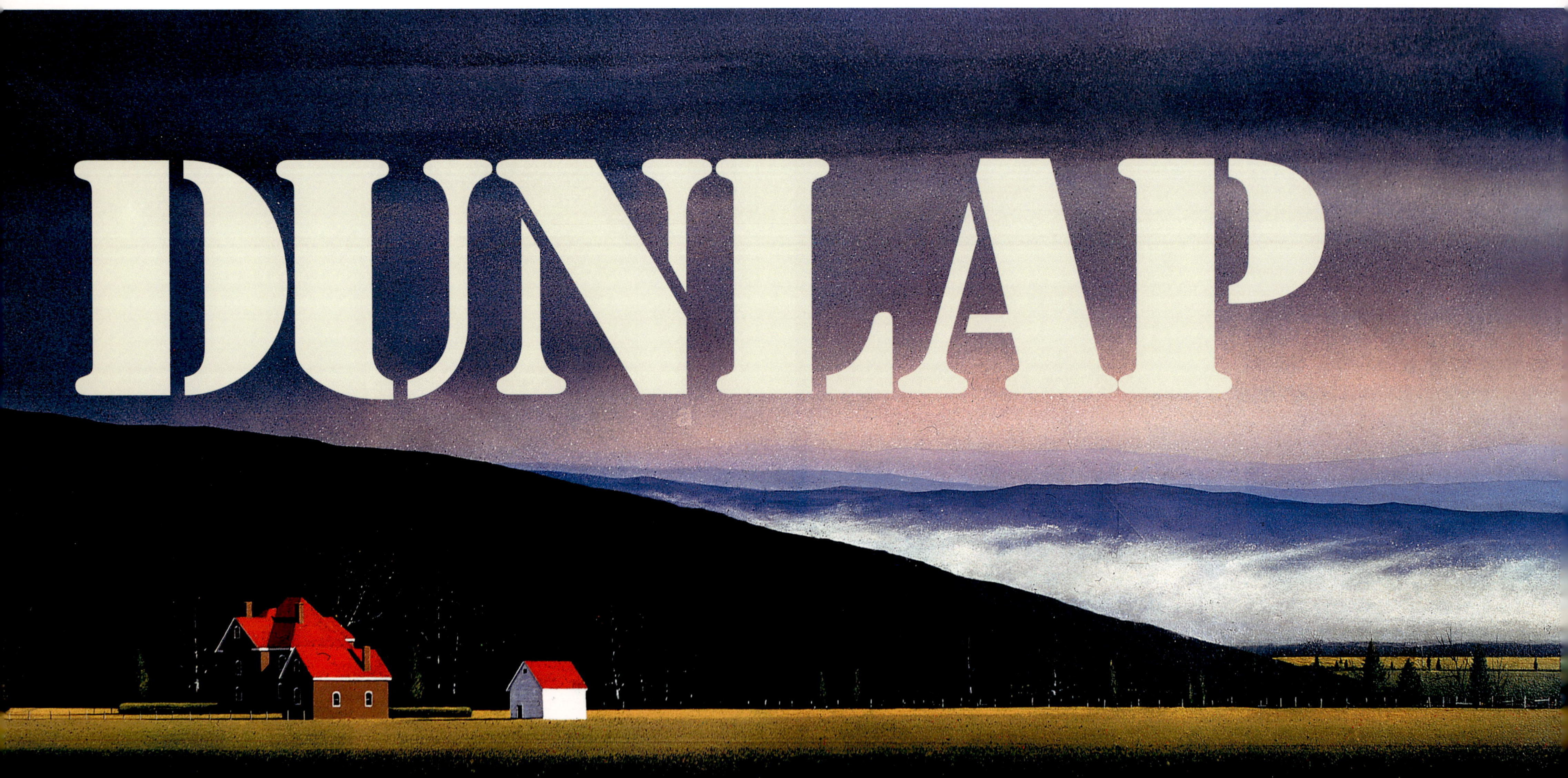
DUNLAP

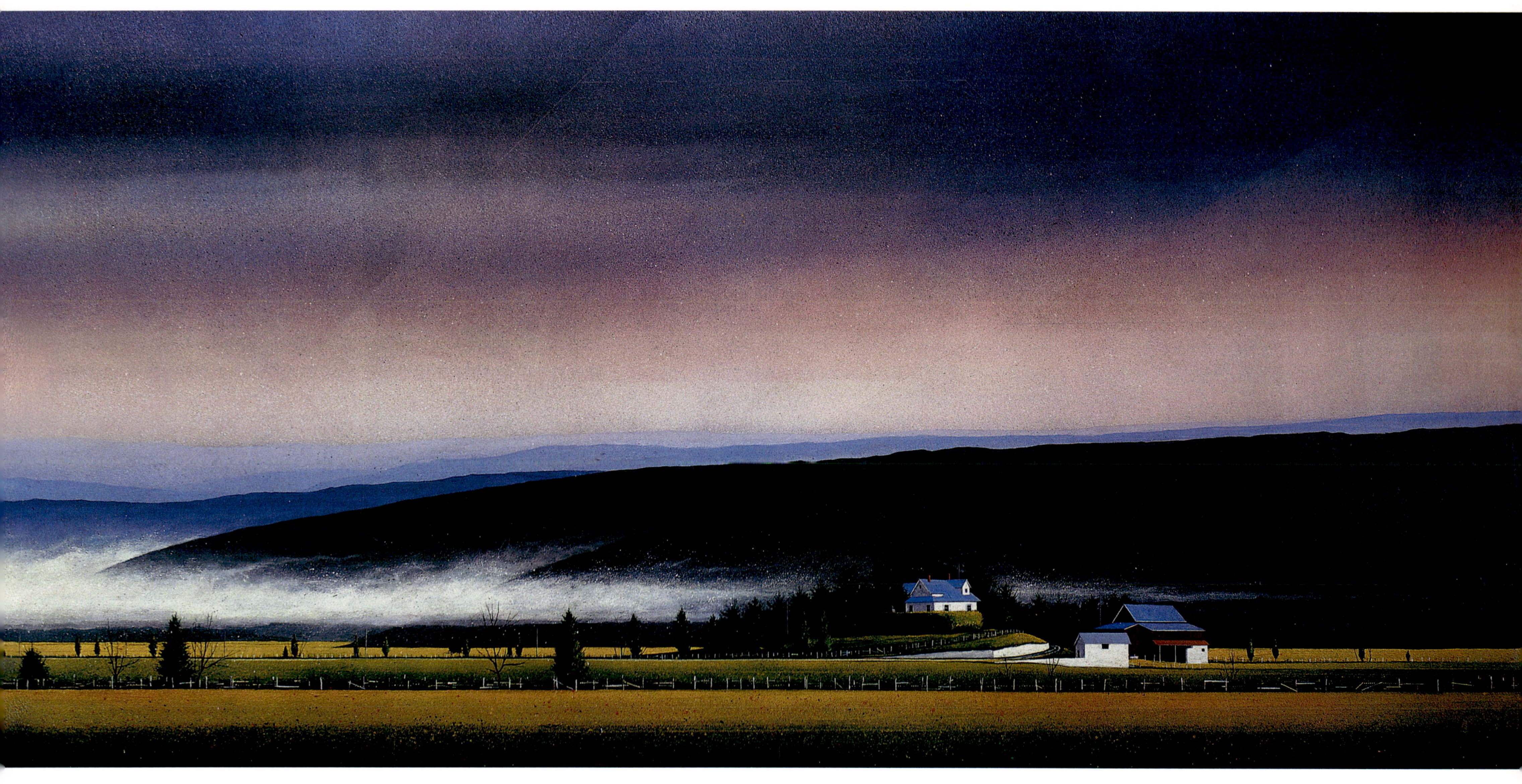

William Dunlap

Foreword by Julia Reed   Essay by J. Richard Gruber   University Press of Mississippi / Jackson

To all those who have come before . . .
and our great mutual place

Major funding for publication provided by

Lawrence and Jan Farrington
Hiatt-Ingram Fund of the Community Foundation of Greater Jackson
Luther H. Hodges, Jr.
James V. Kimsey
Lucio A. Noto

Additional funding provided by

J. Stewart Bryan
F. Borden Hanes, Jr.
Governor Ray Mabus
John N. Palmer Foundation
Lili-Charlotte Sarnoff
Walker Foundation

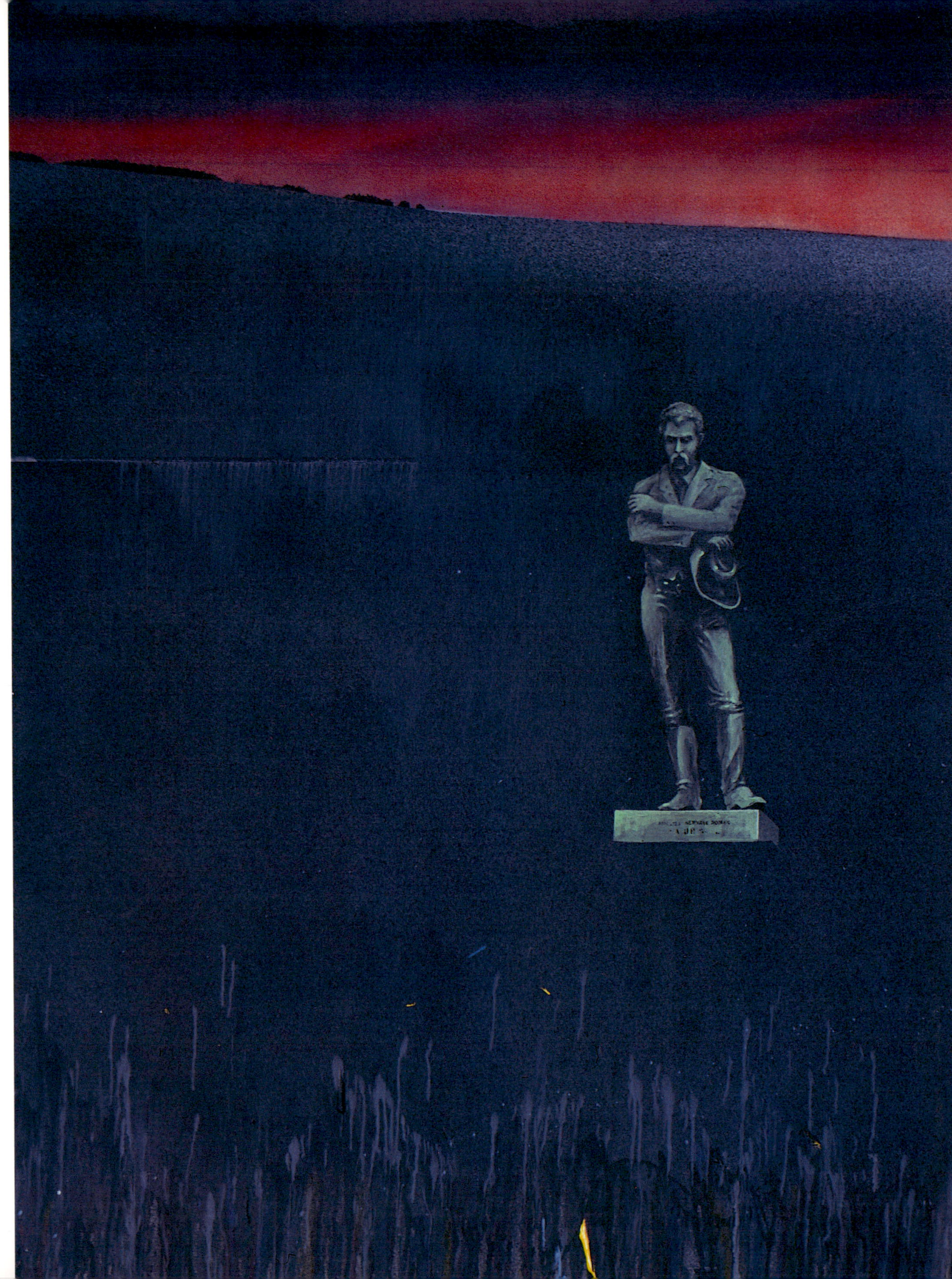

FOREWORD

by Julia Reed

It is astonishing to me that Bill Dunlap and I did not become the close friends that we are now until well into the 1990s. We both grew up in Mississippi, we both, in the words of Willie Morris, traveled "north toward home"—our time in Washington, D.C., where Bill still lives part of the year, overlapped for years. But fittingly, it was on Southern soil, in New Orleans, at Galatoire's to be precise, that our friendship was forged. We met for lunch as two acquaintances with a hundred people in common; seven hours (and many bottles of expensive white burgundy) later I could not remember a time when he hadn't been in my life. These days, we joke that it's a good thing we didn't, in fact, meet during our wilder days—we act bad enough together now.

If to know Bill is to feel as though you've known him forever, let me hasten to add that that's a good thing. He's what the Brits call a life-enhancer. A tireless networker, he's forever dragging me off to meet people I think I don't want to meet, and then of course, they end up enhancing my life too—or at least entertaining me a bit. He has pulled me out of the doldrums, out of tight spots, and sometimes, literally, out of the house to go off on another of our long lunches. I never regret the latter. They are always uproarious (because few people are as funny) and celebratory (because I don't know anybody who loves life more) and creative (many a Dunlap masterpiece has been lost to the Galatoire's laundry). We have toasted the living and the dead, made grandiose plans, and engaged in seemingly brilliant conversation. The maddening thing about Bill is that even in the sober light of the next day, his end of things still seems brilliant.

A fast-talking son of a preacher man, he is not very high on Baptists these days, but I have no doubt he could get a tent full of people speaking in tongues in no time. There are worse things than getting saved by Brother William, and all of us in one way or another have testified before him. Bill is so generous with himself that he makes you want to be too. He has contributed time and energy and art to countless causes, large and small, not least of which, in my mother's view, was the salvation of a cherished bald cypress grove in the Mississippi Delta. My affiliation with, and love for, the Ogden Museum of Southern Art in New Orleans, is a direct result of Bill's benevolent meddling.

Bill is equally comfortable in the rarified air of Gore Vidal's terrace in Ravello, Italy, as on the front porch of his family home in Mathiston, Mississippi, which he stubbornly maintains. Though he's an old-fashioned liberal, I attended a half-dozen parties with him during George W. Bush's second inauguration, our passage made easier by Bill's skill at talking us past barricades my press pass was powerless to get us through. At one event he marched up to a woman he'd never seen before and asked in mock indignation, "Who did that to you?" referring to her eccentric hairdo. I watched dumbfounded, a little afraid actually (this was a formidable woman and her husband was within earshot), but after a beat she gave him a big grin and ten minutes into it I swear he'd sold her a painting.

My favorite quality in people is their willingness to show up. Bill has that in spades. We've been in a lot of places together—at a table with a Nobel Prize–winning neuroscientist, at my rehearsal dinner in an abandoned cotton gin in Tribett, Mississippi, in a swanky skybox at an Ole Miss/Alabama football game (where there was an inevitable Dunlap on the wall). But no matter where we are he always uses his laser eye to hone in on the essence of things and he expresses it in words as well as he does with paint. A month or so after 9/11, he attended a party at my apartment in New York. There were lots of people there to celebrate the publication of a friend's book, as well as the mere fact of gathering after such a horrific event. Bill flew in for the night and wrote me a note afterward, briefly describing an encounter I hadn't noticed between two guests, and it summed up the whole evening brilliantly. It takes hours to decipher his handwriting, but it's always worth it, and this note went into my box of other Dunlap notes, to be taken out and reread on otherwise gray days.

On one literally gray day in Washington, during that same Bush inaugural, Bill arranged a lunch that remains one of my fondest memories. Dressed in his ubiquitous navy blazer, tie, and silk pocket square, he met us at the door of the august Cosmos Club, whose members have included presidents and Supreme Court justices, famous explorers and inventors—and, naturally, Bill. He'd reserved the atrium, a cozy room with bookshelves and gorgeous leaded windows, and around the round table were my parents and my husband, Bill's wife Linda Burgess and their daughter Maggie, and a small group of Mississippi folks including one of our senators and the wife of the governor, whose Mississippi highway patrol driver had an especially difficult time finding the place. Enormous snowflakes fell onto the courtyard outside, the wine flowed, and Maggie, a budding artist already as at home in the world as her parents, entertained herself with her sketchpad.

On that day, like so many others, Bill was the impresario, planning the menu, running the show—but not for any other reason than to gather us all, a group of people who loved and enjoyed each other. Family and friends are of paramount importance to Bill. He knows the importance of being a witness, but he'll also turn up just because you call. When he does, he generally drinks up fine, twenty-five-year-old Macallan whiskey, but in return he supplies that rarest of commodities, good company. What does all this have to do with art, you may well ask. A lot. The generosity, the curiosity and range of experience, the right-on eye and lightning wit, the prodigious gifts of verbal and written expression, they are all what makes him such a great friend and boon companion. But they also make him the artist he is. Who else would consider themselves qualified to comment on "What Dogs Dream"? Hell, he may really know.

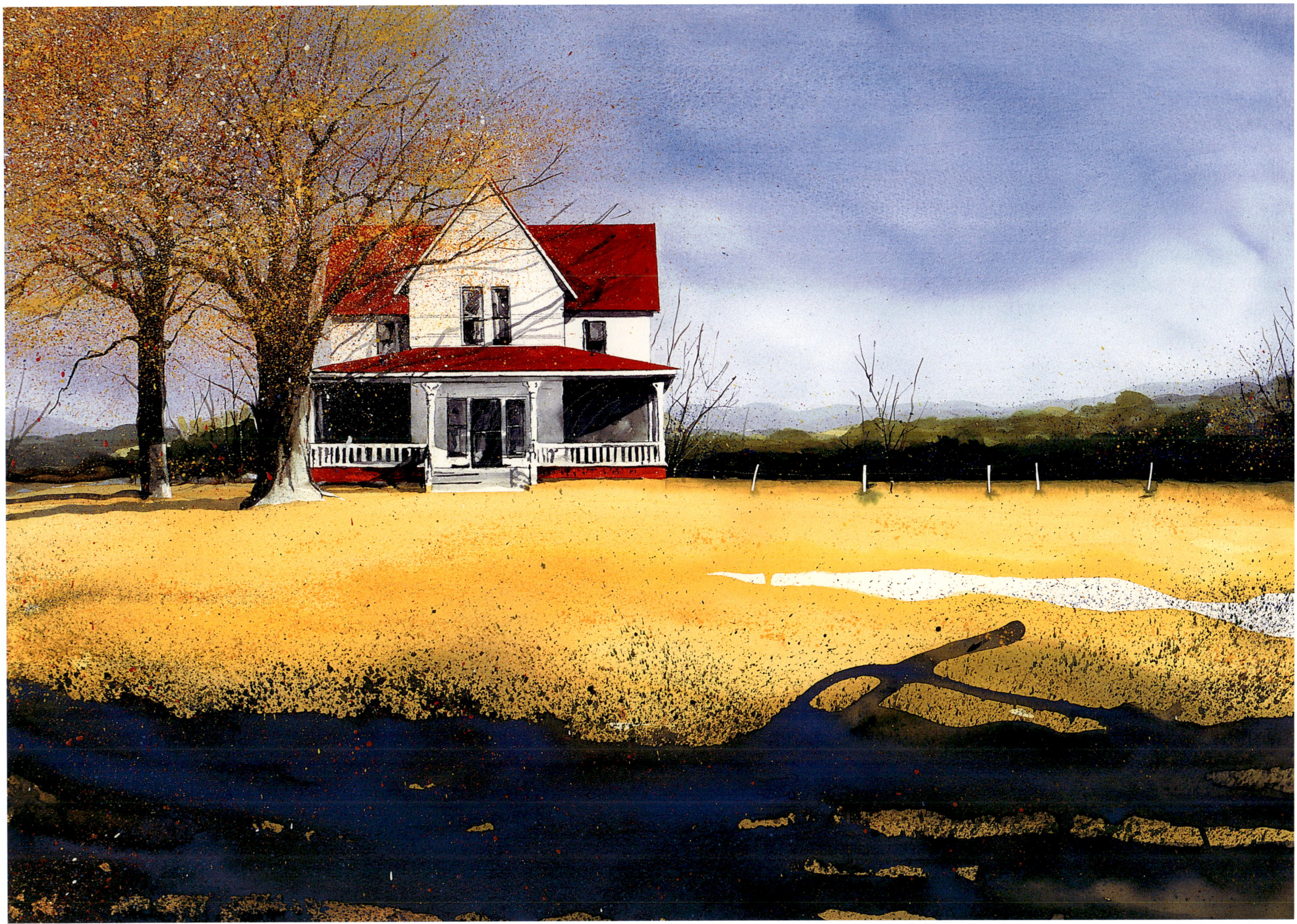

Starnes House, Mathiston, Mississippi, 1971
Watercolor and polymer paint on paper, 22 x 30.
Collection of Museum of Mississippi History,
Mississippi Department of Archives and History,
Jackson. 1974.37. Photograph by Hubert Worley.

Dimensions throughout are given in inches
(height x width x depth).

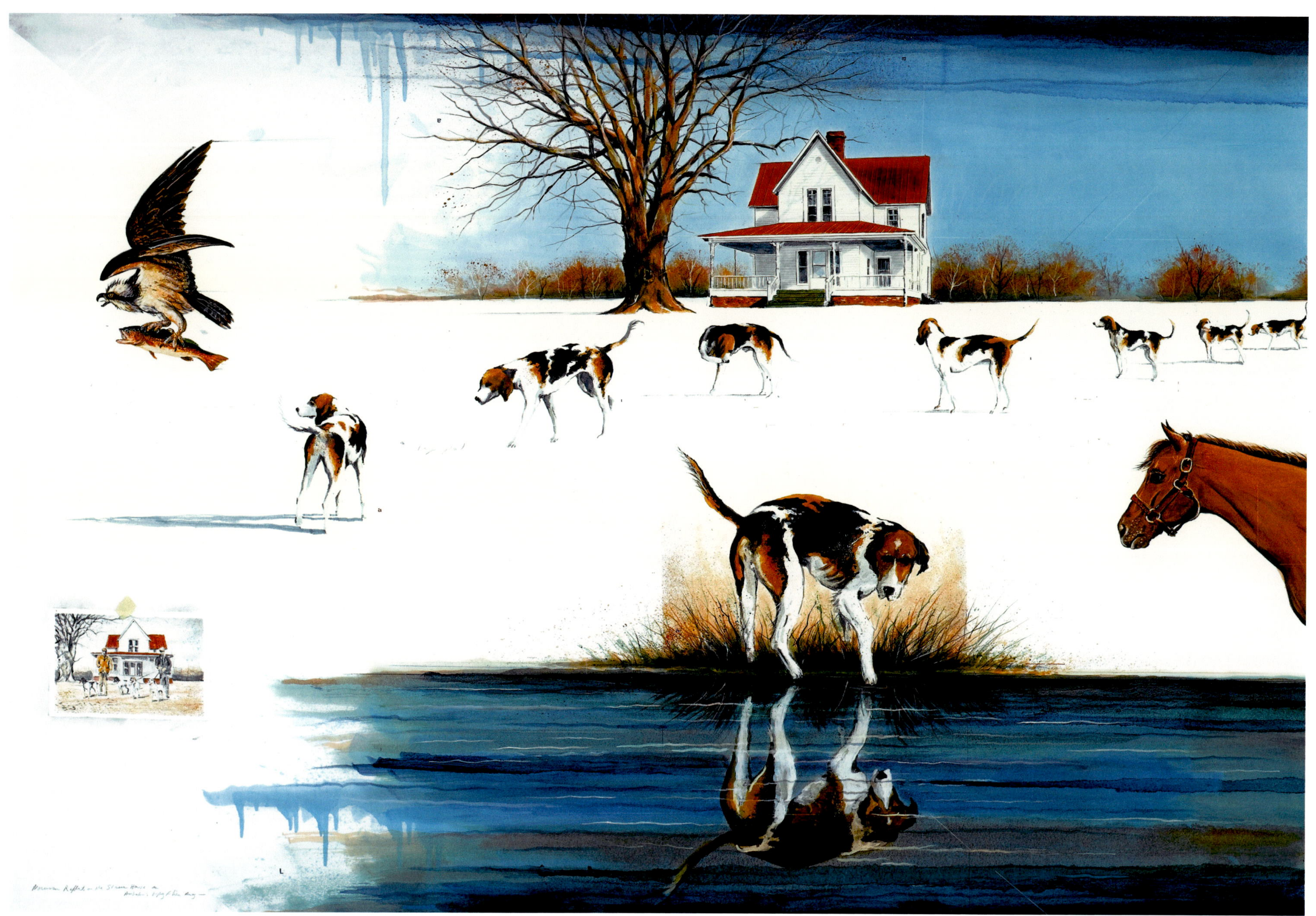

Narcissus Reflects on the Starnes House as Audubon's Osprey Flies Away, 2005
Oil paint and dry pigment on rag paper, 42 x 61.
Private collection. Photograph by John E. Powell.

NARCISSUS REFLECTS ON THE STARNES HOUSE

Bill Dunlap, Art and Life

I

On February 17, 2006, William Dunlap sat in the front row of the auditorium of the new Mississippi Telecommunications Center in downtown Jackson. He studied his program notes preparing to serve as the Master of Ceremonies for the Governor's Awards for Excellence in the Arts. As the room filled, Dunlap greeted award winners, past and present, along with Mississippi's cultural and political leaders.

Those who traffic in the old clichés and stereotypes about Mississippi should be required to attend the Governor's Arts Awards. Since its inception in 1989, winners have reflected the range and diversity of creative talent found across the state and include Leontyne Price, Barry Hannah, Eudora Welty, Richard Ford, Willie Morris, Shelby Foote, Morgan Freeman, Roebuck "Pops" Staples, Samuel Mockbee, Stephen Ambrose, William Eggleston, Charlie Musselwhite, Little Milton, and William Dunlap, himself.

An outspoken and respected native son, Dunlap moved away from Mississippi in 1970, but proudly embraces his roots. Since receiving the award in 1991, he has returned each year to present the awards before standing-room-only crowds inside the Old State Capitol Building. This year, due to damage caused to the building by Hurricane Katrina, the ceremonies were moved to the Telecommunications Center, designed by the Miami firm, Arquitectonica.

Dunlap is uniquely qualified to host these ceremonies. From the Gulf Coast to the Delta to the hill country, he knows Mississippi. He was raised in the small towns and rural environments, has lived in the state's major university town and its largest city, and has met many of its mythic literary, artistic, and musical figures. Each year, the winners whom Dunlap welcomes to the stage reflect the realities of the life and the people he knew growing up here, including high school marching bands, church choirs, professional musicians, artists, craftsmen, and writers, as well as teachers, arts administrators, and patrons.

The Governor's Awards show not only how far the state has come during Dunlap's life, but also how far he has come. He was born in small town Mississippi during the war years, when water fountains were marked "colored" and "white," when the state had no art museum in its capital, and when a professional career in art seemed a remote possibility for a young man from Webster County.

He described this limited art world to his friend and fellow Mississippian, writer Willie Morris, in 1989. "I grew up in what some of my erudite and more sophisticated friends would call a vacuum. There were no museums where I was growing up, no galleries, and no painters that I knew on a first-hand basis." Despite these limitations, he discovered an alternative source of inspiration in Mississippi. "But what there was, was a great concentration of another kind of spirit: there was this extraordinary landscape that one could see."[1] For Dunlap, the landscape would become his inspiration and primary subject in the ongoing series of works that mark his mature career.

II

Mississippi

Driving with Bill Dunlap along Highway 82, through the Mississippi hill country and the Delta, is a memorable experience, one that seems to transcend time while he tells stories. His Mississippi accent lingers over the names of the passing towns and cities—Eupora, Grady, Mathiston, Walthall, Winona, Greenwood, Moorhead, Itta Bena, Belzoni, Money, and Indianola. Dunlap loves to drive these roads, stirring up old memories and often finding both clarity of mind and visual inspiration while moving through the Mississippi landscape. Passing the Natchez Trace Parkway, he describes a favorite childhood experience, listening to the sound of adult voices and observing this landscape while leaning on the front seat, looking over the dashboard of a moving automobile.

Dunlap is thoroughly engaged in contemporary life, yet he was born during a very different time in the South, as these trips through Mississippi remind him. During the 1930s and 1940s, daily life in Mississippi was still structured around an older order, when the Civil War was not just a distant memory. As he tells Ruth Stevens Appelhof, "I am . . . a product of the twentieth century. . . . But I was born in Mississippi near the end of World War II, a time and place far closer in sensibility and pace to the nineteenth century than to the twentieth (thank God) and came of age in the sixties and seventies amid all the social change and political conflict of that era."[2]

Dunlap explains how society and culture functioned when he was growing up. "People did not talk about net worth, cancer, or religion. These issues were not discussed at the table. Folks still bartered goods and services. Thanks to Reconstruction, there was no real money in Mississippi, so it worked out just fine." Recalling Faulkner's famous observation that "the Great Depression came and went in Mississippi and no one even noticed," he adds, "That was our world during the 1950s, 1960s and into the 1970s." When he discovered Eudora Welty's Depression-era photographs, published in *One Time, One Place* (1971), he saw remarkable parallels. "Miss Welty made these during the 1930s, and it was seemingly the same storefronts, the same people, the same Mississippi we were occupying. But that's changed now."[3] This sense of having one foot in each of two very different centuries, by the artist's own admission, is reflected in his preferences and influences in the American art world. "My dual influences were the American painters—Church, Bierstadt, Homer, and Heade—as well as the Abstract Expressionist, Conceptual, and Pop Artists of our time," he informs Ruth Appelhof. "I have no stake in torching the Temple of Art in the name of what's happening now, but I feel the need to make some sort of peace in my own mind between the often naïve optimism of nineteenth-century art and the cold irony of the twentieth—to build bridges between the very best of that past and what matters and makes sense to me from the present."[4]

Mississippi's history and traditions formed Dunlap, as they did all those who left, by choice or necessity, to seek opportunities elsewhere. During the 1940s, Mississippi and the South teetered between two eras of radical transition. As historian James Cobb has suggested, "The years from the boll weevil invasion of the early twentieth century through the beginnings of the Great Migration of blacks to the North and the descent into the Great Depression might be seen as the harbingers of a great turning point, a protracted drama for which the New Deal and World War II constituted the final acts."[5]

Considering these social conditions, William Faulkner looked to the future: "A change will come out of this war. If it doesn't, if the politicians and people who run this country are not forced to make good the shibboleth they glibly talk about freedom, liberty, human rights, then you young men who have lived through it will have wasted your precious time, and those who don't live through it will have died in vain."[6] These words, written around the time of Dunlap's birth, also suggest the impact Mississippi writers like Faulkner and Eudora Welty had upon Dunlap's strongly rooted sense of place, as well as his mature aesthetic vision. He still holds them in high regard, as Barbara Rose has noted. "He will straightforwardly admit that he finds inspiration in regional themes and popular traditions that dominate the imagery and stories of the great Southern writers like Eudora Welty and William Faulkner, to whom he gallantly refers as 'Miss Welty' and 'Mr. Faulkner.'"[7]

William Ralph Dunlap was born on January 21, 1944, in Houston, Mississippi. "The town of Houston had the nearest hospital. Coincidentally, my mother was in the same room in this hospital where my father, 3½ years later, would die. It was not really so ironic given it was a very small hospital at the time." He was delivered by Dr. Gore, his mother's uncle. Every year, on his birthday, his mother recounted the story of Dunlap's birth, tinged with family wit, as he recalls. "It was so warm for January. . . . I sat out on the lawn with Sam Jr. and your cousin Linda until we left for the hospital. Mother said, 'You all look like two children on their way to a picnic.' Well, it was no picnic! You were overdue and a breech birth. And you have been running late and showing your arse ever since."

His parents came from old Webster County families—his mother, Margaret Cooper Dunlap, from Mathiston and Eupora; his father, Sam Coleman Dunlap Sr., from Grady. Like her mother before her, his mother was a teacher, and they came from a long line of farmers, educators, doctors, and lawyers, Scots-Irish migrant families that included Gores, Colemans, Smiths, Coopers, and Johnsons. His father, during the difficult war years, worked in the automobile business and was known as a distinctive local character. In September 1947, when Dunlap was three and a half years old, Sam Sr. died. The artist has few firsthand memories of his father, and knows him best from family stories and photographs, but he explains, "As an artist, you create what you don't have. It's why I initiated the Family Portrait series. I had heard great stories about my father—and had a number of family photographs. He was, by all accounts, a high-spirited, good-humored fellow, given to practical jokes and impersonations. He was learning to fly and would buzz the town of Eupora, dropping various objects on the unsuspecting citizenry. He and several of my uncles were in the automobile business. They would have been the first generation off the farm."

After his father's death, Dunlap's mother moved the young family back to her parents' home in Mathiston. They lived in the house of his maternal grandparents. She completed a degree in English literature from Mississippi State University and then moved to nearby Eupora where she taught high school. During his earliest years, the artist, who has since become widely known for his rapid and heavily animated style of speaking, was a quiet, withdrawn child. "I was thought by some members of my family to be retarded," Dunlap explains. "I started to speak and walk rather late. In retrospect, I didn't have anything to say or place to go. I just looked at things and played alone, but I was paying attention. Of all the senses, for me seeing overrides everything. I don't know if there's a visual equivalent to perfect pitch, or if there is, if I have it. But I do know that one sense can override the others. For me it's always the eye."

The life of small town Mississippi during these years grew increasingly more vital for the young Dunlap. He would later describe details from his childhood to writer Mary Lynn Kotz, who grew up in Mathiston as a friend of the family. "The chinaberry tree was always kind of mystical. And the legion of old dogs. And old people. There was old Mr. Hemphill, who somehow always showed up for Sunday lunch for as long as I can remember—Sunday dinner, as it were. He had a low tolerance for children,

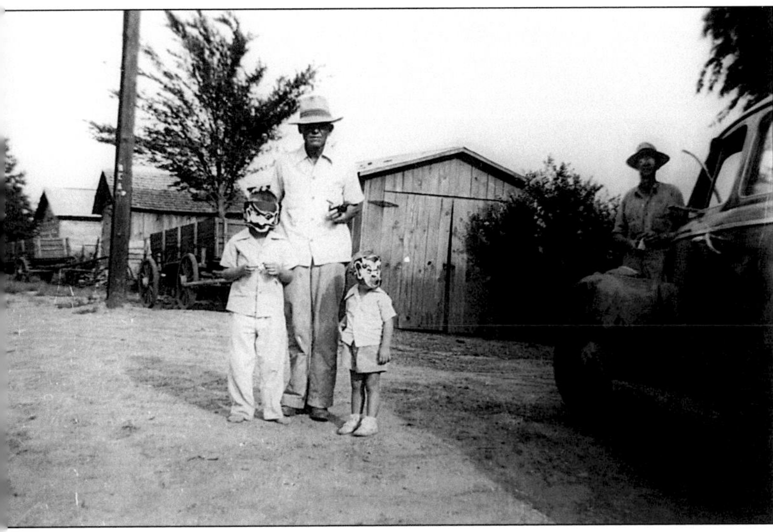

1

2

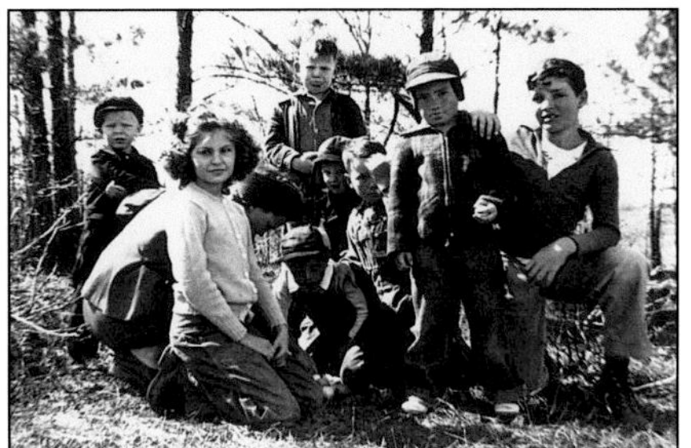

3

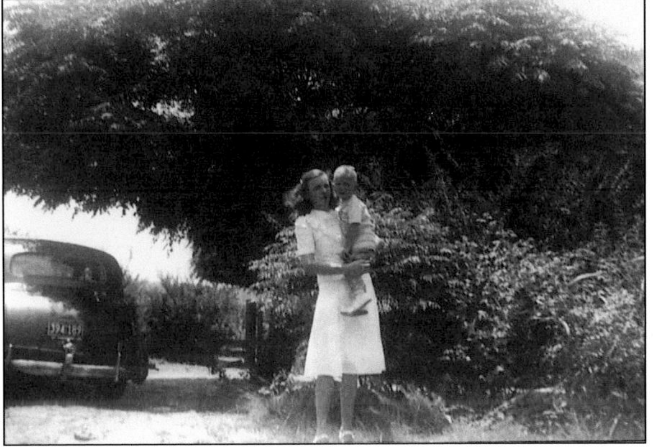

4

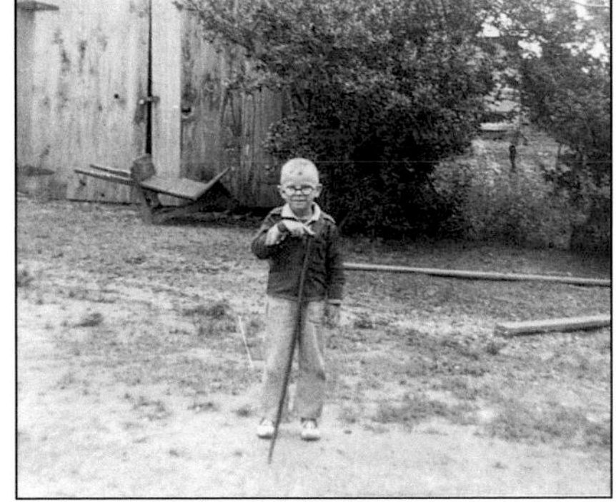

5

Fig. 1. (From left) Sam Dunlap Jr., C. L. Cooper Sr., William Dunlap, and Sam C. Dunlap Sr. (behind car). Mathiston, Mississippi, 1946.

Fig. 2. Alphonzo Hemphill (left) and C. L. Cooper Sr. with dog, 1946.

Fig. 3. William (far left) with wild children in Mathiston, 1947.

Fig. 4. Margaret Cooper Dunlap with son William, 1946.

Fig. 5. Artist at age four and a half, with grandfather's cane and glasses, 1948.

wore false teeth, pronounced Japan 'Jay-pan,' and he had a peculiar odor about him that Old Prince always picked up on."[8]

This place shaped him, as did the peripatetic life that was to follow. As he has suggested, the real and the mythic may have merged for him. "What's real and what's illusion seems to me to be a part of the larger question," he explains to Appelhof. "What was imagined? There was something quite special about growing up in Mississippi when I did, amongst that large, gregarious family of mine, full of terrific storytellers, characters of every stripe, and packs of wild cousins, in a network of interchangeable small towns and communities that seem so innocent now. The weather and the woods were so open and inviting, and everything of significance seemed to occur out-of-doors. All of that fed my imagination and sense of fantasy so it's hard to know what is real—maybe it all was. That's the exact quality of whimsy and inexplicitness I want in the work—the paintings and the constructions."[9]

Noting the influence of time and place on his art, Barbara Rose has observed, "Resonant memory was to become the theme of his work." Dunlap's obsession to collect objects, the objects he describes in his art as "found and fashioned," is a natural extension of this resonant memory. Growing up in an older South, he was familiar with worn and "charged" objects, those given meaning by human use and tradition. The iconography of the found objects associated with his art, according to Rose, "is layered and dense, based on his own specific experiences as well as traditional American myths and metaphors. . . . More often than not, the objects—shells, stones, gourds, branches, animal skulls and skin—are found in nature, souvenirs of the artist's travels and adventures, charged with personal association and historic memories."[10]

When Dunlap's mother remarried in 1952, the family began a series of moves across the Deep South, setting into motion a pattern of relocation and return that is a constant in Dunlap's life and art. They first moved to Port Arthur, Texas (where Robert Rauschenberg was born and later said, "they didn't know what art was there"). When his stepfather later "felt the call to preach," he moved the family to Fort Worth where he attended Southwest Baptist Seminary. Two years later they moved to Charleston, South Carolina, where he was affiliated with the First Baptist Church of North Charleston. In 1958, the family returned to Mississippi and a succession of churches and teaching positions, first in Gloster and Amite County, then in the Delta towns of Belzoni and Moorhead, and finally in Rankin County, near his stepfather's home of Morton.

Dunlap attended Morton High School, graduating in 1962. During his high school years, he worked on the farm of A. B. Wilson, caring and providing for forty head of Hereford cattle. Dunlap acknowledges the positive influence that Wilson had on his life. "Mr. Wilson was a wise and articulate man, a philosopher really, with a world view I came to admire and understand. He was the most task-oriented man I'd ever known, and working with him was always an adventure for the mind and body."

During these formative years, when relocation and starting over were the pattern of his life ("I attended eleven schools in twelve years"), Dunlap and his brother Sam developed a second, more grounded pattern, spending summers with their grandparents and extended family in Grady and Mathiston. Although Dunlap learned to adapt and make the most of the family moves, summers in Webster County served as an idyllic constant in an otherwise unpredictable annual cycle. Here he was part of a larger family and cast of Mississippi characters, securely

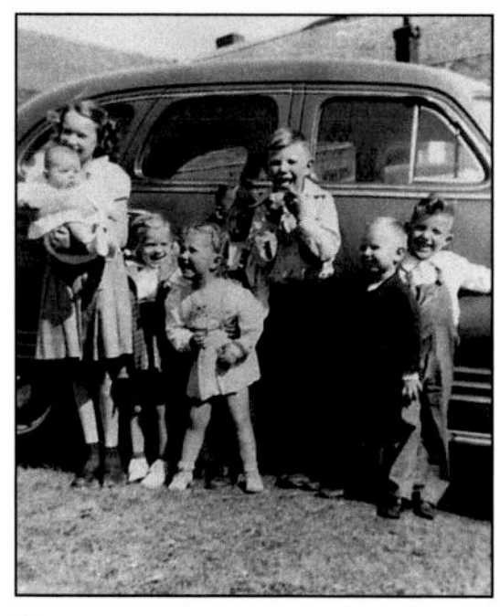

6

Fig. 6. Sam and William (center right) with Dunlap cousins in front of Old Iron Sides in Grady, Mississippi, 1946.

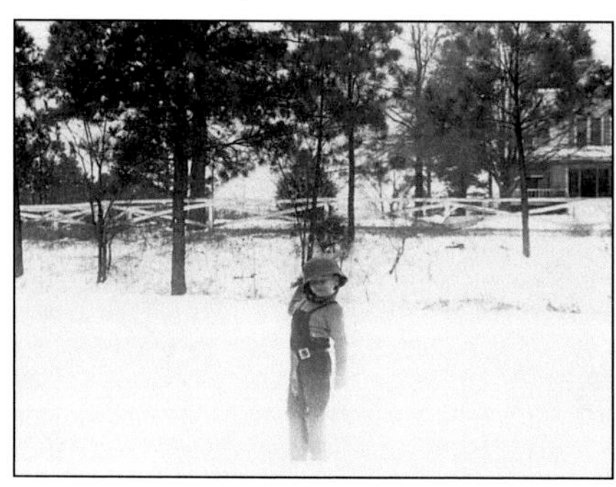

7

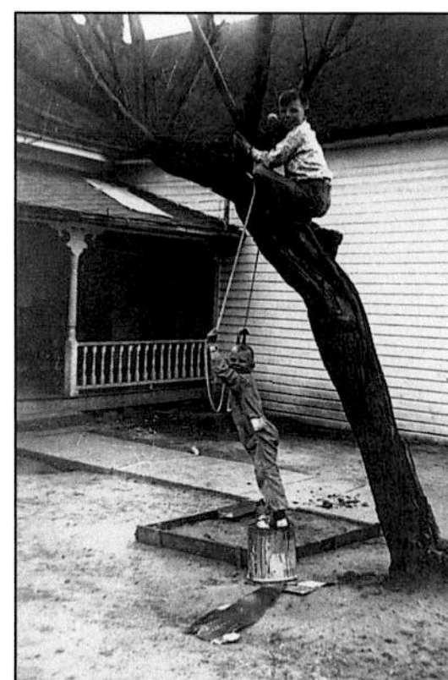

8

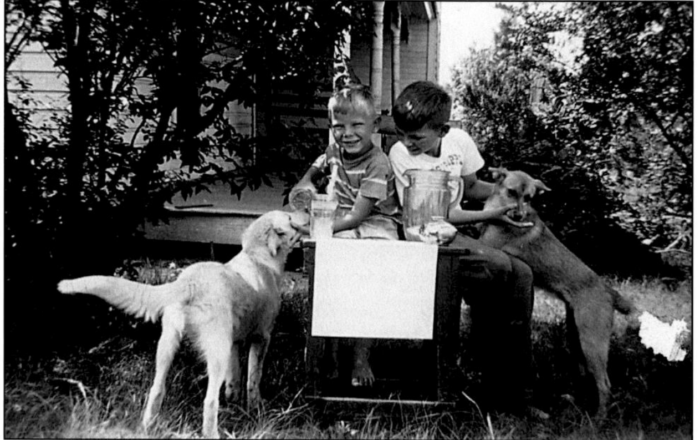

9

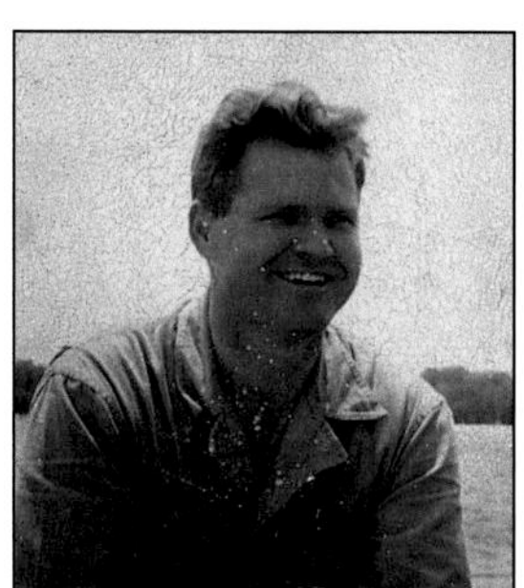

10

Fig. 7. William in front of Starnes house wearing WWII gear, ca. 1951.

Fig. 8. Sam Jr. in chinaberry tree and William standing on can.

Fig. 9. William (left) and Sam with Prince and Yellow Pup at lemonade stand in Mathiston, 1950.

Fig. 10. Allan B. Wilson, 1917–1964.

part of a small-town community. "We would get up in the morning and just leave, run around barefoot and shirtless. We'd get home about supper, and nobody seemed to care. . . . Everything was going to be okay. In retrospect, there was far more supervision than we realized. Black people, white people, they all looked out for us."

If his attachment to the landscape of Mississippi nurtured one of his central artistic subjects, so too did his early and continuing association with the Southern dog, beginning in Webster County. His grandfather, Cas Cooper, raised Walker hounds, and the family home was filled with all types of dogs, purebred and not. He and his brother had fond memories of these dogs, including their pets, Prince and Yellow Pup. Although Prince was killed when Dunlap was seven years old, the dog remains alive in his memory. In a recent essay, he writes, "Later that summer [1951], I watched as Prince ran after and caught a car. My grandfather and I buried him in the woods behind their Webster County, Mississippi, home. I can still find the spot—and on occasion, do."[11]

His grandfather was a respected breeder of Walker hounds, the dogs featured in many of Dunlap's most important paintings (including *Panorama of the American Landscape*, *The Bounty and Burden of History*, *Narcissus Reflecting on the Starnes House as Audubon's Osprey Flies Away*) and are used as the surrogate for man (and himself) in his works. In "What Dogs Dream," a catalogue essay for an exhibition devoted to his dogs, which opened in March of 2006 at the Morris Museum of Art, he recalls, "That same grandfather was a foxhunter of the old school. He bred and hunted generations of pure-blood Walker hounds. With names like Lucky, Mary, Speck, Sally, and Bo, these dogs were all legs, lungs, nose, and heart. They lived to run." On hunting days, as he describes, they were loaded into pickup trucks and driven to the fields.

"The men would release the hounds at some preordained spot and then ride the ridge roads all night listening for the telltale sound of the lead dog opening on a fox. The race was on, not to be watched but rather followed by ear. From this high-pitched cacophony of the 'dogs' mouth,' the men could identify whose hound was ahead, whether they had struck a gray or a red, and whose farm they were tearing up. The 'race' was one man's dog against the others, the fox almost peripheral to the real contest at hand.

"By dawn, with the prey gone to ground and hounds quiet, the men would blow their truck horns and shout their dogs' names. My grandfather's pack came to the call of an old hunting horn that had been his father's. The foxhounds would come straggling in, exhausted, tongues hanging out, limping and bleeding from barbed-wire cuts."[12]

If the "resonant memory" of his early Mississippi experiences is a central component in Dunlap's art, experiences such as these reside at the very core of that memory. And, at times, old realities surface, literally, from the Mississippi soil. "I was back at the old house place not long ago. We'd cut some timber and the ground was all distressed. The sweet gum tree where Prince is buried survives. Near where the kennel had been, the glint of a piece of metal caught my eye. It was a brass nameplate still attached to a decaying leather collar. It read, 'C. L. Cooper, Mathiston, Mississippi, Phone 3451.'"[13] In a gesture that illustrates how memory, history, and reality are fused in his art, Dunlap placed this dog collar near his painting, *The Bounty and Burden of History*, in the large installation he created for the Ogden Museum of Southern Art's 2000 exhibition *Objects: Found and Fashioned*.

Equally important for Dunlap's life and his art is the large frame structure in Mathiston known locally as the Starnes house, located across the road from his grandparents' home. It serves in the twenty-first century as his Mississippi home, adjoined by a studio converted from a historic wooden church. The Starnes house has become an iconic image in his work, not unlike the classic vernacular houses seen in Edward Hopper's paintings. He explains why this house has been central to his memory from a very early date.

"When my father died, we went back to live with my maternal grandmother, a schoolteacher, and my grandfather, Cas Cooper, who operated a sawmill. We lived in the old Hemphill house on old Highway 82, right across the street from the Starnes house. It was one of the first images I remember. Mrs. Starnes was an ancient lady,

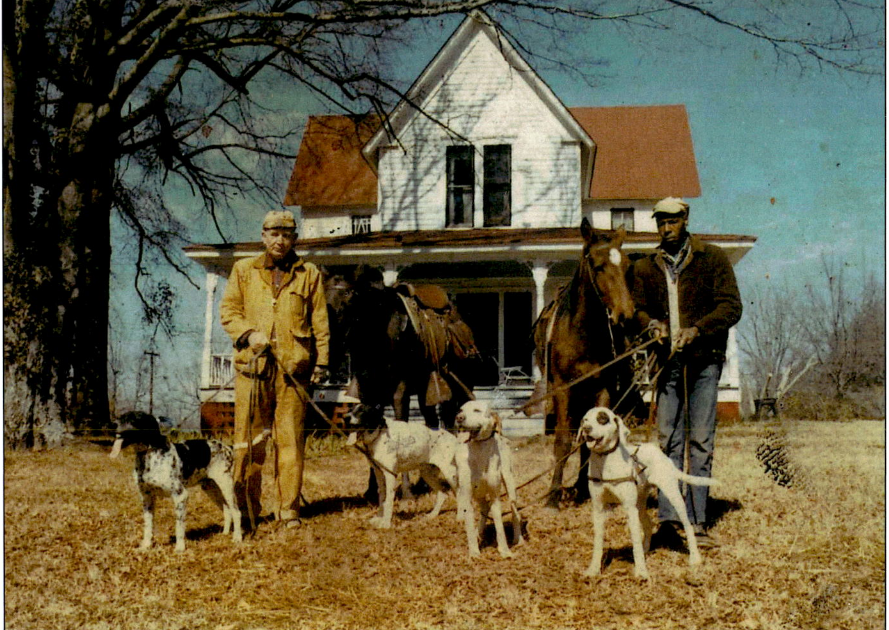

Fig. 11. Bill Starnes (left) with horse Fly, and George Cunningham with dog Spook (far right), prior to hunting trip. In front of Starnes house, 1971.

11

afflicted with palsy, who always sat on her porch. I would slip away and cross this dangerous road, crawl through the fence and go up onto the porch, eat her ginger cookies and listen to her stories. Eventually, someone would come across and get me, tan my hide, but, sure enough, I would go back.

"It has always been an image in my work, an obsession really. The house is a classic up-county, Mississippi carpenter Victorian, two stories, with a red, high pitched-roof. I liked the style of it. It was built on the pattern of a cross. Bill Starnes, the son, lived there with his sister, Mary. He was a graduate of Annapolis and had been at Pearl Harbor. He came home, practiced law, and bird-hunted. We remained friends until he died.

"Just as the bulldozer was about to take it down to build a new Piggly Wiggly store, one of his friends, Fred Bush, called me. He knew my work and my appreciation for the house. He told me the options. To save it, I bought the Starnes house immediately. Later, I moved an old Church of Christ on the property, which would become my studio."

Throughout the high school years, athletics, especially football and track, remained important to him, as did outdoor life and all the traditional pursuits of young men in Mississippi. He also became interested in music during his high school and college years. While he had been drawing since childhood, opportunities for exposure to art were limited to the occasional trip to the Lauren Rogers Museum of Art in Laurel. The Mississippi Museum of Art, where he is now a board member, did not open in Jackson until 1978. During his final year at Morton High School, he and his classmates went to New Orleans on their senior class trip. The city offered him the opportunity to visit the Delgado Museum (now the New Orleans Museum of Art) as well as art galleries in the French Quarter.

Dunlap graduated from Morton High School in 1962, the year that William Faulkner died. Mississippi, in social turmoil since the 1954 *Brown v. Board of Education* decision, entered a widely publicized period of racial unrest. Emmett Till's body was discovered in August of 1955, creating a national scandal for Mississippi. During the early 1960s, Freedom Riders traveled across the state to register black voters. Events escalated in the fall of 1962, when James Meredith enrolled at the University of Mississippi, an event that set the campus into a riotous confrontation with federal authorities. Curtis Wilkie, a student at Ole Miss then and friend of Dunlap now, describes the event. "Army trucks carrying troops in battle gear began lumbering onto the campus. . . . Bearing rifles with bayonets, helmeted soldiers swarmed through a western gate near a dormitory where Meredith had been sequestered throughout the night. . . . Overhead we could hear the drone of a massive airlift, as troops descended, one after another, on the Oxford airport."[14]

While the state's racial wars unfolded in the national spotlight, Dunlap became immersed in music, one area where Mississippians, black and white, played and worked together as a matter of course. For two years, he attended Hinds Community College on a track and band scholarship. In high school he had played drums in the marching band. At Hinds he traveled widely with a stage band and the Hinds Hi-Steppers, performing annually at the Miss America pageant and making regular trips to New Orleans, Washington, New York, and Canada. On these trips he explored museums and galleries and visited the New York World's Fair, where he saw the *Pietà* in the Vatican Pavilion, works by Goya and Velázquez in the Spanish Pavilion, and an extensive Pop Art survey. He also heard Miles Davis and Charlie Mingus in Greenwich Village jazz clubs.

After two years at Hinds, he transferred to Belhaven College in Jackson, located in the same urban neighborhood where writer Eudora Welty lived. Here he encountered an influential professor, William Derrett, who saw potential in the young Dunlap but worried about his study habits (his music remained a major distraction). Derrett introduced him to Welty and Robert Penn Warren and stressed basic writing skills to Dunlap, "doubting I would ever be able to write an intelligible sentence in English." Reinforcing his distinctive sense of place was the fact that after studying Eudora Welty in his Belhaven classroom, he could leave the building and see her, literally across the street, as she came and went from her house at 1119 Pinehurst Street.

After one year at Belhaven, he transferred again, to Mississippi College, a Baptist school in Clinton, whose art department was headed by kinsman Sam Gore. Like all students, he was required to attend regular weekly chapel sessions, where, he later noted, he completed some of his best erotic drawings. He graduated from Mississippi College two years later, in 1967, with a bachelor of science degree. Barry Hannah, his college classmate, later featured

Fig. 12. Hinds Community College sprinters: Dunlap (right), ca. 1963. Photograph by Robert Pickenpaugh.

Fig. 13. Members of the Imperial Show Band at Cal Neva Lodge in Lake Tahoe, 1967: (from left) Bill Dunlap, Tommy Tate, and Bucky Barrett.

Fig. 14. Self-portrait photo: Imperial Show Band on the Road: (from left) Dunlap, Bucky Barrett, and Jimmy Hodo, somewhere on Route 66, summer of 1967.

Fig. 15. Dunlap (right) and George Alexander pour aluminum at the foundry of the University of Mississippi Art Department, 1967.

Fig. 16. Aluminum cast of Noyes Long bust, 1968.

Fig. 17. Dunlap in OSHA-approved outfit for foundry work, 1967.

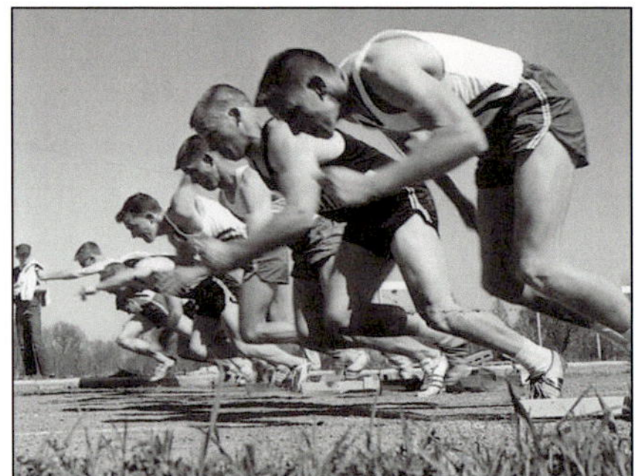

12

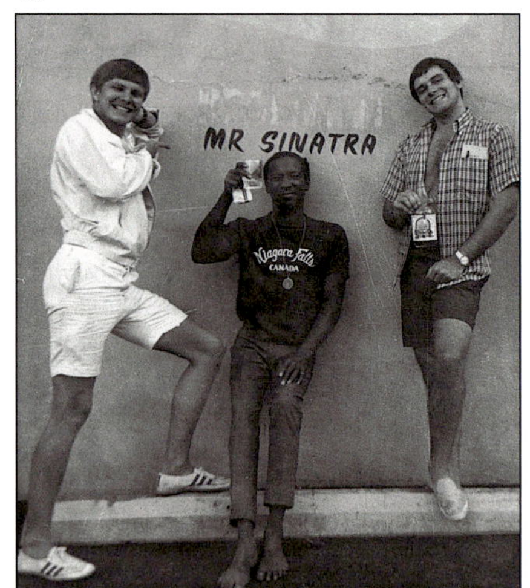

13

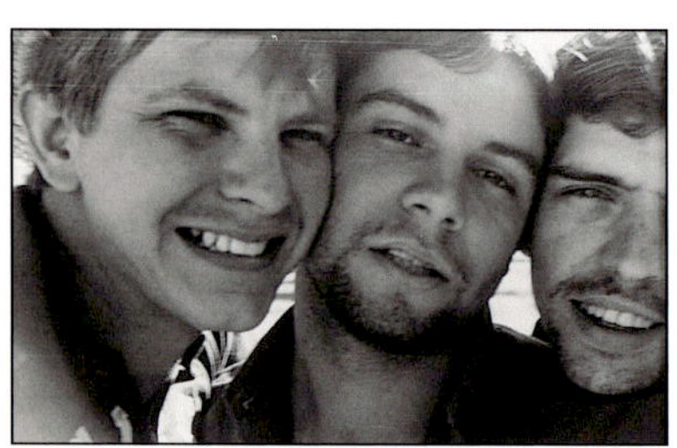

14

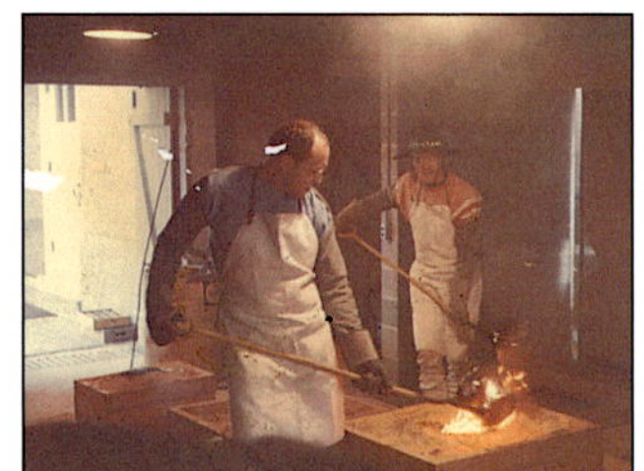

15

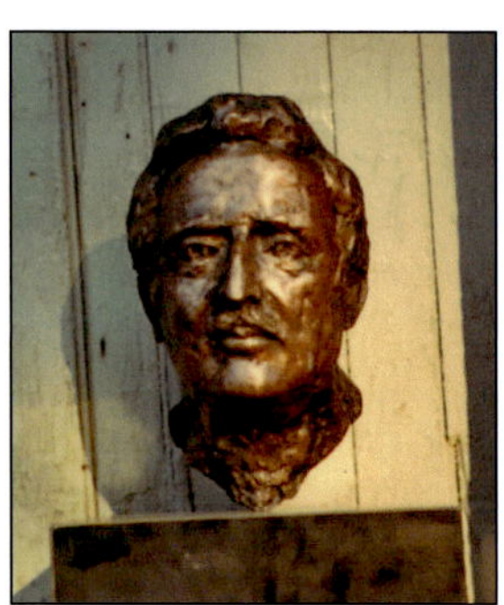

16

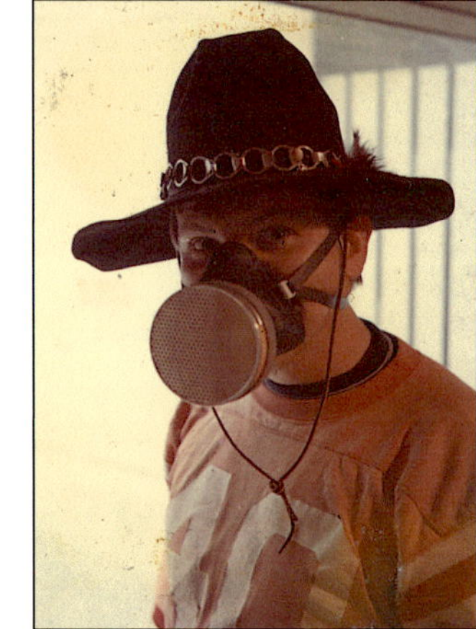

17

Mississippi College in his novel, *Geronimo Rex*. However, by this time, his college education seems to have paled in comparison to the education and experiences he was gaining on the road as a professional musician.

By 1966 he became the drummer for Tim Whitsett's Imperial Show Band, a large rhythm and blues stage band that traveled to New York, Las Vegas, Lake Tahoe, Hollywood, and the Great Lakes. Defying the standards of the period, Whitsett added a black singer, Tommy Tate, creating what was in effect the first integrated R&B band in Mississippi. Because of his active work in the Imperial Show Band, it took Dunlap five years to complete his college degree. The band paid Dunlap well and exposed him to new places, including a broader range of museums and galleries. In his touring days he traveled across the western landscape of Route 66, saw Jackson Pollock's first retrospective at the Los Angeles County Museum, and the exhibit *Sculpture of Sixties*, curated by Jane Livingston. She became a close friend and colleague after Dunlap's move to Washington.[15]

Although he had intended to stay with the band, Dunlap changed his mind quickly after a member of his local draft board contacted his mother. His student deferment was ending, just as the war in Vietnam was escalating, so he immediately enrolled as a graduate student at the University of Mississippi, where he was given an assistantship. He studied with Noyes Long and Dean Aydelott and ran the campus foundry while creating sculpture in bronze and aluminum. One of his early sculptural projects was a sensitive portrait bust of his teacher, Noyes Long, cast in aluminum in 1968. Sculpture had a distinguished history at Ole Miss, including the earlier presence of David Smith as a visiting artist.

In addition to cast sculptural forms, he also explored the use of bent and twisted metal in constructed sculpture, some of which were then discarded by workers from the university's maintenance department, who mistook them for trash. He also experimented with etching and lithography, working with Jack Lemon, the founder of Landfall Press. In 1967, after the death of his grandfather, Clough Dunlap, he was given a series of family photographs, which inspired him to begin his Family Portrait series. His initial goal in this series was fairly clear. "These photographs became source material for a series of etchings, prints, oils, watercolors, and drawings," he explains. "I wanted to make them anonymous enough to be 'every family,' but specific enough to be my experience."

In 1968, Dunlap married Bobbye Jean Kitchens, whose father, O. W. "Pappy" Kitchens, would later achieve fame as a self-taught artist, in no small part due to Dunlap's crusading efforts on his behalf. Dunlap continued to travel and play with bands and came under the influence of Larry Rivers, who opened up significant new directions in his approach to imagery and the use of materials. He also became more aware of national artists with ties to the South, including Robert Rauschenberg and Jasper Johns. Over the years, Dunlap has retained strong ties to the Ole Miss art department, returning regularly to the campus, and has remained friends with many of his fellow graduate students, including George Alexander, John Davis, Herschel George, Bill Lester, and Robert Marsh.

After graduating with an MFA in sculpture and print-

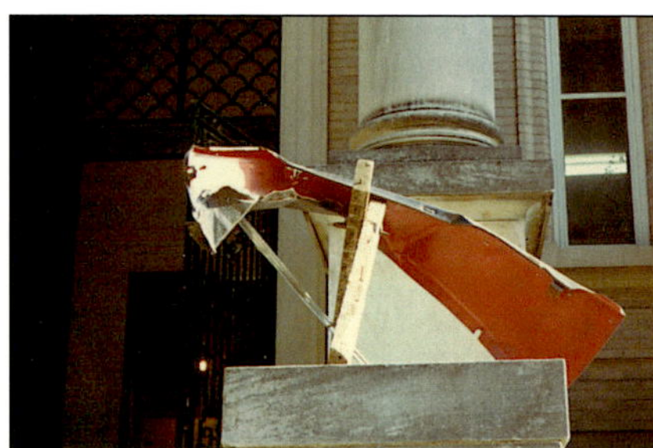

18

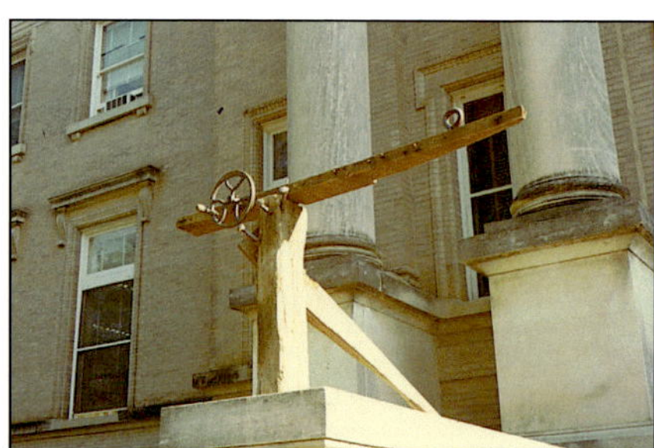

19

Figs. 18–19. Dunlap's found object sculptures, Bryant Hall, University of Mississippi, 1968. Summarily removed by physical plant workers.

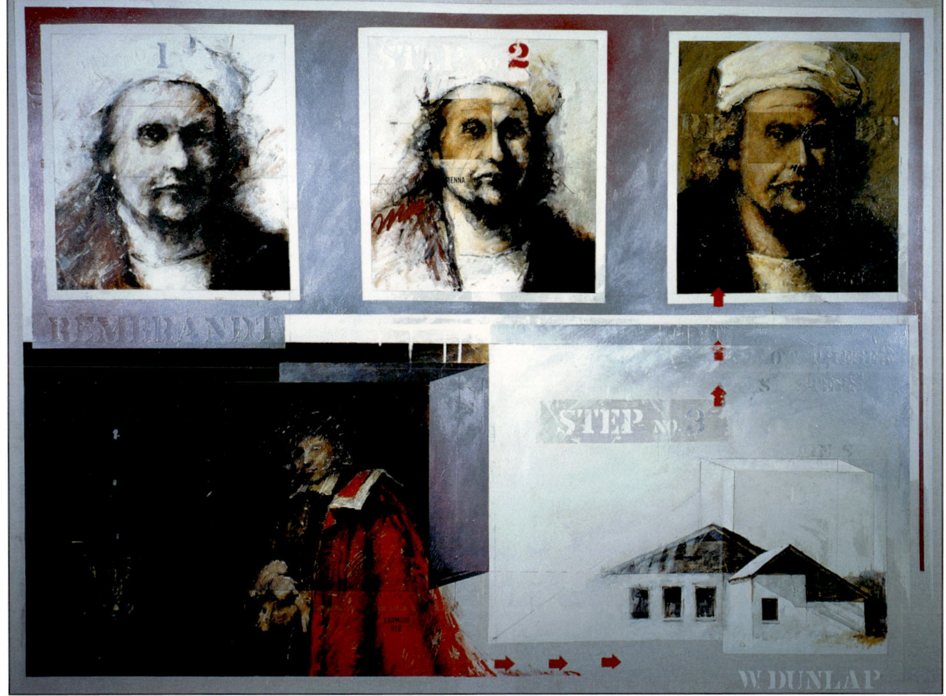

20

Fig. 20. *Learn to Paint Like Rembrandt in Three Easy Steps*, 1971. Polymer paint on canvas with found brushes, 60 x 78. Private collection. Photograph by Jack Kotz.

making in 1969, he returned to Hinds Community College to begin a teaching career that continued through the 1970s. While at Hinds, Dunlap, who had received little formal training in painting (during a time when critics announced that "painting was dead"), began to teach himself to paint.

This was the critical next step in his artistic evolution, initiated in Mississippi before he moved to North Carolina. "I was not really a painter. I had taken some watercolor courses at Mississippi College," he admits. "But I wanted to paint, so I just taught myself by trial and error and by reading and research. I had seen Larry Rivers's work, and I was impressed by it." Inspired by Rivers's recycling of Old Master images, Dunlap began to explore art history and to experiment with appropriating imagery. His Old Masters Re-Considered series incorporates references to Rembrandt, Vermeer, and Velázquez.

In one of his initial works, Dunlap opened a critical new path in his art, one that he would explore throughout the 1970s in North Carolina and, in many ways, to the present. As part of his process of becoming a "self-taught" painter of Old Master portraits, he created a three-part Rembrandt portrait, titled *Learn to Paint Like Rembrandt in Three Easy Steps*, a milestone in his early career. He was inspired, in part, by the release of a new book catalogue published by Abrams, featuring a Rembrandt portrait on the cover. As he recalls, "At that time, it was the closest I had been to a Rembrandt painting."

"I was making paintings that were not portraits of places, but they did incorporate that sense of place," he explains. "'Hypothetical Realism' is the term I coined, tongue-in-cheek but nevertheless fairly accurate. These places are not real but they could be. At this time, Larry Rivers, working in New York, was recycling images from magazines, cigar boxes, and the like. One of my paintings, *Learn to Paint Like Rembrandt in Three Easy Steps*, dealt with the irony of being a twenty-seven-year-old kid, just out of graduate school, suddenly finding himself a college professor. How absurd was that? I recalled the elementary Walter Foster *Learn to Paint* and *Learn to Draw* books and divided a Rembrandt self-portrait into three segments—one drawn, one glazed, and one with artificial crackling to give the appearance of age. That is the joke. Learn to paint like Rembrandt, age the work 375 years, and you have a bona fide masterpiece."

North Carolina

In 1970, Dunlap left Mississippi and Hinds Community College to accept a position at Appalachian State University, in Boone, North Carolina. He remained there until 1979. Though the significance of Dunlap's connections to Mississippi is widely known, the importance of his relationship to North Carolina is less recognized. Four states have been most important to him, and he recently ranked them: Mississippi, North Carolina, Virginia, and Florida. (New York City is another story.) North Carolina is second, only to his native Mississippi. Here, he explored his family's roots in the Scots-Irish culture of the mountains; he developed his mature imagery and teaching methodology; he was inspired by the environment, landscape, and culture of the Appalachians; and, here, he developed a national platform for his art as well as his entry into the art world of New York and Washington. The decade of the 1970s proved to be critical to the development of the art and the public persona of Bill Dunlap.

Dunlap's professional transition to North Carolina was an easy one, made possible by his mentors from the University of Mississippi art department. "I came of age as an artist in North Carolina," he notes. "My two most important professors, Dean Aydelott and Noyes Long, had been at Mississippi, but they were too hot for that place, and they ended up at Appalachian State. I got the fateful call and went to join them." Also there when he arrived were two former Ole Miss graduates, Larry Edwards and Warren Dennis. In many respects, the position at Appalachian State was a clean slate and a solid platform, ready for his evolving approach to new Southern art forms and his related philosophies regarding the role of the artist in the contemporary South. Equally important for Dunlap at this time was his developing relationship with the contemporary art initiatives at Southeast Center for Contemporary Art (SECCA) in Winston-Salem, North Carolina, which continues to the present.

Dunlap and B. J. Kitchens decided to live away from

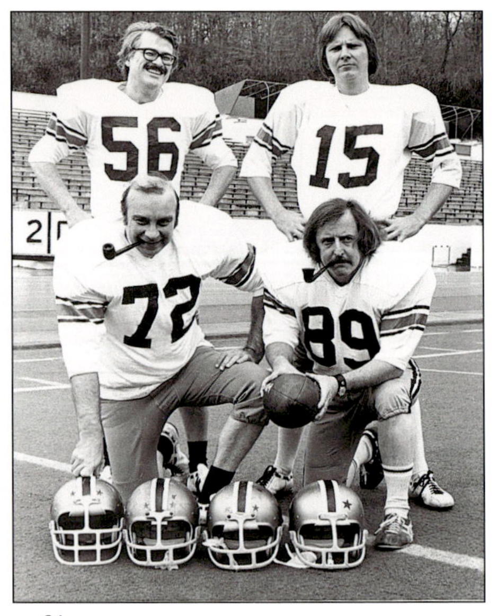

21

Fig. 21. Appalachian State University art department "Mississippi Mafia" in publicity photo for "Fantastic Four" exhibition, ca. 1977. Warren Dennis (#56), Bill Dunlap (#15), Larry Edwards (#72), and Noyes Capehart Long (#89).

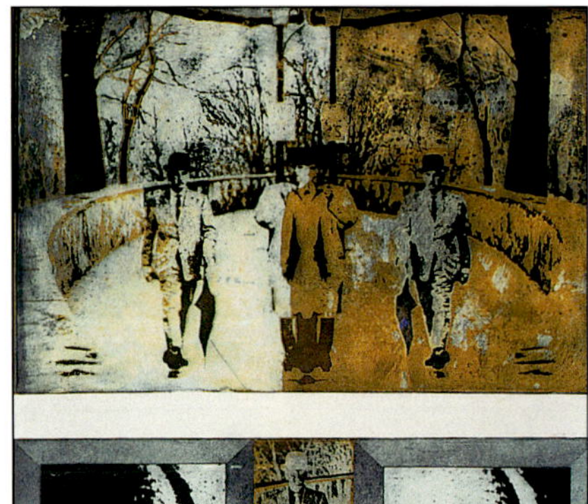

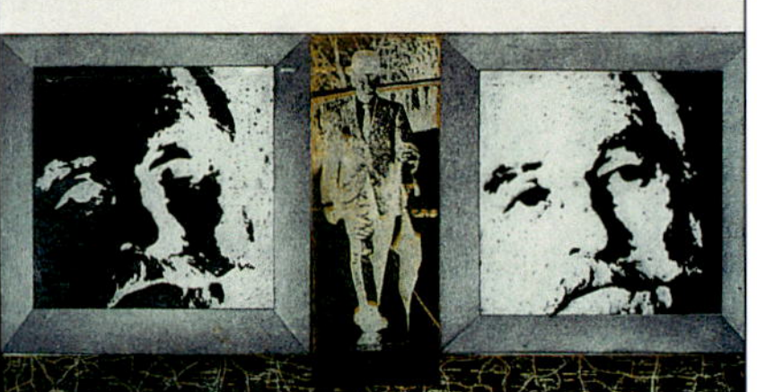

22

Fig. 22. *Faulkner Commemorative Print*, 1972. Three-color intaglio, 32 x 24.

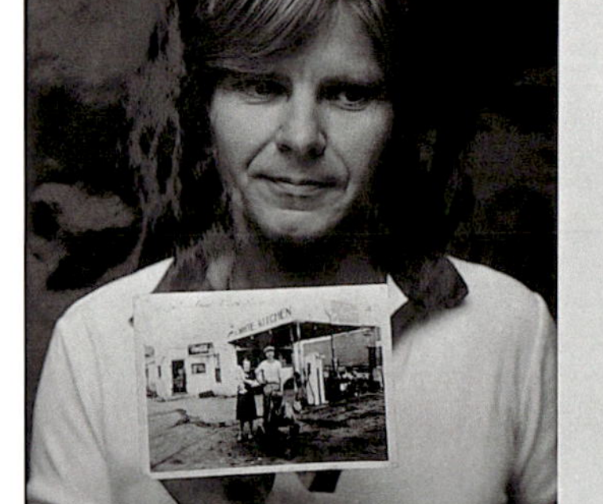

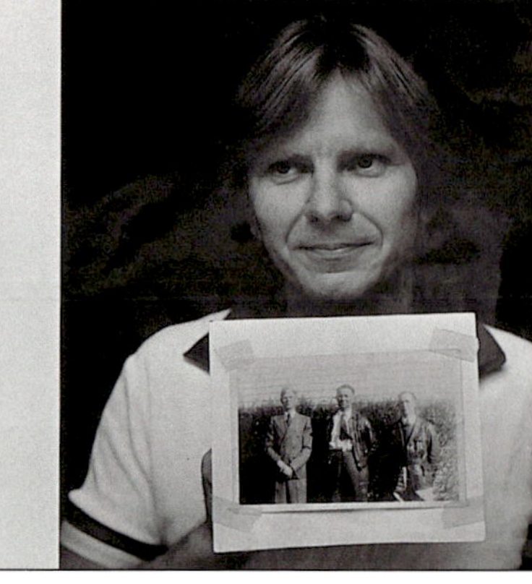

23

Fig. 23. Antecedents Series Polaroid, 20 x 24, 1984. Photograph by John Reuter, Polaroid Studio, Boston, Massachusetts.

the Boone campus and found a house in Blowing Rock on the edge of the Blue Ridge Parkway. "The highway means so much to what I am doing. Those old game trails turned Indian trails turned settler trails that are now national parks—the Natchez Trace and the Blue Ridge Parkway—have become crucial." Dunlap found comfort and familiarity in the placement of these old roads, especially in contrast to the modern interstates that were beginning to cross the South. "They lie lightly on the land, but they've been very important in my life, as roads from place to place, and also as vistas. The interstate system shows the landscape from the engineer's frame of reference. The same landscape can look very different from a farm-to-market road, a gravel road, or from a canoe on a stream."

The placement of the house in Blowing Rock was particularly inspirational to his art, offering unique perspectives on an ever-changing natural environment. "The weather fronts from the east would wash up against the ridge, and back to the west, there would be the sun. Sometimes the weather from the west would be vicious and come in hard and cold. I've seen the clouds roll up to the hill in front of my studio and pour over into the clear piedmont below. It's fantastic to see as is snow in July. I have walked around in shorts in January. It's very, very strange and unpredictable and more than a little dangerous." This natural beauty of the place was enhanced by his next-door neighbor, John Foster West, a noted Appalachian poet and novelist who became a friend, collaborator, and source of inspiration.

Dunlap was born in Mississippi along the Natchez Trace, the historic route between Nashville and New Orleans, and the influences of culture and trade were a central part of the region's history. In North Carolina, he settled on the Blue Ridge Parkway, an equally important pathway, one that linked the mountains and culture of the Appalachian South. In North Carolina he explored his own family's history of migration. "The people are the purest form of my gene pool. The settlers were Scots-Irish who had been denied access to the Scottish highlands. Royalists, dispossessed by Cromwell and set adrift, floated around like the ancient Hebrews. Once they arrived in this country, the tidewater aristocrats had no use for them, so naturally they took to the mountains." From here, the Scots-Irish migrated to Georgia, Alabama, Mississippi, Texas, and farther west.

In the mountains of North Carolina, Dunlap felt comfortable, at home. He also was able to look at Mississippi from a new perspective. During his time in North Carolina, he immersed himself in the full range of Southern literature, placing the Mississippi masters within a larger context. Once he settled into his new working environment, he returned to his evolving subjects—the Family Portrait series and the Old Masters series—and added a new figure, William Faulkner, another "Old Master." Mary Lynn Kotz has suggested that Dunlap's reading of Faulkner and the influence of the mountains and the quality of light there created surprising results. "The landscapes that emerged offer much more: a subtext of tension, of loneliness, of expectancy." Continuing, she describes these complex landscape images: "Faulkner's themes are repeated by Dunlap: the land abides, surviving all of man's attempts to cordon it off with boundary lines; man only presumes to own the land. Over these landscapes Dunlap superimposes grids, boundary markers, surveyor's maps, often drawn in pencil. Odd letters and numbers dangle from the sky. A fragmentary inscription is written in pencil across a field. Tiny arrows and words in agate type reveal themselves to anyone who gets close enough to examine the painting."[16]

The Family Portrait series expanded as Dunlap continued to incorporate the photographs he had received in 1967 into his work. While still painting the old masters, he created new photographic portraits using these family images. Several distinctive family portraits emerged from this period. One was inspired by a haunting image from around 1946, a worn and muted photograph of his father and his brother Sam. This was first translated into a drawing showing father and son, isolated in a landscape, with

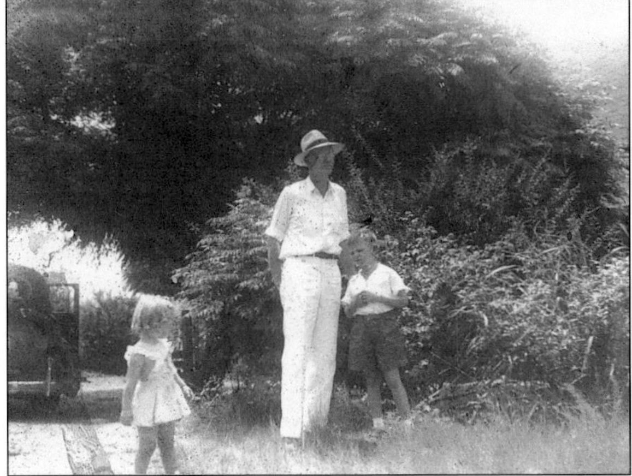
24

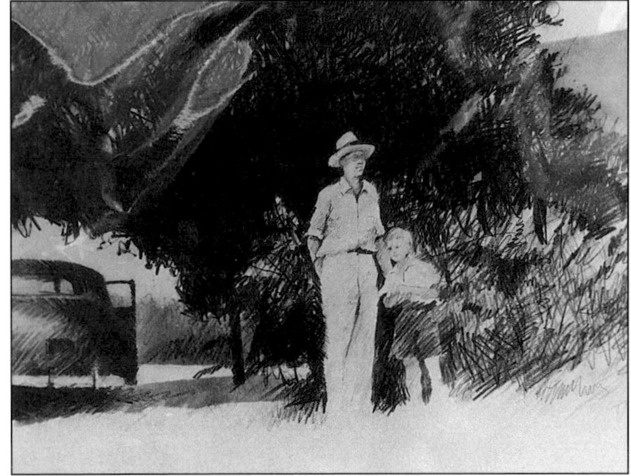
25

Fig. 24. Sam Coleman Dunlap Sr., Sam Jr., and Linda Dunlap (a cousin) in Mathiston, 1946.

Fig. 25. Working drawing from family photograph. Detail, graphite on paper, 1972.

Fig. 26. Dunlap family in Grady, Mississippi, ca. 1940. Source photograph for Family Portrait Series.

Fig. 27. Blowing Rock, North Carolina, ca. 1976.

Fig. 28. Self-portrait with Picasso 90th birthday celebration shirt. Blowing Rock, 1973.

a car nearby, its door open. The father, in white clothing and a light hat, poses formally, looking off into the distance, removed, as the son stands close to him, looking into the picture plane. This drawing served as the study for a painting, which placed the father in complete isolation, flanked by two other family compositions, one with a young woman like the one in the photograph, another featuring a family group. A different work is based upon a cropped 1940 photograph in front of the Dunlap house in Grady, Mississippi. A studio photograph of the artist seated in front of the painting suggests his place within the larger context of family. Dunlap bought this painting back from its original owners and now keeps it in his Mathiston studio.

During these first years in North Carolina he unified his aesthetic concerns in a series of prints, drawings, paintings, and collage compositions, and increasingly used photography as a tool. He experimented with self-portraiture, using his image instead of the old masters, and pop culture, attaching a black velvet painting (before velvet painting was advanced by Julian Schnabel in the 1980s) in his *Award Winning Painting*, which incorporated one of his early award ribbons. He also initiated the Landscape and Variable series, including the images of a barn in snow in *Landscape and Variable* (1973). A major painting from this period, forecasting directions in his later art, is *The Last Mississippi Painting*, a carefully painted composition incorporating elements of the Old Masters series, the Portrait series, vernacular architectural forms, and a skewed canvas grafted onto the main panel. In this bravura work, Dutch Masters combine with Mississippi family portraits—sketchy images derived from photographs (and memories) of father and relatives (specific and metaphorical)—merging on a fluid ground, filled with dripping paint marks and stenciled lettering.

Many of Dunlap's later themes and methods of working were contained and suggested in this large, ambitious early work. In a text accompanying an illustration of *The Last Mississippi Painting* in a 1986 exhibition catalogue (*Reveries & Mississippi Memories*), he writes, "The Mississippi of my youth was populated with giants and heroes—larger than life characters who were anything but Value Neutral. As I remember there was little consensus among them, but they *stood* for something. Right or wrong . . . it didn't matter. These folks were recalcitrant and colorful and I miss them. Some told stories—fables and parables that proved useful tools to live by—a few even wrote them down—William Faulkner once observed that people in Mississippi 'don't read books—they write them.'"[17]

Mississippi, his family, and the larger culture of this region remained essential concerns during these years, reflected in both traditional and nontraditional works, including *Starnes House, Mathiston, Mississippi*. For his artist's demonstration at the Mississippi Arts Festival in 1973, Dunlap, wearing a pristine white suit, in conscious mimicry of old-time Southern politicians such as former Mississippi governor James K. Vardaman, created a urethane foam sculpture on the floor of the Old Capitol. From

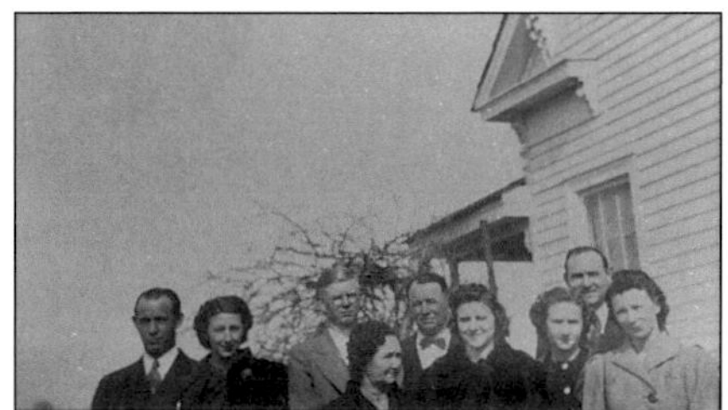
26

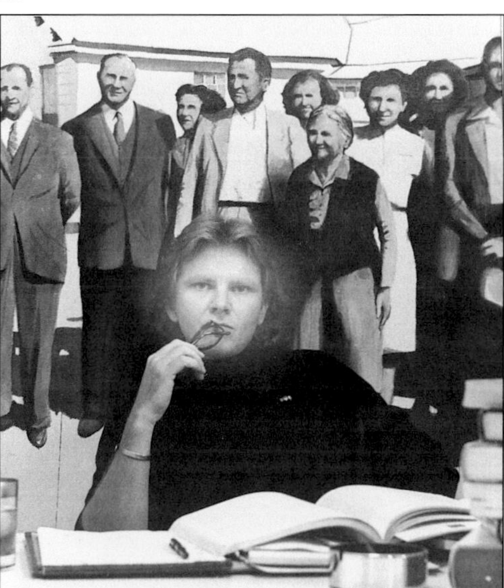
27

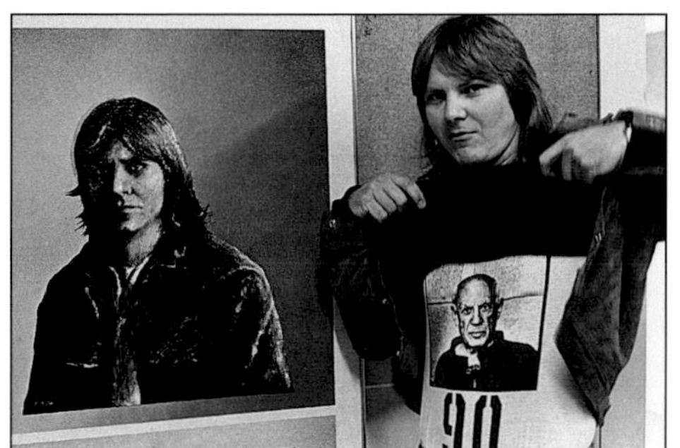
28

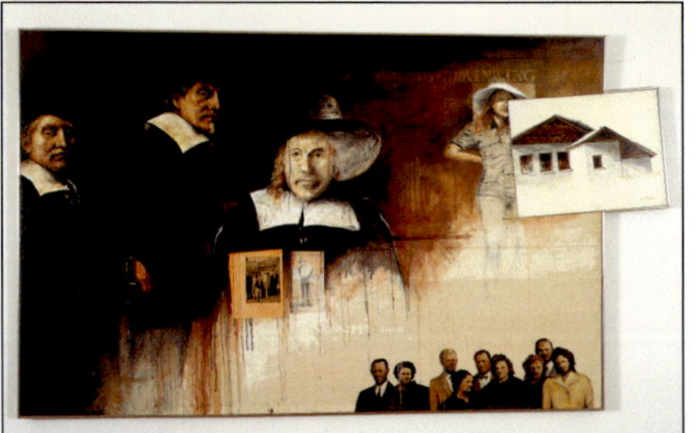

29

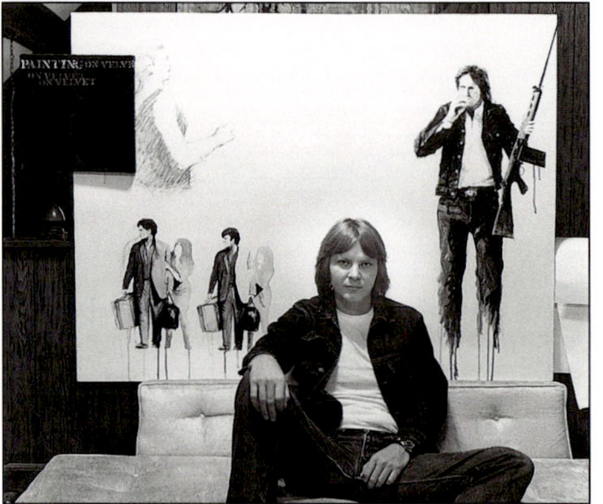

30

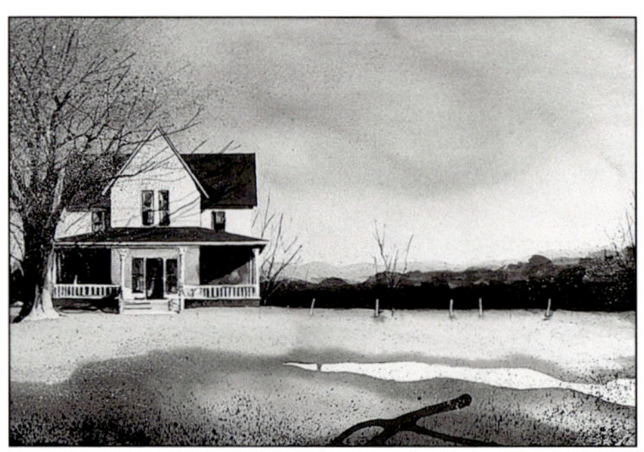

31

Fig. 29. *The Last Mississippi Painting*, 1972–73. Polymer paint and collage on canvas, 66 3/4 x 112 3/4. Private collection. Photograph by Hubert Worley.

Fig. 30. *Award Winning Painting*, photo in Blowing Rock, 1973. Polymer paint and found objects on canvas.

Fig. 31. *Starnes House, Mathiston, Mississippi*, 1971. Watercolor and polymer paint on paper, 22 x 30. Collection of Museum of Mississippi History, Mississippi Department of Archives and History.

Fig. 32. Old Capitol Museum in Jackson, Mississippi, 1973.

Fig. 33. "Dunlap for Governor" performance piece, Mississippi Arts Festival, 1973.

the same dais, he presented a performance art piece, "Dunlap for Governor." This unique fusion of contemporary art and political antics featured the installation of self-portrait posters, stenciled with "Dunlap for Governor" and "Impeach Dunlap," across the landscape of Jackson. His political platform was built around one concept, "good taste." He promised to remain in the Blue Ridge Mountains and send the occasional instructional postcard to the legislature. Needless to say, he was not elected.

Dunlap had been raised with country dogs and his grandfather's purebred hounds. In North Carolina, dogs began to enter his art as subject matter, though these were mountain dogs. Some were shown playing or hunting in the snow. The one portrayed in *Jude the Obscure* was a neighbor's dog that Dunlap befriended and admired. The four-panel composition presents the dog and his shadow moving through a range of distances, apparently approaching the viewer. In some panels the dog is overlaid with lines and grid patterns, characteristic of Dunlap's landscape compositions. Like Prince, the revered dog of his childhood, Jude was killed in his natural environment. Dunlap created this work as a landscape meditation on loss and memory, as well as a lamentation of one dog's animated spirit (p. 48).

Beginning in 1974, Dunlap founded and directed (until 1979) the ASU-NY program, an urban extension

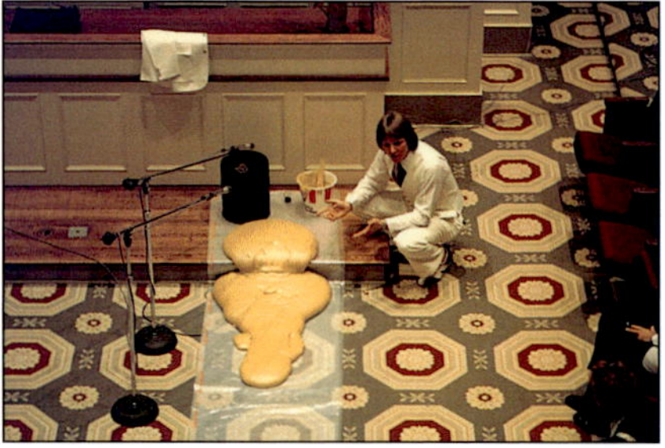

32

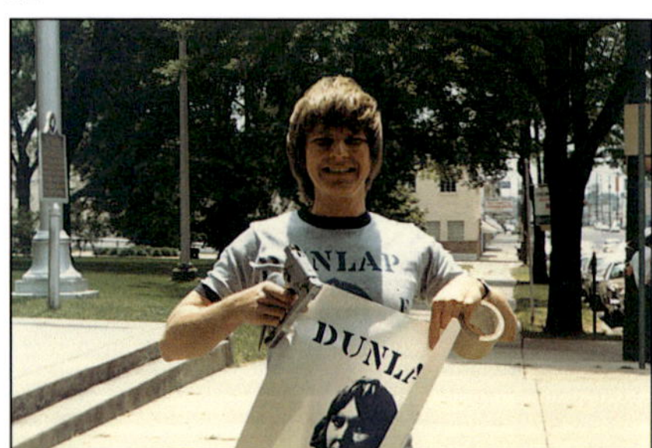

33

campus of Appalachian State University. Recognizing that Southern universities such as Wake Forest owned villas for student exchange programs in Venice, he created something new, a Southern arts residency program in New York. The concept evolved as he traveled in and out of New York's art world. He returned to Boone and presented the idea to his department chair and the university's development office. When ASU agreed, he returned to New York and rented a loft at 67 Vestry Street, in New York's emerging Tribeca district. "This was when SoHo was really taking off—and they could have immediate access to it," Dunlap explains. "You could fly from Greensboro, North Carolina, to New York for forty dollars, so the kids were going back and forth for ten-day periods of time."[18] The artists John Chamberlain and Marisol were located in the building. It was not unusual for ASU students to confront the very artists they had been studying in art history in a social situation.

In 1975, one year after starting the ASU-NY project, Dunlap was appointed director of the University Gallery. He also became active in the university's Artist/Lecture series, bringing to the ASU campus such notable visitors as James Dickey, Tom Wolfe, Vito Acconci, Marcia Tucker, and Margaret Mead, as well as Black Mountain College alumni Jonathan Williams and Lyle Bonge. In 1977, Dunlap became the director of Appalachian House, a second ASU extension campus, located on 3rd Street S.E. in Washington, D.C. The innovative projects he developed and guided at Appalachian State helped bridge the distance between Boone and the nation's leading art centers and brought the ASU art program national recognition.

By the middle of the 1970s, Dunlap was convinced that evolutionary developments were taking place in the South's art world. However, as he traveled and explored the larger art world, he saw little recognition of these advancements. In 1976, when Jimmy Carter entered office as a new president from the South, Dunlap and Jane Livingston organized the first Southern Rim Conference, focusing upon Southern regionalism and the changing role of art in the South. Held at ASU's Camp Broad Stone with support from the NEA, this conference was an effort to document the emergence of a new generation of art and

34

Fig. 34. First Southern Rim Conference, Camp Broad Stone, Valle Crucis, North Carolina, 1976.

Fig. 35. (Front) Paul Schimmel, Bill Eggleston; (back) Dunlap, Bill Fagaly, Warren Dennis, Jane Livingston, John Alexander.

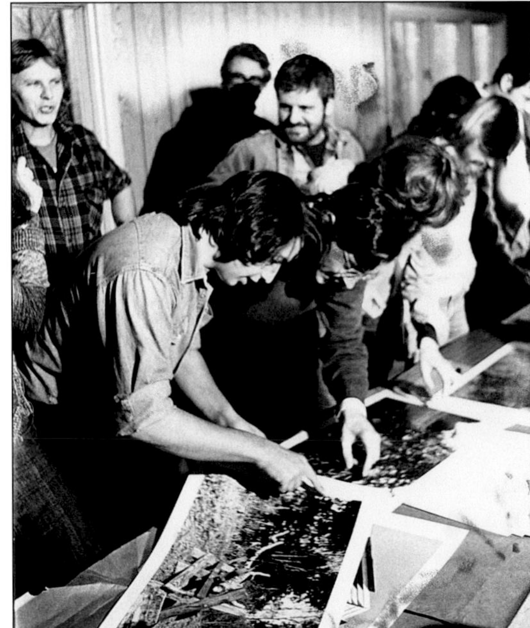

35

artists from the South, including William Eggleston, who brought his new series, devoted to Plains, Georgia, and the places and events he witnessed during the election year. The gathering in the mountains has become legendary, taking on mythic stature. Participants such as Terry Allen, John Alexander, Bill Christenberry, Eggleston, Bill Fagaly, Livingston, Ed McGowin, Charmaine Locke, Jerry Noe, Paul Schimmel, James Surls, and Marcia Tucker have since become widely recognized figures. Three years later, this event served as the focus of a controversial symposium, "Recurring Regionalism: The Southern Rim," presented by Dunlap at the 1979 College Art Association of America Conference in Washington, D.C.

In October 1983, Southern Rim 2, organized by Linda Burgess, was presented by Birmingham-Southern College and the Birmingham Museum of Art. The program brochure describes "a legacy that is owned by the American South," based upon "a strong oral tradition" and "story-telling" that was reflected in the "scores of writers who have emerged from the region." This tradition "greatly influenced its first generation of visual artists. . . . Emerging from the region are numbers of artists whose work is imbued with a strong sense of narrative . . . tapping the same source previously mined by their literary counterparts."[19] Participants included John Alexander, Jo Harvey Allen, Terry Allen, William Christenberry, Harry Crews, Willam Dunlap, Fannie Flagg, Frank Fleming, Ke Francis, James Hill, Mitchell Kahan, Mary Lynn Kotz, Jane Livingston, Ed McGowin, Jim Roche, James Surls, Marcia Tucker, and Jonathan Williams.

During the 1970s, while he explored the old pathways along the Blue Ridge Parkway at a slower pace, Dunlap became immersed in another way of seeing America. Increasingly, he began to see the landscape "through the windshield of a car, with an adult beverage in hand," extending his experience of a changing Southern landscape as cities and suburban areas expanded along the rapidly growing interstate highway system. He abhorred the destruction of the rural landscape and the vernacular architectural forms in these environments, as well as the encroachment upon historic sites and prominent Civil War battlegrounds. Yet, as he tells Mary Lynn Kotz in 1989, these road trips, when he put thousands of miles on his car traveling between North Carolina, Mississippi, New York, and Washington, became central to the advancement of his vision of the contemporary American landscape. "I get excited about road trips, because information comes out of them. When the light is just right, and a building or boulder catches my eye, or a certain green pops out of the woods, I will stop and aim my camera. When I get back to the studio, that film brings back the experience and I make art about that. But also, when I am in motion at about sixty miles per hour and the landscape is sliding by, I do my very best abstract, analytical thinking. I figure things out."[20]

As a result, he developed a new series of horizontal paintings, Off the Interstate, which he exhibited in Washington and New York (pp. 54–55). In the spring of 1976, he exhibited some of them, including *Off the Interstate—Winter* and *Winter Light*, along with his Hybrid Series of abstract collaged landscapes, at the Adams Davidson Galleries in Washington. The Hybrid Series reflected his movement away from the portrait tradition and toward mapping, gridding, and marking the landscape, both literally and abstractly. Looking back in 1981, when paintings such as his *Early Light—Fog Bound I and II* were featured in the exhibition, *More than Land or Sky: Art from Appalachia* at the National Museum of American Art, he describes the importance of these works. "I was born in northern Mississippi, in those red clay hills at the southeastern-most base of the Appalachian range. The Natchez Trace, a game trail for the French, Scottish, and Irish settlers on their way south, ran through my home town. It's now a National Park, as is the Blue Ridge Parkway, which follows the same Appalachian Trail, used also in its turn by some of the same game, and by Indian, immigrant, and government road builders. . . . My work is all about the landscape that flanks these two officially converted old roads. As a member of the postwar generation set free by . . . the automobile . . . I've seen the landscape between New Orleans and New York become a peripheral blur—something glanced at out the window at high speed, a unique perspective—and one that makes the pursuit of absolute clarity more difficult, but no less rewarding."[21]

In certain ways his sentiments echo those of the earlier Hudson River School painters, who questioned the impact of industrialization upon the pristine American landscape of the early nineteenth century. Looking at this period of his art, Barbara Rose indicates that this is where Dunlap "first identified a 'sense of place' as his theme,"

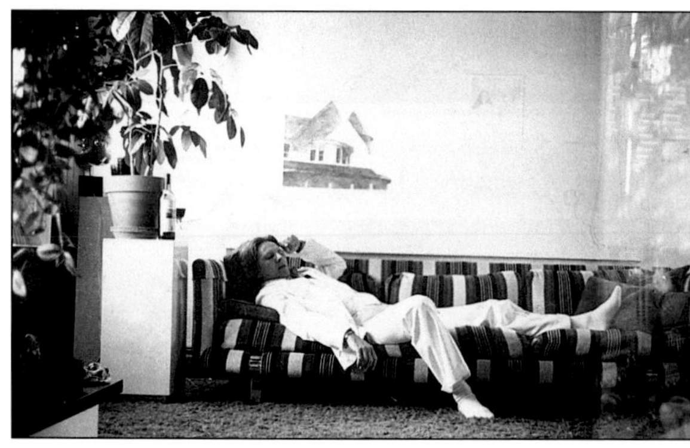

36

37

Figs. 36–37. Blowing Rock, North Carolina, 1975. Hybrid Series in background.

Fig. 38. Works in progress, McLean, Virginia, 1981. Photograph by Lisa Berg.

Fig. 39. Portrait mask of James Dickey, aluminum cast made in 1974. Photograph by Terry Parke.

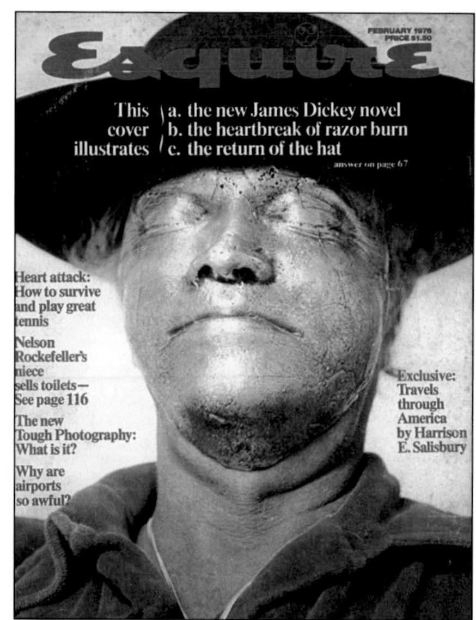

39

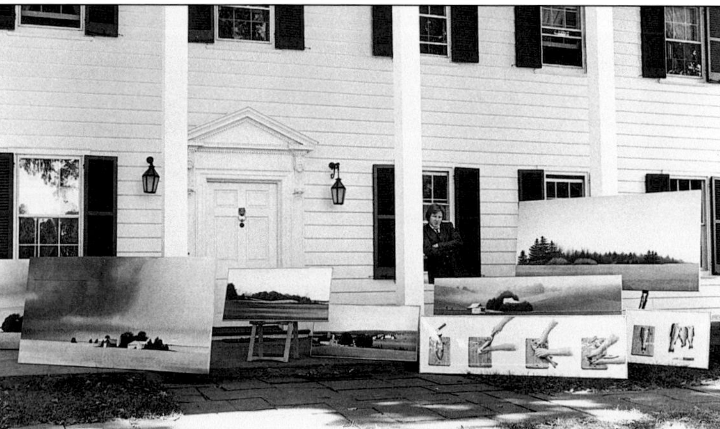

38

and adds that he could have "spoken of a sense of time as well," creating images that "evoke the rapidly disappearing past." She, too, draws comparisons to the evolution of the American landscape painting tradition in his work of this period.[22]

By the middle of the 1970s, he also looked to specific details and smaller elements of the landscape environment—focused images of trout, irises, and diverse other isolated objects. Though he had fished little since childhood, he began to trout fish in the company of friends in North Carolina and found fish to be an increasingly worthy subject for his art. In 1978 he created a large work, *Rainbow Trout Farm*, that showed, in six steps, how to clean and fillet a fish (p. 47). Rather than portray a single fish as a still life, he created a complex piece that suggests time and an evolving process, recalling works such as *Learn to Paint Like Rembrandt in Three Easy Steps*. A photograph from the period shows the range of his works, in subject and scale.

During the 1976–77 academic year, Dunlap took a sabbatical leave from ASU to spend time in New York and Washington, exhibiting and exploring the possibilities of a full-time career as an artist. At the Corcoran in Washington, he visited with Jane Livingston, William Christenberry, and Ed McGowin, associates who would become increasingly important allies. Earlier in 1976, he had gained some notoriety when his cover piece for *Esquire* magazine, a cast portrait mask of James Dickey, caused the poet to be temporarily blinded when seepage of calcium from the plaster caused an alkaline burn on Dickey's corneas.[23]

In 1978, Dunlap arranged for ASU students to work with Christo and Jeanne-Claude on the Wrapped Walkways project in Kansas City, and he expanded his exhibition activities in galleries across the country. Continuing art historical projects devoted to the European masters, in 1978 he created *Reluctant Water Lilies*, in response to seeing a Monet exhibition in St. Louis, and another exploration testing the range of his own technical skills (p. 48). He launched a new series devoted to American masters, including Andrew Wyeth, who was initially the subject of prints such as *Christina at the Beach*, completed in the early 1970s (p. 43). Later, in 1985, he paid tribute to the Brandywine School's unique landscape imagery in *Famous American Art Place #47* (p. 61).

In 1979, Larry Edwards invited Dunlap to accept a position as Professor of Art and Director of Special Projects at Memphis State University. Dunlap moved from ASU, but retained strong ties to the students, faculty, and programs there. In Memphis, which has long been tied to the culture of Mississippi, he advanced friendships with William Eggleston and rediscovered his earlier ties to the music and literary world there. He lived out of the city in the Germantown area, before it developed into an expansive suburb, and while there filmed a documentary, *Memphis, Home of the Blues*, on a neighboring hog farming operation, one of a series of experimentations in film. He completed a large painting, *Landscape with "Have Mercy,"* incorporating his off-the-interstate landscape imagery with a portrait of himself and a legendary figure he had met in South Carolina, nicknamed "Have Mercy" (pp. 52–53).

Memphis was in a transitional period during this time, before the revival of downtown began with the reopening of the Peabody Hotel, when matters often still centered on the death of Martin Luther King Jr. there, in 1968, at the Lorraine Motel (now the site of the National Civil Rights Museum). After a year in Memphis, Dunlap ended his teaching career.

III
Washington and New York

In 1980, Dunlap moved to Ranleigh Manor House, in McLean, Virginia, a historic estate owned by his friend John Harbert, where he maintains a studio. During a 1995 interview in Washington, he explains why he initially moved to the city. "I had great good friends up here and an opportunity to put the studio together on a piece of property in McLean. And my intention then was to spend some time in the mountains of North Carolina where I still had a house and a wife. And this would be sort of my northernmost outpost. But as things turned out, the wife wandered away and took the house with her. So I ended up living here." He also discovered that he was highly productive as an artist in this new environment. "New York is more seductive for me. I think Washington's a better place to work and a better town for conversation than New York. The museums here are very giving, very open. The more I'm around an environment like this the better I'm bound to be."[24] Notwithstanding his move to Washington, Dunlap continued to spend time and work in New York. Linda Burgess soon moved to Manhattan, and their relationship strengthened. Together they had a series of lofts downtown, culminating with the purchase of a space at 548 Broadway in 1988.

The 1980s and 1990s proved to be important for the evolution of Dunlap's national and international stature. During this period he created the *Panorama of the American Landscape*. He explored new subjects, expanded earlier themes and experimented in new media, while exhibiting widely and selling works to important collections. He received a range of awards and fellowships which enabled him to travel extensively. After he was divorced from his first wife, he was remarried, to Linda Burgess, in 1988. That year, he launched his career with WETA as a television commentator and writer. During the 1990s, he received the Mississippi Governor's Arts Award then initiated his role as Master of Ceremonies for that event. In 1995, Linda and Bill's daughter, Maggie, was born. And, in 1999, his mother died following a long illness. He and Linda sold their loft and studio in New York.

The Washington art world was inviting for an artist from the South. William Christenberry, Ed McGowin, Sam Gilliam, and Robert Stackhouse, as well as members of the Washington Color School, were active here. These younger artists had rejuvenated the Henri, Middendorf, Angus White, and Adams Davidson Galleries. Nationally prominent museums such as the National Gallery of Art, the National Collection of Fine Arts, and the Phillips Collection were an important presence, but none were as crucial for these artists as the Corcoran Gallery. There Jane Livingston and other curators advanced an innovative series of exhibitions and programs. In 1976, the American bicentennial launched the larger trend to recognize American art and artists in a new range of exhibitions, collecting, scholarship, and publications. A changing American art market followed, one that would open new opportunities for Dunlap and his contemporaries to explore their Southern narrative themes.

A significant number of important Southern exhibitions were presented at the Corcoran Gallery of Art. Fellow Mississippi artist Ed McGowin pioneered the opening of Washington museums to a contemporary Southern aesthetic with his 1975 *True Stories* exhibition at the Corcoran. In 1982, *Black Folk Art in America: 1930–1980*, organized by Jane Livingston and John Beardsley, focused on self-taught artists from the South, a genre that was unknown to most Americans then. The next year, William Christenberry was the subject of a career survey, organized by Walter Hopps at the de Menil Museum in Houston, that filled the Corcoran's exhibition galleries. This was a significant career event for Christenberry, who is now recognized as a dean of the Washington art world.

Elsewhere, three milestone exhibitions contributed to advancing Southern art and artists to national audiences. Mississippi native William Eggleston was the subject of the first exhibition of color photography and a related publication, *William Eggleston's Guide*, presented by the Museum of Modern Art in 1976. In 1983, the Virginia Museum of Art organized a large traveling exhibition, *Painting in the South: 1564–1980*, accompanied by a scholarly catalogue. And in 1984, the Columbia Museum of Art in Columbia, South Carolina, organized another survey exhibition, *Art and Artists of the South: The Robert P. Coggins Collection*, also accompanied by a catalogue. The Coggins Collection became the foundation and inspiration for the first museum of Southern art, the Morris Museum, in Augusta, Georgia, which opened in 1992. Two related developments were the founding of the Center for the Study of Southern Folklore in Memphis in 1972, and the founding of the Center for the Study of Southern Culture by William Ferris at the University of Mississippi in 1977.

Dunlap was well aware of these advancements in the field of Southern art and culture and became increasingly involved with those organizing these initiatives during the 1980s. As his intuition had suggested in 1976, when he organized the first Southern Rim Conference at ASU, there was growing national interest in the art and culture of the South, just as the related political and economic resurgence of the region brought the South greater stature in the nation's capital, his new home. From Washington, always closely allied with the history and culture of the South, he was well positioned to become increasingly active in the social and political evolution of these national issues.

Dunlap continued his driving trips between Washington, New York, North Carolina, and Mississippi with regularity. The automobile served as more than a vehicle for his travels; it was a source of inspiration for his art and his thinking about his larger aesthetic vision and philosophy. Traveling through the landscape was crucial to the work he developed in the early 1980s. During this period he also became immersed in the history of the Civil War, expanding upon his childhood exposure to the war in the West. He drove throughout the Shenandoah Valley and visited Antietam, Gettysburg, and Chancellorsville to paint and photograph Civil War battlefields.

In this period, he continued to focus on smaller, more specific aspects of the environment, as reflected in paintings of individual trees in his American Landscape: Tree Trunk series. In 1981, he explains that these works emerged from the Off the Interstate series, when he studied a tree line in the late fall, trying to isolate a specific tree trunk "when the light comes in low, out of the south . . . and it bounces off of everything it doesn't bleach white. Well, these trees out toward Middleburg were just

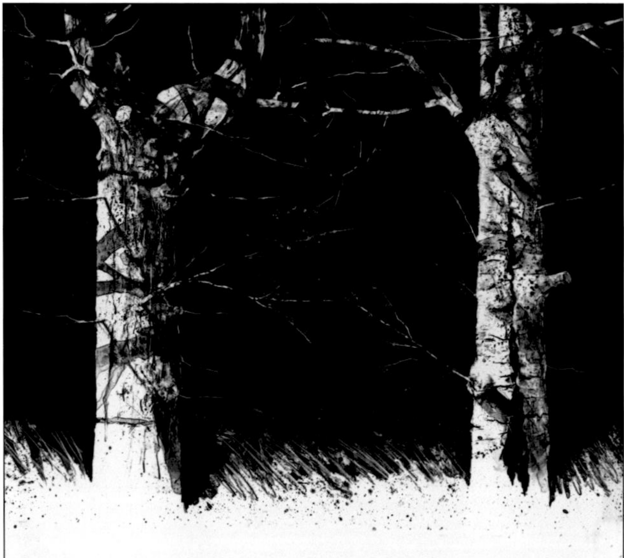

40

Fig. 40. *Double Trunk,* 1982. Lithograph, printed by Bill Lagattuta, Tamarind Institute, 16 x 16. Collection of Dr. Eleanor Gill, Olive Branch, Mississippi. Photograph by David Adamson.

as white as they could be. . . . It occurred to me that that look . . . that moment, if you will, was worth spending some time with."[25]

Later, in 1992, he suggests why he had developed such a specific and lasting interest in trees. "These old scarred and gnarled trees stand like sentinels: noble, even when felled by the likes of lightning or infestation. . . . I'm no genus snob when it comes to trees. I do not prefer the birch to the beech, the water oak to the willow, the sweetgum to cottonwood, nor even George Inness's glowing mossy trunks to Jacob Van Ruisdale's peeling painterly bark. . . . I cannot remember when I haven't been drawn to trees. . . . That which I climbed as a child, I now paint." And he concludes by noting the appeal of an isolated tree. "I find most haunting the visage of a single illuminated trunk on the edge of a wood not far from the road. It calls and beckons one to enter a heretofore unidentified sacred grove to be granted some special knowledge. A given in my personal mythology is the tenet that trees know all there is to know."[26]

In 1981, his landscapes were exhibited at the Smithsonian's Museum of American Art in *More than Land or Sky: The Art of Appalachia*. Dunlap said of a hunting trip that same year with John Harbert's family in eastern Oregon, "It was the first time I had been in the woods with a gun since I was sixteen or so. For me hunting had become a dark symbol of so much that was wrong in the sixties and seventies." The haunting image of severed isolated deer heads became central to his art in following years. Raised in Mississippi during the violent conflicts of the Civil Rights era, Dunlap's interest in the Civil War escalated during the 1970s and 1980s, when he recognized parallels to the violence of the war in Vietnam and the path of violence and destruction in American society. Using and expanding the deer head imagery, in 1982 he created *Three Deer Head for Antietam*, (pp. 62–63) a metaphorical image reflecting the penchant for violence in America, and a critical step, as was *Oversized Mule Deer* (1983, p. 62), in the evolution of his imagery for *Panorama of the American Landscape*.

He expanded his work with other artists, as evident in his participation with Christo and Jeanne-Claude in their *Surrounded Islands* project, created in Miami's Biscayne Bay. Using a special Polaroid camera located in Boston, in 1983 he worked with John Reuter to develop the Antecedents Series, a photographic series inspired by his family photographs. In 1984 and 1985, Dunlap served as an adjunct curator, working with curator Francis Fralin on a photographic exhibition and publication at the Corcoran Gallery, *The Indelible Image: Photographs of War—1846 to the Present*. On this project he discovered a photograph by Dr. William A. Bell, *Sgt. Wylliams, G Troop, 7th Cavalry. Killed in battle with the Cheyenne Indians. June 26, 1867*. This image of a flayed corpse filled with arrows would become an icon for Dunlap and appear in a number of his works.

In 1984, the year he began making lithographs with printer David Salgado at Trillium Graphics in San Francisco, his divorce from his wife, Bobbye Jean Kitchens, became final. Earlier, with the support of Jane Livingston and Bill Fagaly, Dunlap had helped her retired father, "Pappy" Kitchens, see his art included in museums and gallery exhibitions from Washington, D.C., to New Orleans.

A major breakthrough for Dunlap came in 1985, when Jane Livingston initiated a series of contemporary art projects in the classical rotunda of the Corcoran Gallery. In recent interviews, Dunlap discusses the evolution and significance of this expansive project, including the invitation from Livingston, who asked him what he might create, if he was given the space. "The space cries out for a contemporary cyclorama. I had seen the *Battle of Atlanta* as a child and had just visited Paul Philippoteaux's *Battle of Gettysburg* cyclorama and knew a great deal about the nineteenth-century cyclorama phenomenon." When she called to inform him that he had been given the commission, the realization set in that he had never worked on such a scale, and he pondered how to begin. Then he commissioned an architectural student to build a model of the rotunda as a starting point.

In addition to his historic research, he took a major new step when he cut up reproductions of his own earlier work and created new collages from these. He did not want to work from traditional models, but wanted to look for sources in his own imagery. "I wanted to find the straight line that ran through the heart of my own work," he explains. "The deer hunt in Oregon had been a profound experience. I made a piece using deer heads lined up into infinity, reflecting the irony of coming out of the Oregon woods and picking up a newspaper only to learn that Anwar Sadat had been assassinated by his own bodyguards and finding below the fold a headline announcing the largest deer harvest in Oregon's history."

Driving up and down the Valley of Virginia, along Interstate 81, provided the other important visual impetus. "On certain spring days, driving north toward Washington, the verdant landscape would suddenly turn. A weather system had dropped snow on both sides of the road. Then, several miles later, it would clear up and be green again. That experience contributed to my idea of having a sense of opposites in the panorama, with green on one side and white on the other, under a constant sky, with the battlefield of Antietam as a central subject."

Dunlap worked all winter on the panorama, creating

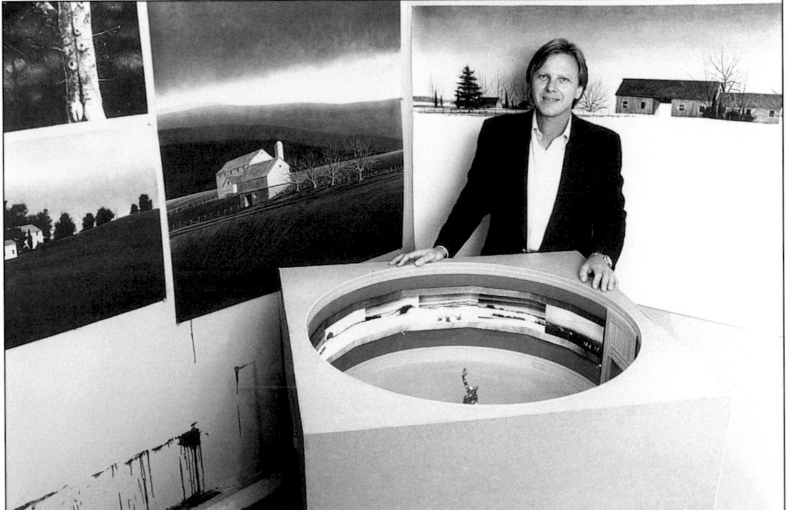

41

Fig. 41. Model of panorama made for rotunda of Corcoran Gallery, 1985. Photograph by Lisa Berg.

Fig. 42. The artist in his studio with panels from *Panorama of the American Landscape*, 1985. Photograph by Lisa Berg.

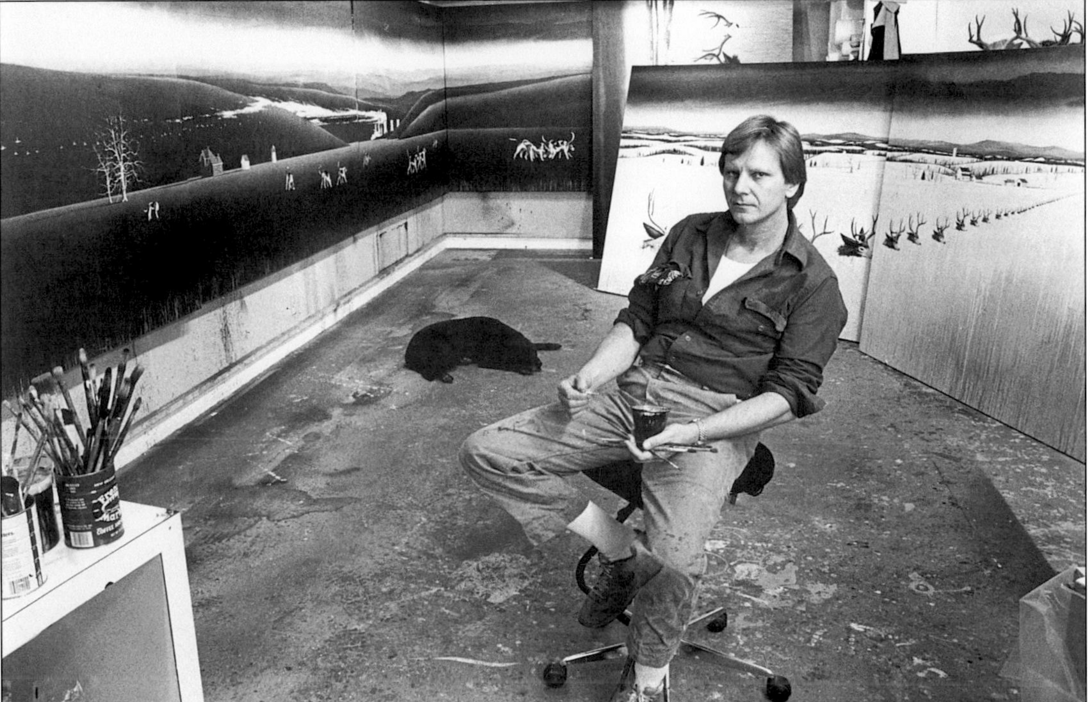

42

a system of fourteen equally sized panels. Only later, after a critic pointed it out, did he realize the relationship to the fourteen stations of the cross. He selected a size that was large but manageable (66″ x 94″), allowing him to move each canvas without assistance, creating what he calls his own golden mean. "I was the Vitruvian man. The length and reach of my arms became the deciding scale of the panels in the panorama." He could work on no more than four panels at once, so each canvas had to be capable of standing on its own as an individual work. His goal was for the total to become greater than the sum of its parts. He used a diverse range of both traditional and contemporary techniques to create the panels—painting, pouring, spraying, and dripping.

By specifically looking back and becoming a student of his work and the sources that led him to develop his imagery and iconography—he was able to transcend his own art history and experiment with his subjects in ways similar to his earlier experimentation with the old masters and the larger history of art. He also felt free to introduce new images and icons, distinctive images that permeate his work to the present—Walker hounds, classical architectural forms from Palladio and Jefferson, and the polluting smokestack of industry in nature. He expanded his use of the marked grids and map lines on the painted landscape, the manmade and real-estate-defined landscape of the nation.

His inspiration came, in part, from a trip to Atlanta when he was eight years old, as he tells Mary Lynn Kotz. "My grandmother took me to see the *Battle of Atlanta* cyclorama in Grant Park. It was a terrific illusion, with the background painting slipping into a diorama of tiny soldiers, horses, and wagons in the foreground. It made an indelible impression."[27] He also studied the panorama at Gettysburg and John Vanderlyn's view of Versailles at the Metropolitan Museum in New York.

Dunlap's fourteen panels are divided into two seven-panel compositions. A verdant Virginia hunt-country environment, filled with Walker hounds and fox hunting imagery, along with a bird of prey and its quarry, dominates one half, and the other is dominated by a row of deer heads, aligned and disappearing into the distance, in a stark and snow-filled symbolic and accurate rendering of the Antietam battlefield. One central figure is evident, a standing monumental image, perhaps an ambiguous "hero" of war, placed on the pedestal. Is this a Southern general or political leader, or a Northern one? Or is there another explanation for the presence of this isolated figure in this expansive composition? The history and geography of the Shenandoah Valley, which Dunlap had absorbed over years of driving through the region, and the history of Antietam and the Civil War infuse the composition. More than 23,000 Americans died there in America's bloodiest single day of battle (pp. 64–69).

Though dogs had entered his pictorial imagery in North Carolina, the panorama first introduced the Walker hound as a major subject and symbol. "This is important," Dunlap affirms. "When I visited the Middleburg hunt, I went to the kennels to draw and photograph the dogs there. These Virginia dogs, I was pleased to discover, were from the same bloodline as my grandfather's Mississippi dogs." Dunlap used these dogs not just because of their familiarity, nor because of their presence in the Virginia landscape. "These Walker hounds are the ultimate hunters, and deer the ultimate prey." In the background, behind the dogs and the deer, are rural houses and barns, derived from prototypes in his Off the Interstate series, with one form resembling the Starnes house.

Dunlap selected two main images as the focus of

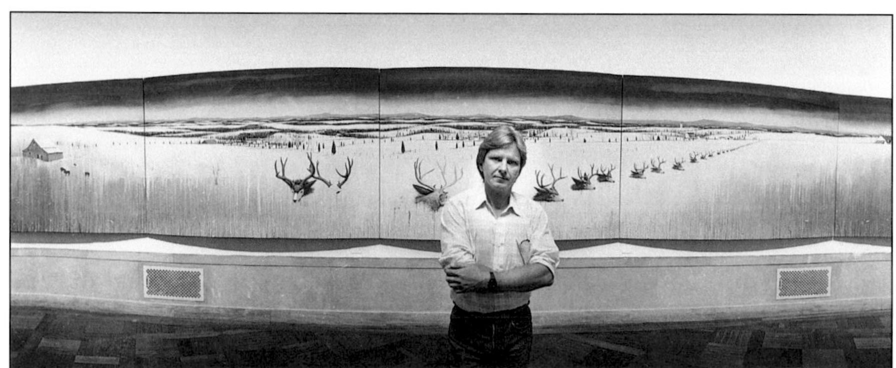

43

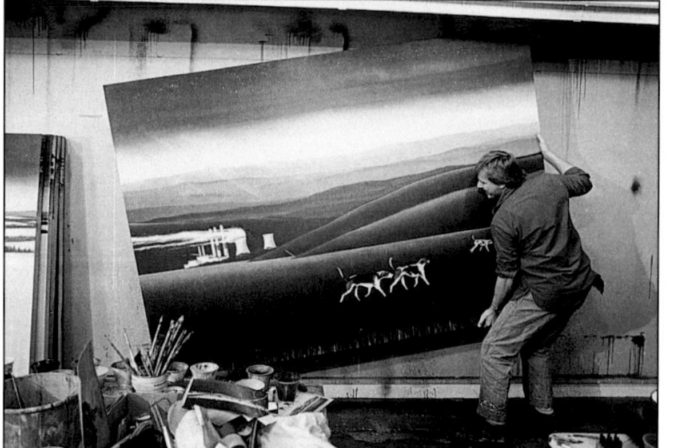

44

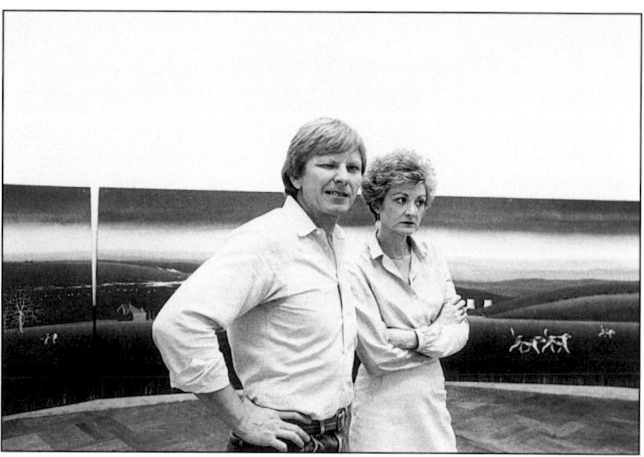

45

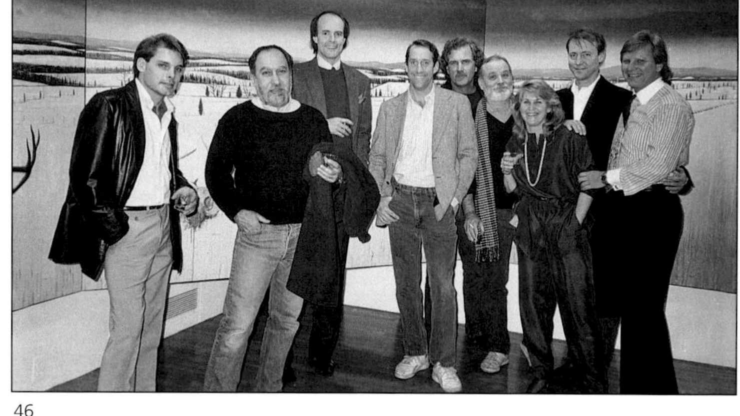

46

Fig. 43. Artist with panels from *Panorama of the American Landscape* at the Corcoran Gallery, 1985. Photograph by Robert Epstein.

Fig. 44. Work in progress in studio. Photograph by Jack Kotz.

Fig. 45. Dunlap and Jane Livingston during installation at Corcoran Gallery, 1985. Photograph by Jack Kotz.

Fig. 46. The S.W.A.T. Team: (from left) Richard Roederer, David Itchkawich, John Davis, John Alexander, Mac Whitney, Brian Doyle-Murray, Linda Burgess, Paul Manes, and Bill Dunlap at Sherry French Gallery, 1985.

each half of the panorama. On the winter side, he used *Three Deer Head for Antietam*, expanding the range and number of heads into an infinite space. On the opposite side, he used the cooling tower and factory image, derived from *Agrarian Industrial Complex*, an image reproduced on the cover of *Harper's* magazine. He did not invent these images for the panorama but selected them from existing concepts. "They were there," he explains. "They were working drawings. When I looked back through my work, I decided to use them as primary subjects. I made collages from that earlier work and installed them in the model. Everything else flowed from those two key images."

With the panorama, he combined his diverse artistic interests and explorations into a singular work, created specifically for the historic rotunda of the Corcoran Gallery. Dunlap, a trained sculptor, had essentially taught himself to paint after graduating from the University of Mississippi. The challenge of confronting the iconic figures of art history and working their images into his own compositions was of primary interest. In the panorama, he discovered a way to create a contemporary version of the traditional American historical painting, one that reflected the scale, cultural relevance, and historical stature of American landscape and historical paintings of the nineteenth century. Earlier, several contemporary artists, including Ronald Bladen, Gene Davis, Robert Stackhouse, and William Christenberry, had created large-scale sculptural compositions in and around the Corcoran. Dunlap, looking both to the history of the building and American painting, proposed not a sculptural form but a monumental new type of painting, his contemporary cyclorama, one that sought to evoke a strong sense of place.

This work might be interpreted as Dunlap's response to Church, Bierstadt, Moran, and other American landscape painters, as well as to the Luminist painters who inspired him after he attended John Wilmerding's exhibition, *American Light: The Luminist Movement, 1850–1875* at the National Gallery of Art. This panorama may also be seen as an updating of the mural revival of the Depression era, when small town post offices and federal buildings across the country, supported by the federal government and its Works Progress Administration (WPA), brought original art to large public audiences. These types of murals are on view across Mississippi, as evident during a recent visit to the Eupora post office with the artist, where a restored WPA mural, painted in 1945 by Tom Savage, was on view in the lobby.

When designing the panorama, Dunlap had no plans to exhibit the project in other locations. After its initial presentation, however, requests and opportunities began to appear, and he agreed to traveling the work. It was shown in New York, Connecticut, North Carolina, Colorado, Mississippi, Tennessee, and beyond. When it opened in New York at the Sherry French Gallery, many of his artist friends appeared in support of his exhibition and the project. One group of friends, aligned from the days of the Southern Rim Conference, were photographed at the opening and described by John Alexander: "This is the SWAT team—Southern White Art Trash—out to support Dunlap."[28] Accompanying him were Paul Manes, Terry Elkins, Richard Roederer, and Linda Burgess, Dunlap's future wife. Twenty years after its unveiling, *Panorama of the American Landscape* has moved comfortably into the twenty-first century, most recently exhibited at the Gibbes Museum of Art in Charleston in 2004 and 2005. An exhibition at the Ogden Museum of Southern Art in New

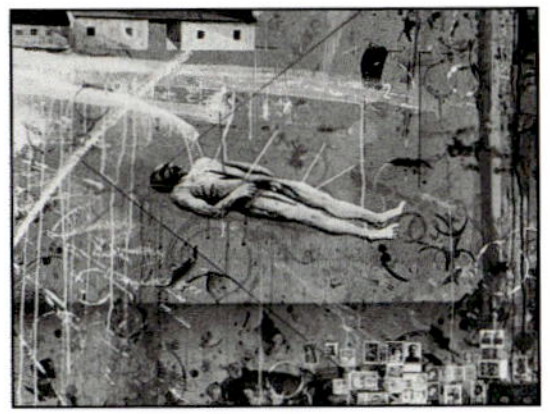

47

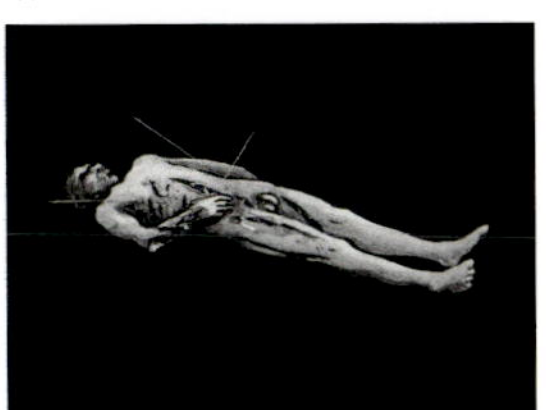

48

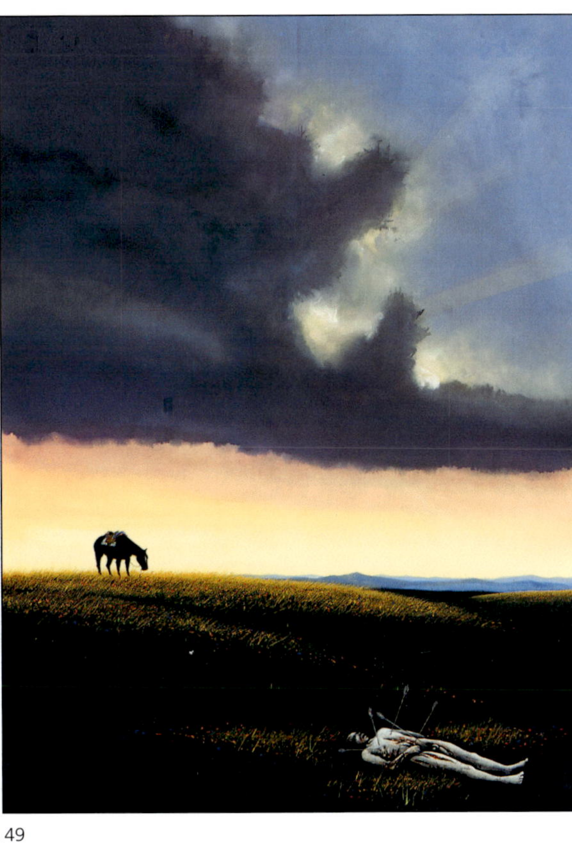

49

Fig. 47. Detail from *Meditations on the Origins of Agriculture in America*, 1987. Wood, canvas, polymer and oil paint, steel, snake skin, wire, flag, 48 x 96 x 24. Private collection. Photograph by Jack Meyer.

Fig. 48. *St. Sebastian of the Plains* (initial study), 1986. Initial study of Sergeant Wylliams from Dr. William Bell's carte de visite photograph, 1876. Polymer paint on canvas, 24 x 28. Private collection. Photograph by Jack Meyer.

Fig. 49. *Landscape and Variable: Indian Paint Brush*, 1987. Polymer paint on canvas, 96 x 67. Private collection. Photograph by Hubert Worley.

Orleans is scheduled for the fall of 2006. The Mississippi Museum of Art is planning to construct a special area to exhibit the panorama in its new building.

After the panorama was completed, Dunlap returned to the studio and created a series of significant canvases and a body of new constructions, incorporating in some of them the image of Sergeant Wylliams. *Landscape and Variable: Indian Paint Brush*, completed in 1987, depicts the lone figure, pierced by arrows, low on the ground, a waiting horse on the horizon line, beneath heavy clouds. "I found it the most hypnotic and compelling image I encountered during all those months of looking at bloody corpses in war photographs," he explains to Ruth Appelhof. "For me, it was the most *indelible image*. . . . It speaks volumes to the power of an image to surge past time and place and make connections with us now. . . . He's like some Saint Sebastian of the Plains—an American martyr, a symbolic sacrifice as fresh as the morning newspaper. His plight is as unnerving today as it was in 1867 when his photograph was mailed back East from Kansas for propaganda purposes. And I'm not through with him yet. I may one day find the very arrow that killed him—and put it in a construction, of course."[29]

Two additional pieces from this period, both incorporating images of Sergeant Wylliams, are notable within the larger context of his work. *Landscape and Variable: Deer Hide—Willow Seek* is a painted construction that combines diverse subjects of this era, including Sergeant Wylliams, a horizontal landscape composition with a house and barn, a Walker hound in a skewed, attached panel, and another attached segment, incorporating wood, deer hide, and a willow ball (p. 70). A large and highly charged construction, *Meditations on the Origins of Agriculture in America* is built upon his earlier concept of "found and fashioned" objects (p. 73). "This came directly from the studio," he explains. "The background is a four- by eight-foot plywood table top from my studio. It became very roughly textured, and rather than discard it, I put it up on the wall and waited for something to happen. And it did." He painted a landscape with architectural forms, derived from structures he had seen driving through New Jersey, across the top. He stuck a knife into the wood, piercing and violating the picture plane. And beneath a skewed landscape painting he placed "a little corner of the Confederate flag as a powerful symbol. People were, and are, upset by it. Using that immediately identifiable corner of the illegal flag spoke volumes about agriculture in America and its origins."

Large works that combined his painting and sculptural abilities became increasingly evident, as in *Large Mouth Founding Fatherland* from 1989 (pp. 84–85), featuring an iconic range of high and low art forms—the painted head of George Washington (painted by Dunlap after another old master, Gilbert Stuart), a painted still life and a landscape, and actual found objects, including a mounted fish, an old electric fan, and a carved wooden Coca-Cola bottle. During this period images of flowers and fish became increasingly evident (*Landscape and Variable: Season Change Iris Watch*) at about the same time that he discovered a Civil War Minnie ball while working in the iris bed of his Virginia garden. He returned to the three extra stretched canvases he had prepared for the panorama. Works such as *Landscape and Variable: The Bounty and Burden of History* are a summation of the iconic themes and subjects contained in the larger fourteen-panel composition.

Considering the importance of *The Bounty and Burden of History*, Alex Nyerges describes it as "a classic example of Dunlap's landscape painting as a Southern narrative art form." Looking at the foreground of the painting, Nyerges indicates that Dunlap "depicts fruit, such as watermelon, as evidence of the bounty . . . in America. . . . The fruit is . . . a direct quote from the work of Raphael Peale, inspired by an exhibition of intimate still lifes at the National Gallery of Art, 1988–89. A classic Walker hound, symbolizing the bounty of hunting, looks mournfully at the collection of fruits scattered on the ground. This scene is clearly a commentary questioning the meaning and cost of our success." After pointing out the presence of the hilltop mansion in the painting, recalling both Palladio's Villa Rotunda and Thomas Jefferson's Monticello, and the controlled vista associated with such structures, he points

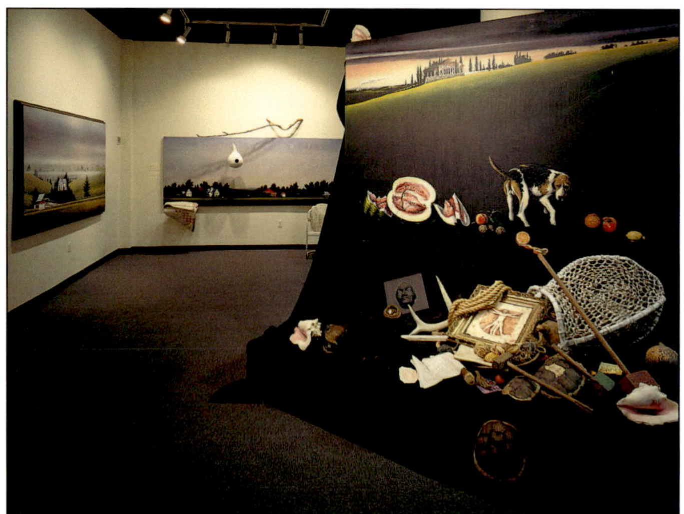

50

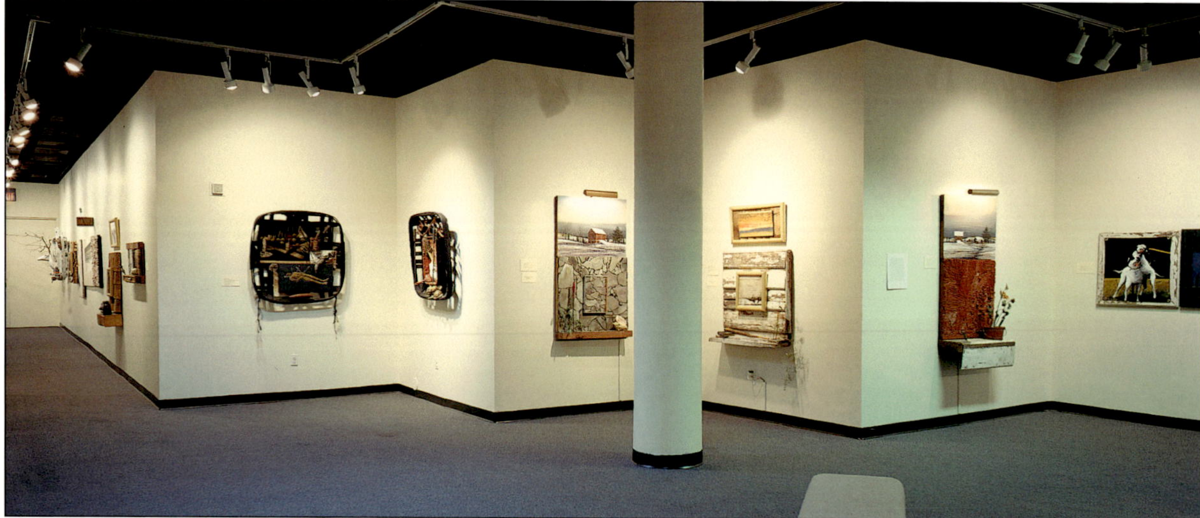

51

Figs. 50–51. *William Dunlap: Re-Constructed Re-Collections* exhibit, 1992. Art Museum of Western Virginia, Roanoke. Photographs by Jack Kotz.

to another type of structure. "In planning Monticello, Thomas Jefferson gave great attention to what we now term 'viewshed,' that land which was visible from high atop his building site. This landscape shows a similar viewshed; however, an industrial cooling tower spewing steam intrudes in the upper left corner of the scene. Doing double duty as a visual intrusion into this otherwise bucolic landscape and as a metaphor for progress and its cost to society, the smoke stacks take the landscape from traditionally bucolic underpinnings into a realm of social commentary not unlike Geroge Inness's depiction, a century earlier, of progress in the guise of the great iron horse, the locomotive."[30]

During this period Dunlap traveled extensively and received considerable professional recognition. Awarded a Rockefeller Foundation International Fellowship, he served as a Resident Scholar at the Bellagio Study Center. While in Italy, he and Linda Burgess married in a small private ceremony. They traveled together across Italy, visiting architectural and artistic landmarks and landscape environments. In 1988, he also began working as television and arts commentator with WETA in Washington, a profession that would open new directions for him in the broader Washington arts world. The program, *Around Town*, was advanced by Peggy Cafritz, who invited Dunlap to make an appearance on the show. "Peggy knew that I did not mind carrying on in public and wasn't short on opinions," he explains. "And she said, why don't you come on and talk about art? So I came on, and I think the first show that I did was the *Andrew Wyeth Helga* show . . . the next week Jackson Frost called me back. So I've been doing it pretty much ever since. And it's a wonderful concept. . . You get a handful of people who can talk. It's about conversation, but it's also about what's going on culturally in the environment, in a given time frame."[31]

This opportunity offered Dunlap a way to expand his role as an arts advocate in the Washington area, and allowed him to review national exhibitions and projects taking place in the South and regions beyond Washington. He began writing articles for magazines as well. In 1989 he published a book with Willie Morris, *Homecomings*, which included an interview between the two, essays by Morris, and a folio of paintings by Dunlap, including three works with the image of Sergeant Wylliams (*Landscape and Variable: Deer Hide—Willow Seek*, 1987; *Meditations on the Origins of Agriculture in America*, 1987; and *Landscape and Variable: Indian Paint Brush*, 1987). In the interview with Morris, Dunlap describes his future plans for working in his Mississippi studio. "I would like to be here several months out of the year, in the fall and the spring certainly. My wife Linda [Burgess] has a studio in New York, I'm in Washington, so it makes sense to have a place on neutral ground. We can work wherever we are."[32]

In 1992 and 1993, *William Dunlap: Re-Constructed Re-Collections*, a exhibition organized by Ruth Stevens Appelhof for the Art Museum of Western Virginia, traveled in Virginia and in Mississippi. It featured a number of Dunlap's major paintings and constructions from the 1980s, as well as the emerging Object Lesson series. (pp. 95–97). Describing these works in the exhibition catalogue, Bill Kovach writes: "With his constructions Dunlap seems to have physically completed the bridge and provides for this generation an exciting new connection with the past. By engaging us in a discussion with ourselves about the tension which exists between the land and those of us who live and prey on it, Dunlap is helping us

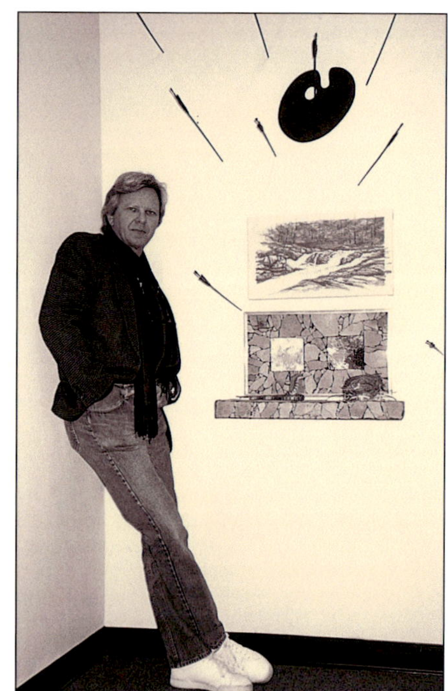

52

Fig. 52. The artist with *Genesis of the Art Wars*, Sherry French Gallery, 41 West 57th in New York, 1994. Photograph by Linda Burgess.

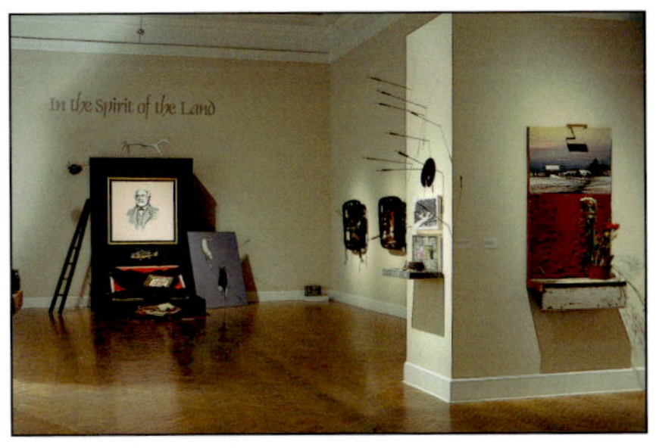

53

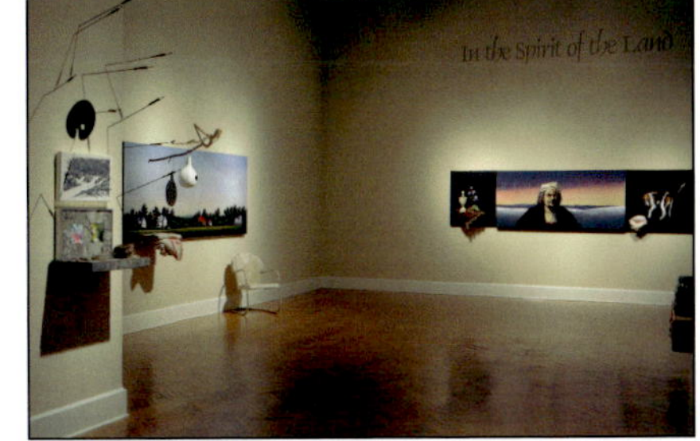

54

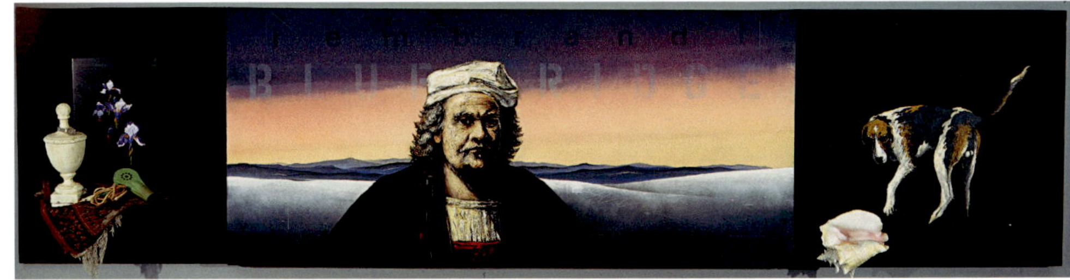

57

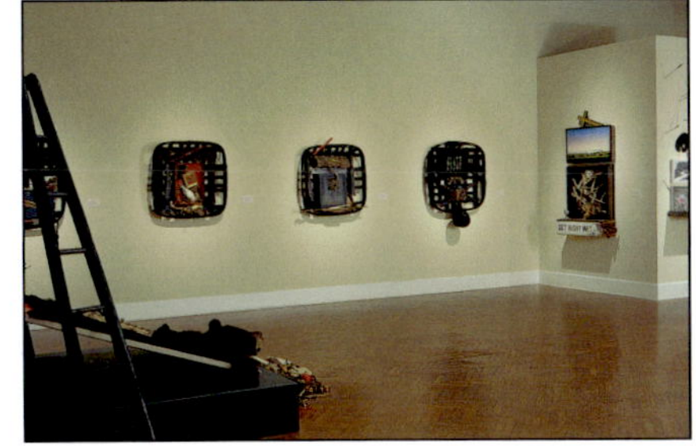

55

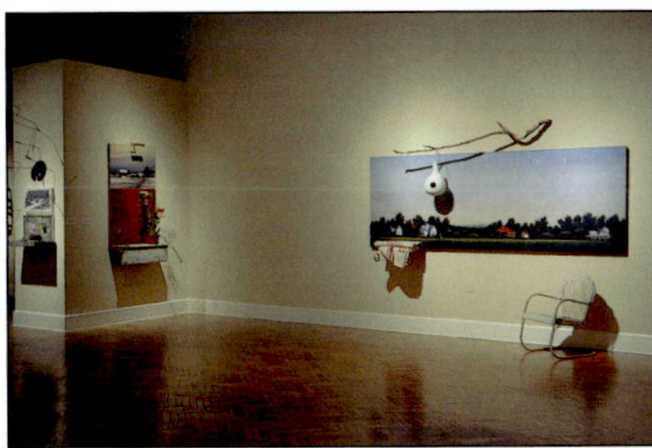

56

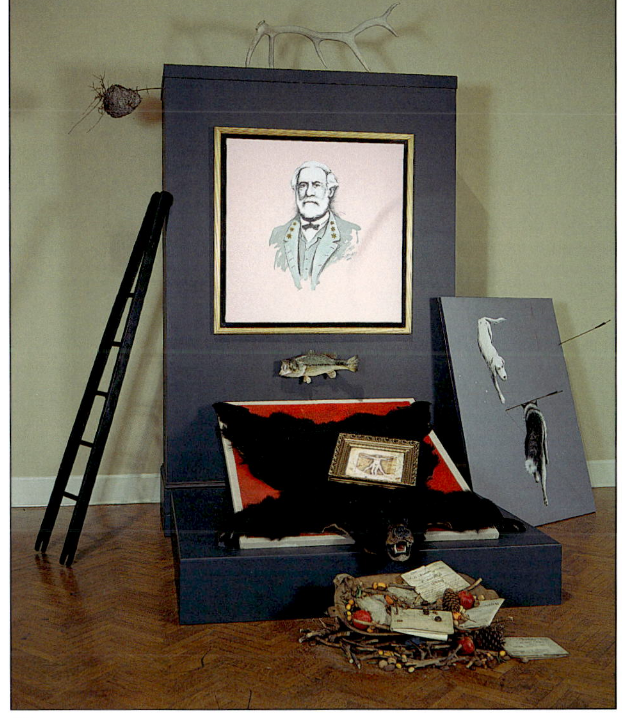

58

Figs. 53–56. *In the Spirit of the Land* exhibit, 1995–96. The Corcoran Gallery of Art, Washington, D.C. Photographs by Jack Meyer.

Fig. 57. *Rembrandt in the Blue Ridge*, 1994–95. Polymer paint on canvas, wood, shell, fabric, metal, found materials; triptych, 36 x 146 x 8. Collection of Jim and Liba Lambe, Roaring Gap, North Carolina. Photograph by Jack Meyer.

Fig. 58. *Vitruvian Bear,* 1995. Found objects, hornet nest, elk horn, ladder, large mouth bass, black bear rug, parchment, glass, paper, 98 x 72 x 72. The Corcoran Gallery of Art, Washington, D.C., *In the Spirit of the Land* exhibit. Photograph by Jack Meyer.

understand the nature and limits of our place here."[33] Speaking of the development of the series, Dunlap further notes, "My friend, the poet Jonathan Williams, said he could write poems but he'd 'just as soon stumble upon them, in the great *out there*.' I too can paint objects, but it's just as satisfying to find them and then incorporate them into larger, more grandiloquent work. I'm just trying to jog people's memories."[34]

One work from this period, *Genesis of the Art Wars*, served as Dunlap's response to the culture wars surrounding the controversial cancellation of Robert Maplethorpe at the Corcoran Gallery of Art. It incorporates an arrangement of arrows around an artist's palette, while below a landscape painting is installed above a construction made of slate, with materials as diverse as a bird's nest and a snake incorporated into the composition. Critics responded to these works in a number of ways, often including references to Dunlap's narrative interests and his kinship to the spirit of the great Southern writers. Artist Ed McGowin, reviewing works from this period, writes: "Bill Dunlap's paintings could be a history lesson for the historian. The pervasive sense of the past and the importance of it are recorded over and over in his art and evokes powerful memories of places the viewer has never been." A specific work from this period, *He'll Set Your Fields on Fire* (p. 100), intrigued McGowin, who observes, "A statement of madness by juxtaposing a mounted squirrel and a microphone in the context of a landscape painting and skull with snake skin is retold by the religious icons of the Christian cross on its side and 'Get Right Wit' (get right with God) sign. The total effect of the narrative on this viewer is that history proves the world is capricious." Concluding his review, McGowin offers a succinct summation of Dunlap's context and goals, "There are echoes of great southern writers, Faulkner, Welty, Williams; and great southern artists, Johns and Rauschenberg; leading to a personal statement that is articulate as it is complex. Meaning is layered. Logic is elliptical going around the center at varying speeds. For the viewer making the connections in Dunlap's art requires the same leap of faith that the artist makes in the production of the work. There is an absence of rhetoric or ideology to indoctrinate a conclusion. The skill and facility are deceptive and provide no net for the artist or the viewer. It is there simply to allow you to look at a very complex code. After that you are delightfully on your own."[35]

In 1995, the Corcoran Gallery invited Dunlap to return for another exhibition, *William Dunlap: In the Spirit of the Land*, curated by Jack Cowart with a catalogue essay by Barbara Rose. In a press release for the exhibition, Dunlap describes the new work by saying that "it combines elements of painting, sculpture and assemblage in such a way as to provoke connections and dialogue between our perceived historical past and the critical concerns of our current time and place."[36] Connecting to his own art history and his earlier works, he brought Rembrandt back into his art in the 1994 work, *Rembrandt in the Blue Ridge*. As Rose suggests, Dunlap painted Rembrandt skillfully, but reflected the artist's profile as "not only a cheap reproduction but also as a popular icon worshiped in the temples of art," creating in this work a

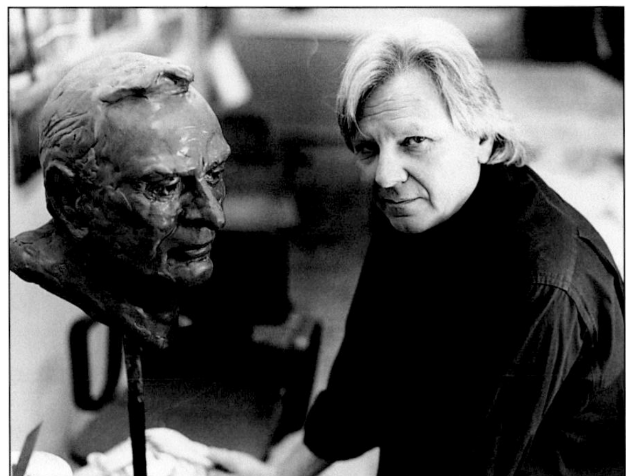

59

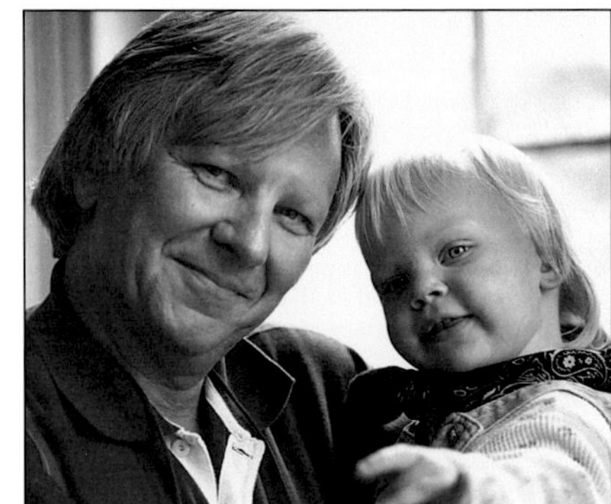

60

Fig. 59. Clay bust of Gore Vidal in studio in McLean, 2002. Photograph by Carol Harrison.

Fig. 60. Dunlap and daughter Maggie, 1997. Photograph by Stephen R. Brown at Polly Kraft's studio.

"thrice removed and decontextualized image [that] is a painted image of a mechanically reproduced reproduction of an old master." Calling the resulting work "uncanny," she concludes, "In Dunlap's work, the play between ironic mockery and sincere admiration creates a tension that is consistently intriguing. The association of Rembrandt with the Virginia hills suggests multiple meanings: perhaps the greatest European painter, whose name is synonymous with the idea of the masterpiece, may be on the losing side of the battle between art and nature at the very heart of the American aesthetic. For a man like Dunlap, who loves art and nature equally, choosing one over the other must surely have been difficult. His reconstructed Rembrandt dominates a weirdly uninhabited Blue Ridge landscape painted in a documentary factual style reminiscent of nineteenth-century American painting."[37]

In 1994, Dunlap received the Lila Wallace Foundation International Arts Fellowship, and he and Linda moved to Bangkok to study and compare Cha Praya-Mekong culture to that of the Yazoo-Mississippi River Delta. They traveled as well through Vietnam, Cambodia, Burma, and Southeast Asia. In 1996–97, he returned to Vietnam and co-curated an exhibition, *A Winding River: Contemporary Paintings from Vietnam*, for Meridian International Center in Washington, D.C. And the following year, *Outward Bound: American Painting on the Brink of the 21st Century* traveled in Asia.

During the mid-1990s, Dunlap found that he was spending less time in New York, though he still made regular visits to conduct his art business there. The birth of Linda and Bill's daughter, Margaret Staeger Gore Dunlap (Maggie), brought a new focus to their lives, and Bill was making frequent trips to Mississippi to spend time with his ailing mother, who now lived in the Starnes house. In 1999, four years after Maggie's birth, his mother Margaret died. Considering the future educational and social needs of their growing daughter, Bill and Linda sold the New York loft and acquired a new residence and studio in Coral Gables, Florida. The fact of an emerging international art scene in Miami was not lost on them.

IV
Mississippi, Washington, and Florida

Bill Dunlap and Linda Burgess entered the twenty-first century with new priorities and geographic realities with the adaptive reuse of the Starnes house and studio and the refocusing of their relationship to the New York art world. With these changes, Dunlap's profile in Mississippi increased, and as an expanding museum and gallery scene developed in New Orleans, Dunlap became increasingly active there as well. He watched Mississippi change and be reborn, as tourism and casinos flourished across the state and along the Gulf Coast. In places like Clarksdale, where Morgan Freeman opened a restaurant and blues club, he witnessed reverse migration, Mississippians returning home to embrace the best traditions in the state.

In Florida, he and Linda expanded their ties to the museum and art scene in and around Miami. He gradually began to incorporate bits of Florida environment into his work—most literally evident in the palm bracs he began to collect and manipulate. He exhibited these new found object sculptures in New Orleans at the Contemporary Art Center in 2002, at the grand opening of the Ogden Museum of Southern Art in 2003, and at the Søren Christensen Gallery in 2004. To a larger degree, his immersion in the world culture evident in Miami, especially its ties to Latin America, reinforced his global vision and sense of an evolving American culture, including a changing Southern culture.

Dunlap seldom ventured into portraiture, an exception being his commission to paint Mississippi governor Ray Mabus (1988–92). A second exception came when he decided to return to the type of sculpture he had created as a graduate student at the University of Mississippi. In 1999 he proposed to make a portrait bust of writer, distant relative, and friend Gore Vidal. (Dunlap's maternal grandmother, Mary Elise Gore, and Vidal's grandfather, Thomas Pryor Gore, were first cousins.) Accompanied by Washington filmmaker Karen Thomas, who planned a documentary on the process, he visited Vidal's home in Ravello, Italy. In "Bring Me the Head of Gore Vidal," an article published in the *Washingtonian*, Dunlap chronicles the trip and describes the process of creating the bust. "The modeling of a portrait head is pretty straightforward. Earth's own malleable clay is applied to a rigid armature and then shaped and formed by addition and subtraction. Details and textures are achieved with a variety of tools, but none is better than the fingers and thumbs of the sculptor's hands." He goes on to observe, "There's something timeless, even biblical, about forming the image of a man in clay. . . . When the modeling is done, a plaster impression is taken and the original is destroyed.[38]

Dunlap's work since 2003 reflects a process of revisiting and reworking his primary themes and subjects—revising, refreshing, and updating them. And in many cases he has extended the meaning and depth of his subjects, what he commonly calls his "cast of characters," much as Faulkner did. In 2000, not long after his relocation to Florida, Dunlap created a unique installation, *William Dunlap: Objects Found and Fashioned,* at the Ogden Museum of Southern Art's transitional gallery at 603 Julia Street. Starting from a work in the museum's collection, *Landscape and Variable: The Bounty and Burden of History*,

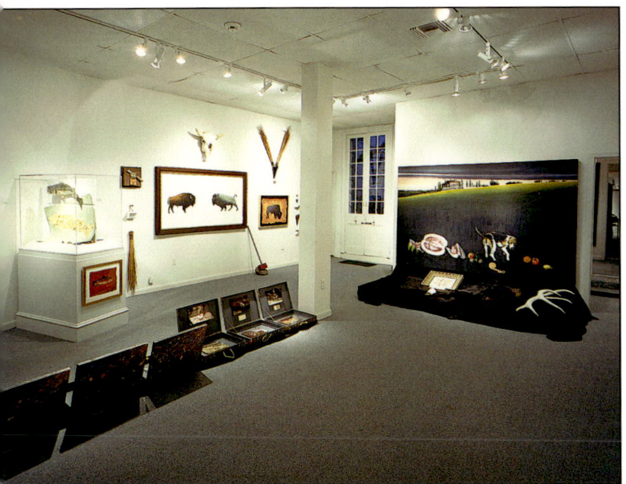

61

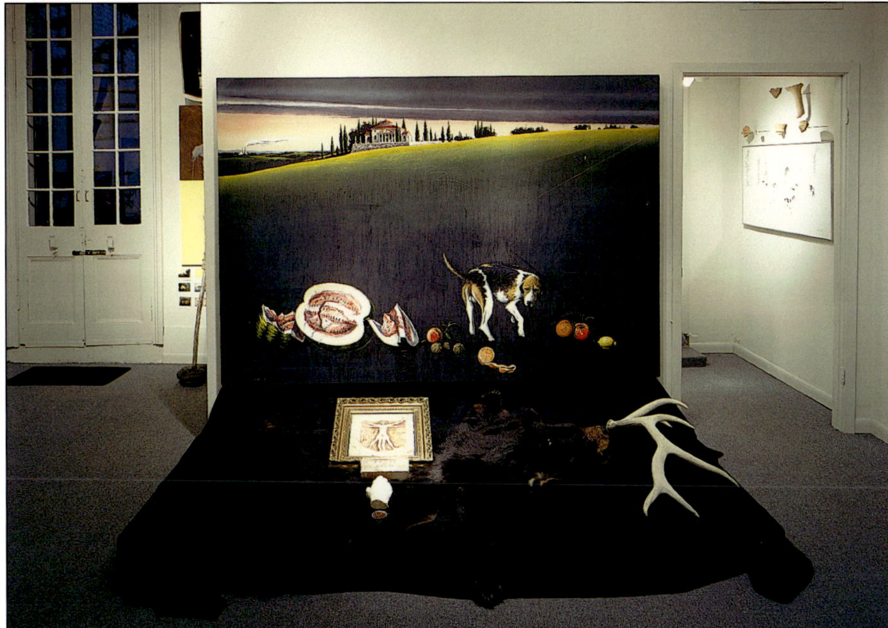

62

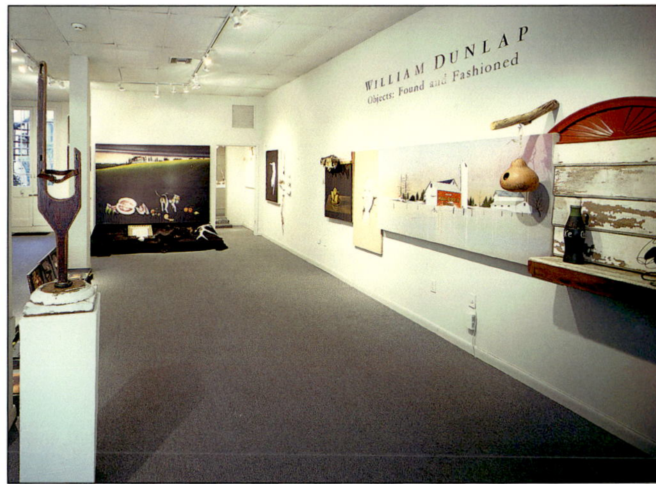

63

Figs. 61–63. *William Dunlap: Objects Found and Fashioned* exhibit, 2001. The Ogden Museum of Southern Art, New Orleans, Louisiana. Photographs by Joe Bergeron.

and several related paintings, he built a large environmental installation, working spontaneously, responding to his own art forms as well as found objects and selected objects from his family's history, including his grandfather's old dog collar. While making this installation, documented by Washington filmmaker Stanley Staniski, he repeatedly emphasized the importance of process, the creative process, and stressed the abiding power of the found object for him. For the first time in many years, a selection of his early North Carolina photographs were featured in a set of box constructions he had created during the 1970s.

New Orleans, a familiar city for him as it has been for many from Mississippi, also began to support his projects and commissions. He was commissioned by Fifth Circuit Judge Grady Jolly to paint a large allegorical canvas for the U.S. Court of Appeals in New Orleans, a work he titled *Young Bull and War Memorial*, completed in 1998. The young bull in the painting passes before an unidentified stone war memorial in a bucolic Southern landscape with a classic Greek revival structure and a church steeple in the remote distance (p. 106). During this period he began to exhibit at the Galerie Simonne Stern and was selected for inclusion in the New Orleans Museum of Art triennial exhibition, where he delivered a performance lecture, "Dialogue, Monologue, Travelogue, Hollow Log." And continuing his earlier association with the Contemporary Art Center, initiated during Ted Potter's tenure as director, in homage to Juan Miro, he presented an installation of painted Florida bracs, *Miro, Miro on the Wall*, in 2002.

That same year he was honored as one of the University of Mississippi's distinguished alumni, shortly after fortieth-anniversary ceremonies marking James Meredith's enrollment at the university. During the homecoming parade through downtown Oxford, which circled the courthouse square, Dunlap was honored like a returning football hero, riding in a parade in a convertible with his wife and his daughter. He joined the university's Chancellor in his private box for the football game, surrounded by celebrities and Mississippi politicians. An exhibition of his work was featured at Millie Moorhead's Southside Gallery, located on the courthouse square, along with an exhibition of another prominent artist from the South, Benny Andrews.

When the Ogden Museum of Southern Art opened in the summer of 2003, Dunlap (and his art) played a central role in the grand opening ceremonies and related events. He hosted a panel discussion by Southern artists that was connected in spirit to his earlier Southern Rim Conference at ASU, where in 1976, he explored the existence of a new Southern visual aesthetic in a remote North Carolina mountain retreat. By 2003, with the opening of the Ogden Museum of Southern Art, and the earlier opening of the Morris Museum of Art in Augusta, Georgia, in 1992, there was no longer a question about the importance and vitality of Southern art.

Though he often returns to Mississippi, Dunlap has never been simply nostalgic or sentimental about his native state; he recognizes its dark past as well as its positive history. Nor has he only looked back. Since his birth there, Mississippi has become more progressive in economic development and racial equality, and Dunlap remains closely attuned to these issues. This is reflected in a range of recent commissions and projects, including his commissioned work for the offices of the Nissan plant in Canton, Mississippi. The sprawling facility is located in a rural area he once mapped as a college student working under the hot sun on a road crew building Interstate 55. He was commissioned as a mature artist to paint the same landscape for a Japanese corporation that he could never have imagined existing in his home state in 1963.

The Nissan plant in Mississippi is part of a distinctively different Southern landscape, one that has evolved in response to globalization, international commerce, and rising new populations. Mississippi has become a leader of the industrial New South, joining other progressive states.

Fig. 64. *Delta Dog Trot, Landscape Askew,* 2003. Polymer paint on canvas, 78 x 144. Collection of Viking Range Corporation, The Alluvian Hotel, Greenwood, Mississippi. Photograph by Tom Joynt.

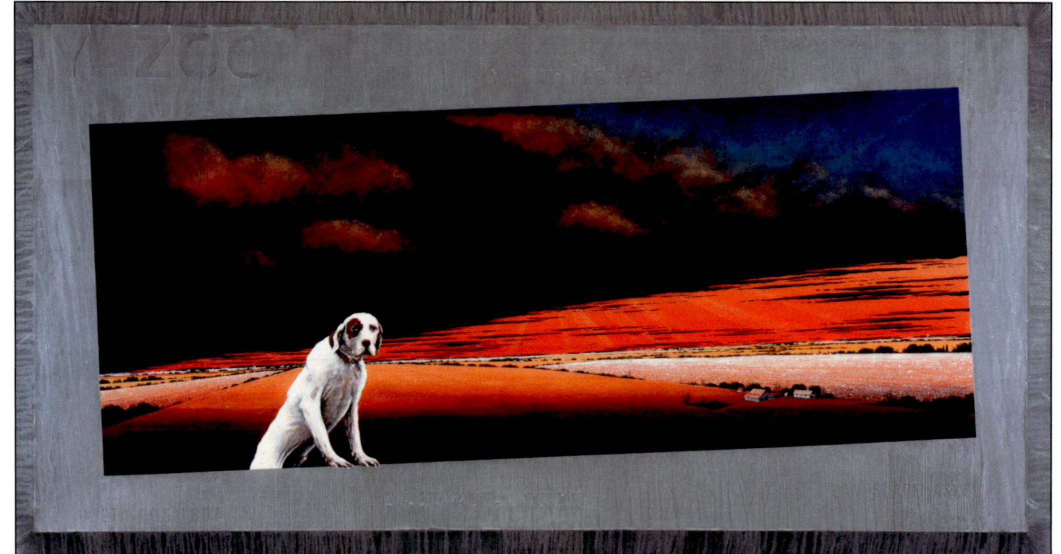

64

A Toyota plant was built in Georgetown, Kentucky; Saturn and Nissan plants were built in middle Tennessee; Mercedes, Honda, and Hundai plants appeared in neighboring Alabama, and BMW built a modern manufacturing facility in South Carolina. The automobile had always been important to Dunlap, and now automotive and truck manufacturing changed the landscape of his state and region. While economic development continues to unfold in his state and region, Dunlap serves as an observer, a recorder of change, and his art will no doubt evolve to reflect the nature of these events.

The changing South is recasting the future of remote areas and bringing a degree of economic and cultural revitalization to small towns and cities. Reflecting this changing landscape of Mississippi and its smaller towns, is a project that Dunlap might not have envisioned a decade earlier, a boutique hotel in Greenwood, Mississippi. Opened in 2003, the Alluvian Hotel was developed by the highly successful Viking Range Corporation, headquartered in Greenwood, to serve as a center for its growing number of destination visitors. Business and upscale leisure travelers come to Greenwood, many attracted by Viking's culinary school and tours of its manufacturing center, where ranges are custom-built for many of these visitors. In 2003 Dunlap made a large painting, *Delta Dog Trot, Landscape Askew*, for the hotel's lobby. In 2005, he contributed *Darkness on the Delta* and *Narcissus—Spa Dog* to the hotel's growing and significant collection of Mississippi artists. Each of these Dunlap works features a prominently placed Walker hound in a Mississippi landscape, a development his grandfather, Cas Cooper, might find interesting, if not amusing.

Delta Dog Trot, Landscape Askew is filled with allusions to Mississippi history, Choctaw Indian history, his beloved dogs, and the history of art. As Dunlap explains in an artist statement about the work, its title in part comes from his response to that region's geography. "My initial childhood sighting of the Delta was from the East coming in on Highway 82. Just as one first catches sight of that flat, alluvial plain, the road banks to the right and, sure enough, the horizon line slips ever so slightly . . . askew!" As to the reason for his inclusion of so many floating words in the composition, he explains that "there's a great deal of text in Western art, from early illuminated manuscripts and religious altar pieces to contemporary conceptual art. The words imbedded in *Delta Dog Trot* not only identify the painting and the artist but give the names of the river system that brought that rich soil south in the first place." And the central importance of the dog is clearly indicated by the artist: "One of the most compelling devices employed by nineteenth-century trompe l'oeil painters was a figure so placed as to seem to come out of the picture plane. That's what I've tried to achieve with the dog, who's white as cotton, life-size and then some, and makes eye contact from any place in the room. All animals, and dogs in particular, play a symbolic role in my work. They stand in for people. I'd like to think they represent the best of us."[39]

In 2003, he was commissioned by Washington's new convention center complex to create *Landscape Askew*, which combined almost all of his iconic images in a single constructed, painted triptych composition. To the left, a Walker hound, striking a pose similar to that in *Delta Dog Trot*, is placed below a worn wooden wall fragment and flanked by a portrait of George Washington and a mountain waterfall landscape. The central skewed landscape panel is once again Antietam in winter. To the right, a Rembrandt self-portrait (signed and identified) is placed next to another waterfall painting. Both sides are bracketed by painted wooded pilasters and balanced by slate panels. In Washington, an international capital city known for its museums and culture as well as for its proximity to the Virginia hunt country and the Blue Ridge Mountains, these references seem particularly appropriate.

Rembrandt, his ultimate old master, is featured in a number of additional major works, all triptychs, completed from 2000 to 2005, including *Rembrandt in Umbria with Etruscan Warrior* (2000), *Rembrandt and Titus—Father and Son* (2002), *All That Glitters . . .* (2004), and *Rembrandt and Spook* (2005). In the earliest of these, *Rembrandt in Umbria*, the artist's self-portrait fills a large central panel and dominates the composition, and in the next, Rembrandt and Titus share double billing, in the title and in the composition. *All That Glitters . . .* moves the Rembrandt self-portrait to a side panel, giving prominence to a Dunlap painting of a classic Rembrandt figure (*Man in a Golden Helmet*), surrounded by a complex range of objects found and fashioned by the artist, with small dog and trout portraits in the left panel. Finally, in the most recent of these, *Rembrandt and Spook*, the dog (Spook) has replaced Rembrandt as the prominent subject of the large central panel (with another Walker hound perched up, looking out of the picture frame), and Rembrandt's self-portrait is reduced to a small side location.

Delta Dog Trot, Landscape Askew was one of the first in a major new series of paintings, prints, and mixed

Fig. 65. *Rembrandt in Umbria with Etruscan Warrior*, 2000. Polymer paint on canvas, slate, bronze, velvet, wood, 30 x 108 x 4. Collection of James V. Kimsey, McLean, Virginia. Photograph by Jack Meyer.

Fig. 66. *Rembrandt and Titus—Father and Son*, 2002. Polymer paint on canvas, wood, slate, leather, metal, found objects; triptych, 30 x 120 x 11. Collection of Lauren Rogers Museum of Art, Laurel, Mississippi. Photograph by Jack Meyer.

Fig. 67. *All That Glitters . . .*, 2004. Wood, canvas, clay, slate, tortoise shell, velvet, leather, gold leaf, tintype, found objects; triptych, 32 1/2 x 102. Collection of Sharon and Bruce Bradley, Washington, D.C. Photograph by Jack Meyer.

Fig. 68. *Rembrandt and Spook*, 2005. Mixed materials construction, triptych, 30 x 120. Private collection. Photograph by Jack Meyer.

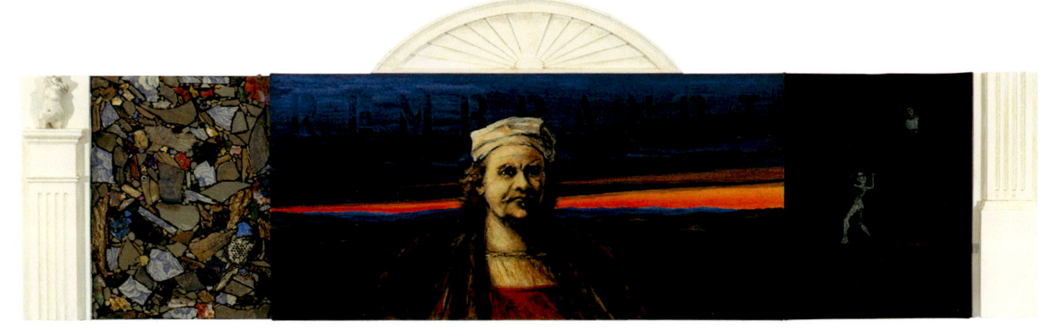

65

66

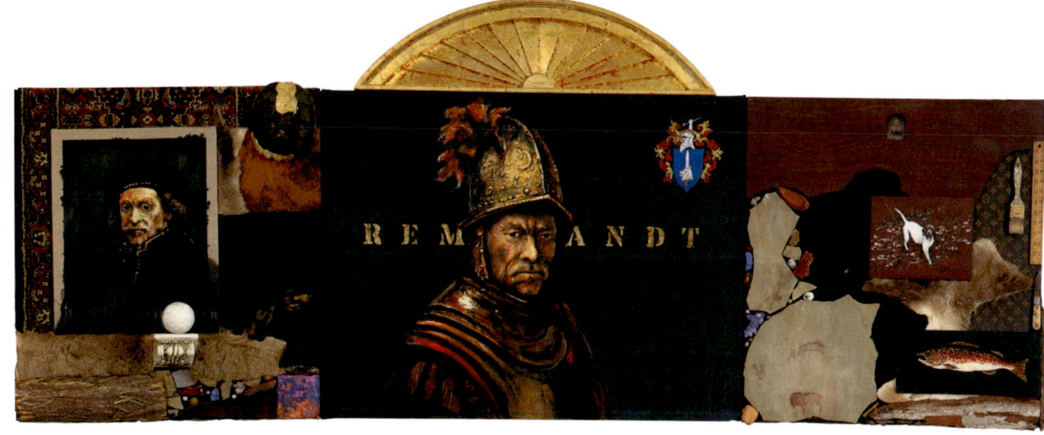

67

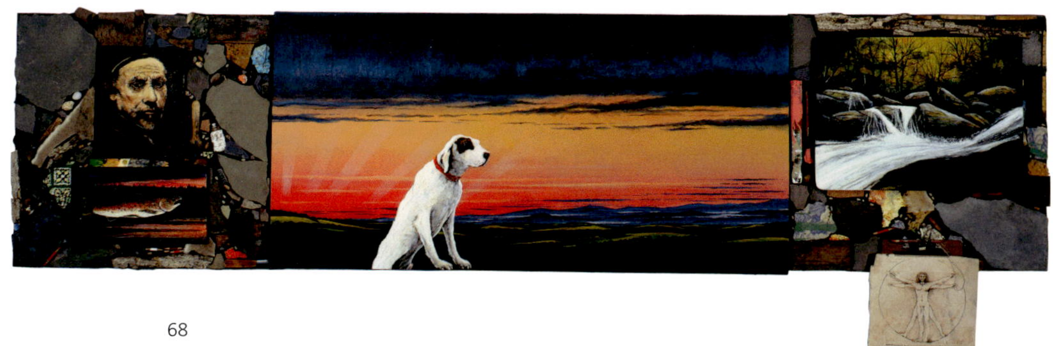

68

media compositions featuring his Walker hounds and their larger environmental context. *White Dog*, a triptych composition from 2003–4, presents its trompe l'oeil white dog, identified both in the painted image and in painted words, perched up high, looking directly at the viewer. In *White Dog Allegory*, from 2005, once again with a painted white dog (moved to the right side) and painted words identifying the dog, a more complex composition is presented, including variations on many of the elements painted in 1988 in *Landscape and Variable: The Bounty and Burden of History*. Also related to *The Bounty and Burden of History* is *Jeffersonian Democracy—A Work in Progress*, with a clearly identifiable Monticello in the background and a pack of wild hounds in the foreground, eating and destroying a watermelon (the "bounty" portrayed in the earlier work, taken in kind from a Raphael Peale painting), with the painted words "Jeffersonian Democracy" hovering above and below the dogs, allowing the viewer to draw his own conclusions regarding the artist's implications.

Many of these works are featured in the Morris Museum of Art exhibition, *What Dogs Dream*, along with *Darkness in the Delta*, *What Dogs Dream: The Ultimate, Eternal, Endless Hunt*, and *Narcissus Reflects on the Starnes House as Audubon's Osprey Flies Away* (all 2005). Writing in the exhibition's catalogue, he offers some insight into his recent and ongoing fascination with these dogs, linking this subject to the larger question of the identity of "Southern" art and the "Southern" artist. "To be a 'Southern Artist' in the manner in which William Faulkner was a 'Southern Writer,' his postage stamp of native soil yielding so rich a crop of universal truths and verities, is high aspiration indeed." He suggests that symbols "offer themselves up at just the right time and place" and goes on to explain why he has selected the Southern Dog as such a symbol. "To self-consciously go out into the Southern woods symbol-hunting could prove as disastrous as a canoe trip with James Dickey. However, were I to nominate a contender for Professor [Ellsworth] Woodward's Southern Symbol Sweepstakes, I don't think we could possibly do better than to elevate the ever-present, ubiquitous, obedient, intelligent, loyal, devoted, dilatory, lazy, noble, faithful, libido-driven, sly, sneaky, benign, slobbering, dangerous, mangy, flea-bitten, rabies-carrying, chicken-killing, car-chasing, egg-sucking, Southern Dog."[40]

These recent works, with subjects ranging from Southern dogs to Rembrandt, were completed before August 29, 2005, before Hurricane Katrina ravaged the Gulf Coast, literally changing the landscape of New Orleans and the Mississippi Gulf Coast, and bringing death and destruction on an unprecedented scale. In November 2005, Dunlap traveled to New Orleans and visited with members of the city's art world, seeking information about needs and ways he and others could help in Washington. He and Mississippi architect David Trigiani then drove to the Mississippi Gulf Coast, the region he knew from his early years. While across this whole coast, destruction and the need to rebuild is evident, architects like Trigiani and national teams have met to develop plans and design rebuilding concepts. However, coastal rebuilding, many months after Katrina, is progressing at a painfully slow rate. The complex, painful, and powerful impact of this national disaster will, ultimately, find its way into Dunlap's art, on some level, as it already has entered his writing, as evident in an essay for the Copley News Service, "What I Saw at the Apocalypse."

He begins by noting the connections between New Orleans and Mississippi. "Growing up in Mississippi, spontaneous road trips to New Orleans were a native son's birthright, no matter one's age, station, or the climatic conditions." He reports what he saw in the devastated Ninth Ward of New Orleans. "As far as the eye could see, this place, once so full of life, hard luck, and laughter, was all brown, motionless, and dead. Future generations who study the great New Orleans diaspora will find its origins here." Arriving on the Mississippi Gulf Coast, this native son "began to look for recognizable landmarks. There were few." The destruction there was equally overwhelming. In his essay, he links the future of these two regions. "New Orleans and the Mississippi Gulf Coast have long been havens for artists, free-spirits, and bohemians. Arguably, these two destinations have more in common with one another than with their respective states. If history is any indicator, their fates are forever intertwined. That large populations will once again mass near the water, and storms will come with predictable frequency, are indisputable facts. The question is simply how to reconcile these two forces of nature."[41]

Before Katrina, then Rita, changed the Gulf Coast South, Dunlap had completed a remarkable new body of work. In March of 2006, at the opening of his exhibition *What Dogs Dream* at the Morris Museum of Art, this survey of dog imagery underscored the importance of the new work, and it demonstrated how closely tied this work is to his own past, to the history of his own art. Just as he had earlier in his *Panorama* for the Corcoran Gallery, Dunlap built upon his own iconography and art history to develop a new level of mature imagery and narrative. This is most evident in *Narcissus Reflects on the Starnes House as Audubon's Osprey Flies Away*, which he considers to be part of a diptych with *What Dogs Dream: The Ultimate, Eternal, Endless Hunt* (pp. 130, 131). As he had done earlier in *Panorama*, he designed the composition of these two works so they could stand alone, yet also could be joined to make a pair of related images, as evident in the alignment of the rows of dogs when the two are installed together. Both panels show a snow-covered winter landscape, filled with barren trees, barns and vernacular house forms, Walker hounds, and evidence of an overpopulation of predators, with few prey.

It is, however, *Narcissus Reflects on the Starnes House as Audubon's Osprey Flies Away* that most embodies the spirit of the *Panorama of the American Landscape*. As in the Antietam panels for *Panorama*, this environment is cold and stark, forbidding to many life forms, except the hunters and a lone symbol of the prey, a fish caught in the talons of "Audubon's Osprey," another layer of art reference at work. Man is not directly present, only felt in his absence. In *Panorama* it was a painted sculptural monument; in this work it is an old image of Bill Starnes and his retainer, shown as hunters, posed with their horses and bird dogs in front of the Starnes house, suggesting that reality and art, fact and fiction, overlap here. Rather than deer heads, the prey in his Antietam panels, here he depicts a large and loosely aligned pack of hounds and hunters and the osprey overhead (just as he painted a single bird of prey in *Panorama*).

In the background, the Starnes house looms. It is, of course, a specific nineteenth-century house in Mathiston, a house complete with histories that intertwined with generations of his family history, yet it is also a mythic, metaphoric structure, just as the architecture of Jefferson and Palladio became less specific, more metaphorical in his art. As a child, he looked up to see the Starnes house from the yard of his grandparents' home; that is the perspective he uses here. The house dominates all below. It also perfectly aligns with Narcissus, the Walker hound in the foreground. In size and in alignment, they are one, or seem to be. Off to the right, the neck and head of a horse with bridle, perhaps one of those he had studied in Virginia for the hunt scenes in *Panorama*, inserts itself, floating over the water. In this complex and layered work he is showing his hand, his "artistry" as a painter, and perhaps revealing himself a bit as well.

Narcissus Reflects on the Starnes House demonstrates what the art world knows by now, that Dunlap can paint like Rembrandt, like Vermeer, like Audubon and other old masters. He doesn't want us to forget that—just as he wants to remind us that he can paint architectural images reflecting the best of Palladio and Jefferson—but here he has underscored the difference between himself and those who came before. He paints the Starnes house, his house, with its Mississippi mythology and its actual history, a vernacular form (yet still a "house on the hill," like Jefferson's Monticello), elevated to iconic stature, equal to those more famous structures. He does so, because he *can* do so. Like William Faulkner, who created and layered his mythic Mississippi in literature, Dunlap, who knows "Mr. Faulkner's" work, does the same with art.

Looking at *Narcissus Reflects on the Starnes House* and comparing it to *Panorama of the American Landscape*, one is reminded of what Jane Livingston wrote after Dunlap worked with her at the Corcoran Gallery. All of his work, on a grand or modest scale, she suggests, "is alike in its having sprung from the artist's restless compulsion to record his own rich associative life. He is, in all the work, as much diarist as abstract composer, and as close spiritually to the American trompe l'oeil masters, Peto or Harnett, as to our great landscape painters, Homer or Kensett or George Inness." Describing his paintings as having "an old-fashioned truthfulness to their craft," marked by a "capacity to register not only what the artist sees, but what he knows," she offers the following conclusion: "It is really only through a long and repeated exposure to Bill Dunlap's work that one becomes fully aware of the depth of literary content in it, and its far-reaching resonances. But, as with all good painting, one needn't know all of the artist's vocabulary to intuitively understand his aesthetic or his intended mythologies. A single work, even a modest landscape or still-life fragment, hints at the full range of Dunlap's extraordinarily sophisticated grasp of the symbolic power of painting. What is never in doubt, of course, is the artist's sheer painterly skill; what we may endlessly question and examine are his meanings."[42]

Dunlap continues to shuttle across the South between his studios in Coral Gables and McLean. He works in the studio when he is not traveling, because despite all the roles he plays, Dunlap is first and foremost a studio artist. His studio, wherever he decides to locate it, is more than a literal space where painting and sculpting take place. The studio is, by his admission, where he allows the art to direct him, where the art guides his technical skills, spontaneously, when the magic, the "mojo," is at work. There, he will discover new ways to respond to the change he has witnessed in Mississippi, in Virginia, in Florida, and across the South. He plans to return to the Starnes house, to work in his old Church of Christ studio, and to Mathiston where "his people" were and are. Today, like one of those Walker hounds he paints, he is keeping an eye (and ear) on the past while he moves forward, heading down the road, tail and nose up, quiet and alert, hunting for prey. He'll find it. He always does. We'll see.

J. Richard Gruber, Ph.D.
The Ogden Museum of Southern Art
University of New Orleans

Notes

1. William Dunlap and Willie Morris, "Dialogue: The Author and the Artist," in Willie Morris, *Homecomings* (Jackson: University Press of Mississippi, 1989), xi.
2. William Dunlap and Ruth Stevens Appelhof, "Re-constructed Re-collections: An Interview," in Ruth Stevens Appelhof, *William Dunlap, Re-Constructed Re-Collections* (Roanoke: Art Museum of Western Virginia, 1992), 2.
3. Interview with the author, February 2006. Unless otherwise cited, all quotes from the artist are taken from an extended series of interviews with author, completed from 2001 to 2006.
4. Appelhof, 2.
5. James C. Cobb, *Redefining Southern Culture, Mind and Identity in the Modern South* (Athens: University of Georgia Press, 1999), 32.
6. Ibid, 36–37.
7. Barbara Rose, "Dunlap's Dilemma, or Why Rembrandt Screamed," in *In the Spirit of the Land* (Washington: Corcoran Gallery of Art, 1995).
8. Quoted in Mary Lynn Kotz, "William Dunlap's Northern Offensive," *Museum & Arts Washington* (March/April 1989), 72.
9. Appelhof, 3.
10. Rose.
11. William Dunlap, "What Dogs Dream," in *What Dogs Dream, Paintings and Works on Paper by William Dunlap* (Augusta: Morris Museum of Art, 2006), 10.
12. Ibid.
13. Ibid.
14. Curtis Wilkie, *Dixie: A Personal Odyssey Through Events That Shaped the Modern South* (New York: Scribner, 2001), 110–11.
15. See www.heybabydays.com/Imperial_Show_Band. Dunlap is noted here as the band's drummer from 1966 to 1969 and credited with two recordings for the band, including "Dee's Village" and "Stand by Me," featuring Tommy Tate.
16. Kotz, "Northern Offensive," 97.
17. William Dunlap, in *Reveries & Mississippi Memories* (Laurel: Lauren Rogers Museum of Art: 1986), no pagination.
18. "Bill Dunlap of WETA's *Around Town*," 14.
19. Symposium brochure, "Southern Rim 2, The Narrative Tradition in the Arts," Birmingham-Southern College and the Birmingham Museum of Art, Birmingham, Alabama, October 20–22, 1983.
20. Kotz, "Northern Offensive," 97.
21. William Dunlap, in Barbara Shissler Nosanow, *More Than Land or Sky, Art from Appalachia* (Washington: National Museum of American Art, 1981), 52.
22. Rose.
23. James Dickey, "Cahill Is Blind," *Esquire* 85.2 (February 1976), 67.
24. "Bill Dunlap of WETA's *Around Town*," 14-15.
25. William Dunlap, in Jan Ehrenworth, editor, *Quadrum Gallery Newsletter* 3 (Spring 1981).
26. William Dunlap, in *Art Encounters* (Autumn-Winter 1992) Vaughan-Goodman Fine Paintings, 18.
27. Kotz, "Northern Offensive," 98.
28. Ibid, 70.
29. Appelhof, 4.
30. Alex Nyerges, "William Dunlap, Continung the American Landscape Tradition," in *William Dunlap, Re-Constructed Re-Collections*, 5.
31. "Bill Dunlap of WETA's *Around Town*," 15
32. Morris, *Homecomings*, x.
33. Bill Kovach, "William Dunlap, Painting in the Southern Narrative Tradition," in *William Dunlap, Re-Constructed Re-Collections*, 8.
34. Ibid, 10.
35. Ed McGowin, "William Dunlap, Paintings," *Eye Wash, The Washington Artist's Tabloid* (April 1990).
36. Corcoran Gallery of Art, press release, "William Dunlap: In the Spirit of the Land," November 1, 1995.
37. Rose.
38. William Dunlap, "Bring Me the Head of Gore Vidal," *The Washingtonian* (November 1999), 148.
39. William Dunlap, "Delta Dog Trot, Landscape Askew," written artist statement, Alluvian Hotel, Greenwood, Mississippi, May 2003.
40. Dunlap, "What Dogs Dream," 11.
41. William Dunlap, "What I Saw at the Apocalypse," original text version, artist's papers.
42. Jane Livingston, "William Dunlap," in *William Dunlap: Recent Works* (Maitland, Florida: Maitland Art Center, 1988), no pagination.

LOOK AT IT

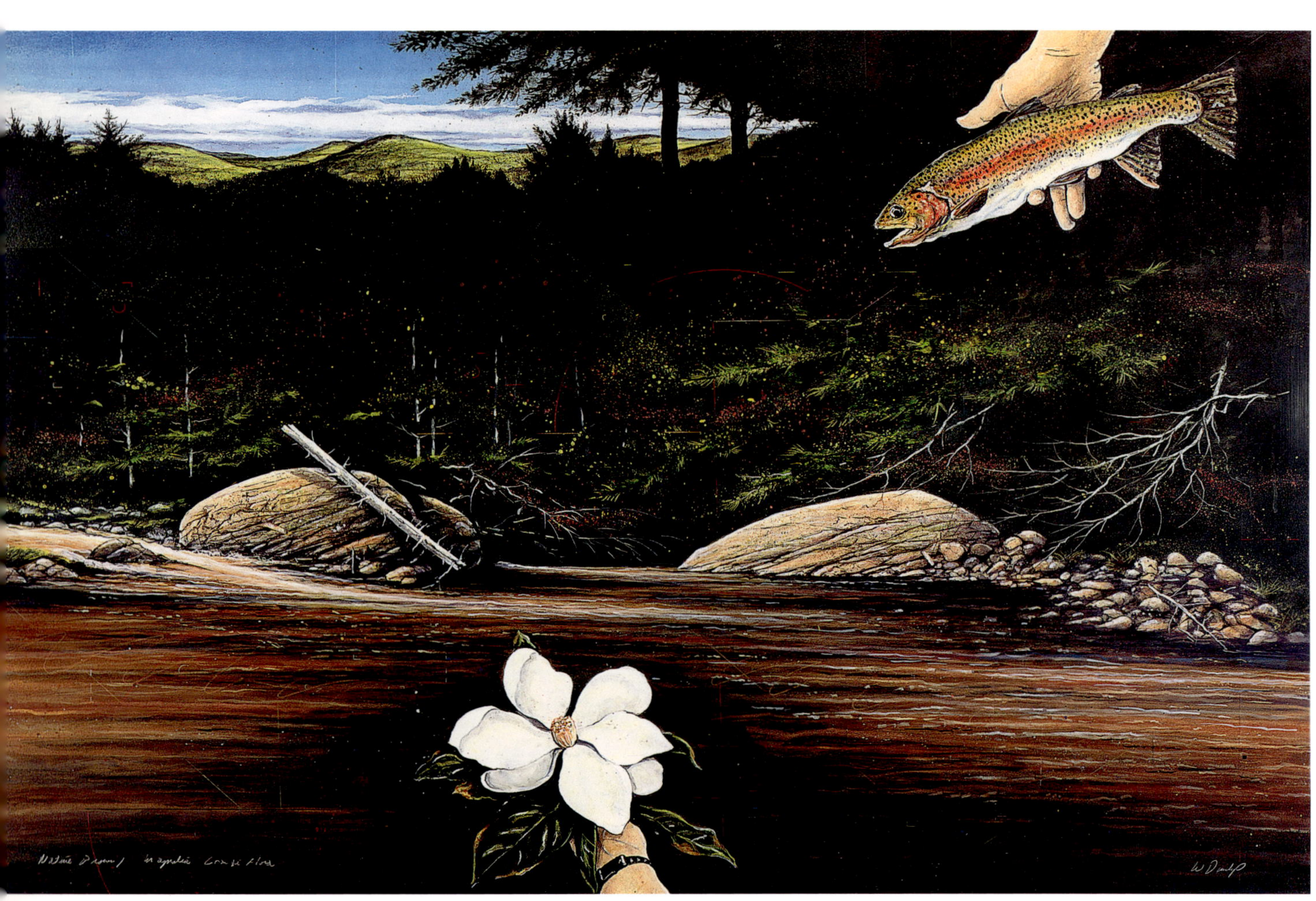

Native Brown—Granda Floria, 2000
Oil paint and dry pigment on rag paper, 42 x 63.
Private collection. Photograph by Don Queralto.

(or *invise id—reputa id,* if you prefer Latin)

In an early site-specific installation, I suspended a dozen cassette recorders at ear level in a darkened hallway of Jackson's Old Capitol Museum. These historic walls had heard the thunderous debates of secession and the oratory of, among others, Jefferson Davis and John C. Calhoun. Now broadcasting simultaneously were recordings of modern authors reading from their works. The effect was that of a hypothetical literary revival meeting with the voices of Robert Lowell, Dylan Thomas, Paul Camus, Ernest Hemingway, Robert Frost, William Faulkner, and James Dickey, all talking at once. Just to be in the conversation has always been my greatest ambition, so this exchange of random ideas ricocheting around the room made perfect sense, if only in the accidental nature of this artificial discourse.

I've attempted to do the same below. Imagine yourself listening to this not-so-random arrangement of quotes about Art from some of the West's finest minds. Look at it and think about it—and I hope it resonates.

> "The great lesson of the cave paintings of Lascaux is that Art is an intuitive, autonomous, and timeless activity and works independently of the development of society."[1] "Every work of Art must have about it something not understood to obtain its full effect."[2] "O you whose intellects are healthy—look at the doctrine which hides beneath the vellum cover of strange verse."[3] "The less amenable the work of art to the intellect, the greater it is."[4] "The better hidden the author's point of view, the

THINK ABOUT IT

better for the work of art."[5] "Perpetual Modernism is the measure of merit in every work of Art."[6] "Although Modern Art always seems to be about the future, the whole enterprise of Modernism can be seen as backward looking."[7] "Knowledge is Power."[8] "Imagination is more powerful."[9] "Remember, the art world is comedy."[10] "In general, I prefer laughter to tears."[11] "Painting is the best way I've found to get along with myself.[12]

As the above exercise amply demonstrates, the making of a book about Art involves the heresy of intermingling words and pictures, the latter said to be worth a thousand of the former. Given our current rate of communication inflation, it may be more like a trillion, and I include my own endeavors in this blanket indictment. Verbalizing about a nonverbal form of communication is tricky business at best. Wrapping the written word around Art is even more difficult, and I don't envy those who do it for a living.

Nevertheless working on this project with the generous, inspired, and highly professional folk at the University Press of Mississippi has given me a great deal to look at and think about, and put me into sweet reverie recalling a time in 1989 when Willie Morris, JoAnne Prichard, and I collaborated there on the book *Homecomings*.

Rifling through old evidence files and tracking down works of art made decades ago has forced a hard look back farther in time than I'm accustomed to or sometimes comfortable taking. Coming into contact with these objects and images again was strangely satisfying. While I felt little pride of authorship, I did experience some compelling moments of absolute clarity. I readily recalled specific events and particular concerns (some since resolved, some not), or obscure bits of news whose occurrence coincided with making the work.

The artist is concerned with the painting he's working on now and is impatient with anything that might divert attention. All this reconstructing the past, while sometimes disconcerting, has, however, brought me to a realization that a glance over the shoulder can, unlike its effect on Lot's wife, bring into focus a future not before glimpsed. Charged images have the power to suspend time and space and to provoke adverse behavior. Eudora Welty did tell us that "all serious daring starts within," and that was certainly the case with me.

In my grandmother's parlor during every summer of my childhood, I pored over stacks of vintage World War II magazines. One title commanded I *LOOK*. Another promised that between its covers there was *LIFE*. These publications were my initial exposure to history, art, popular culture, and that exotic, illuminating, and dangerous world yet to be reckoned with. In retrospect, those bold, dramatically cropped black and white photographs by the likes of Edward Steichen, Carl Mydans, and Ed Clark taught me to see, to look at, and think about pictures. Later I discovered Richard Haliburton's travel books, but that's another story.

I imagined myself making paintings long before I stretched my first canvas. In the time-honored way, I still employ a technology not far removed from the Stone Age. Wooden sticks with animal hair attached, dipped into an emulsion of pigments, are the tools I use to mark on the wall of my proto cave/studio.

The artist makes a thing because he wants to see it, and there can be no more pressing reason. That it might be of some use to others is pure lagniappe. This level of sanctity is, however, difficult if not impossible to sustain in a society constantly bombarded from every direction with static, kinetic, and seductive images. Rather than to be put off by this set of circumstances, I consider myself fortunate to live in a time and place where the quality, quantity, and currency of pictures are as unlimited as they are uninhibited. This image glut can only increase the value of the one-of-a-kind handmade object. Unlike our prehistoric precursors, I have a wealth of influences—an endless image bank and other Art to work with, towards, and against.

So go and sin no more, but do keep in mind that as far as Art is concerned, don't take the words too seriously, just look at it and think about it. . . and hold out for the reverie.

William Dunlap
Coral Gables, Florida, April 2006

1 Paul Rand
2 Samuel Taylor Coleridge
3 Dante Alighieri
4 Johann Wolfgang von Goethe
5 Friedrich Engels
6 Ralph Waldo Emerson
7 Clement Greenberg
8 Thomas Hobbes
9 Albert Einstein
10 Harold Rosenberg
11 John Cage
12 Robert Rauschenberg

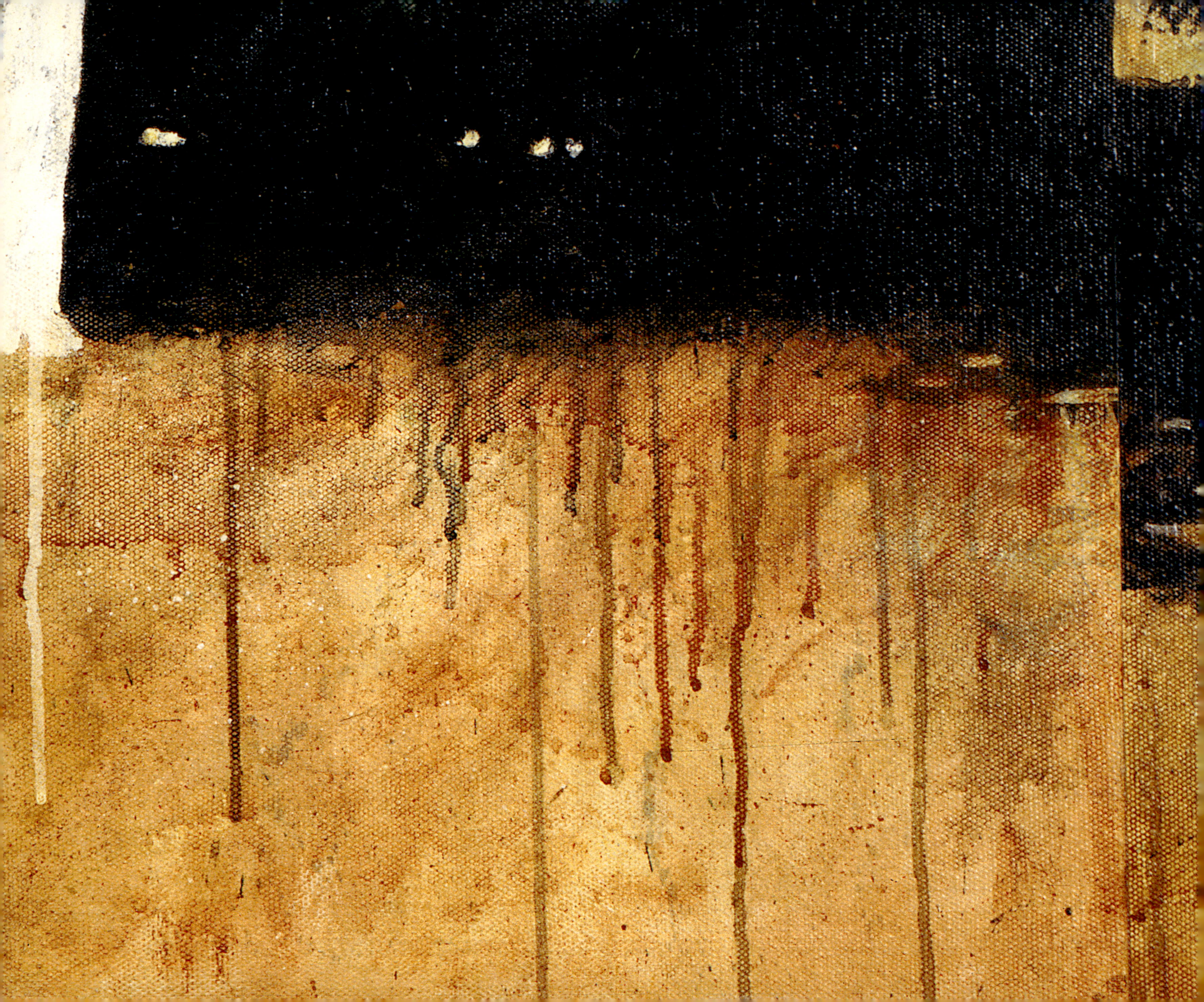

A Family Portrait in Grady, Mississippi, 1970

Polymer paint on canvas, 73 x 39 1/4. Private collection. Photograph by Hubert Worley.

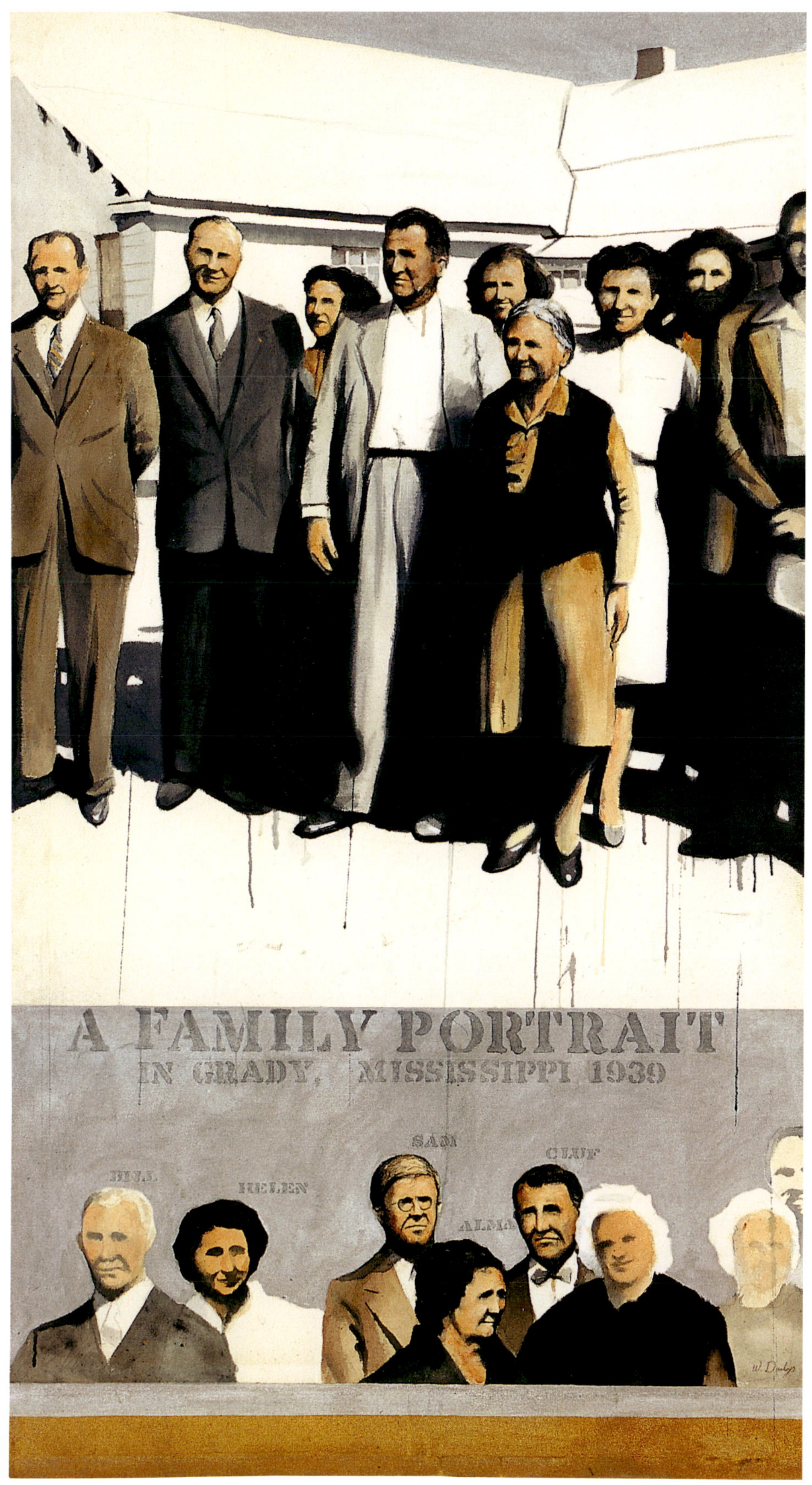

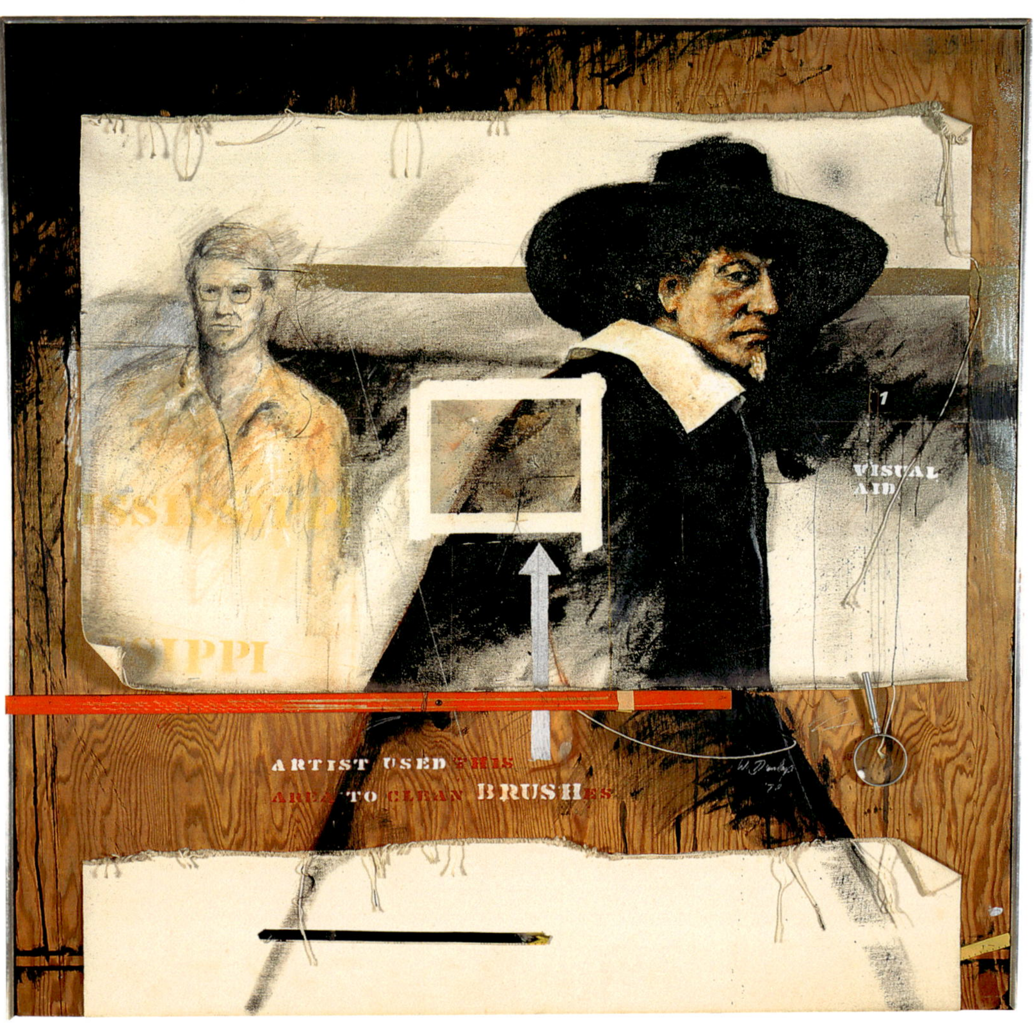

Family Portrait with Visual Aid, 1970–71
Polymer paint, canvas, graphite, plywood, wire, magnifying glass, 16 mm film, staples, 48 x 48. Collection of John Simmons, Puerto Vallarta, Mexico. Photograph by Hubert Worley.

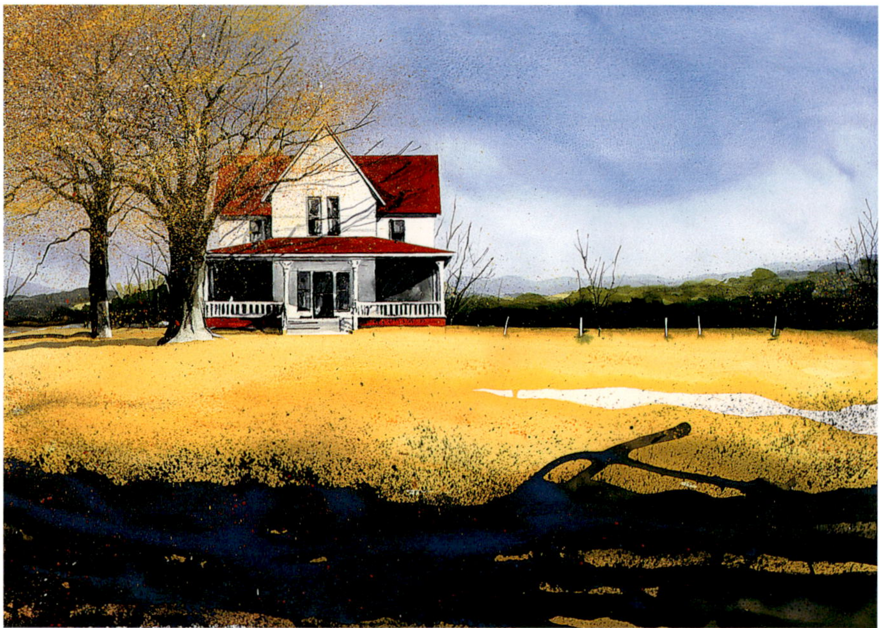

Starnes House, Mathiston, Mississippi, 1971
Watercolor and polymer paint on paper, 22 x 30. Collection of Museum of Mississippi History, Mississippi Department of Archives and History, Jackson. 1974.37. Photograph by Hubert Worley.

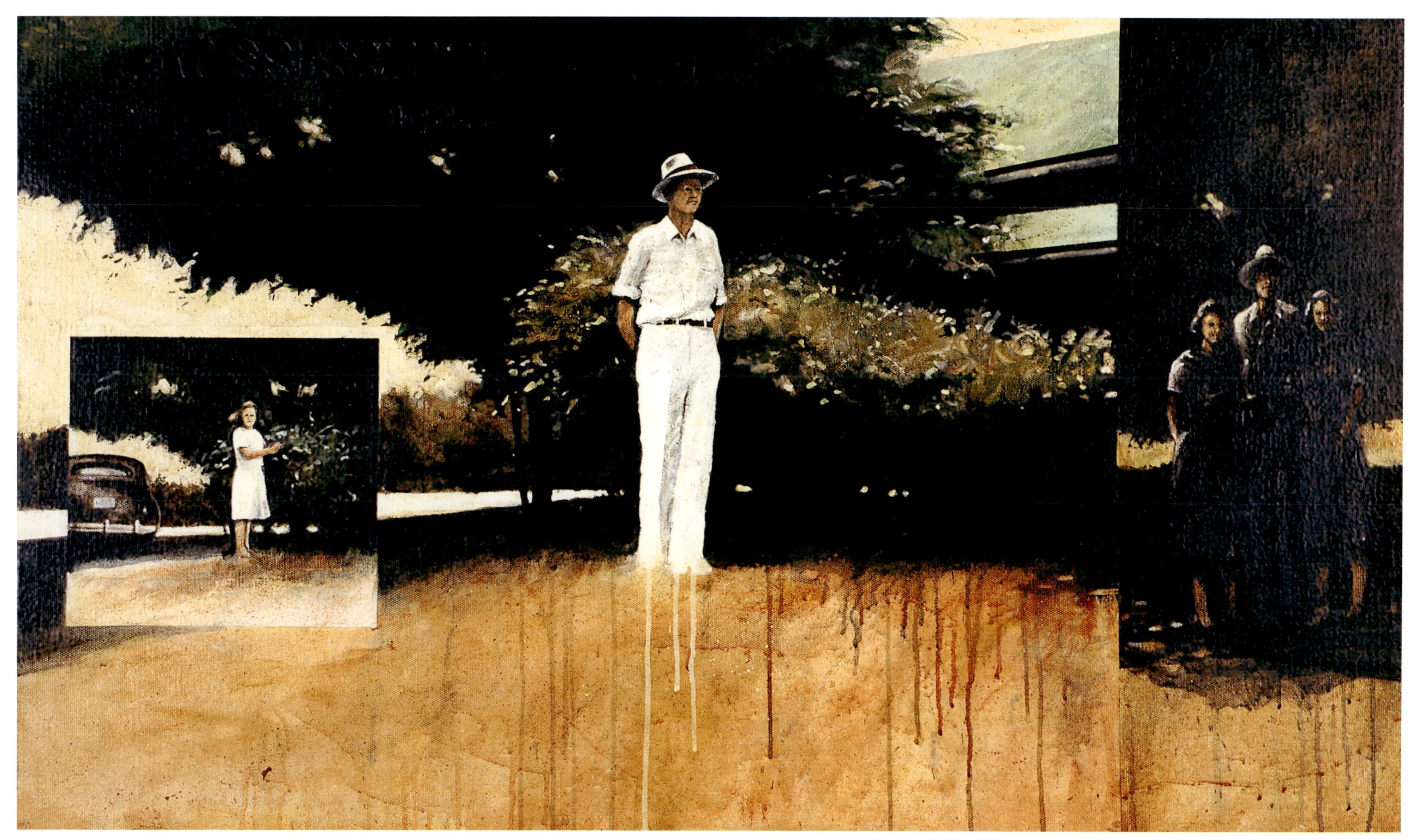

Mississippi Painting, 1971

Polymer paint on canvas, 36 x 60. Collection of Sam C. Dunlap Jr., Nashville, Tennessee. Photograph by Hubert Worley.

Self-Portrait with Father and Fowl, 1971
Polymer paint on canvas, 50 1/4 x 50 1/4 x 3.
Private collection. Photograph by Hubert Worley.

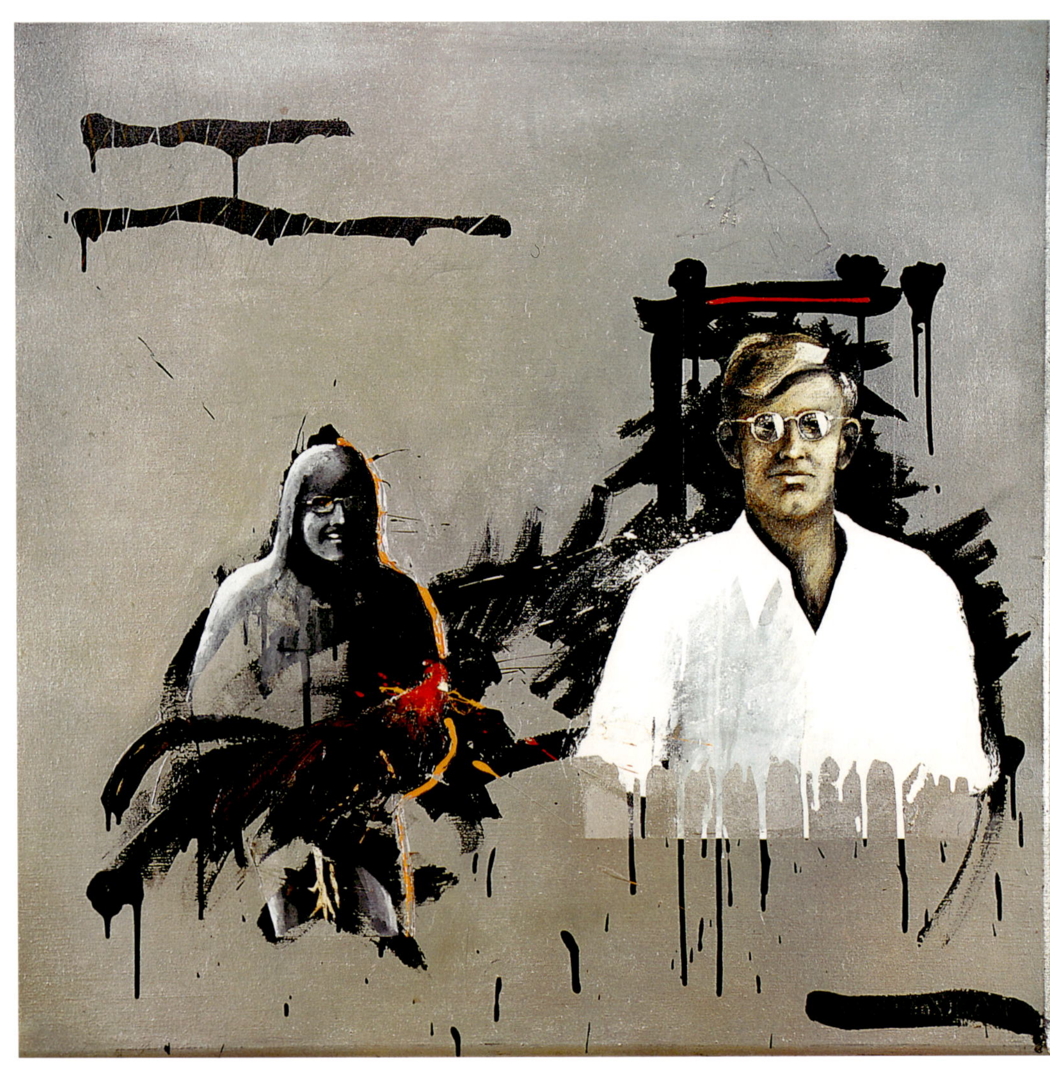

Father and Sons, 1971
Polymer and metallic paint on canvas, 48 x 48.
Collection of Mississippi Museum of Art, Jackson. Gift of Norma Latimer Watkins, in memory of her mother Norma Hosford Latimer Fontaine. 1987.135. Photograph by Lisa Berg.

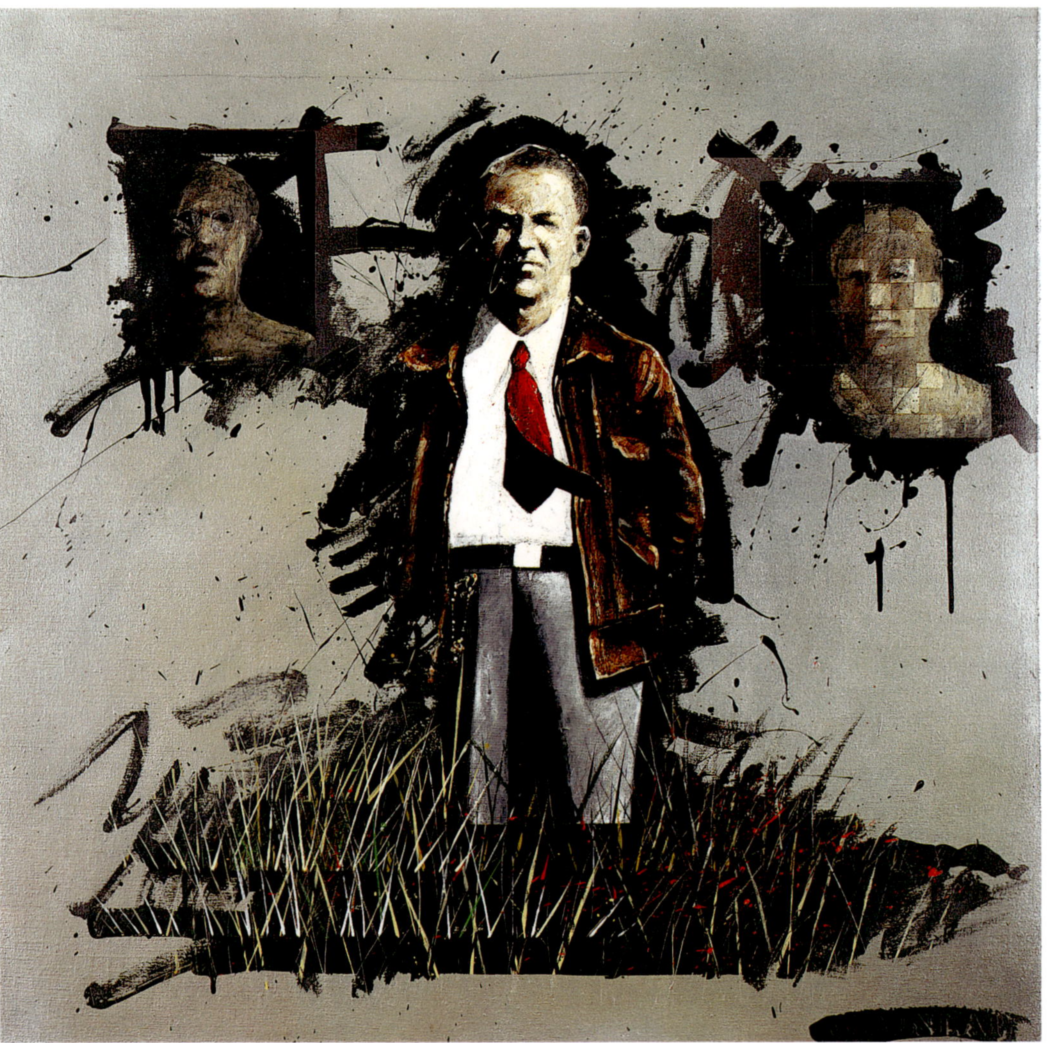

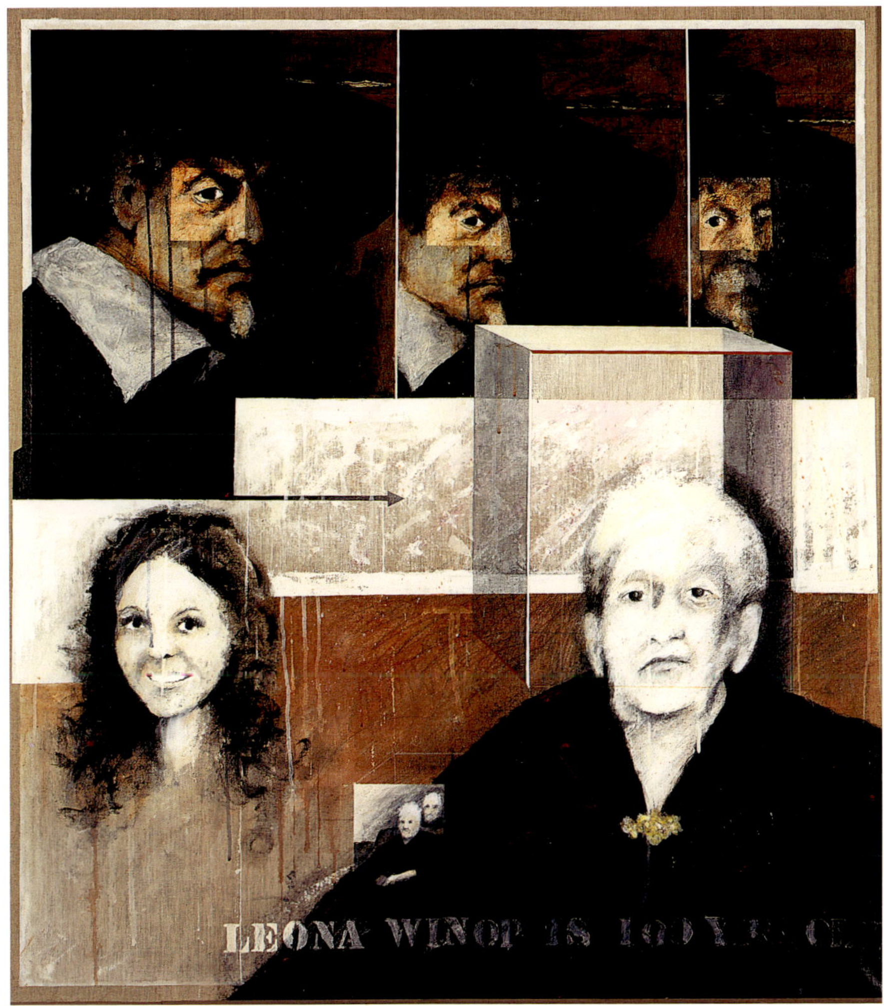

Leona Winor is 100 Years Old, 1971
Polymer paint on linen canvas, 54 x 48.
Collection of Mississippi Museum of Art, Jackson. Gift of Norma Latimer Watkins, in memory of her mother Norma Hosford Latimer Fontaine. 1987.134. Photograph by Hubert Worley.

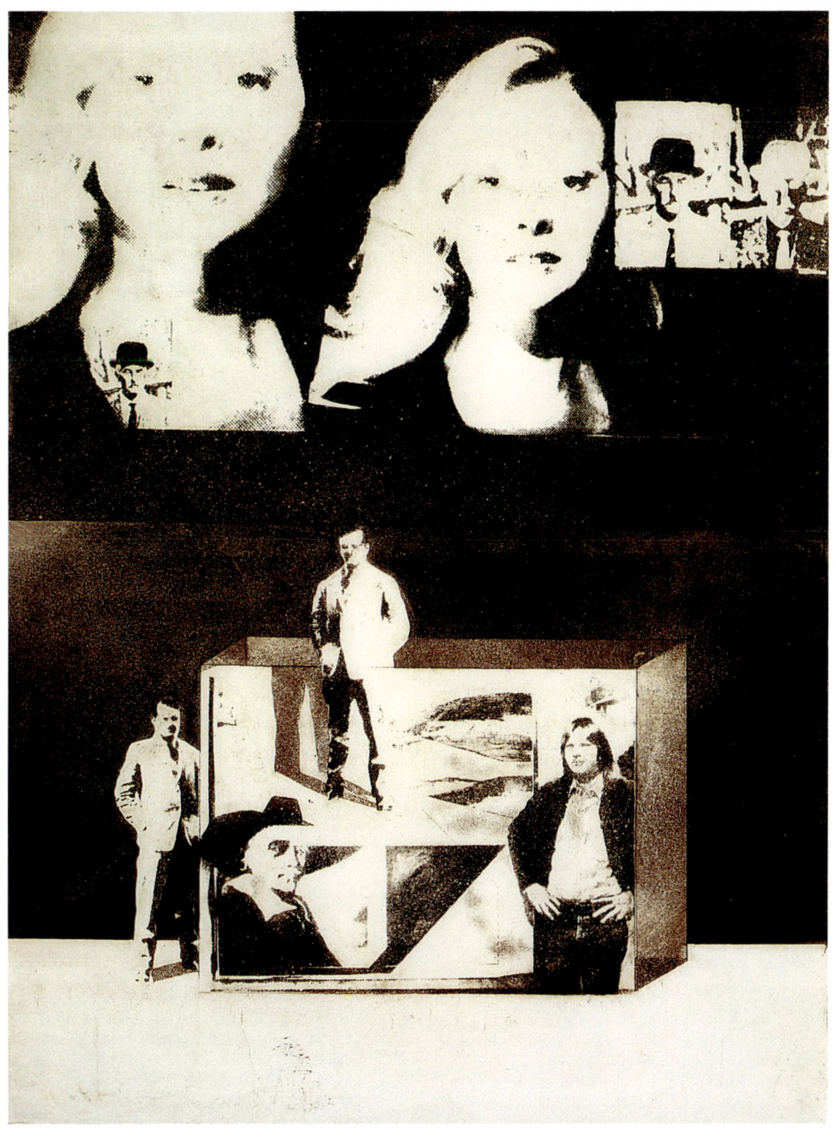

Excellent Company, 1971
Photo etching/intaglio, 23 1/2 x 1/ 1/2.
Collection of Hubert Worley, Jackson, Mississippi. Photograph by Hubert Worley.

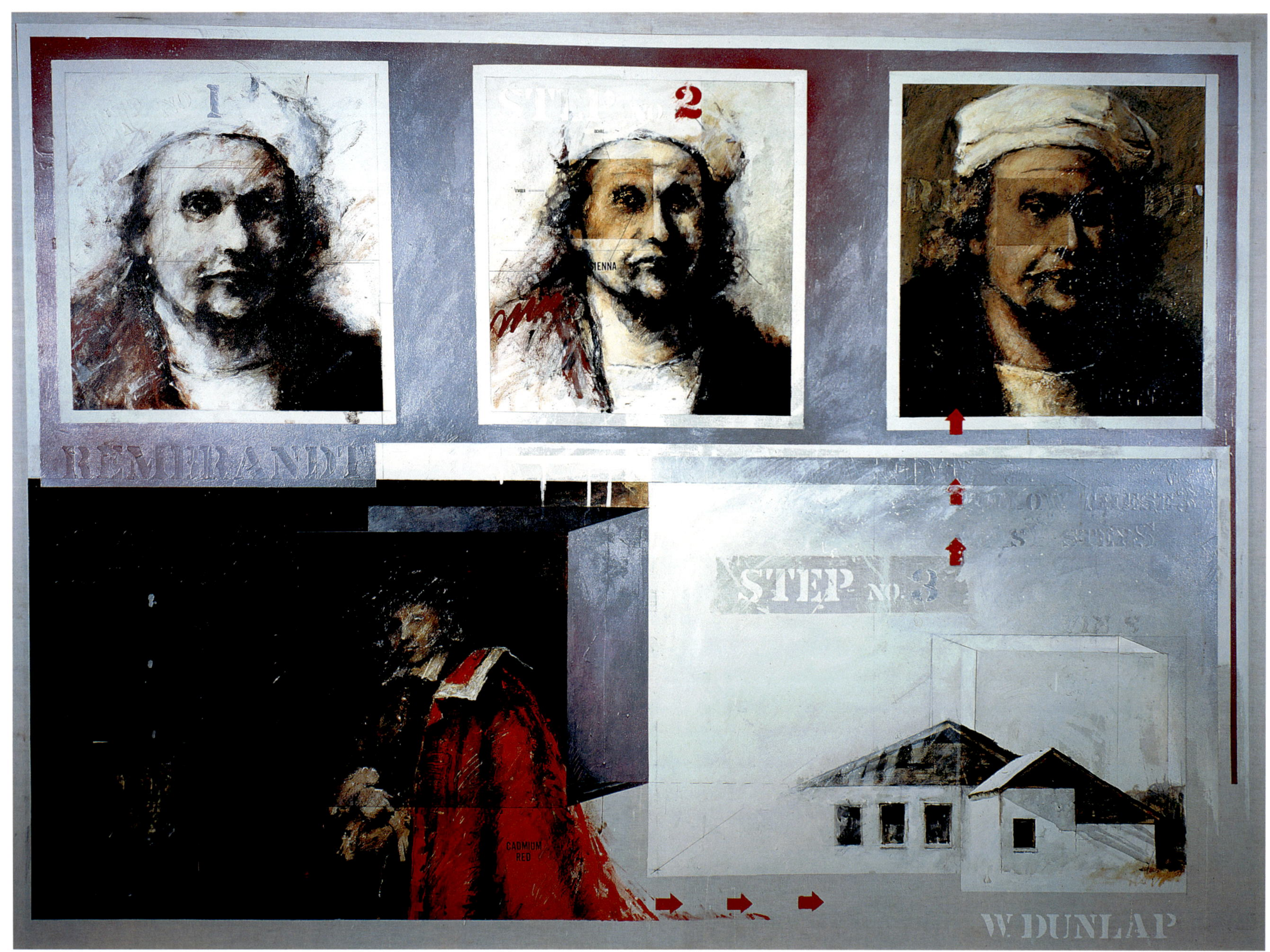

Learn to Paint Like Rembrandt in Three Easy Steps, 1971
Polymer paint on canvas with found brushes, 60 x 78. Private collection. Photograph by Jack Kotz.

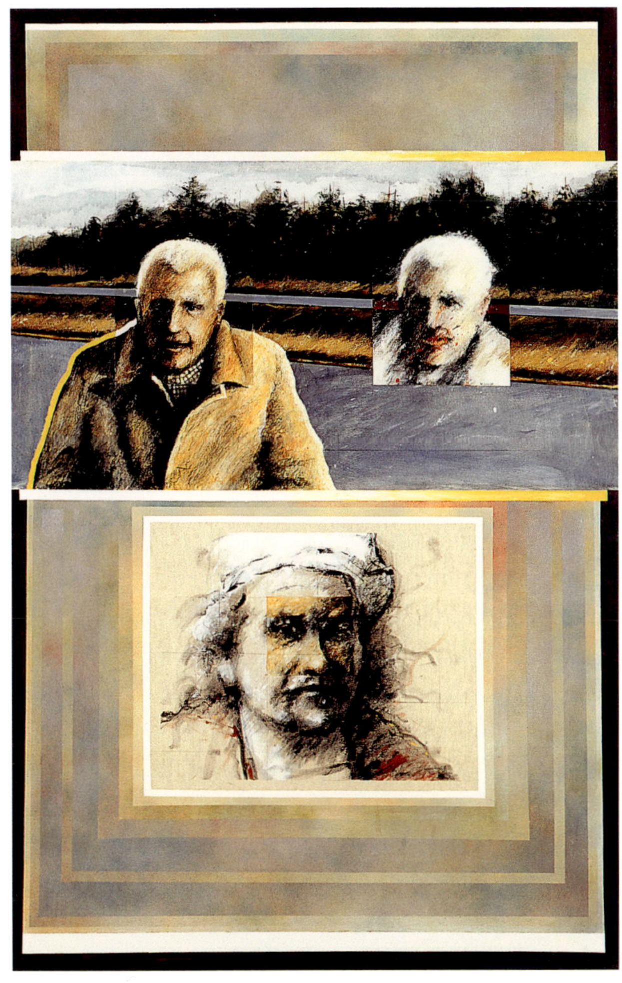

Rembrandt and Roadside, 1972
Polymer and metallic paint on canvas, 73 x 44 3/4. Private collection. Photograph by Hubert Worley.

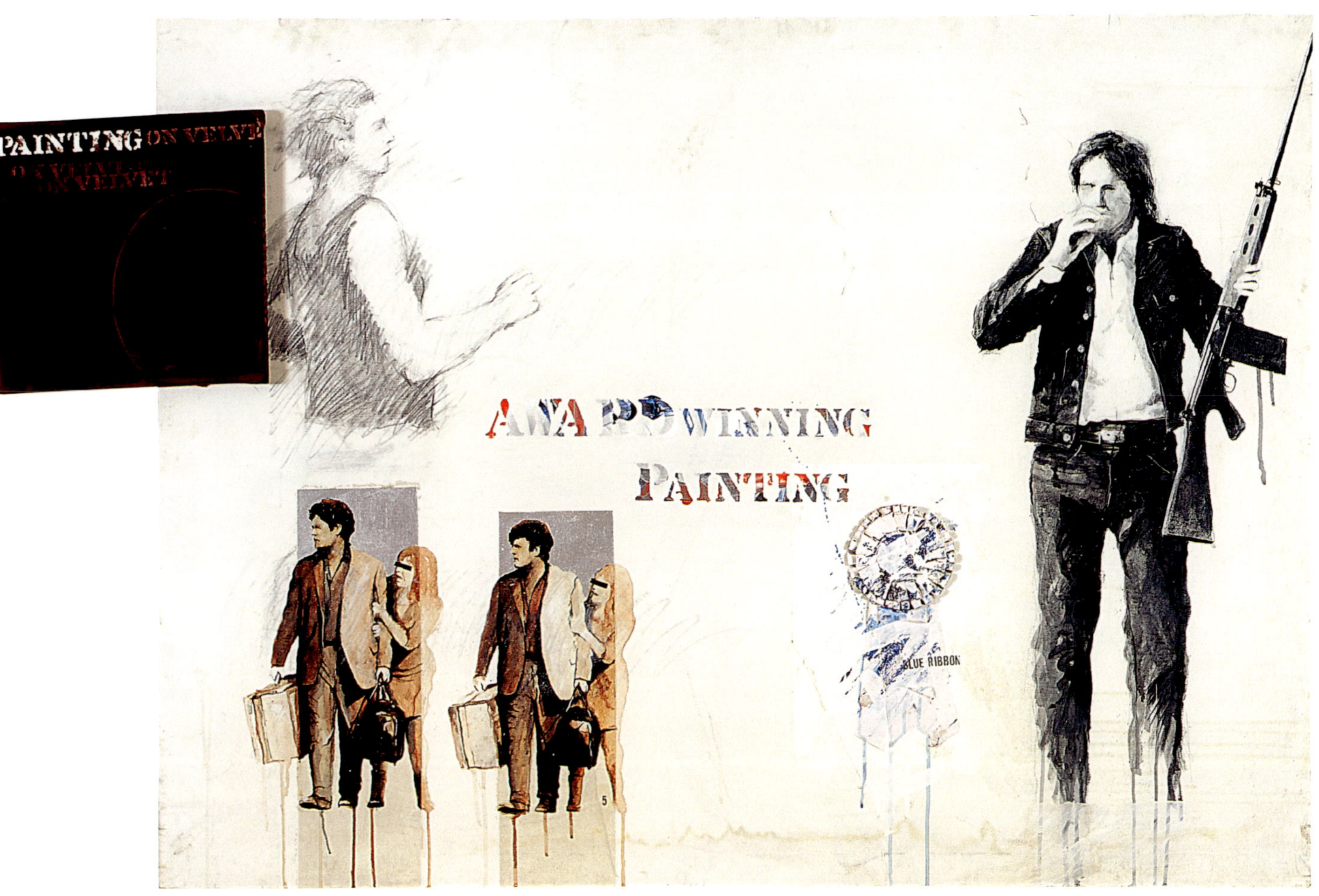

Award Winning Painting, 1972
Polymer paint and found objects on canvas, 45 1/2 x 68 1/2. Private collection. Photograph by Hubert Worley.

Christina at the Beach, 1971–72
Etching/intaglio, 20 x 25, artist proof. Collection of David Trigiani, Jackson, Mississippi. Photograph by Hubert Worley.

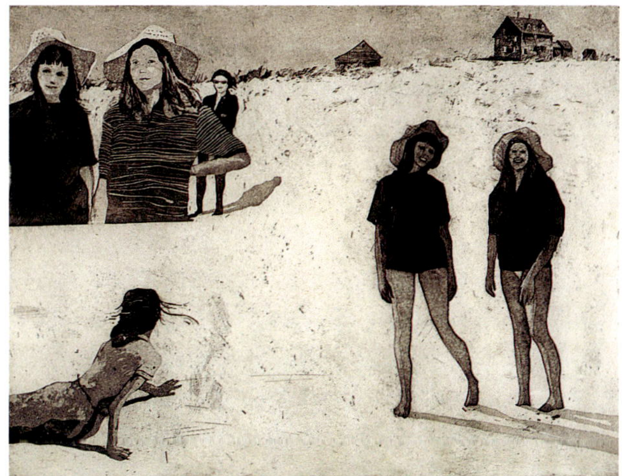

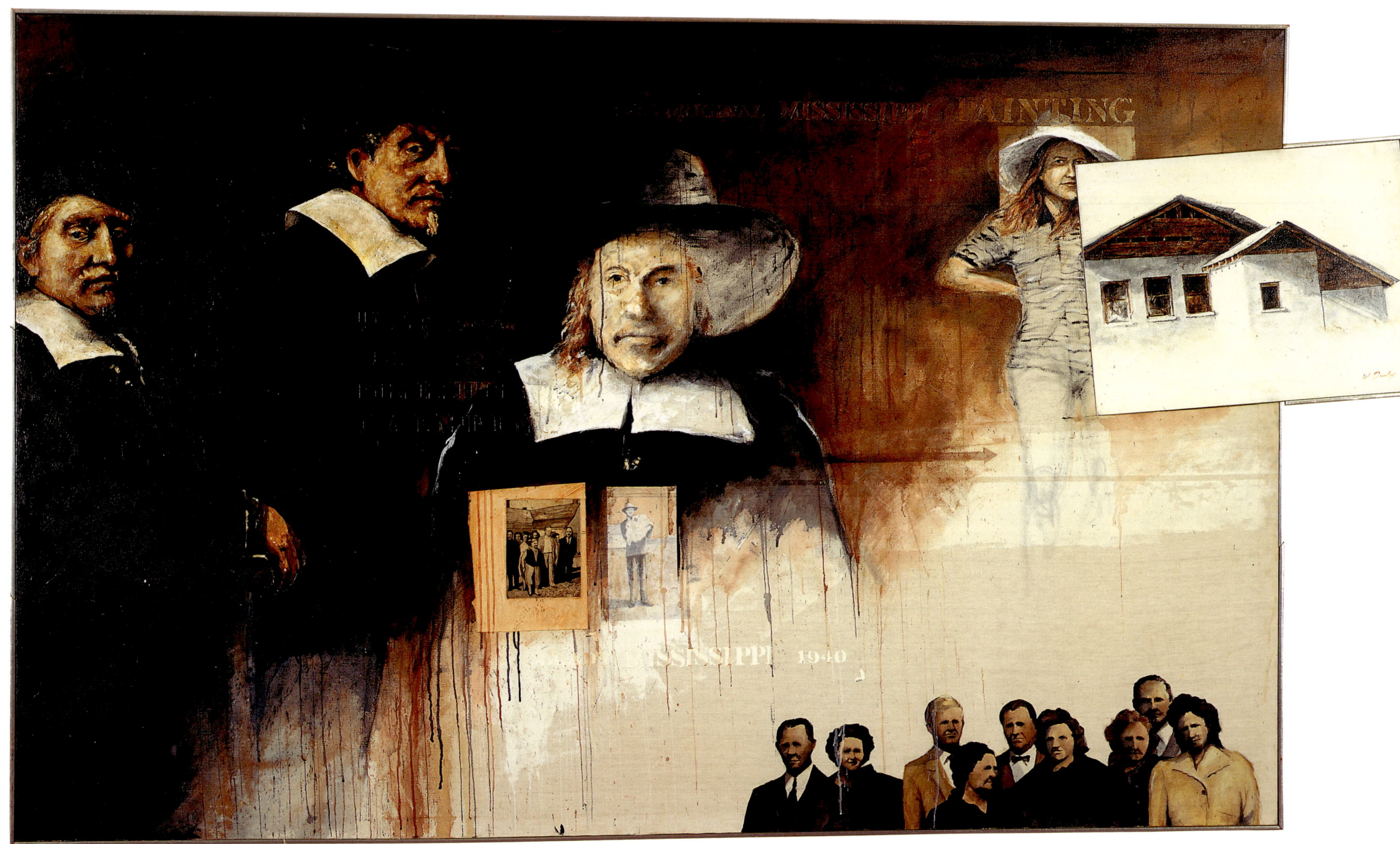

The Last Mississippi Painting, 1972–1973
Polymer paint and collage on canvas, 66 3/4 x 112 3/4. Private collection.
Photograph by Hubert Worley.

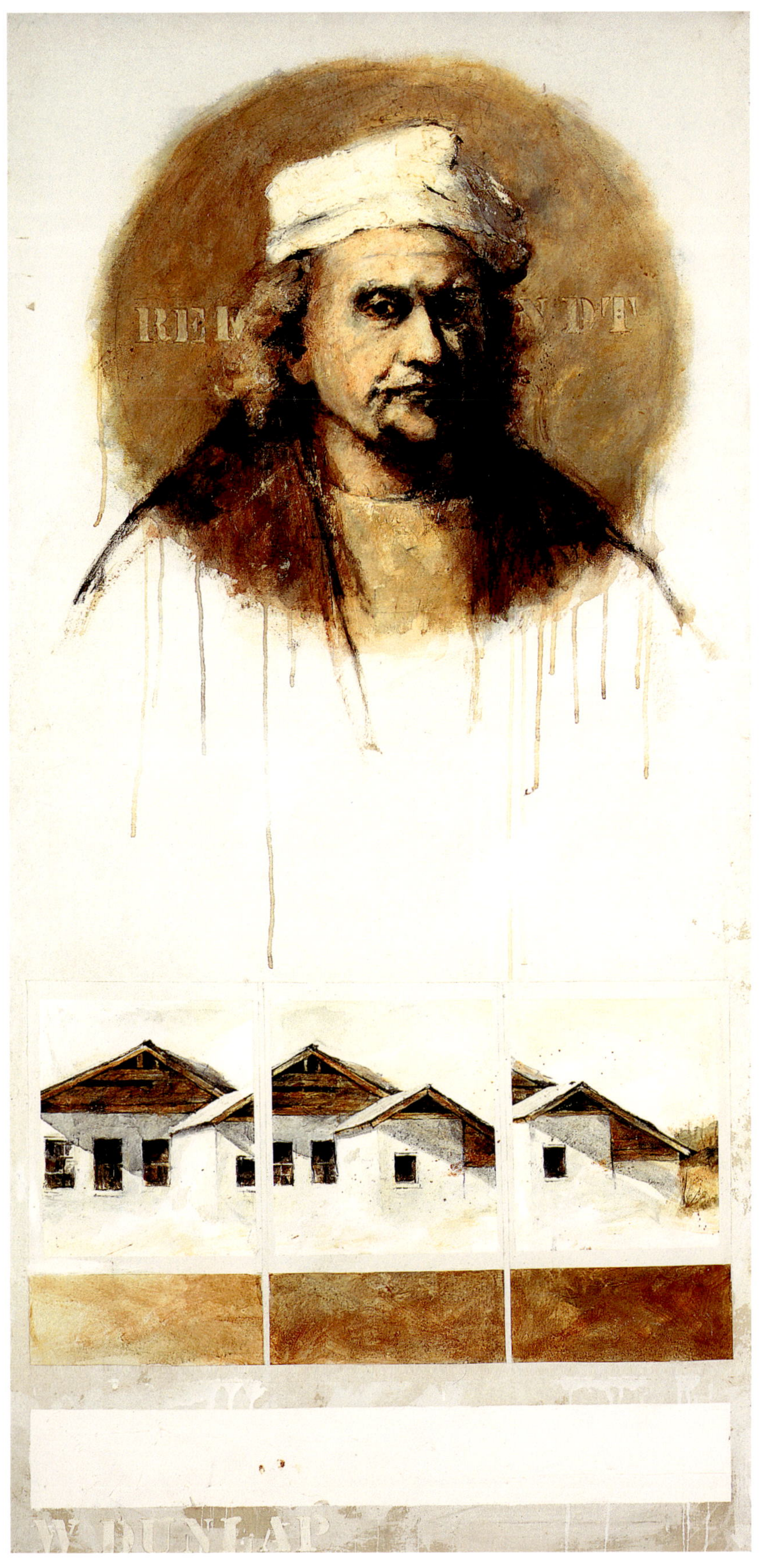

Landscape and Variable—Rembrandt High School Marching Band, 1972
Polymer paint on canvas, 66 x 32. Collection of Mississippi Museum of Art, Jackson. Gift of Norma Latimer Watkins, in memory of her mother Norma Hosford Latimer Fontaine. 1987.136. Photograph by Hubert Worley.

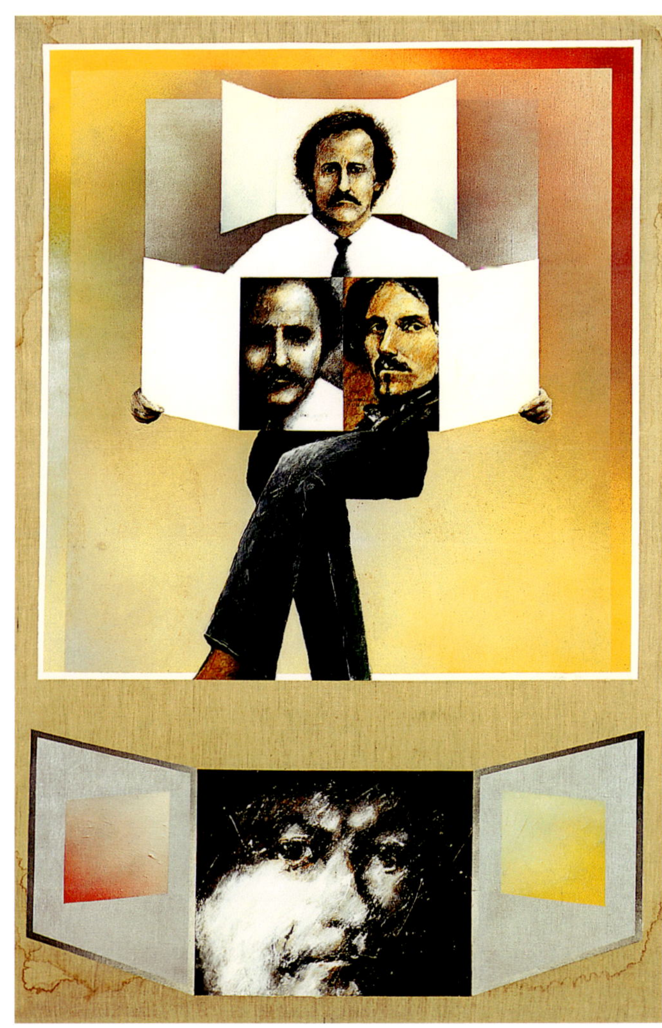

Capehart, Rembrandt, and Delacroix, 1973
Polymer and metallic paint on canvas, 71 x 45 1/2. Private collection. Photograph by Hubert Worley.

Pond Bank, 1973

Watercolor and polymer paint on rag paper, 22 x 30. Collection of David Trigiani, Jackson, Mississippi. Photograph by Hubert Worley.

Landscape and Variable, 1973

Oil paint on rag board, 50 x 55. Collection of Judge and Mrs. E. Grady Jolly, Jackson, Mississippi. Photograph by Hubert Worley.

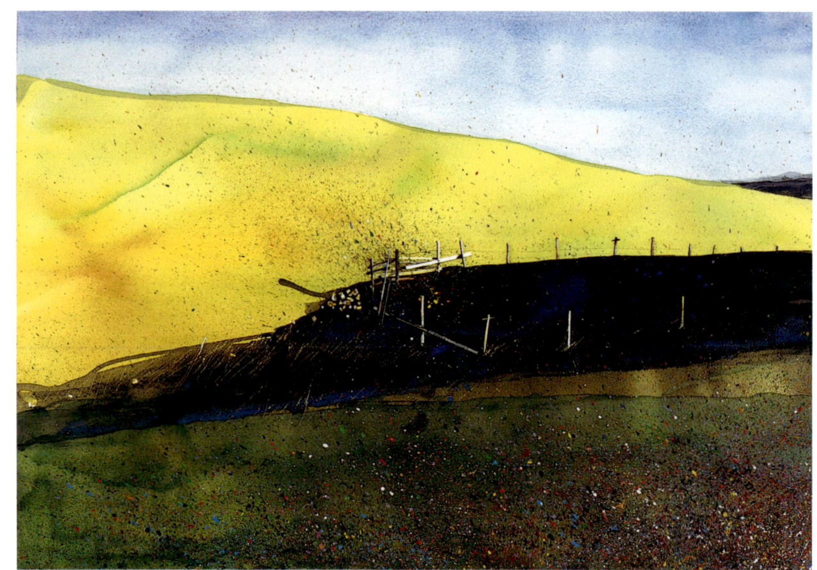

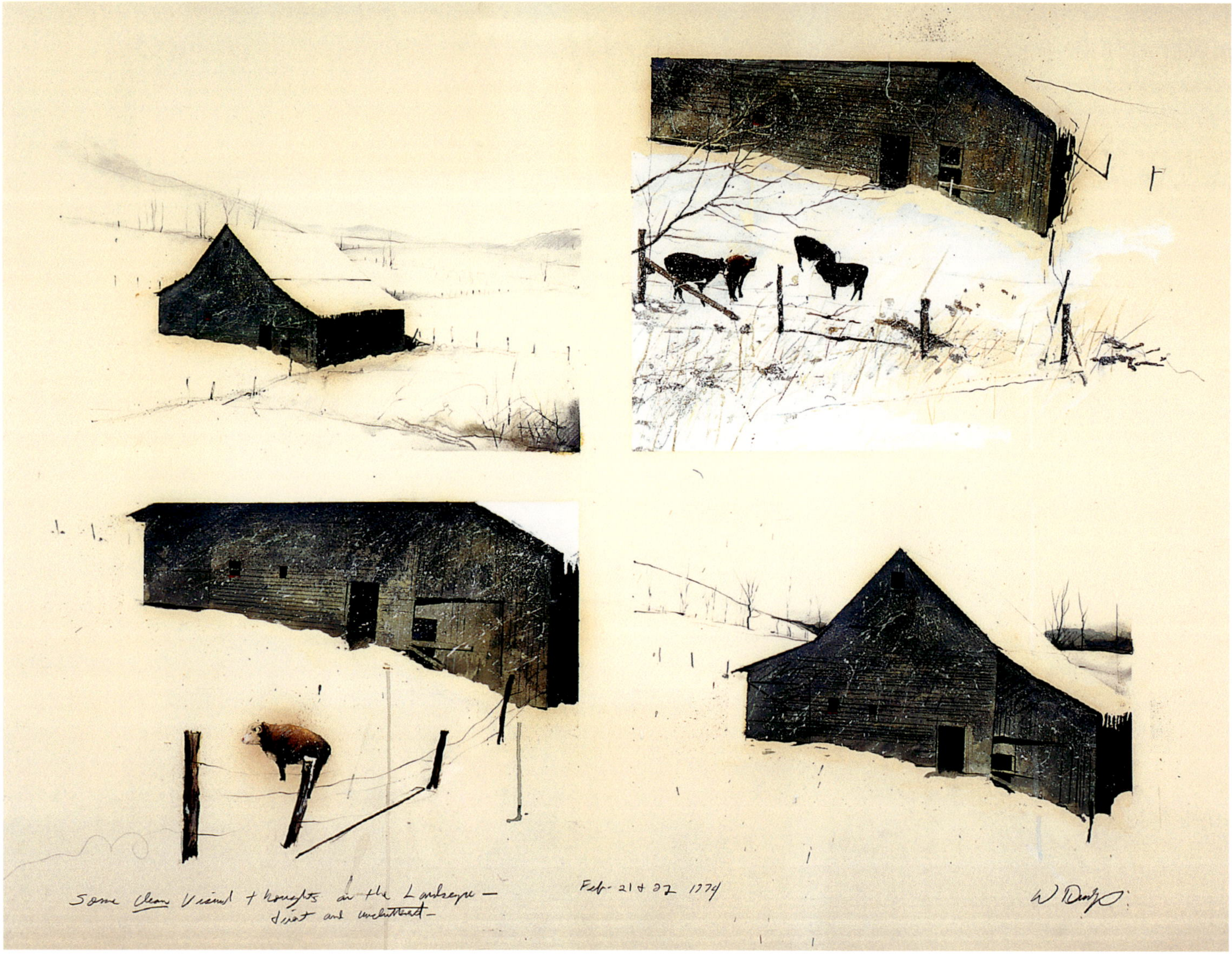

Old Masters Reconsidered: Dr. Tulp and Friends, 1975
Polymer paint on Masonite, 48 x 48. Private collection. Photograph by Jack Meyer.

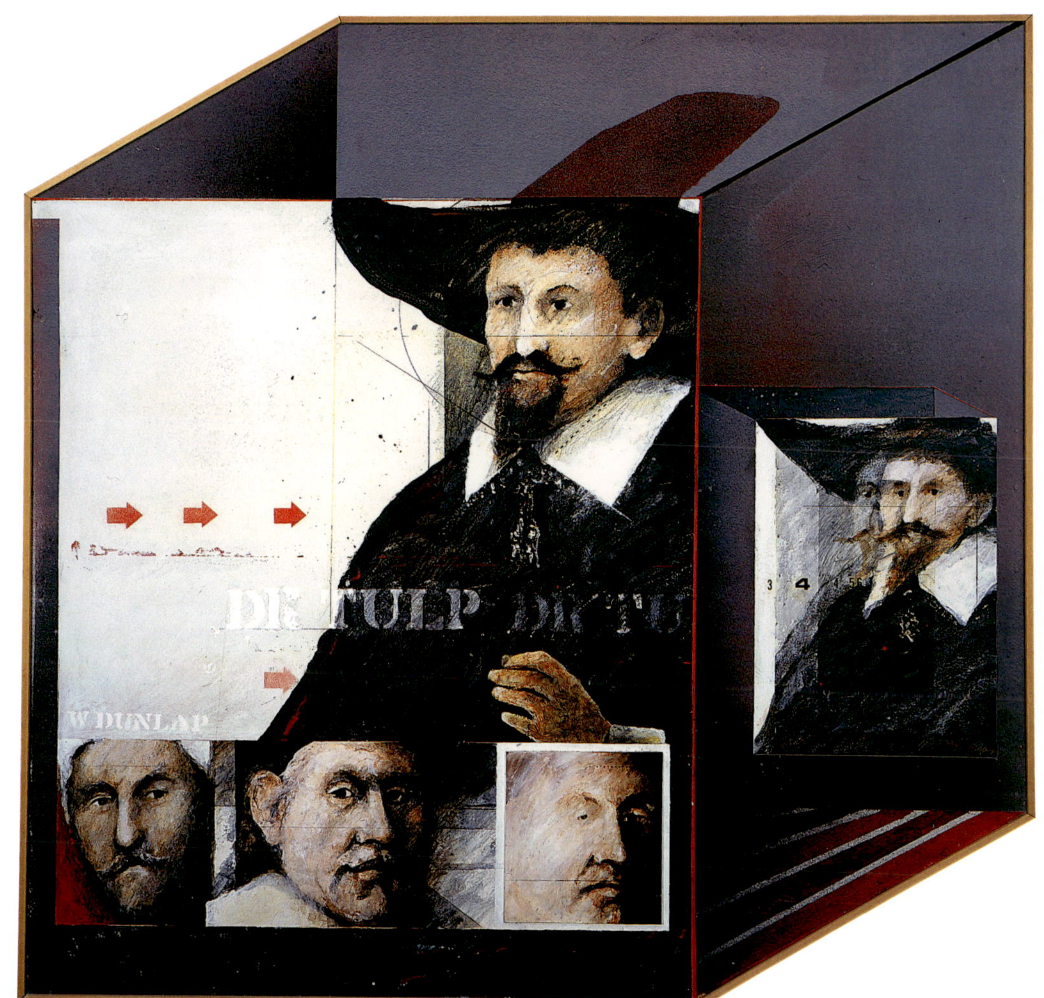

Rainbow Trout Farm, 1978
Oil paint and dry pigment/graphite on paper, diptych, 24 x 118. Private collection. Photograph by Jack Meyer.

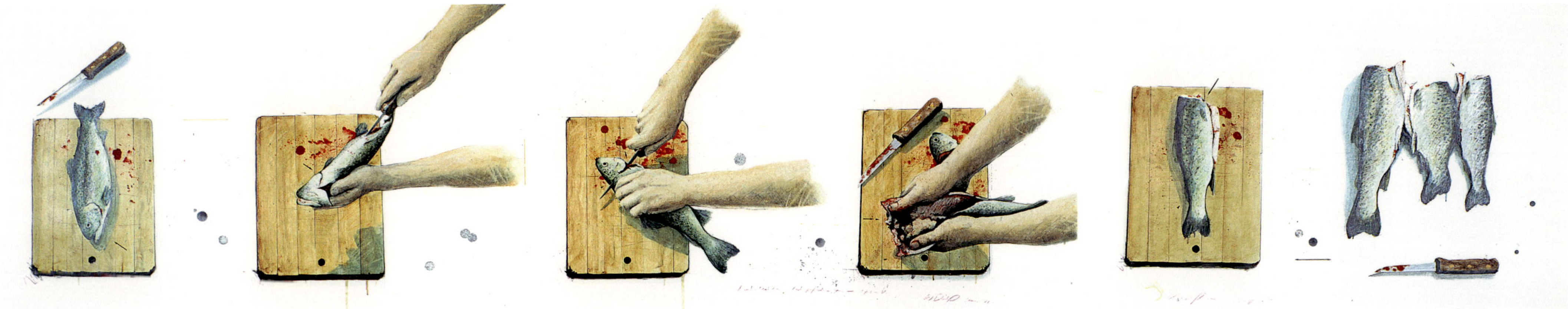

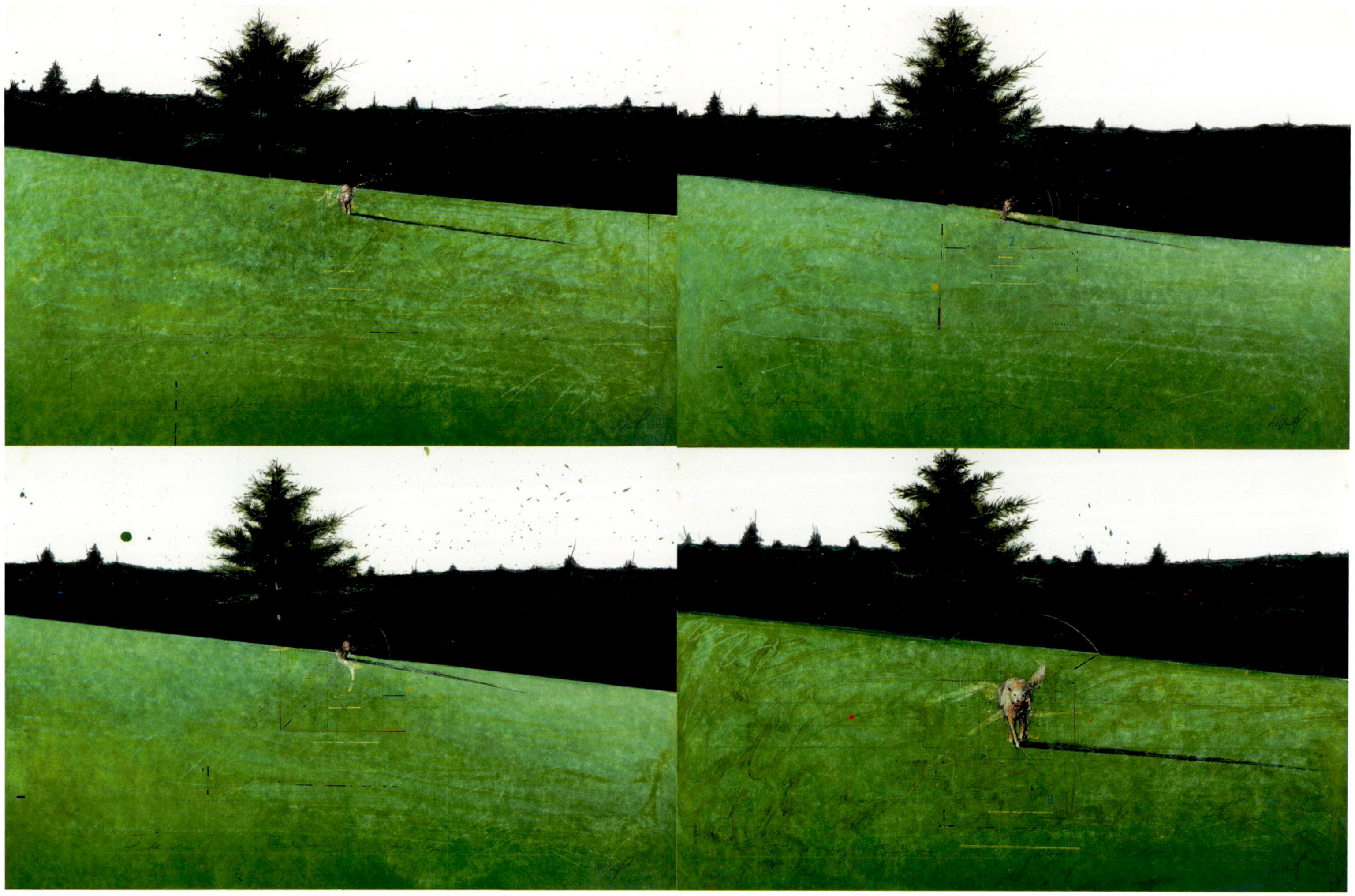

Jude the Obscure, ca. 1976
Oil and polymer paint on paper, 4 panels,
24 x 36 each, 48 x 72 entire. Private collection.
Photograph by John E. Powell.

Reluctant Water Lilies,1978
Polymer paint on canvas, diptych, 48 x 60 each.
Collection of Dr. John Harbert, McLean,
Virginia. Photograph by Jack Kotz.

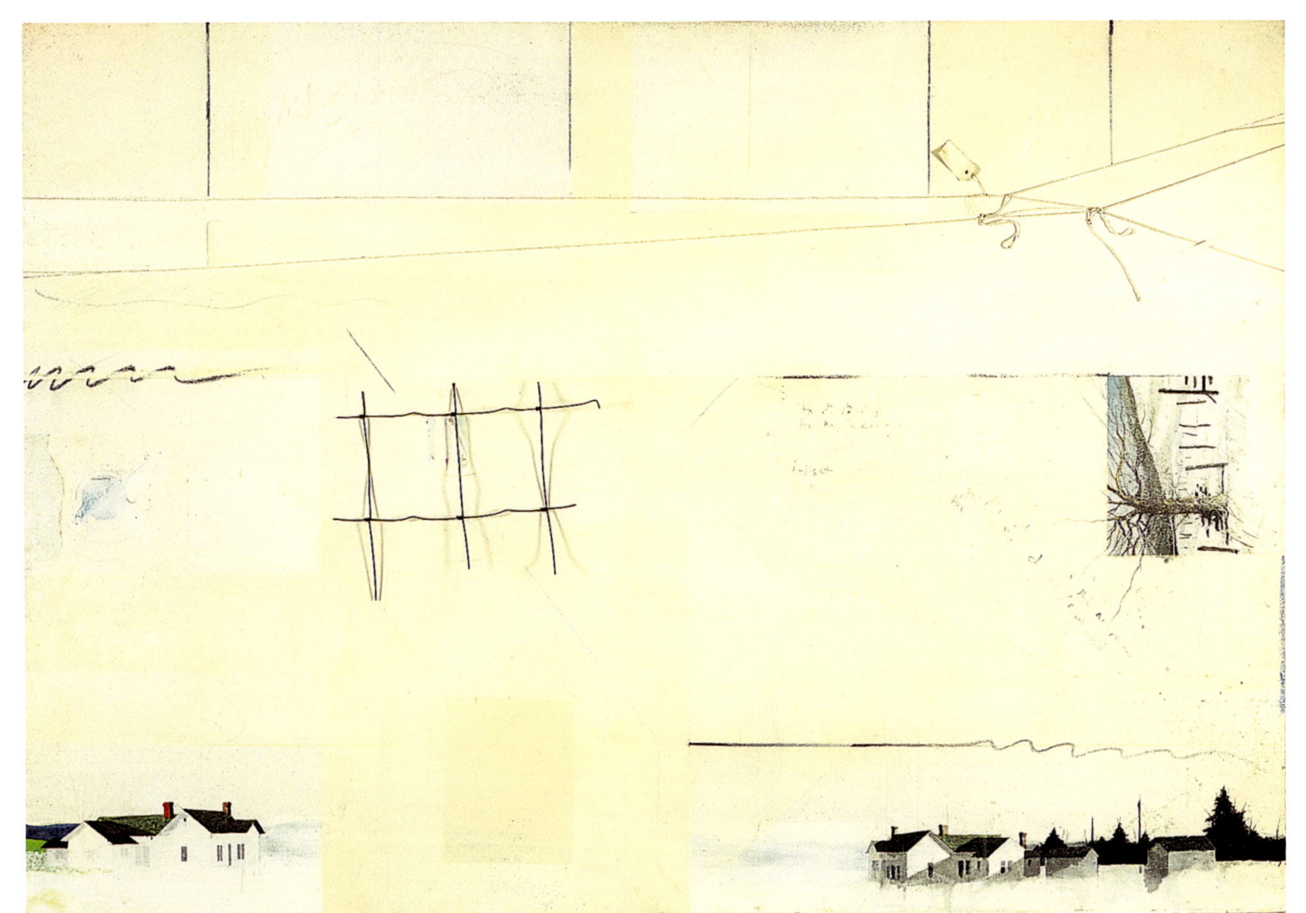

Hybrid Series: II, 1976
Polymer paint and found objects on canvas, 60 x 84 1/2. Private collection. Photograph by Hubert Worley.

Mail Pouch Tobacco, 1978
Oil paint and dry pigment on rag paper, 32 x 72. Collection of Richard Fisher, Galisteo, New Mexico. Photograph by Edward E. Mullen.

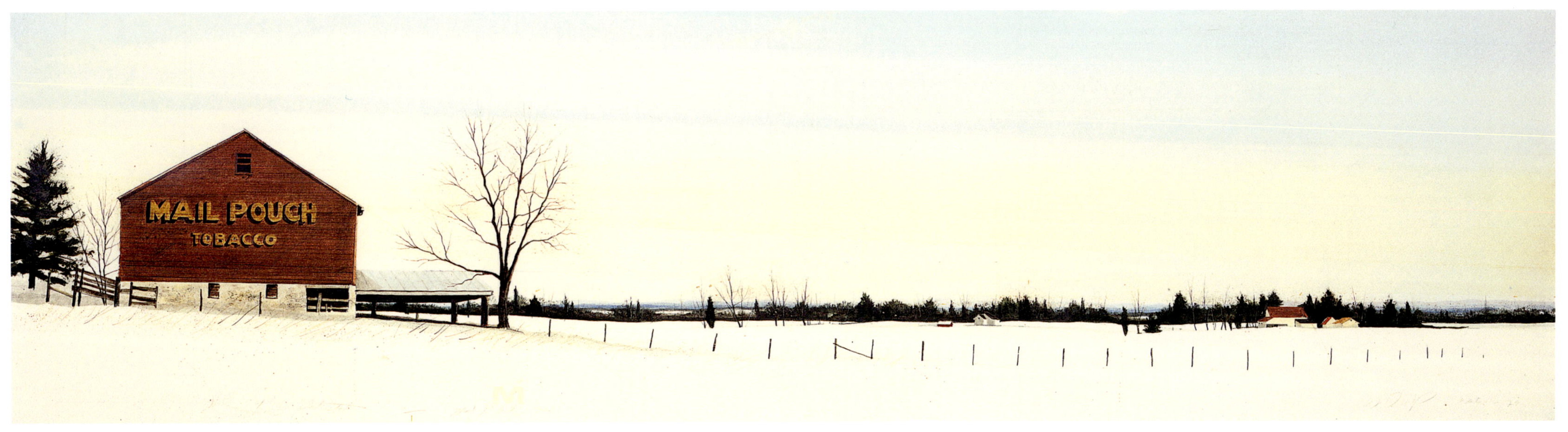

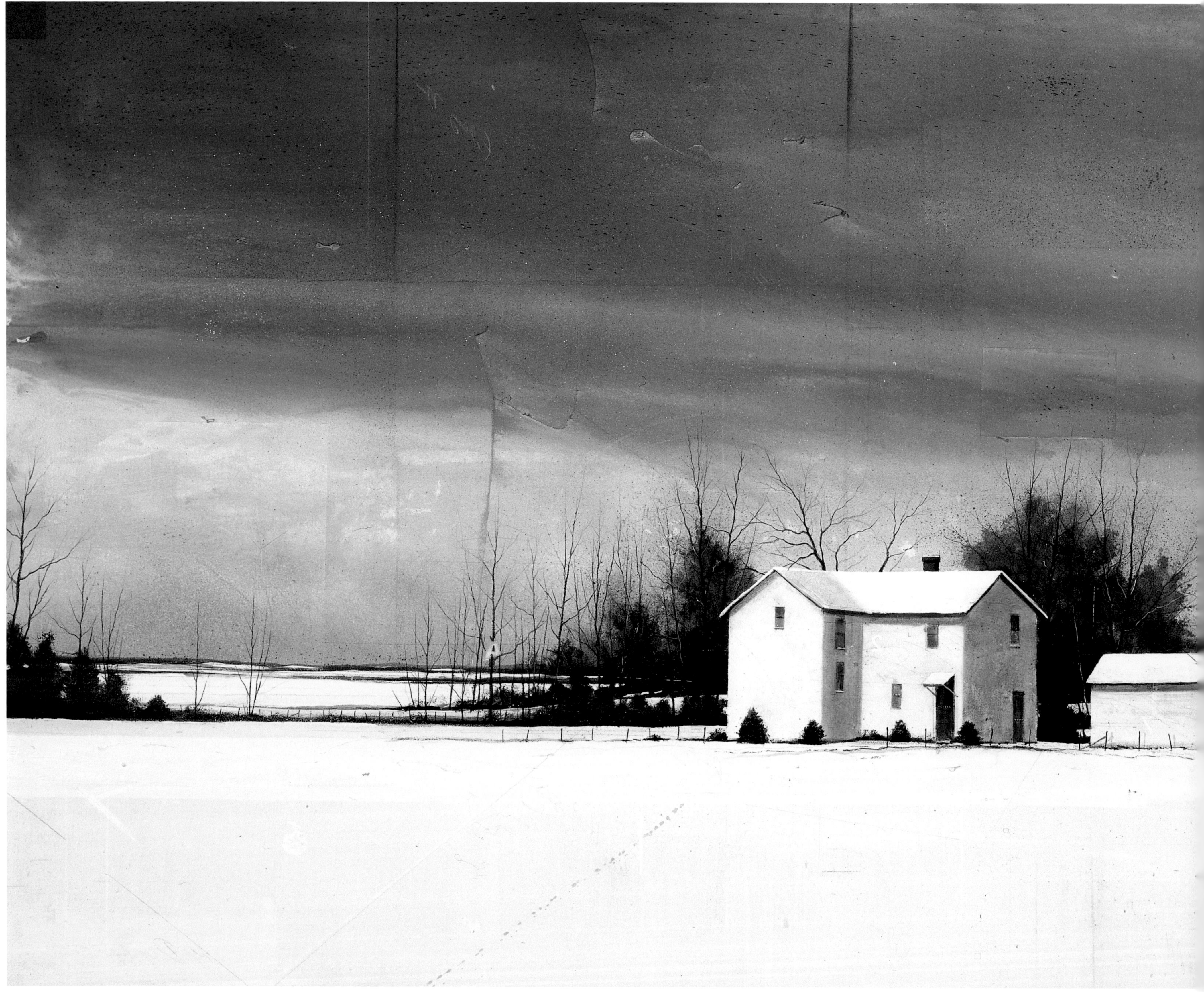

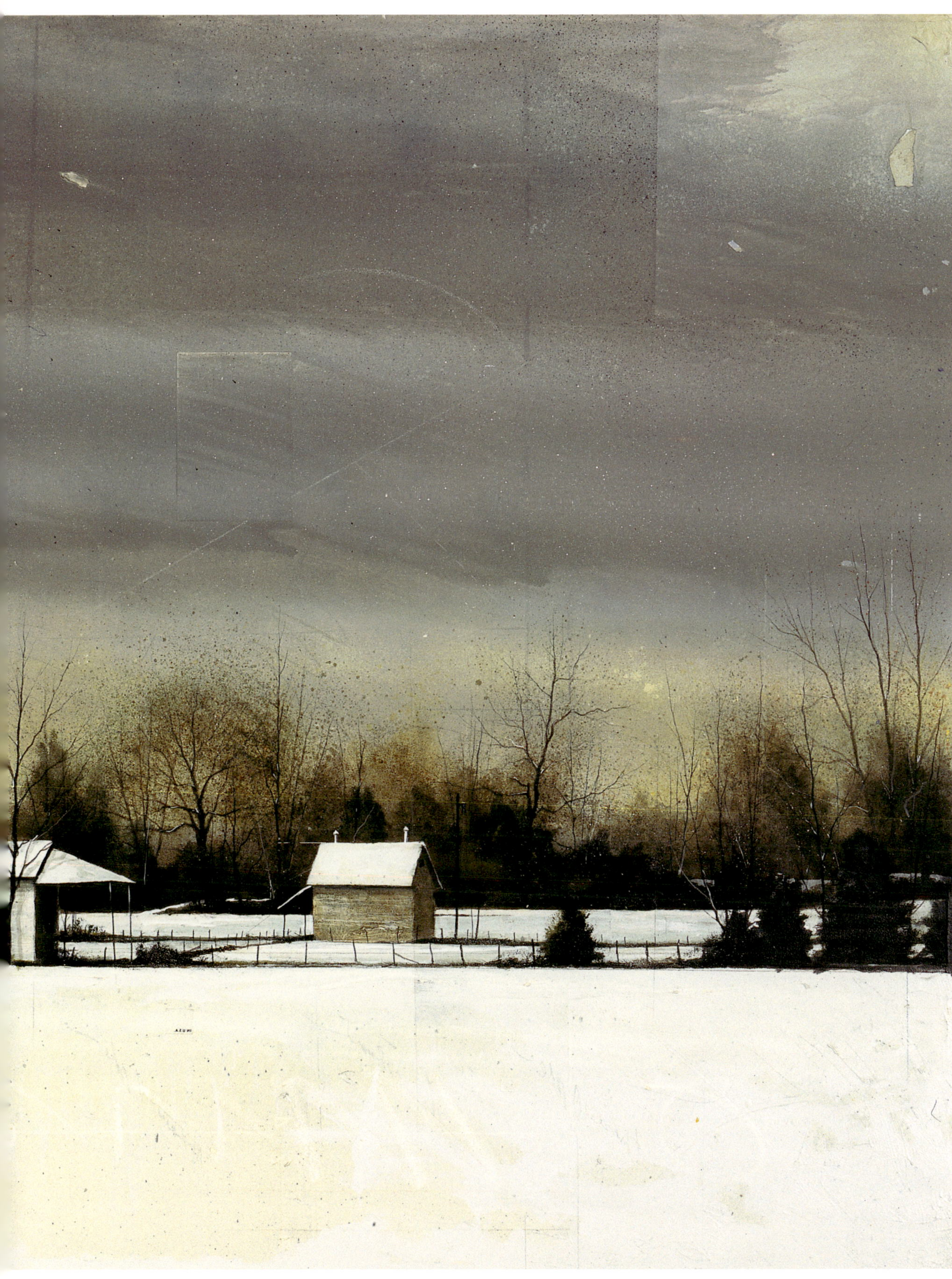

Winter '77 Series, 1977

Polymer and oil paint on canvas, 48 x 96.

Collection of Mississippi Museum of Art, Jackson. Gift of The Gallery Guild, Inc. 1978.001. Photograph by Walter Smalling.

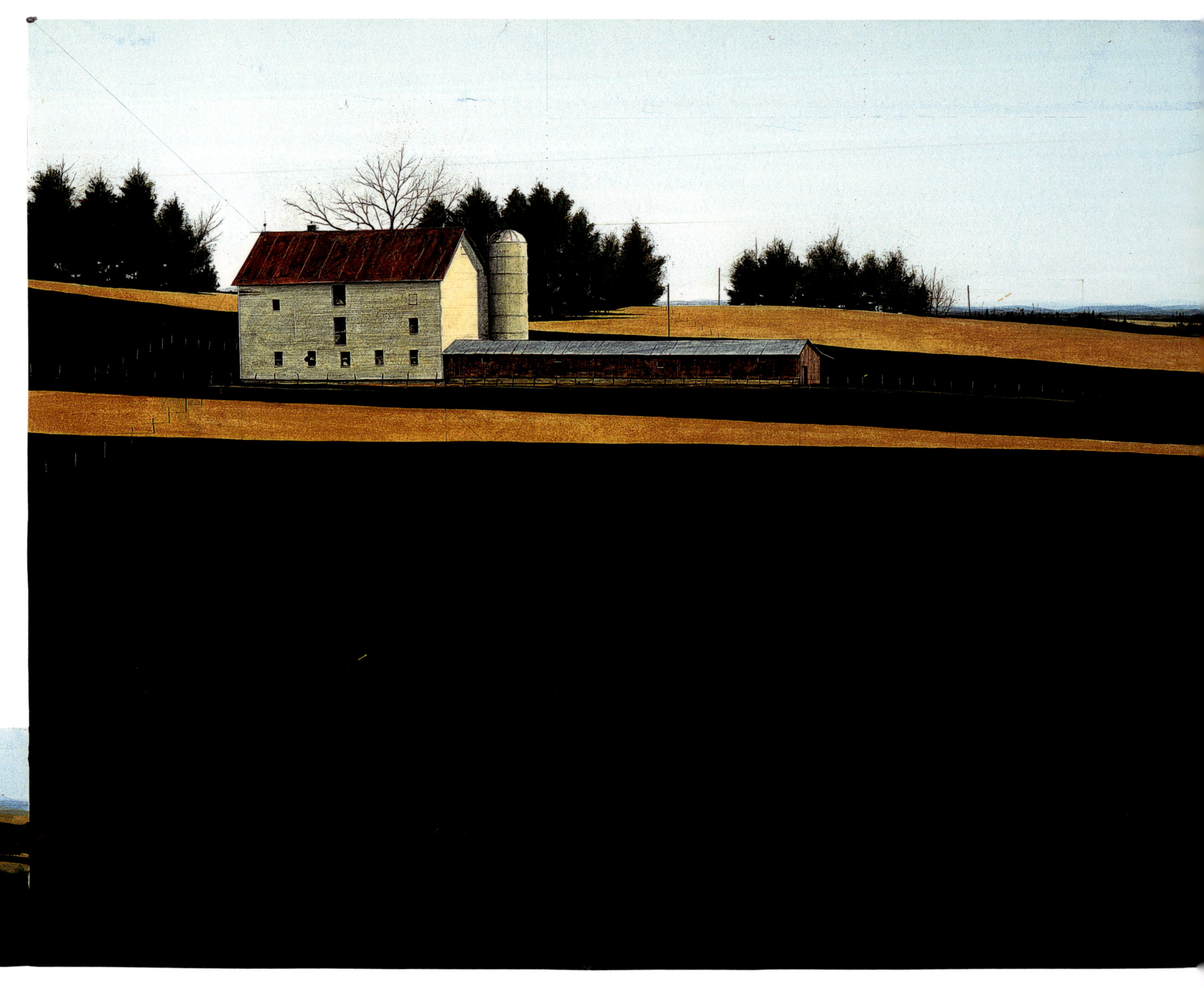

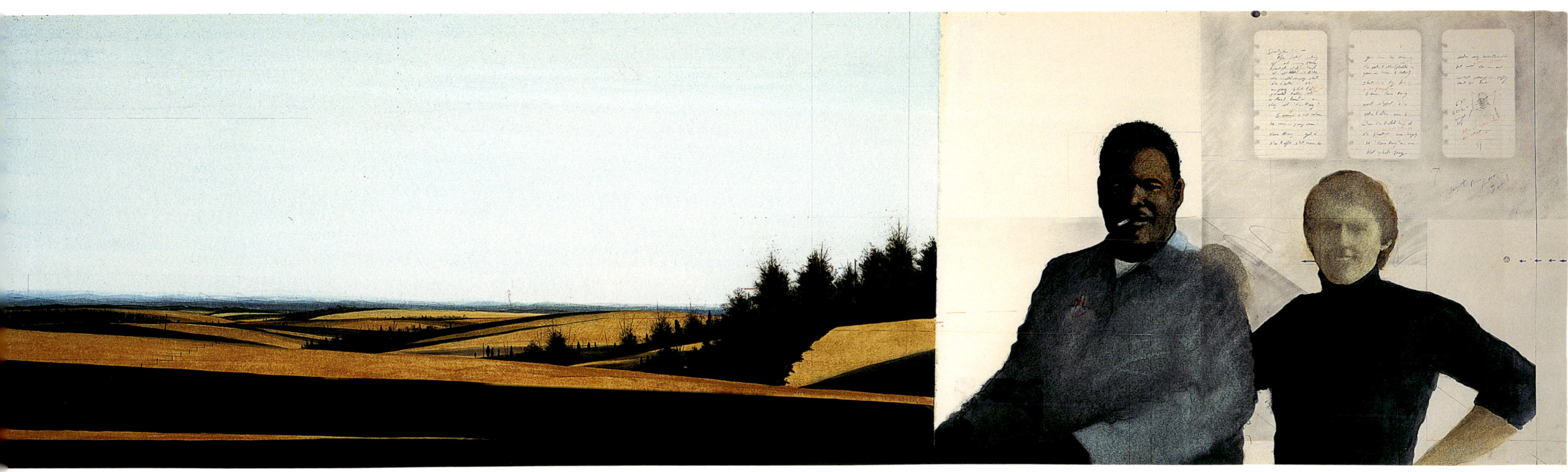

Landscape with "Have Mercy," 1979
Oil paint and dry pigment on rag paper, triptych, 48 x 156 (12 x 18, 48 x 60, 24 x 84). Private collection. Photograph by William Moretz.

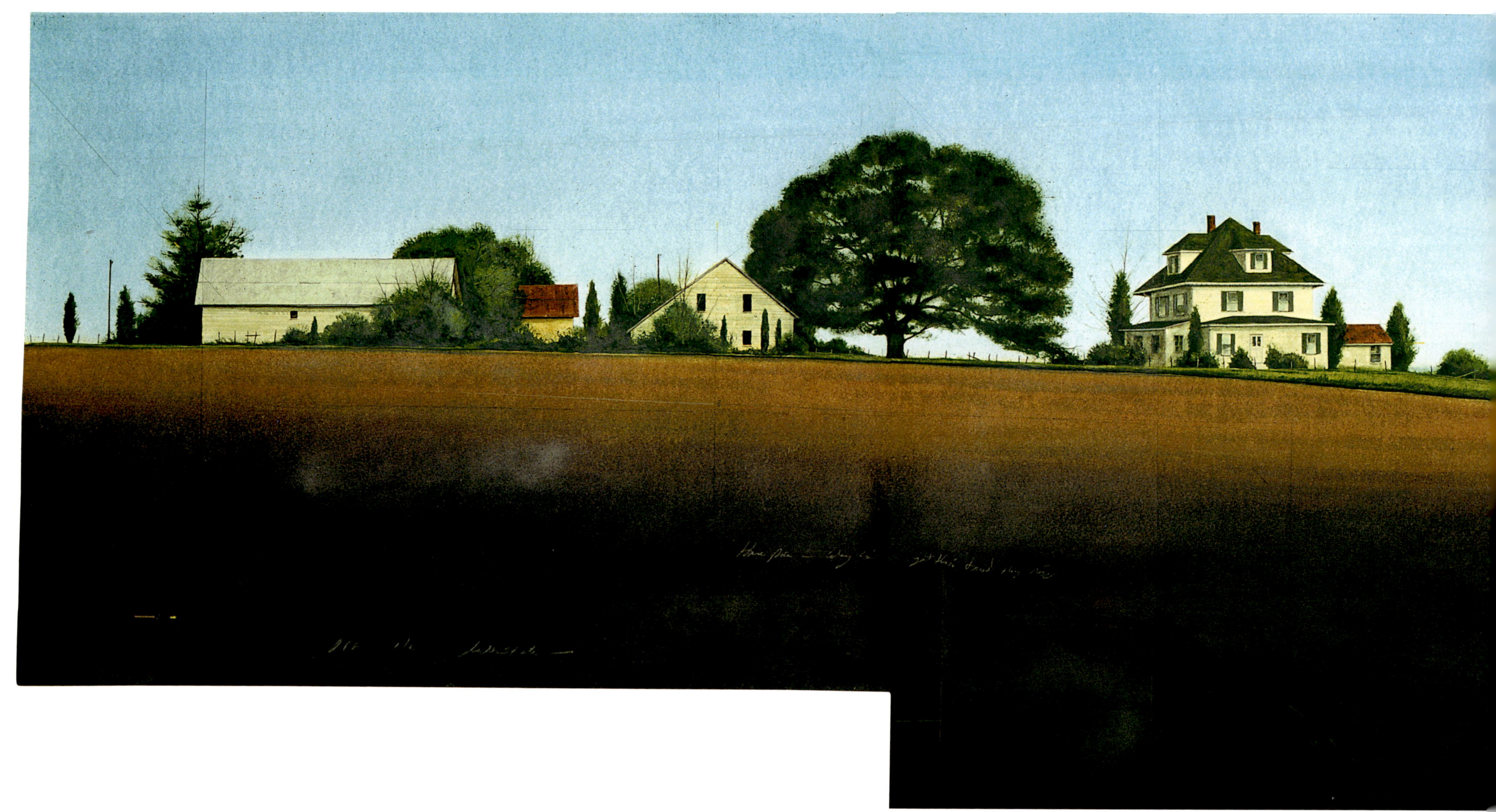

Off the Interstate—Early Spring, 1979
Oil paint and dry pigment on rag paper, triptych, 24 x 155. Private collection. Photograph by William Moretz.

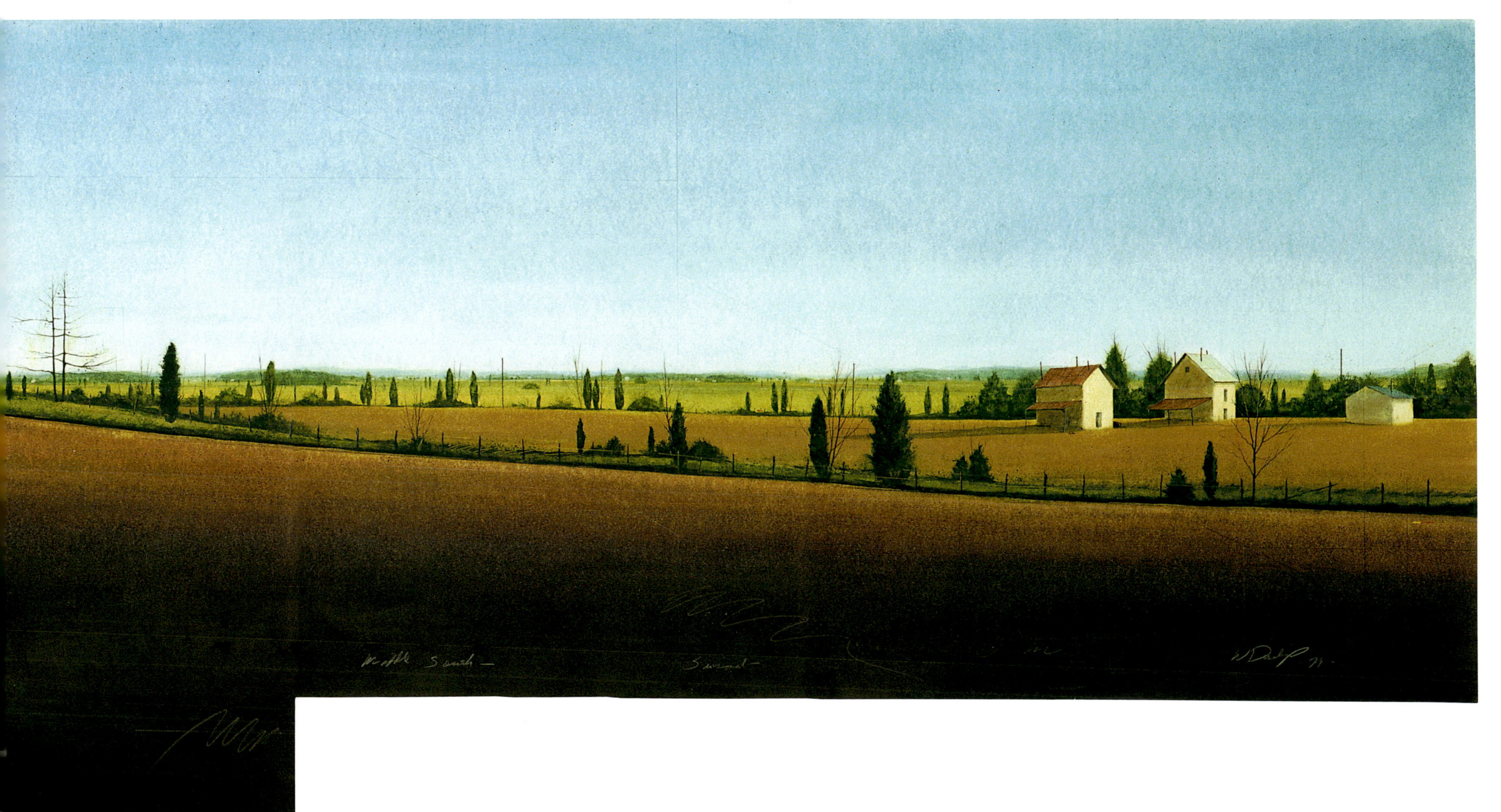

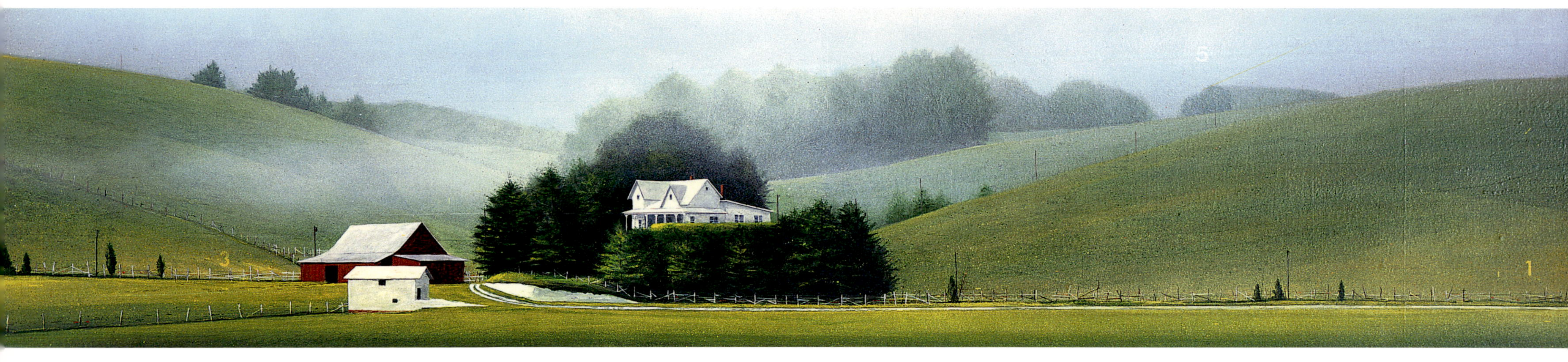

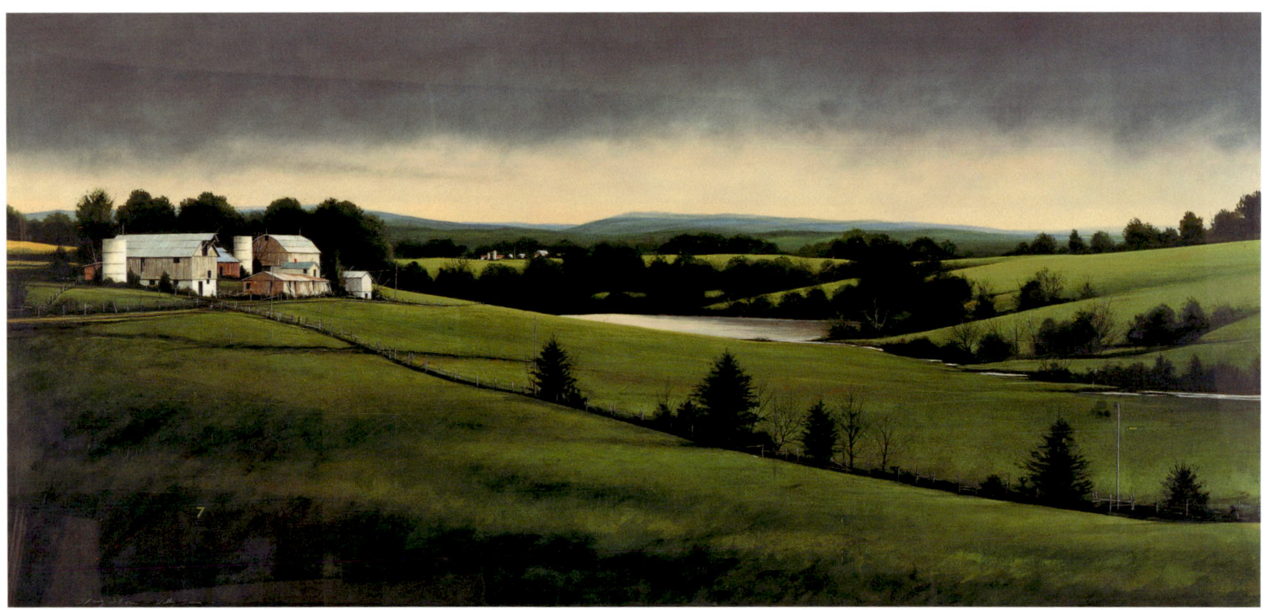

Early Light—Fog Bound, 1980
Polymer paint on wood panel, diptych,
18 x 156. Collection of Fisher Brothers,
New York City. Photograph by Jack Meyer.

Spring Storm—Valley Series, 1982
Oil paint and dry pigment on paper,
44 1/4 x 89 1/2. Collection of The Corcoran
Gallery of Art, Washington, D.C. Gift of the
Women's Committee. 1982.43. Photograph
by Jack Kotz.

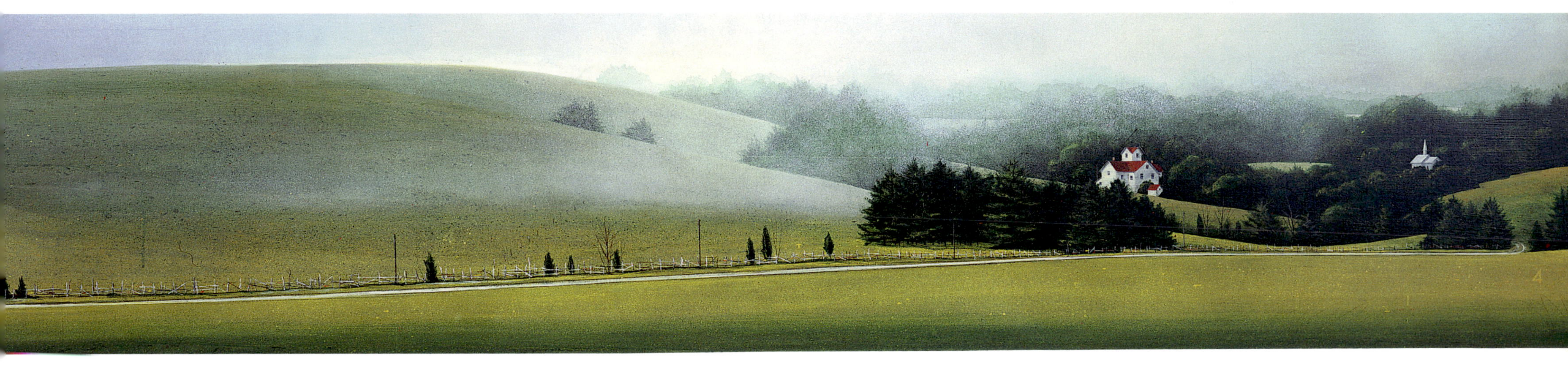

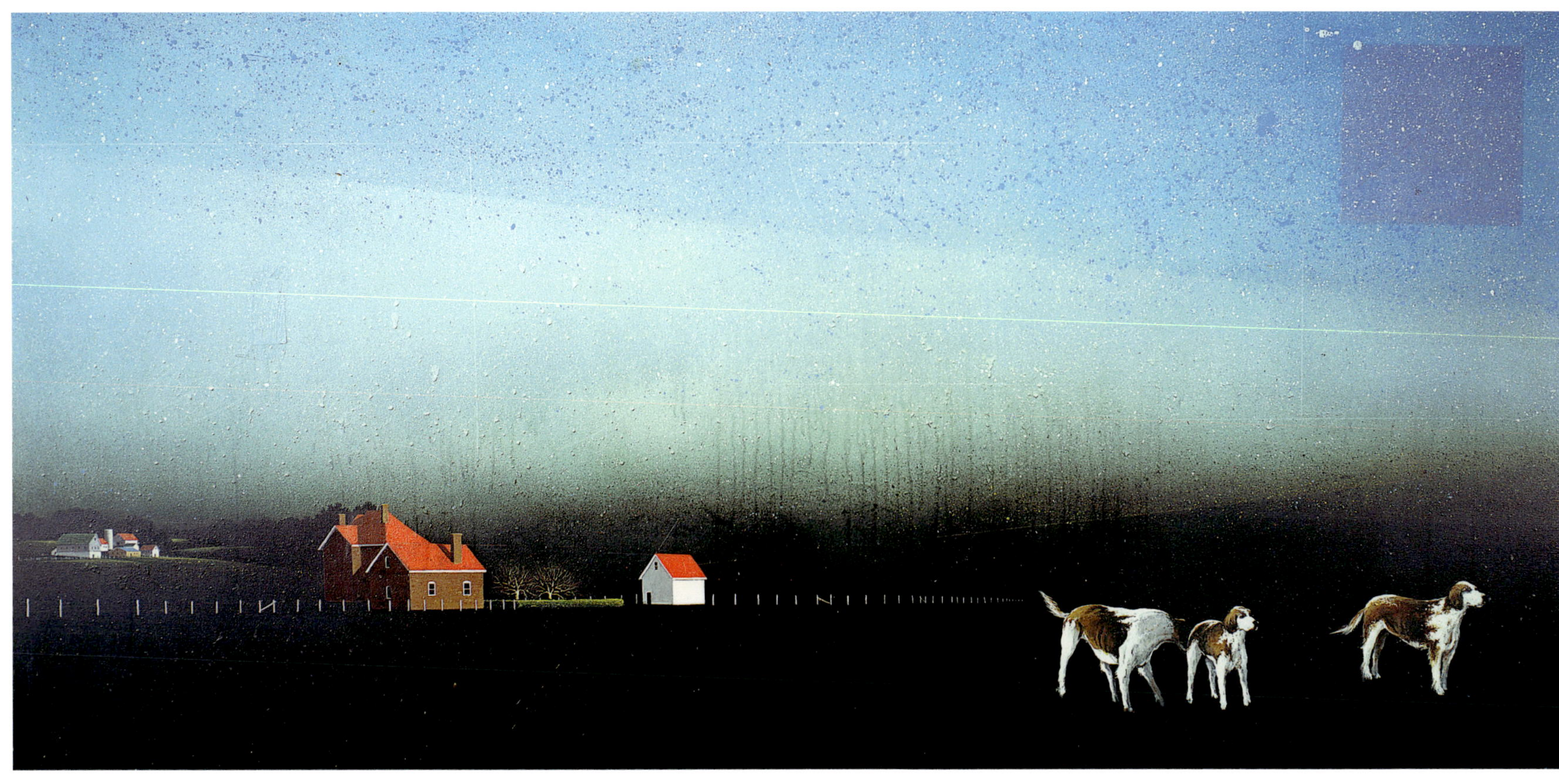

Dog Trot, 1983
Polymer paint on canvas, 48 x 96. Private collection. Photograph by Jack Kotz.

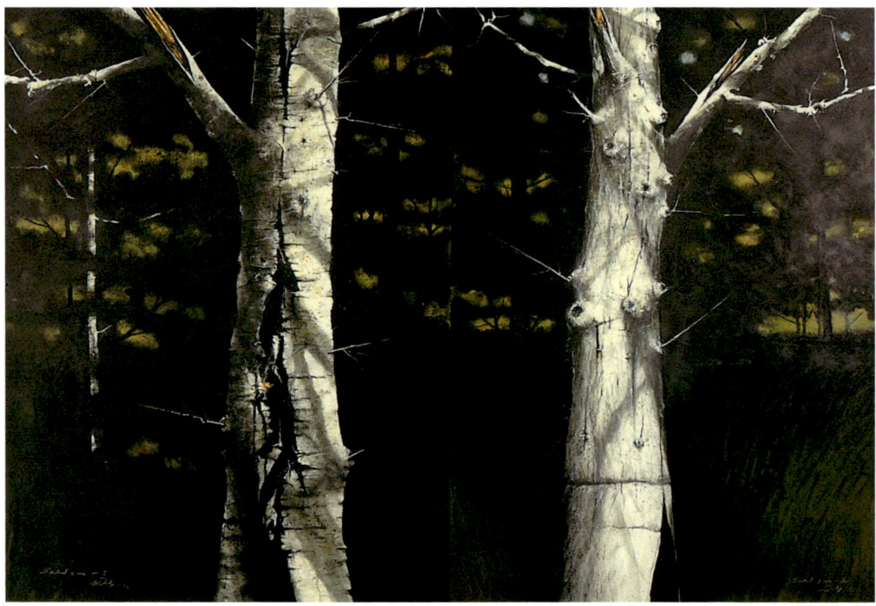

Double Trunk: Trunk Series, 1981
Graphite and oil wash on rag paper, 40 x 52.
Collection of Caroline Vaughan Goodman,
Jackson, Mississippi. Photograph by Jack Meyer.

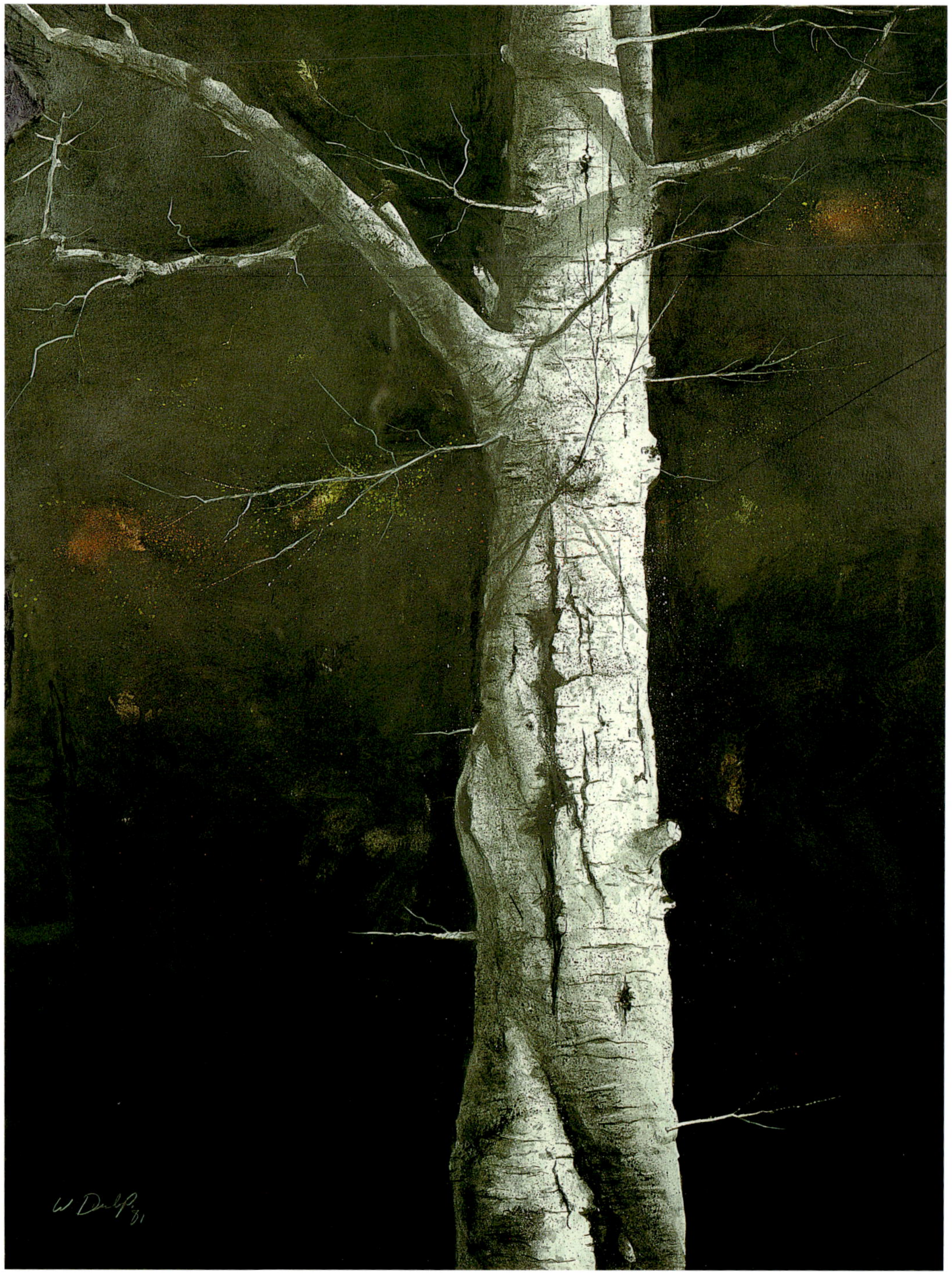

American Landscape: Trunk Series,
1981
Graphite, oil wash, and pencil on rag paper,
40 x 30. Collection of The Metropolitan
Museum of Art, New York City. Gift of the
artist, 1990 (1990.303). Photograph by Lisa
Berg.

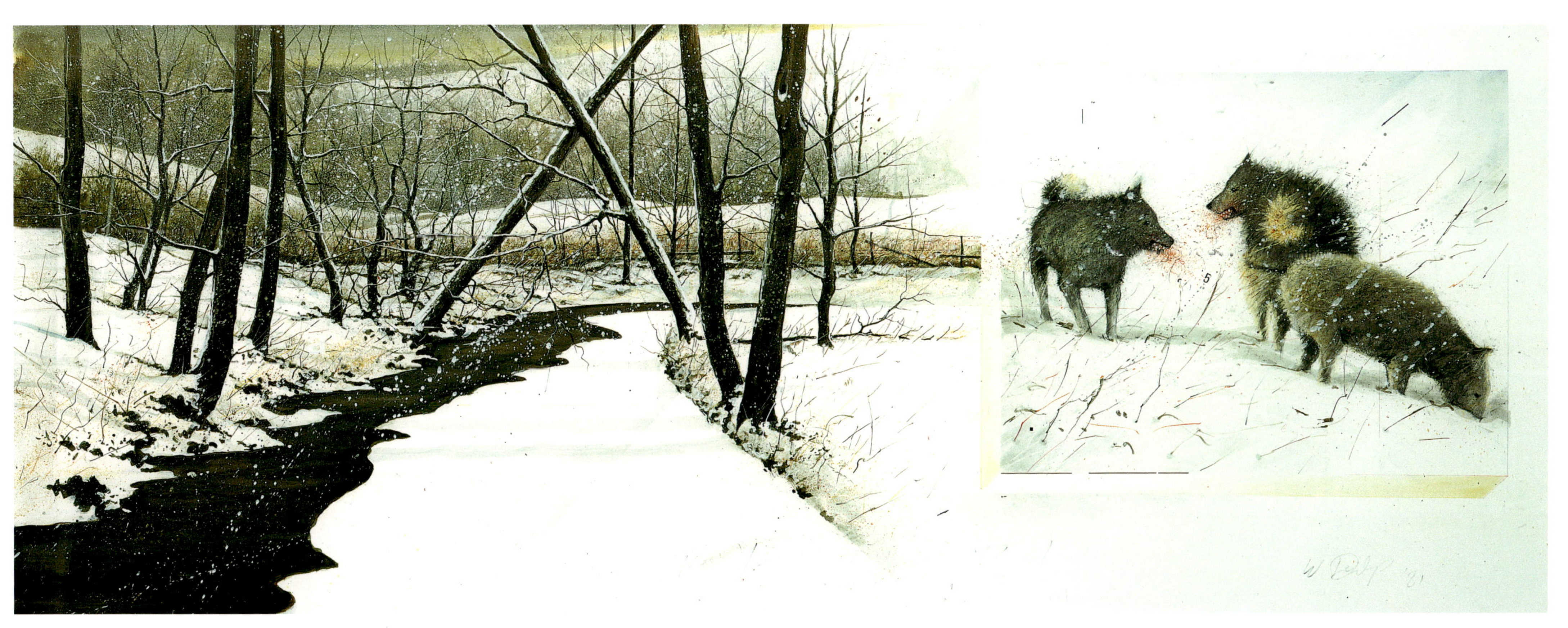

New Year's Day—1981, 1981
Oil paint and graphite on rag paper, 32 x 79. Collection of the Honorable Ann and Donald Brown, Palm Beach, Florida. Photograph by Jack Kotz.

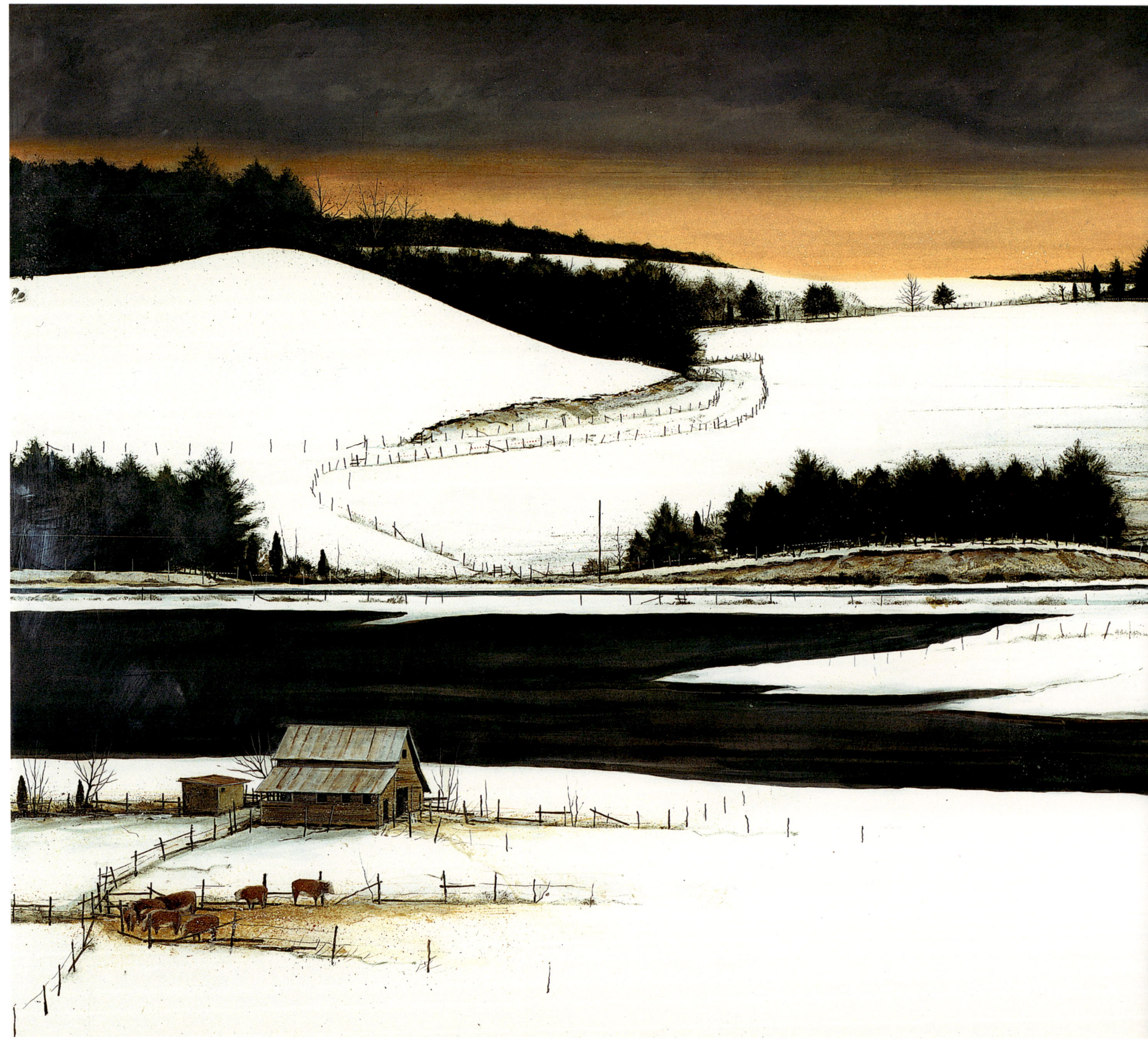

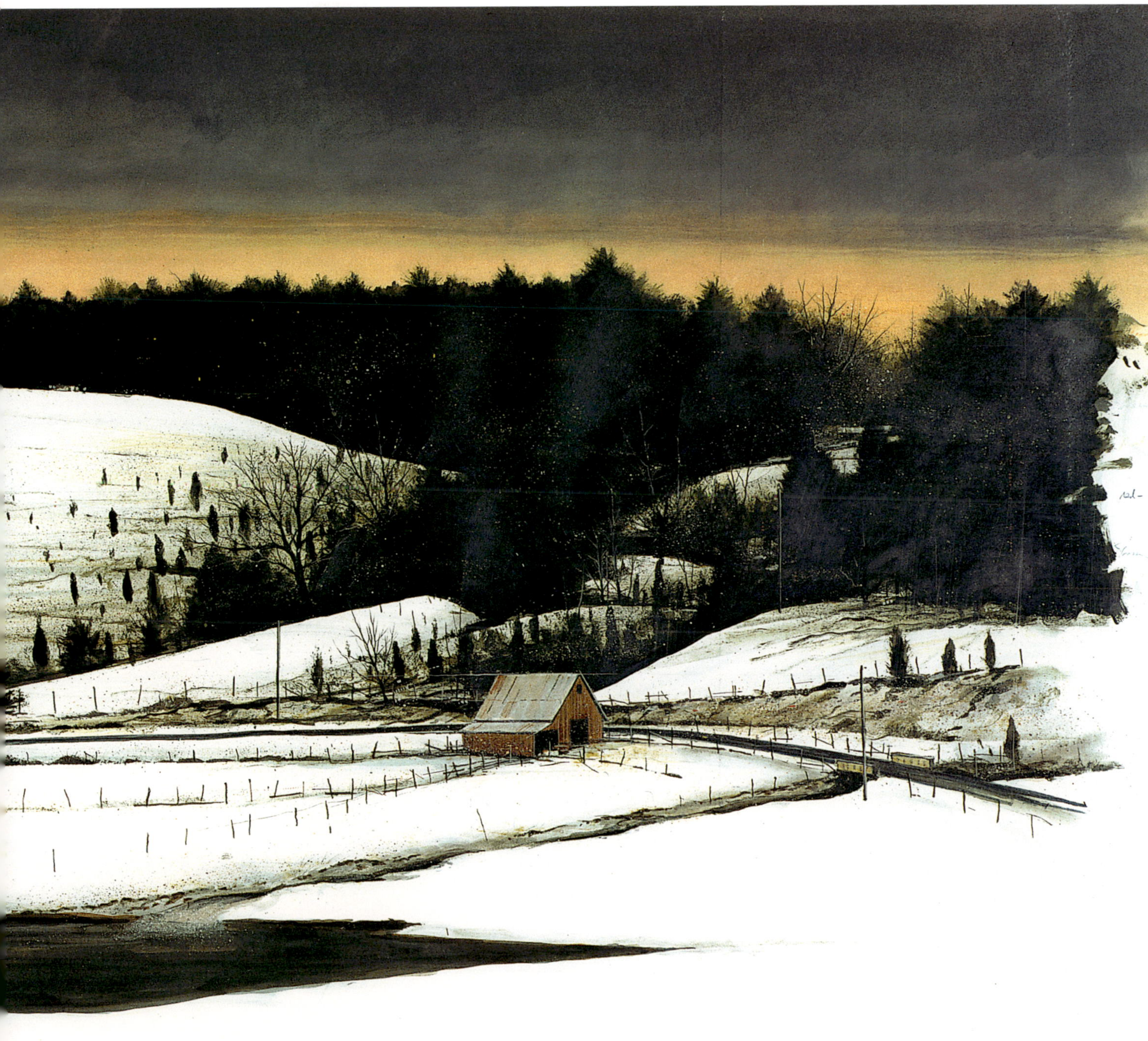

Late Light/Valley Series, 1982
Oil paint and dry pigment on paper, 48 x 96. Collection of Mr. and Mrs. Horst Wagner, Cramerton, North Carolina. Photograph by Jack Kotz.

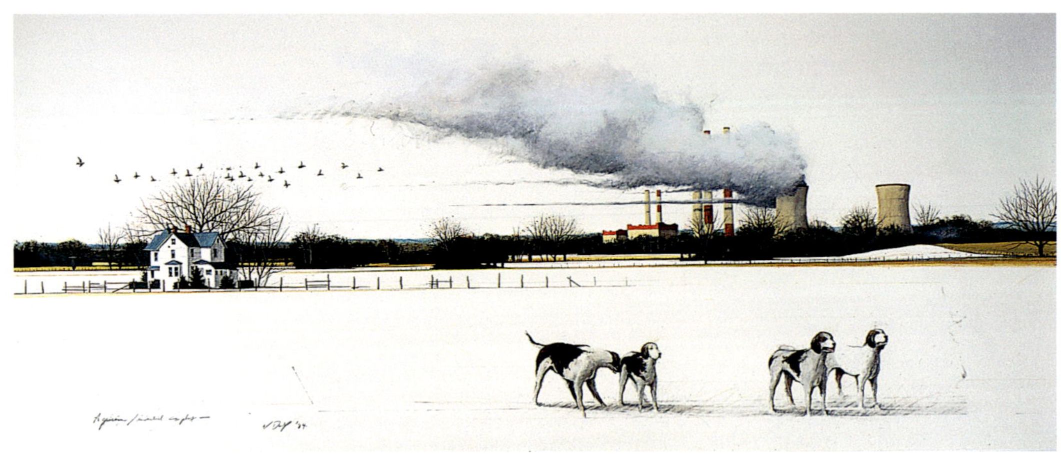

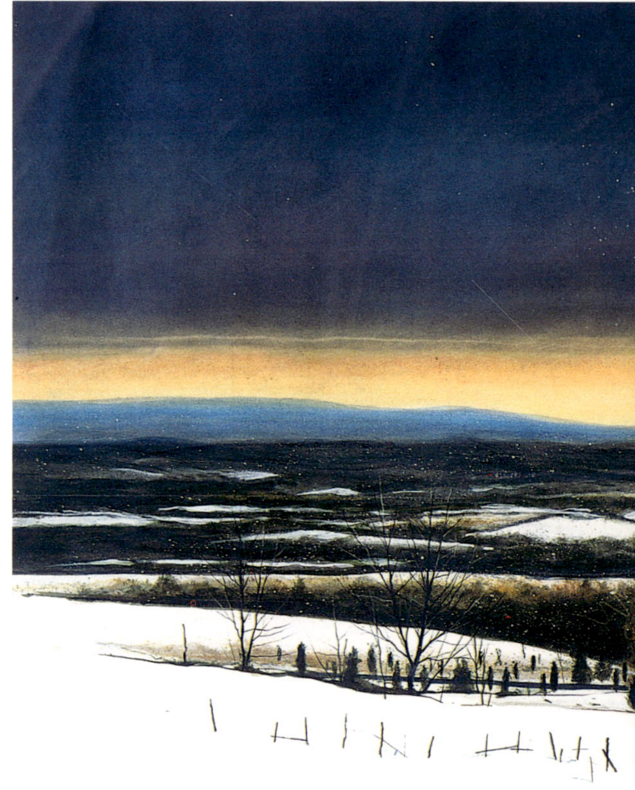

Agrarian Industrial Complex, 1984
Oil on paper, 37 x 84. Private collection.
Photograph by Jack Kotz.

Oversized Mule Deer, 1983
Oil paint on paper, 72 x 48. Collection of Martha Long, Houston, Texas. Photograph by Walter Smalling.

Three Deer Head for Antietam, 1982
Oil paint and dry pigment on paper, 43 1/2 x 93 1/2. Collection of Cornelia and Meredith Long, Houston, Texas. Photograph by Jack Meyer.

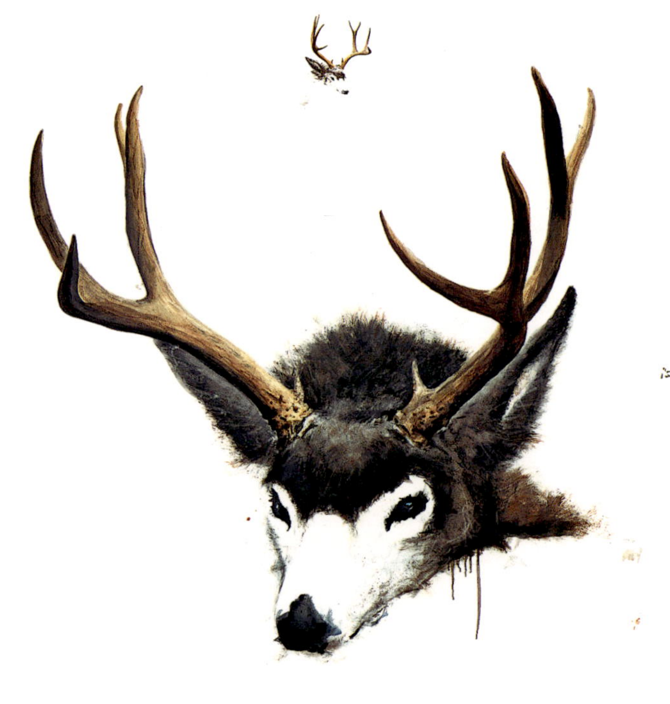

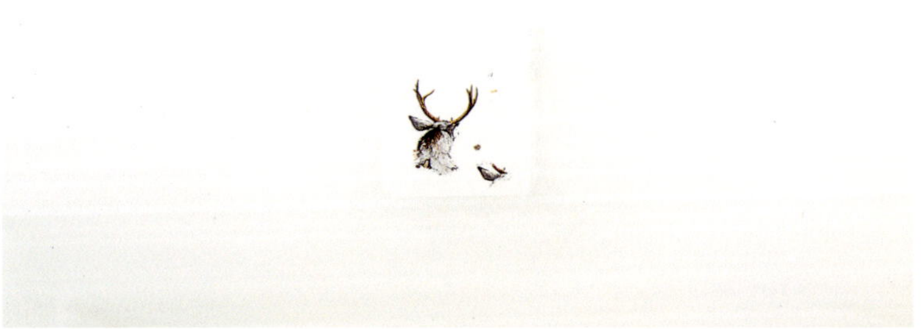

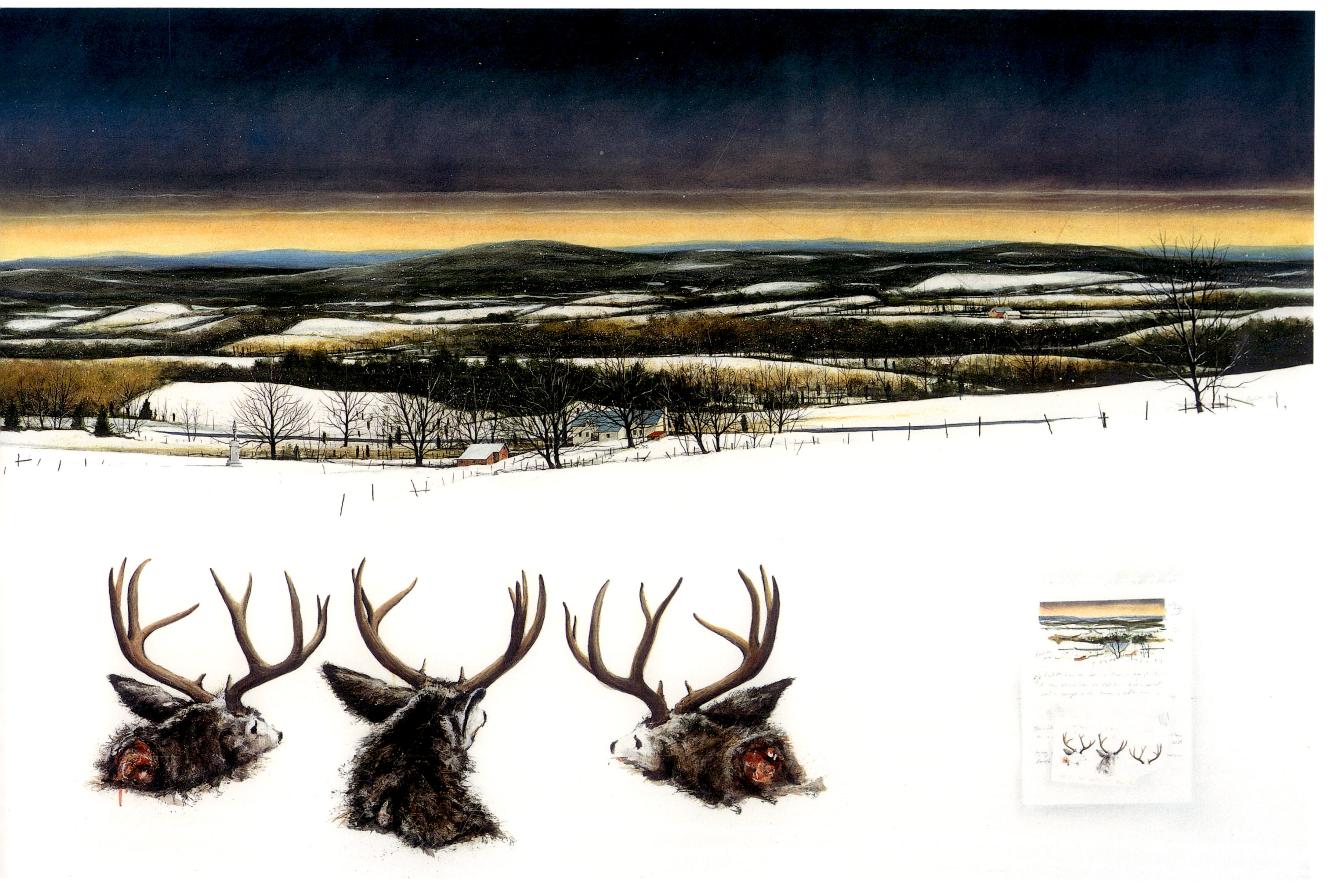

Panorama of the American Landscape

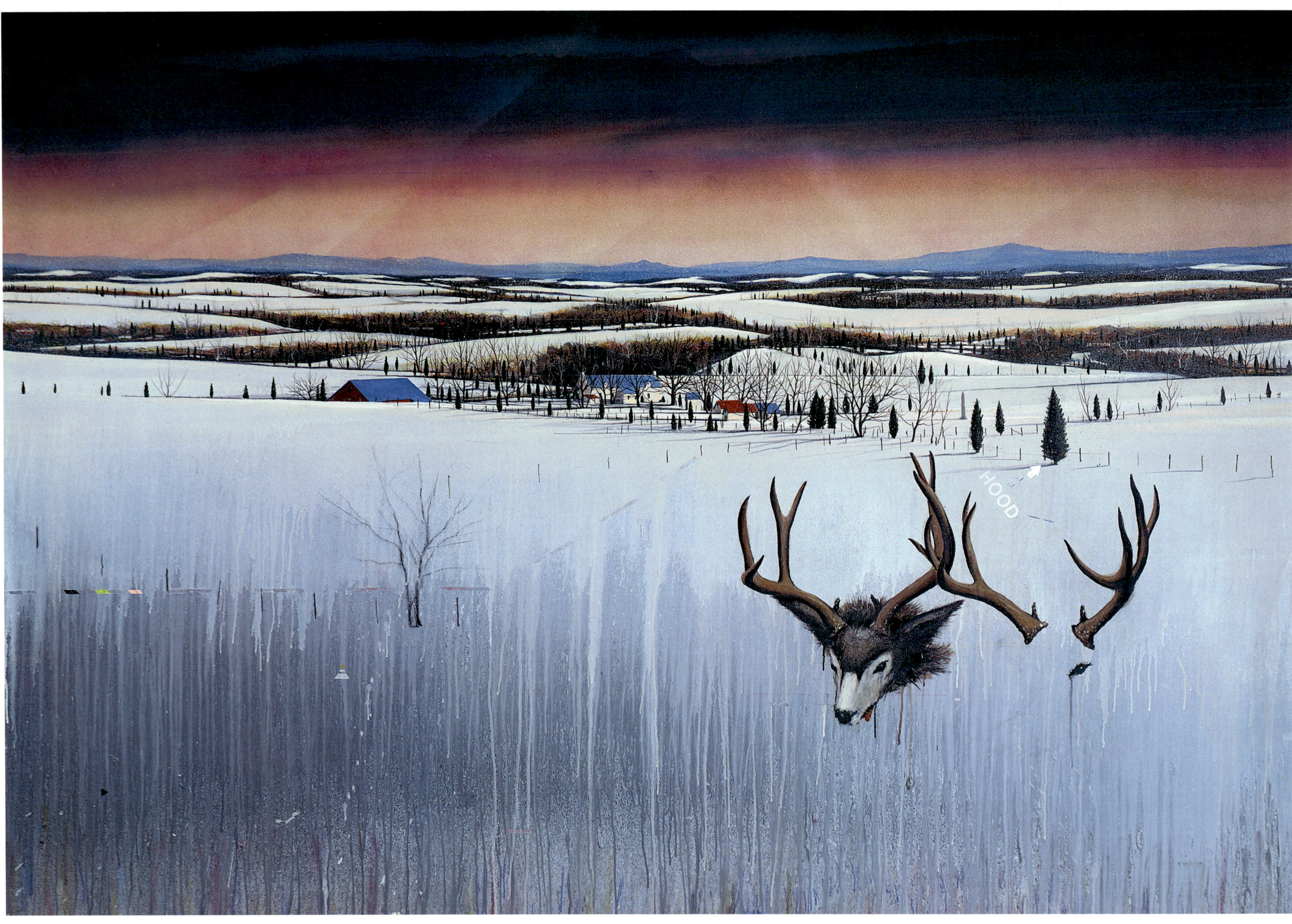

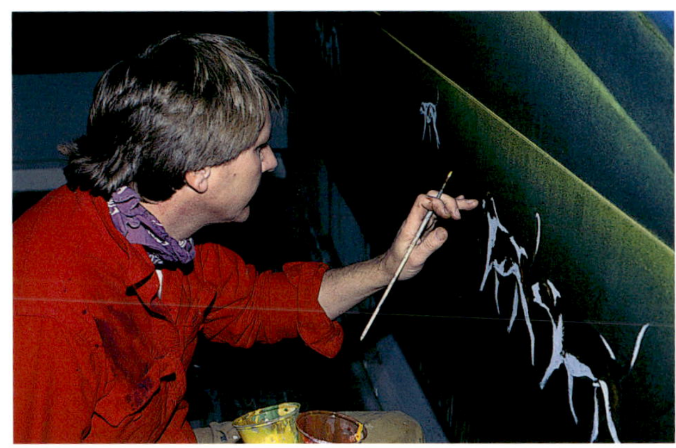

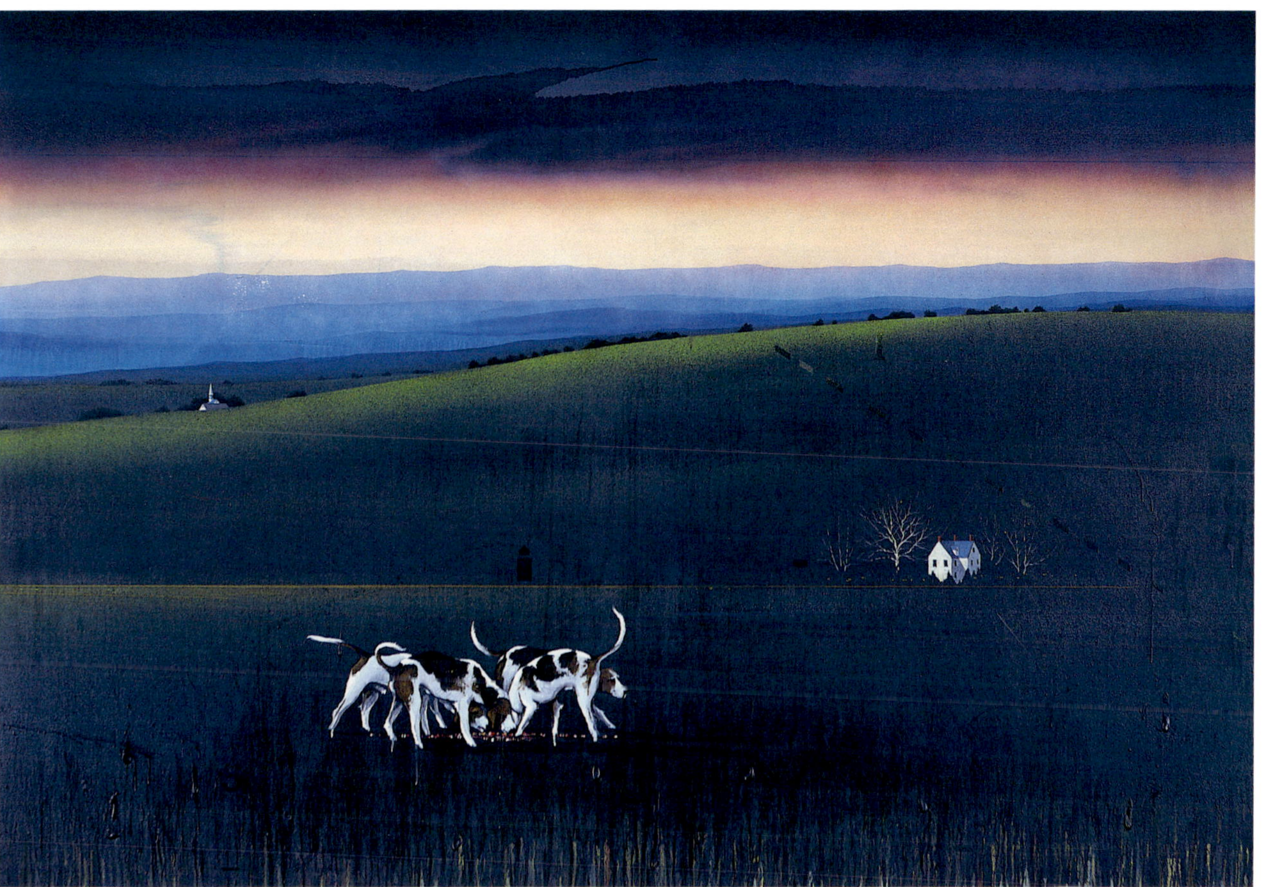

The *Panorama of the American Landscape*, a fourteen-panel painting on canvas, was originally commissioned for the neoclassical rotunda of the Corcoran Gallery of Art in the winter of 1984–85. Infused with the history and geography of the Shenandoah Valley and the Civil War, the circular composition portrays the battlefield of Antietam in the seasons of summer and winter, represented by balanced green and white sections. Dunlap used both traditional and contemporary techniques, applying the polymer paint by brushing, pouring, spraying, and dripping. In developing the imagery for this painting, he experimented with subjects from his previous works and also introduced new images and icons that have continued to inspire his art. The *Panorama* has been exhibited in New York, Connecticut, North Carolina, Colorado, Mississippi, Tennessee, and beyond.

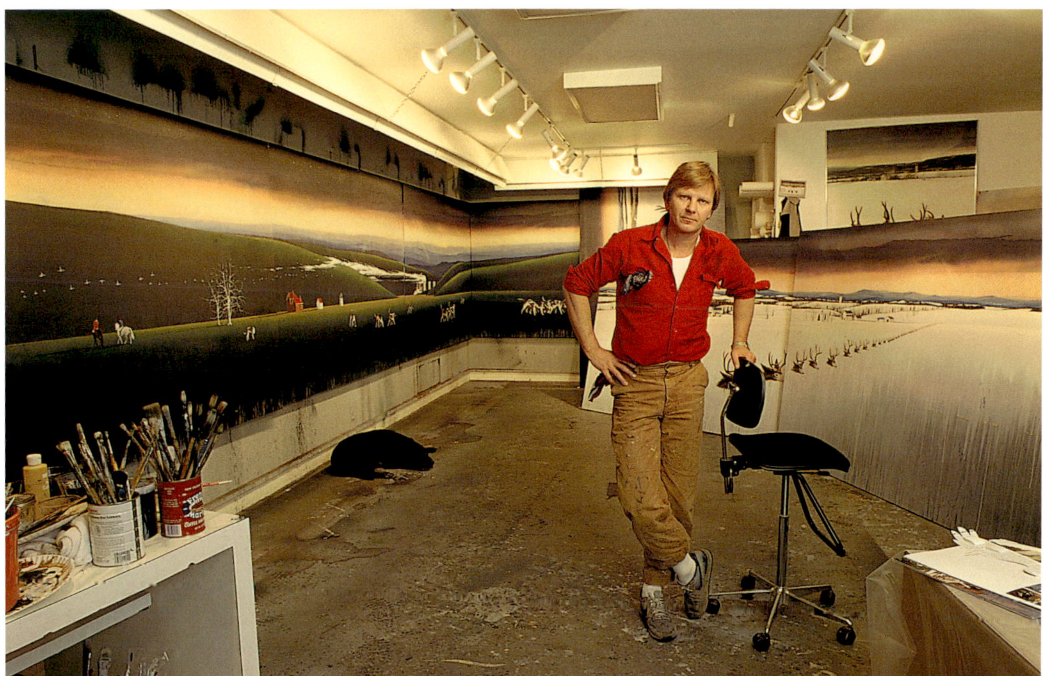

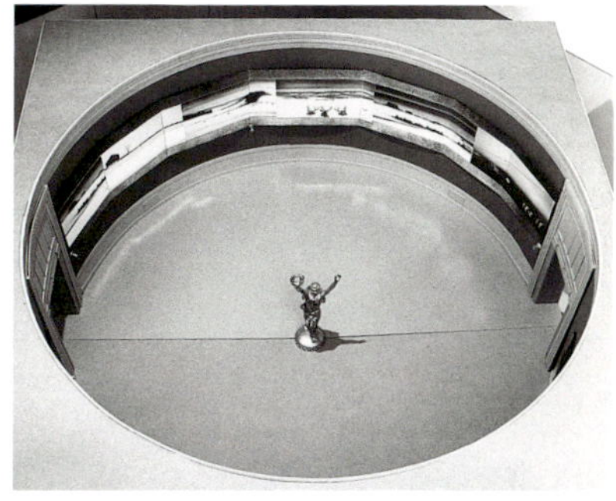

Above: Dunlap began with a model of the rotunda gallery to help plan the panorama. Left and top left: The artist at work in his studio, with panels from the summer side of *Panorama of the American Landscape*. Photographs by Lisa Berg.

Facing page: Detail from a panel of the winter side. Top right: detail from a panel from the summer side. Photographs by Jack Kotz

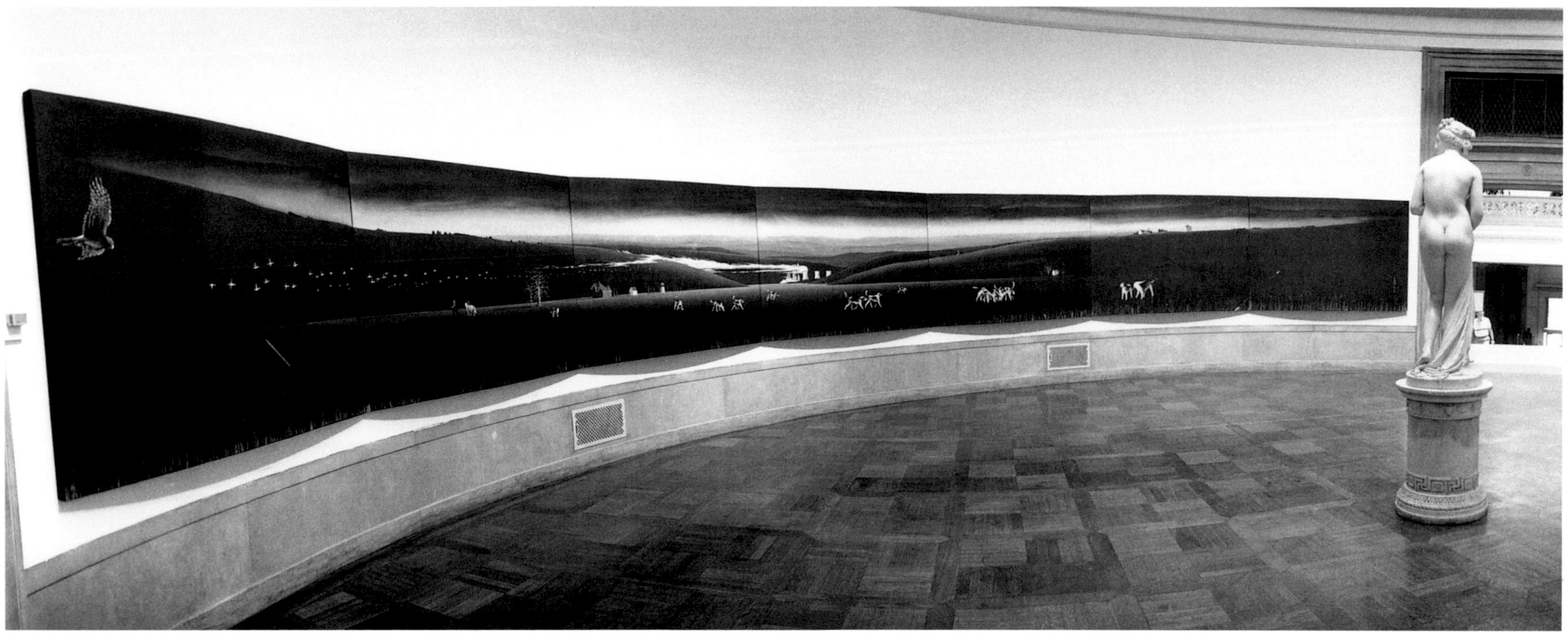

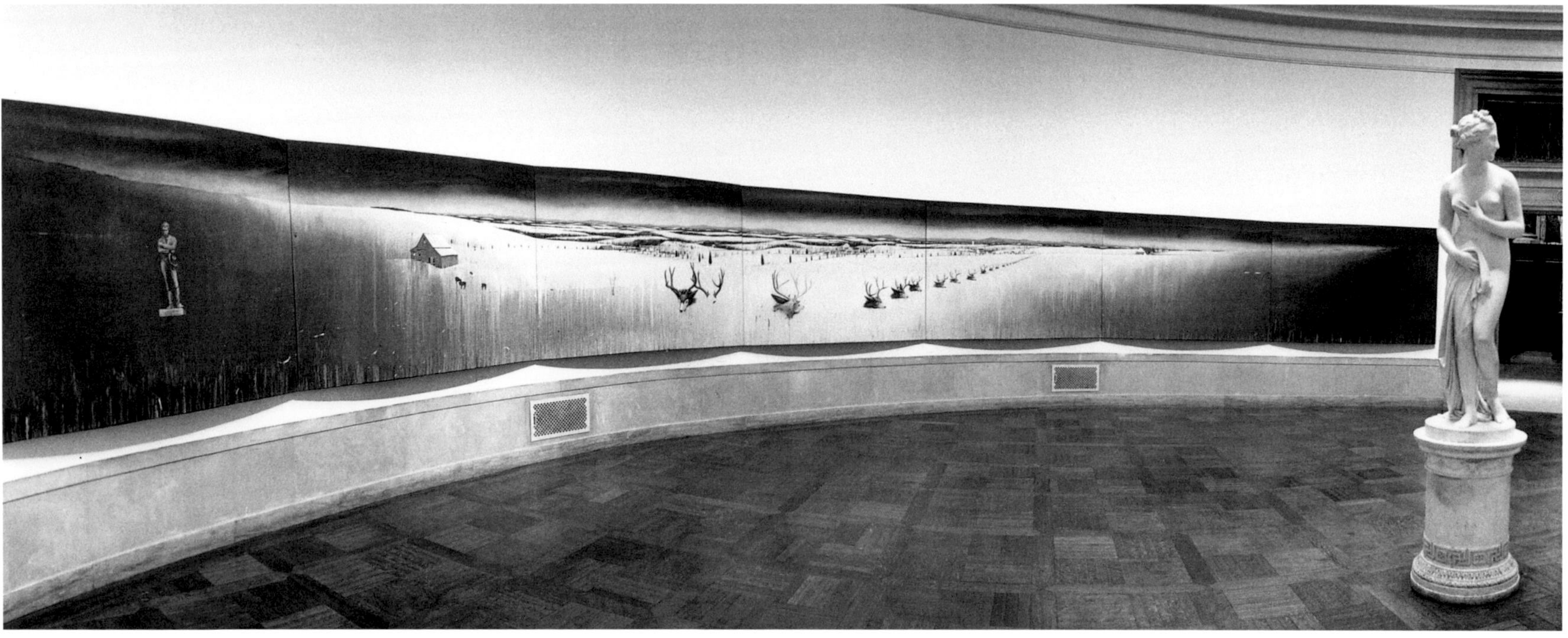

Installation shots of *Panorama of the American Landscape*, 1984–85. Corcoran Gallery of Art, Washington, D.C. Photographs by Jack Kotz.

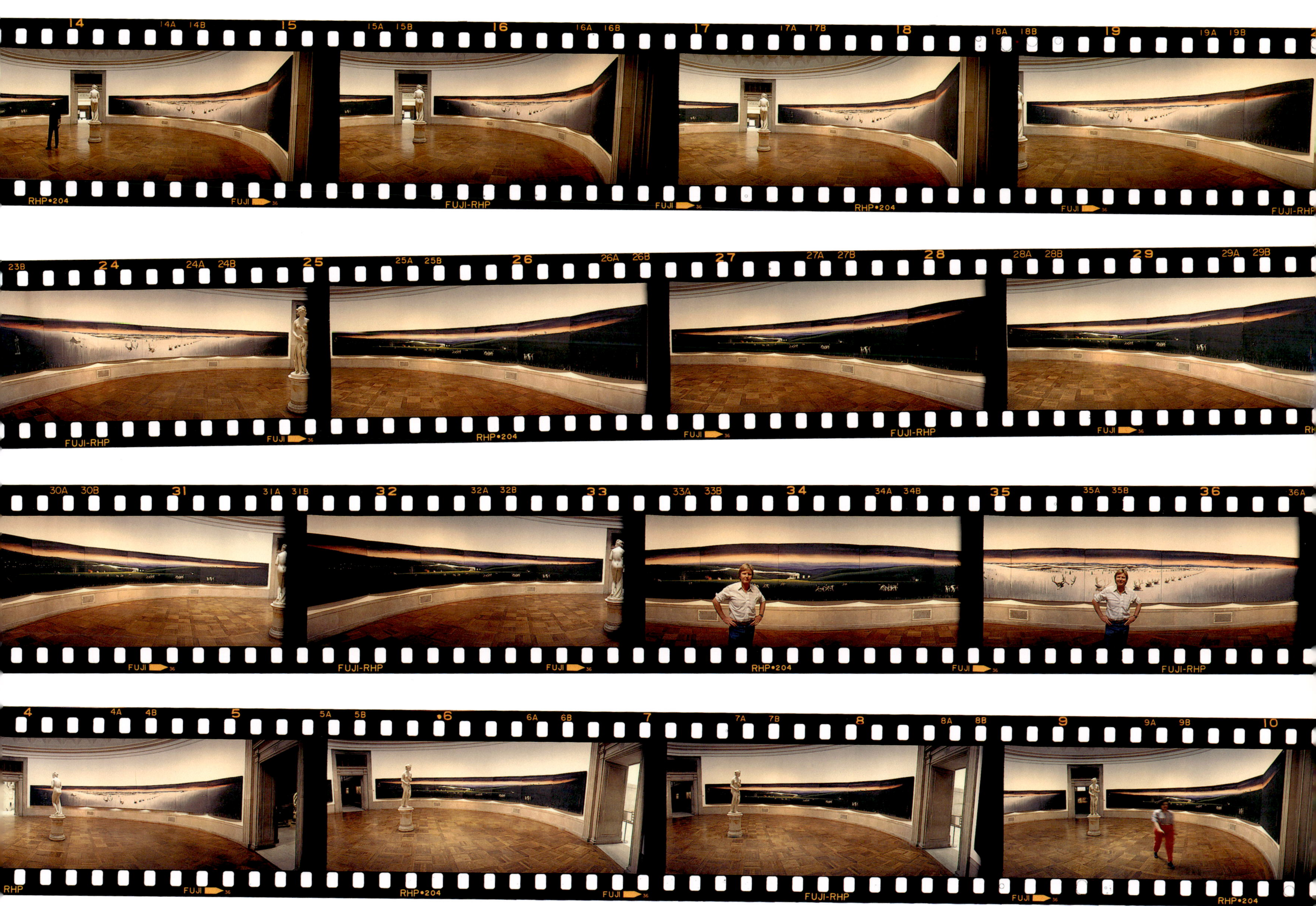
14 14A 14B 15 15A 15B 16 16A 16B 17 17A 17B 18 18A 18B 19 19A 19B
RHP•204 FUJI FUJI-RHP FUJI RHP•204 FUJI FUJI-RHP
23B 24 24A 24B 25 25A 25B 26 26A 26B 27 27A 27B 28 28A 28B 29 29A 29B
FUJI-RHP FUJI RHP•204 FUJI FUJI-RHP FUJI
30A 30B 31 31A 31B 32 32A 32B 33 33A 33B 34 34A 34B 35 35A 35B 36 36A
FUJI FUJI-RHP FUJI RHP•204 FUJI FUJI-RHP
4 4A 4B 5 5A 5B 6 6A 6B 7 7A 7B 8 8A 8B 9 9A 9B 10
RHP FUJI RHP•204 FUJI FUJI-RHP FUJI RHP•204

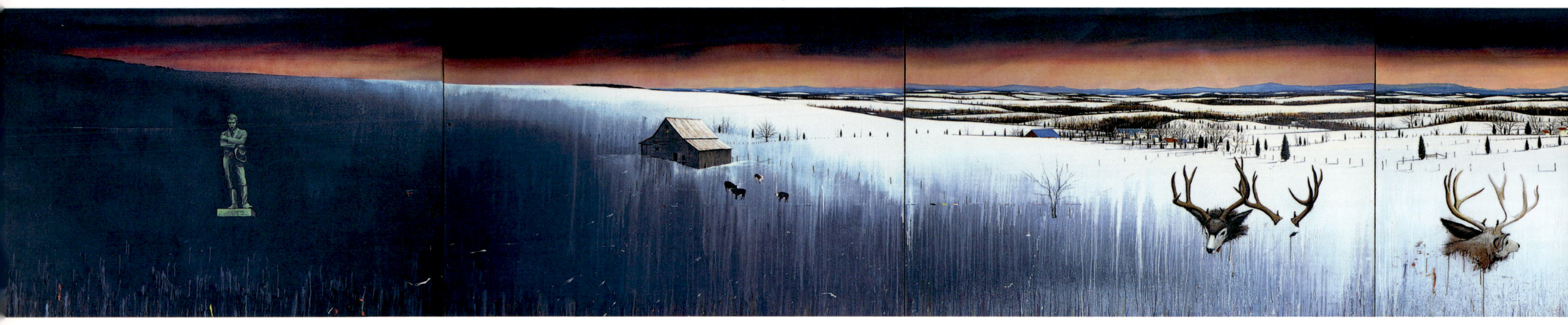

Panorama of the American Landscape,
1984–85
Polymer paint on canvas, fourteen panels,
66 x 94 each. Corcoran Gallery of Art,
Washington, D.C. Photographs by Jack Kotz.

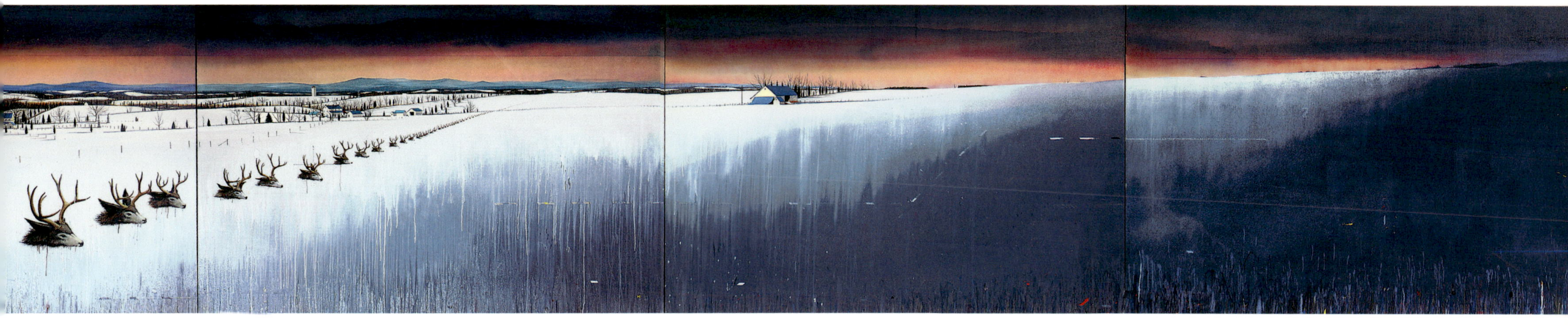

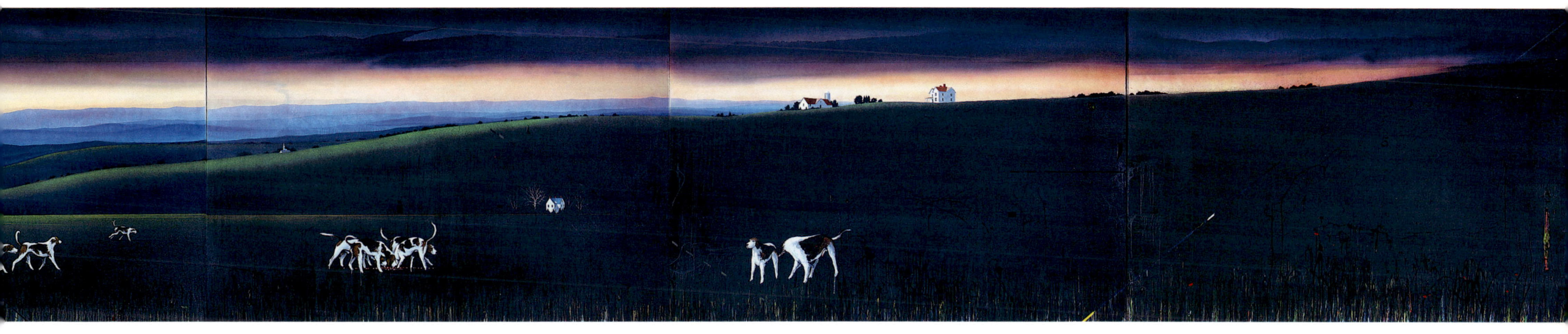

Landscape and Variable: Deer Hide—Willow Seek, 1987
Polymer paint on canvas, metal, deer hide, 30 x 132 x 7. Private collection. Photograph by Adam Reich.

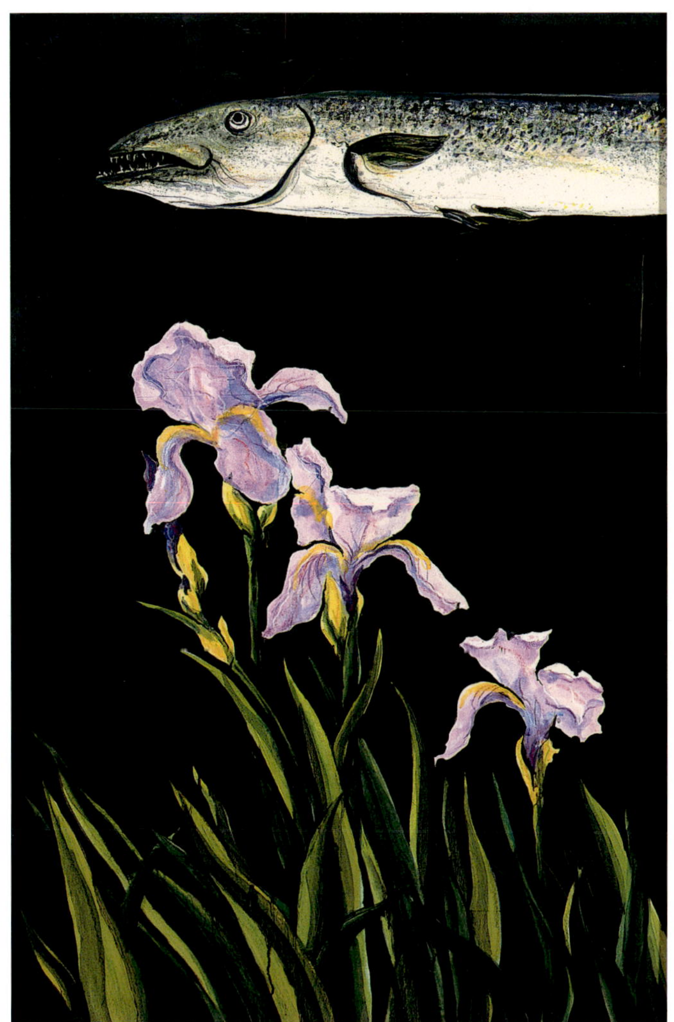

Aqua Garden VI—Iris You Well, 1987
Oil paint and dry pigment on rag paper, 53 x 34. Collection of Margaret and Berney Burgess, Coral Gables, Florida. Photograph by Don Queralto.

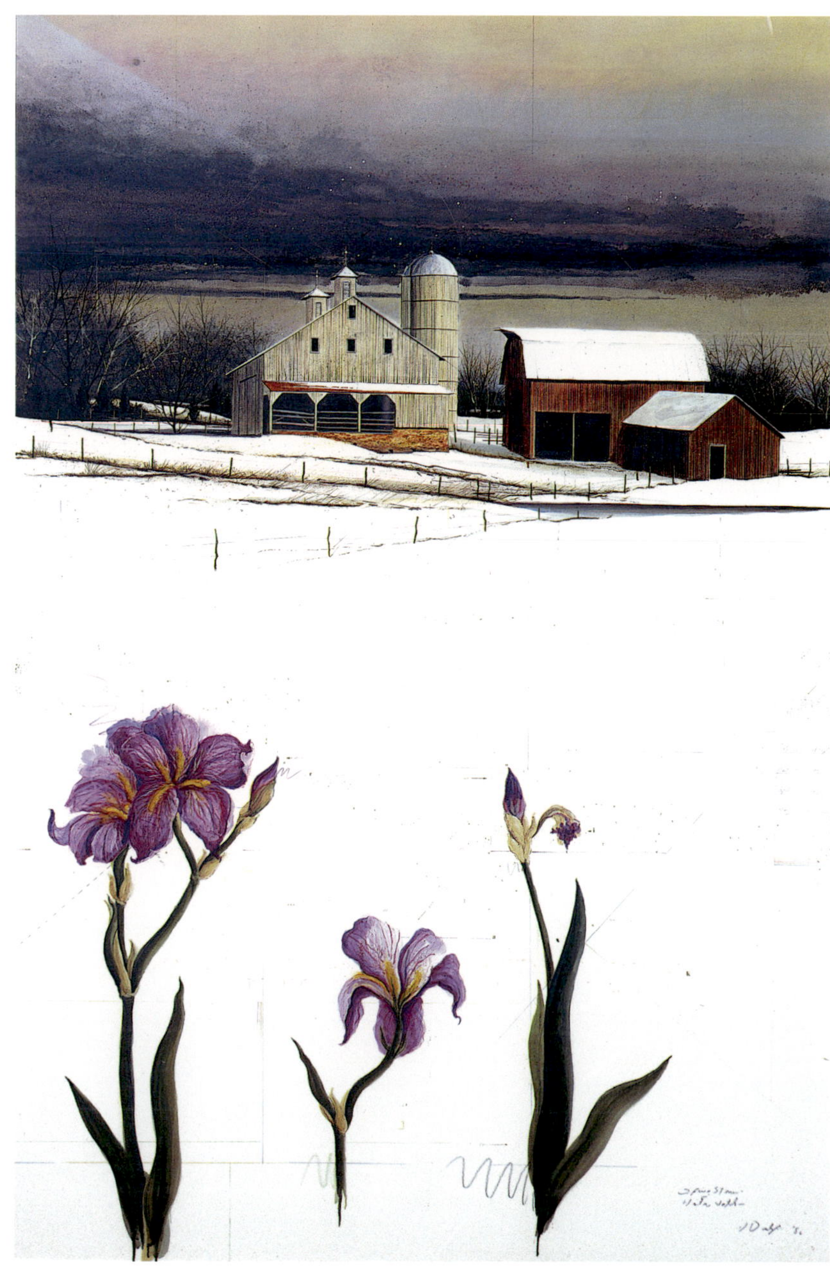

Winter Light—Iris Watch, 1986
Oil paint and dry pigment on paper, 72 x 48. Private collection. Photograph by Jack Meyer.

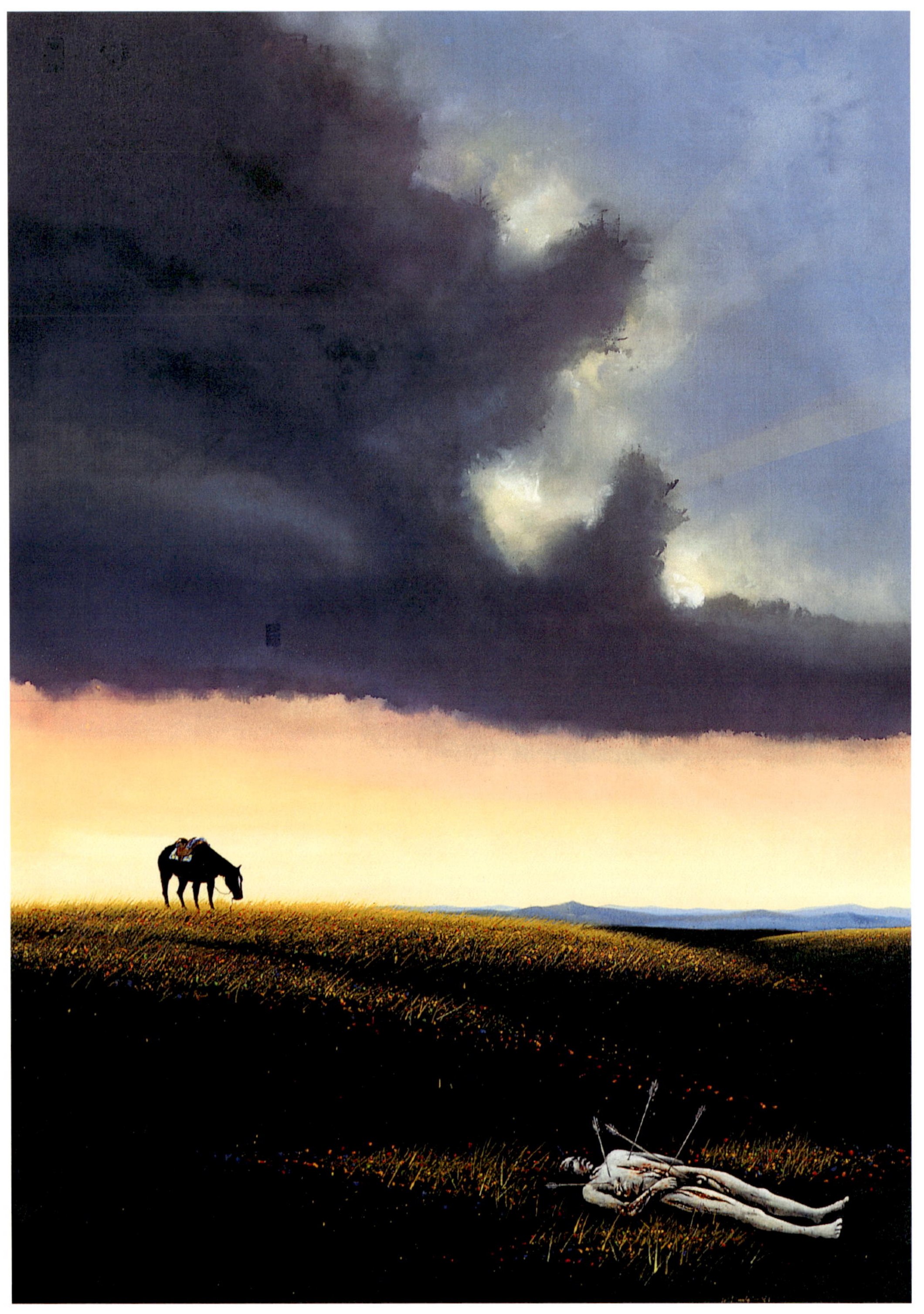

Landscape and Variable: Indian Paint Brush, 1987
Polymer paint on canvas, 96 x 67. Private collection. Photograph by Hubert Worley.

Meditations on the Origins of Agriculture in America, 1987
Wood, canvas, polymer and oil paint, steel, snake skin, wire, flag, 48 x 96 x 24. Private collection. Photograph by Jack Meyer.

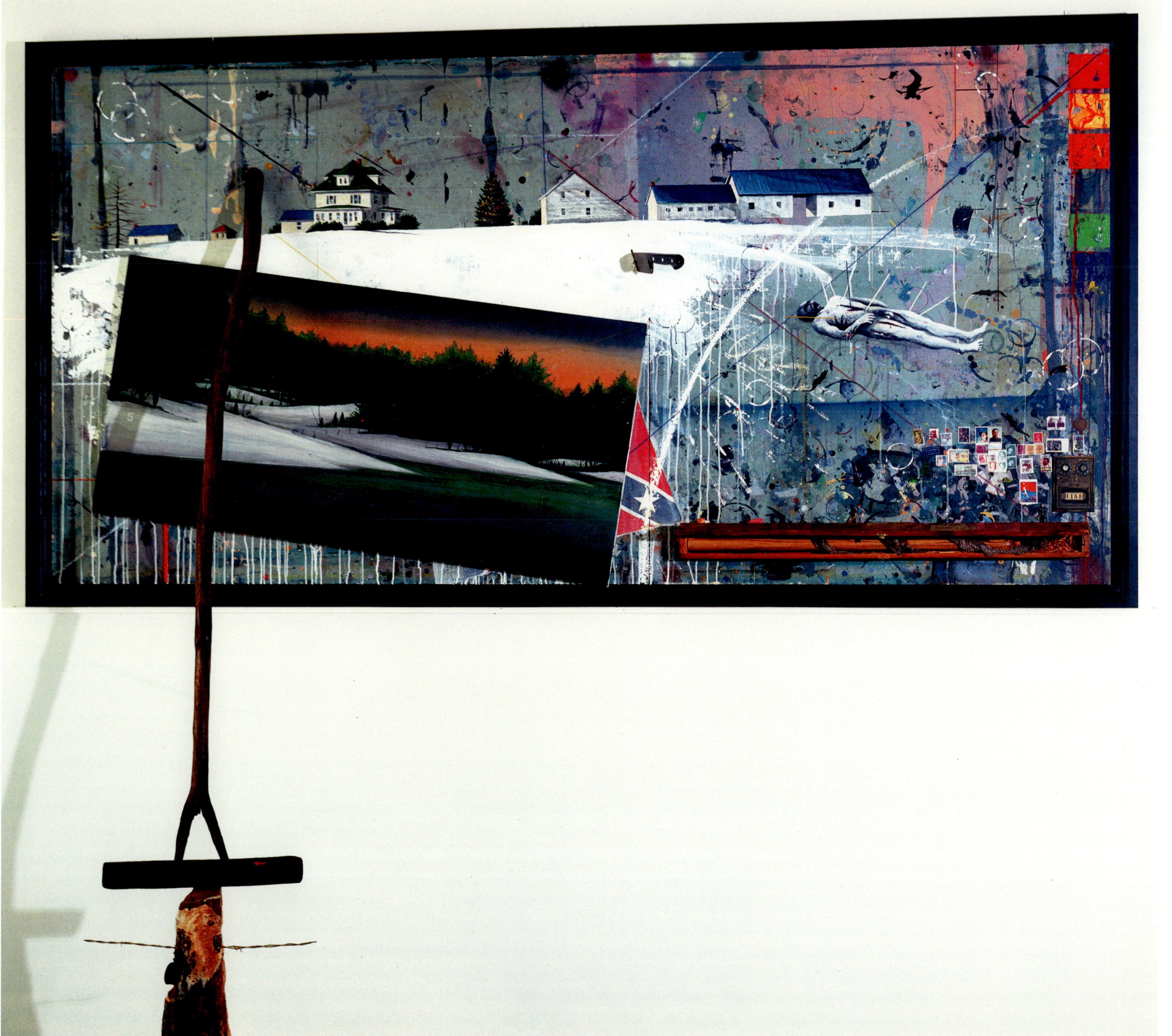

Antietam Cut—Deep Iris Watch, 1988
Polymer paint on canvas, shells, steel, knife, wood, 30 x 160 x 8. Collection of Chuck and Joseph Wise, Jackson, Mississippi. Photograph by Jack Meyer.

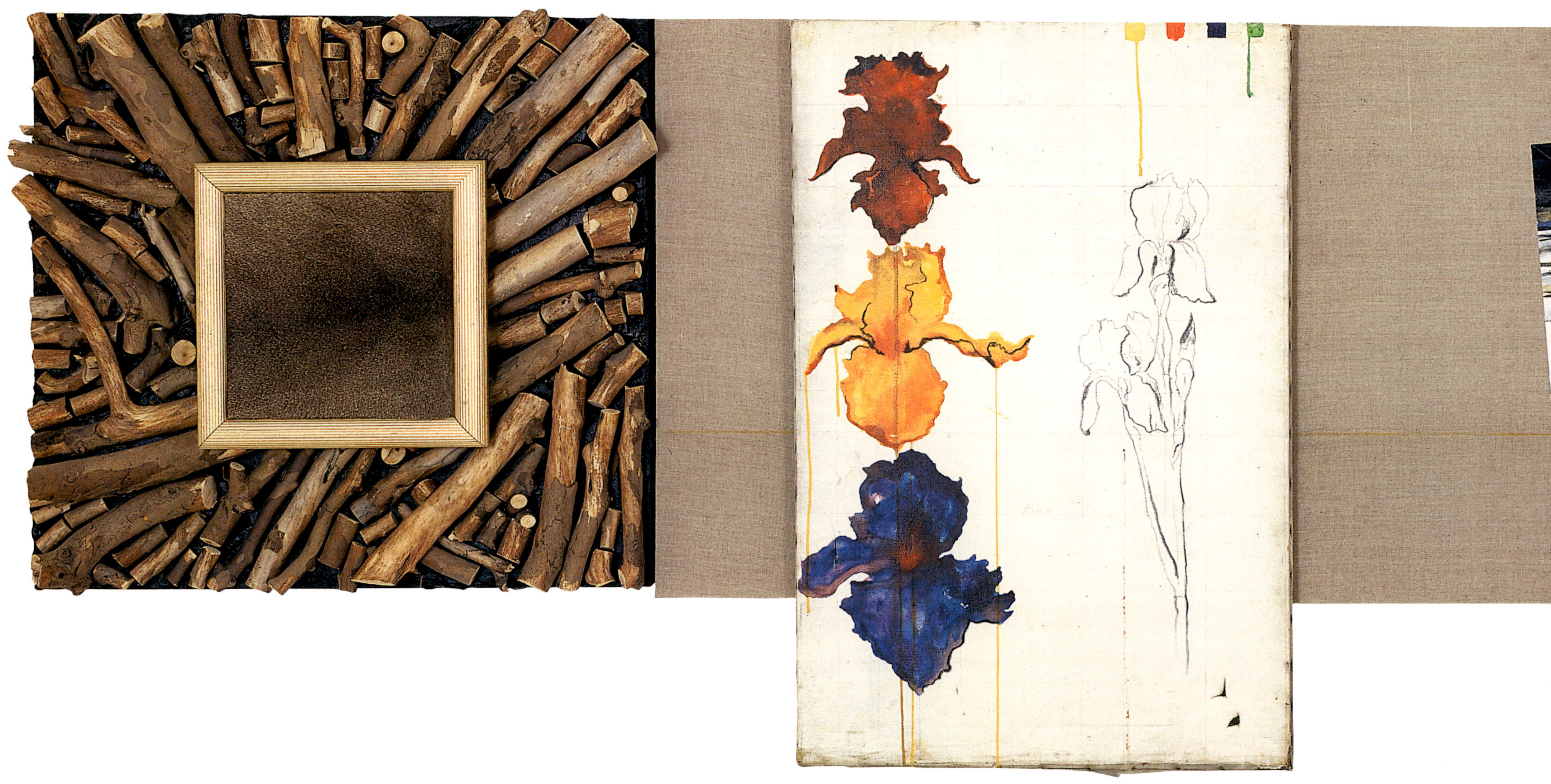

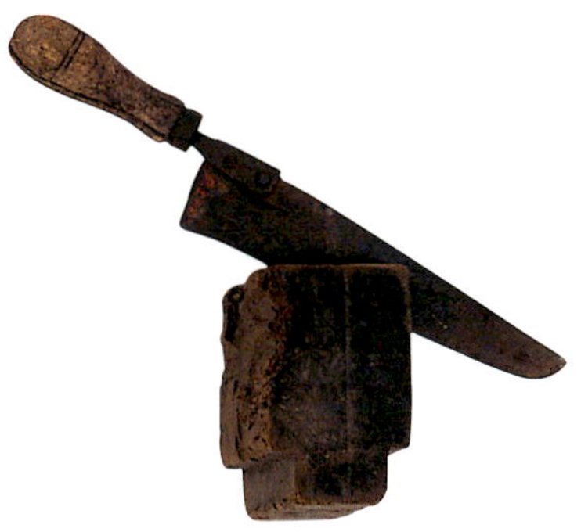

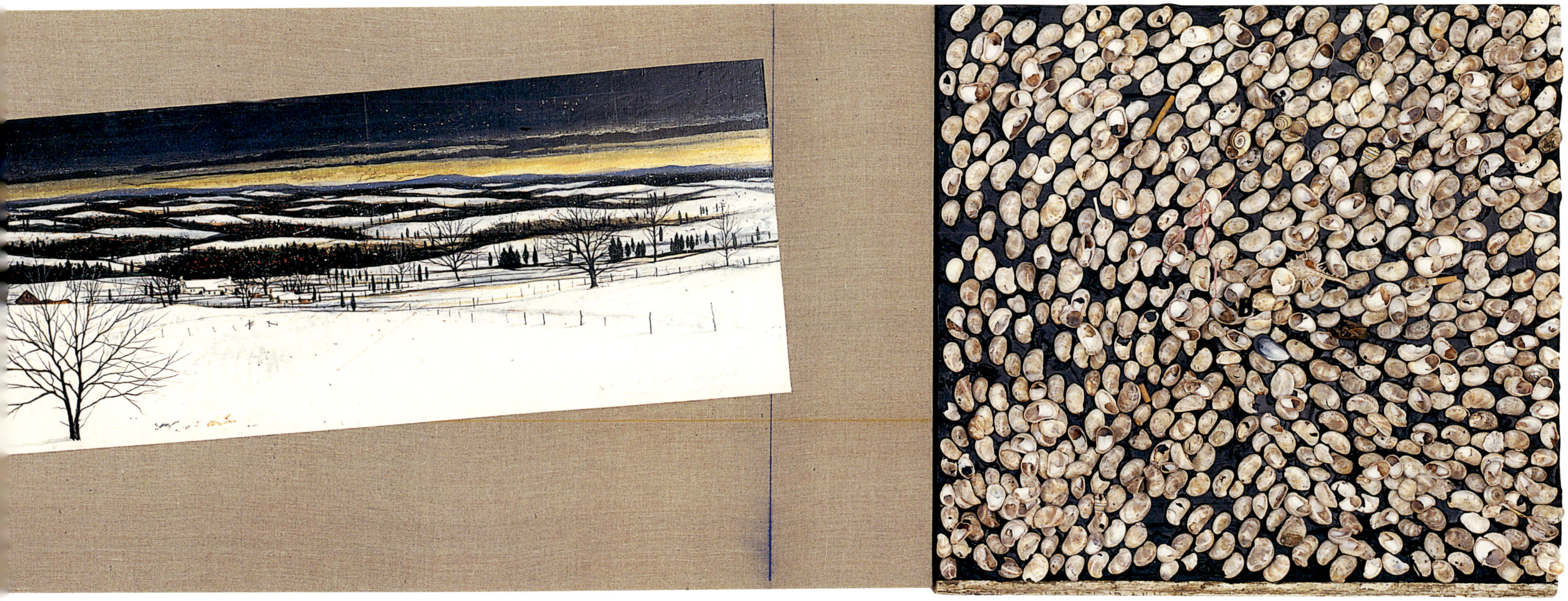

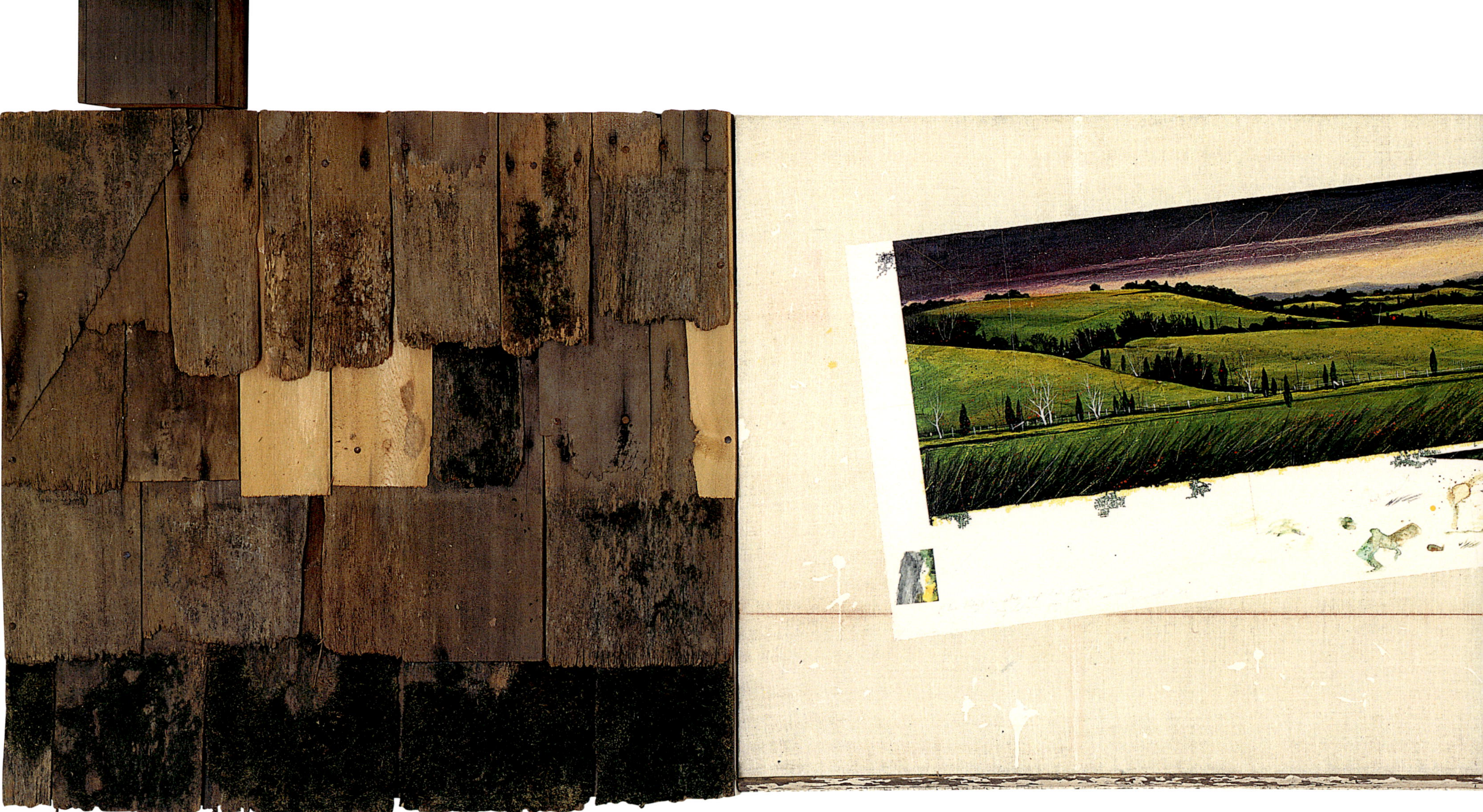

Landscape and Variable: Cedar Ridge—Flight or Fight, 1988
Wood, polymer paint, canvas, glass, photographs, hawk's wing, 30 x 128 1/2 x 6.
Collection of Jim and Liba Lambe, Roaring Gap, North Carolina. Photograph by Jack Kotz.

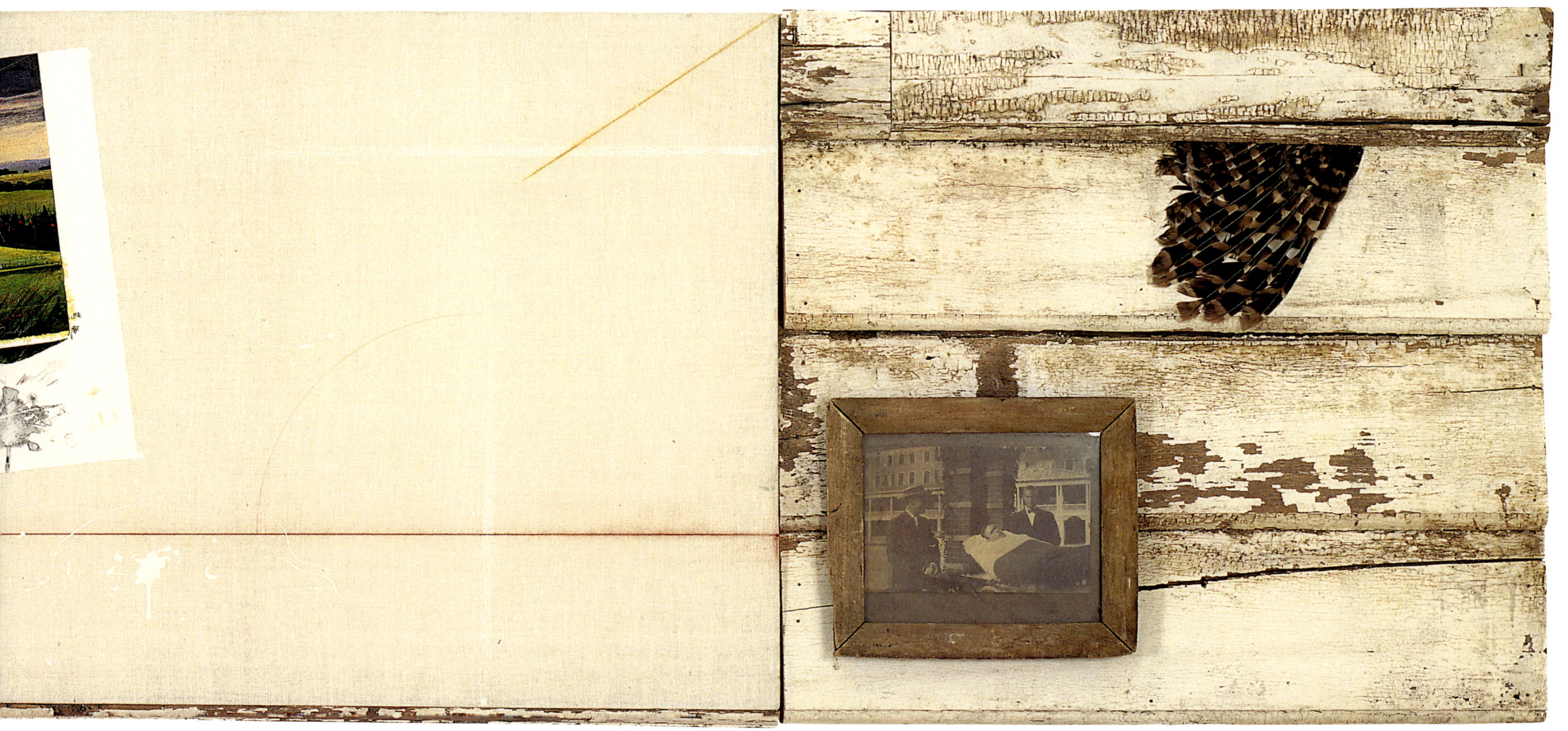

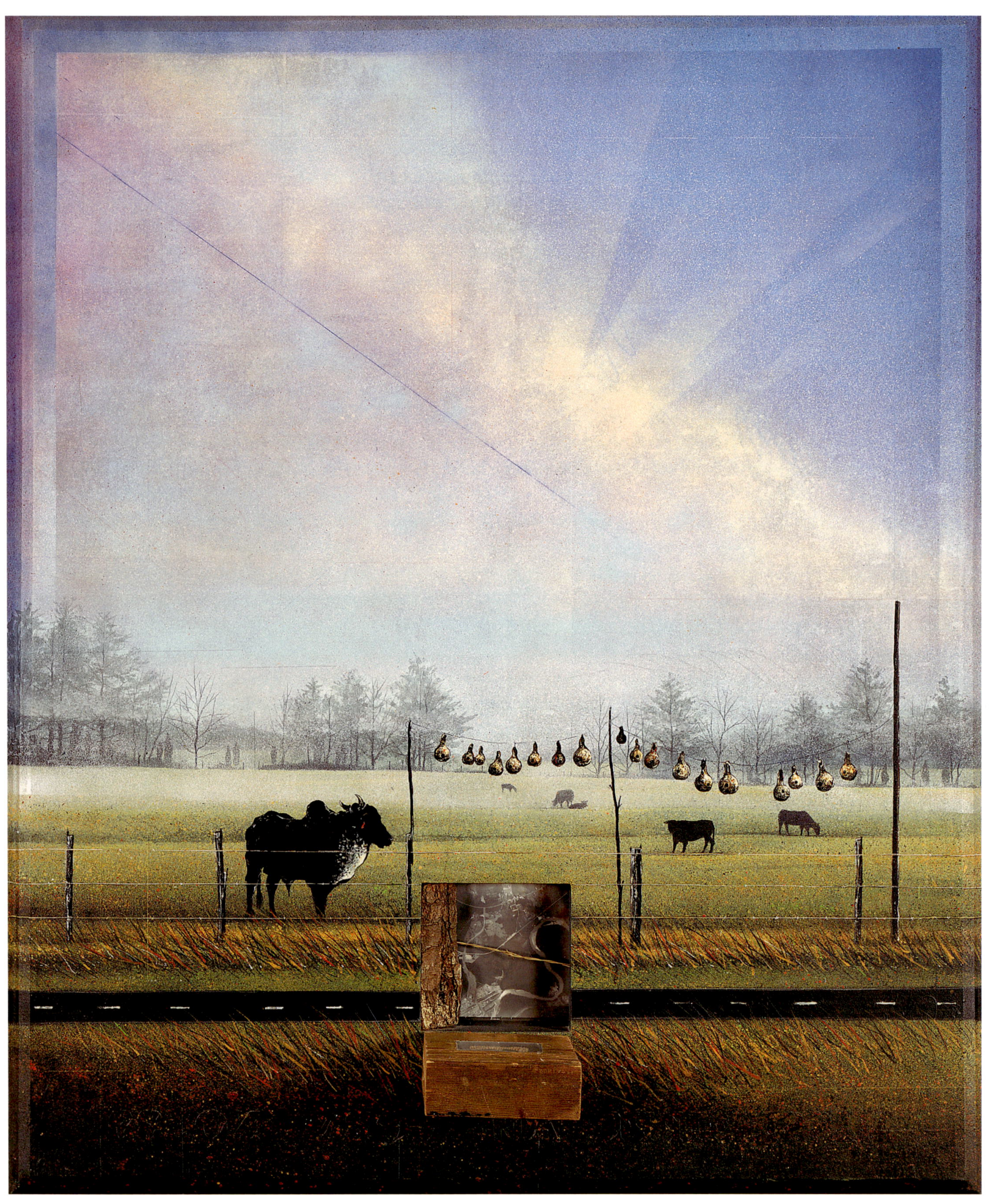

Allegory #39, 1988

Polymer paint on canvas, wood, metal, photograph, 89 1/2 x 63. Collection of Governor Ray Mabus, Ridgeland, Mississippi. Photograph by Hubert Worley.

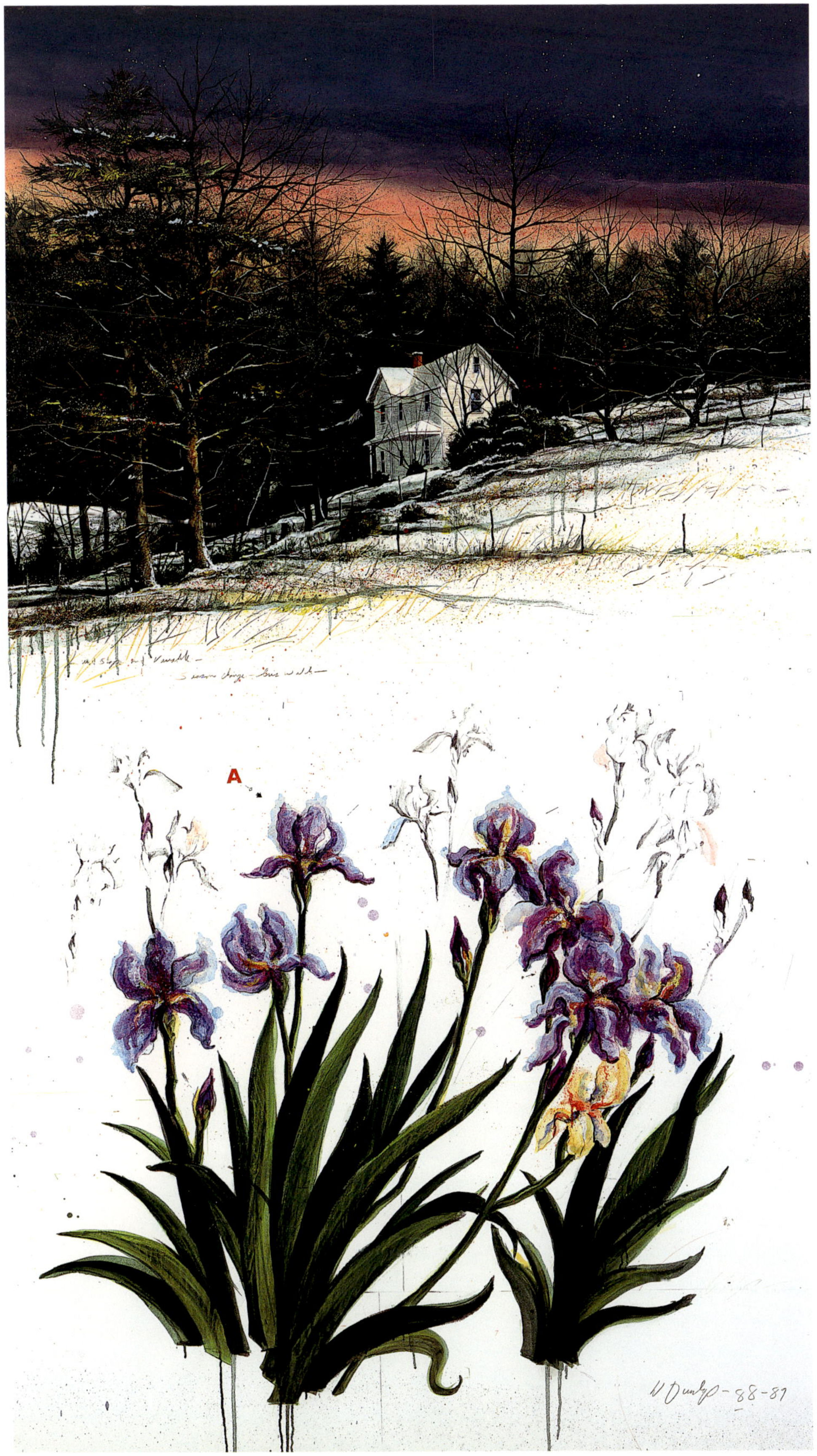

Landscape and Variable: Season Change Iris Watch, 1988–89
Oil paint and dry pigment on paper, 72 x 41. Collection of Margaret and Berney Burgess, Coral Gables, Florida. Photograph by Don Queralto.

Birds of a Feather, 1984
Oil paint, dry pigment, and graphite on rag paper, 40 x 44. Private collection. Photograph by Jack Meyer.

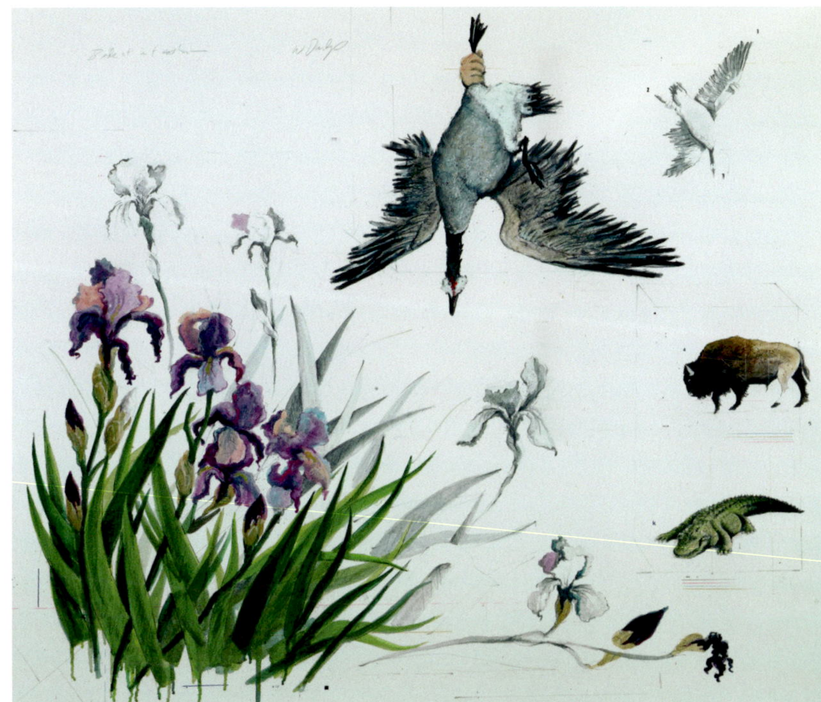

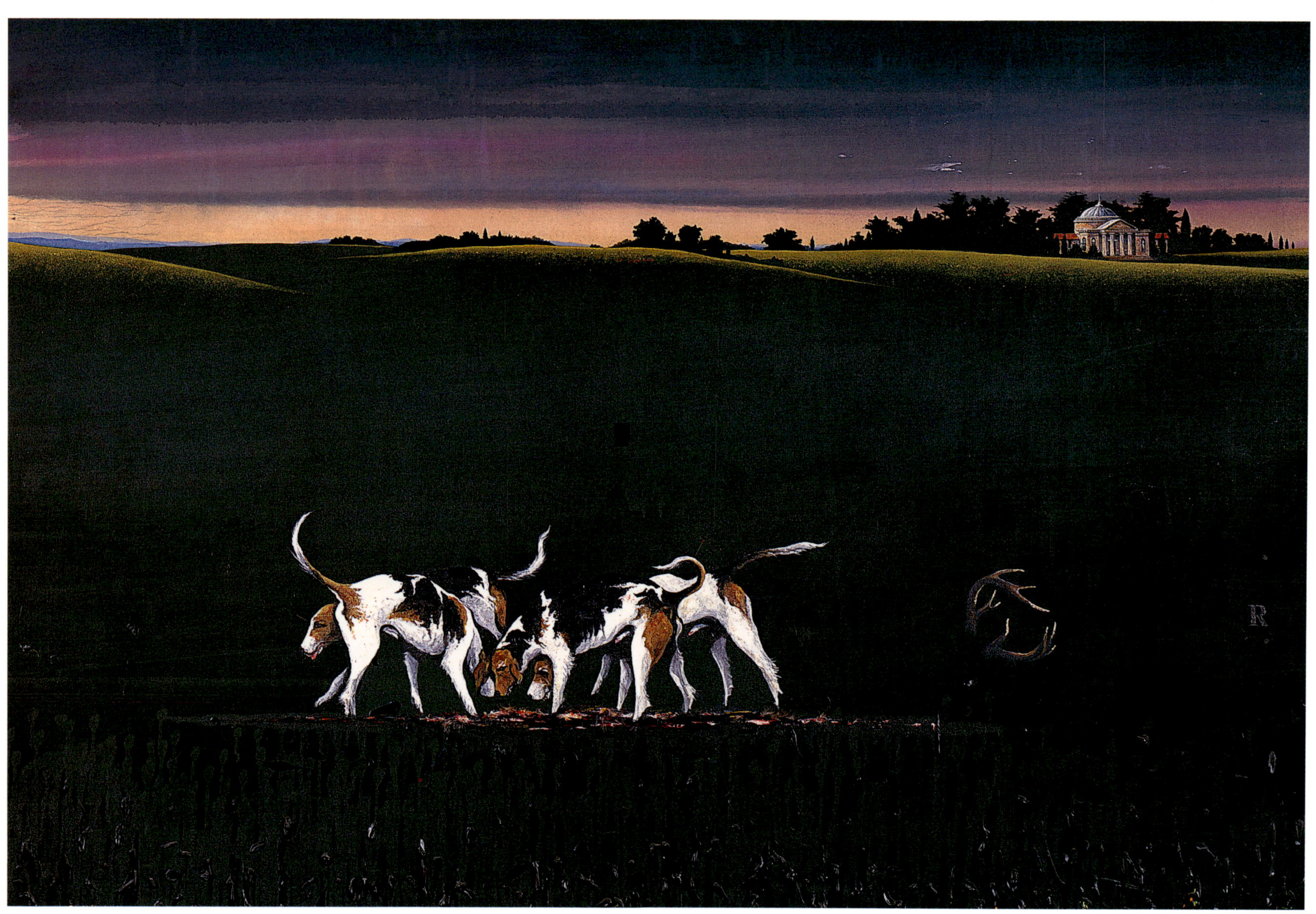

Dog Trot—Deer Demise, 1988
Polymer paint and hair on canvas, 68 x 94.
Collection of Governor Ray Mabus, Ridgeland,
Mississippi. Photograph by Hubert Worley.

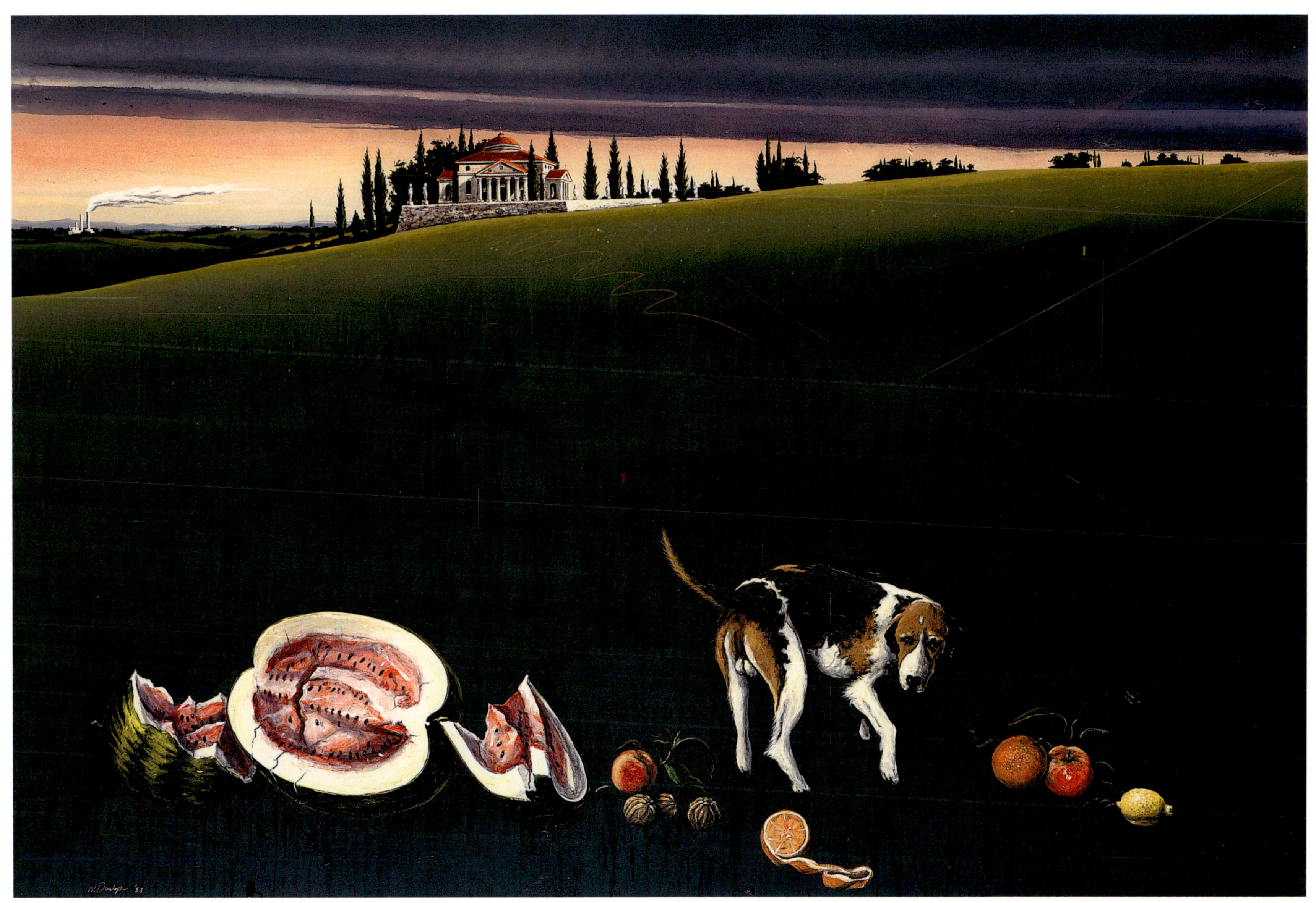

Landscape and Variable: The Bounty and Burden of History, 1988
Polymer paint on canvas, 68 x 94. Collection of The Ogden Museum of Southern Art, New Orleans, Louisiana. Photograph by Jack Meyer.

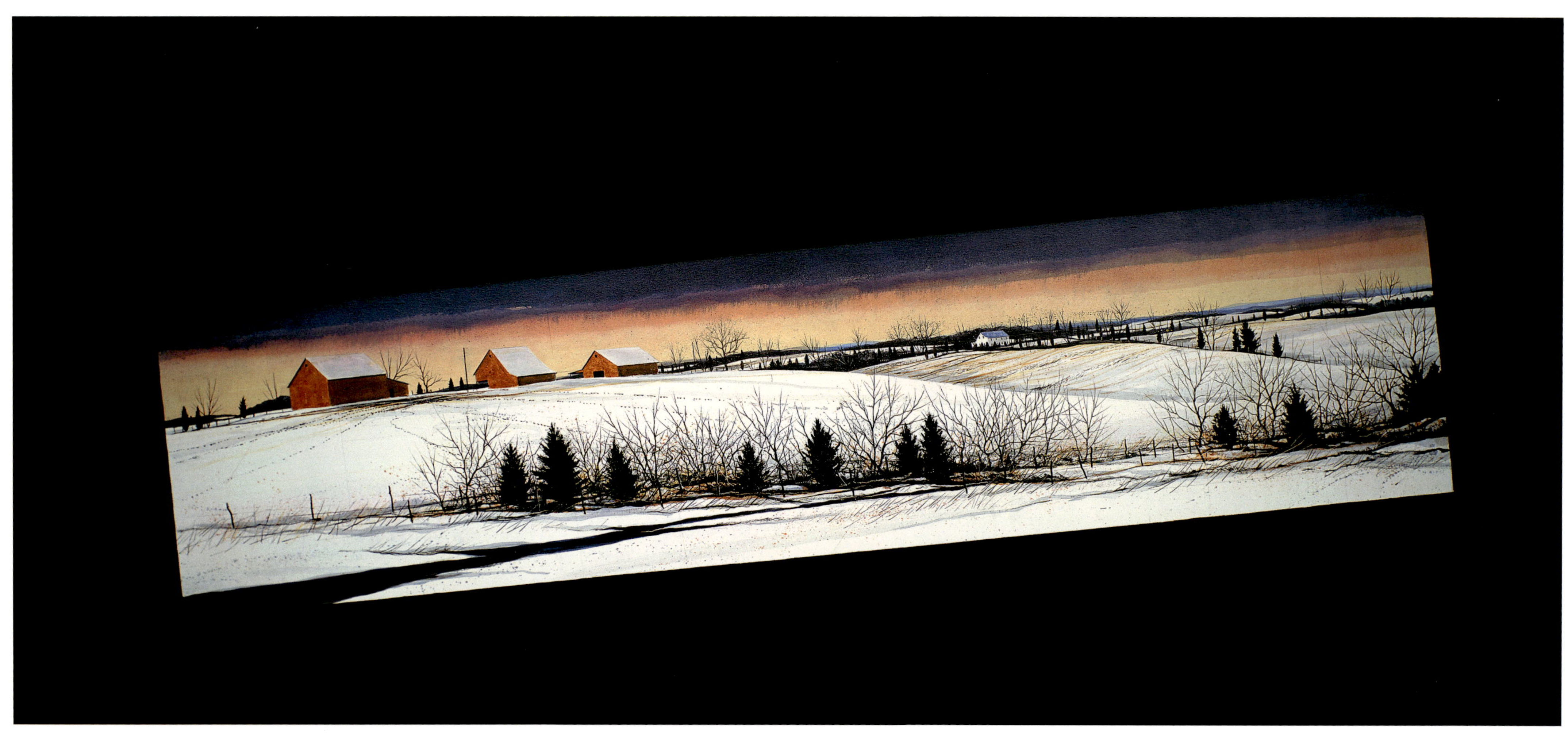

Landscape Askew, 1988
Polymer paint on canvas, 48 x 96.
Collection of James V. Kimsey, McLean,
Virginia. Photograph by Jack Meyer.

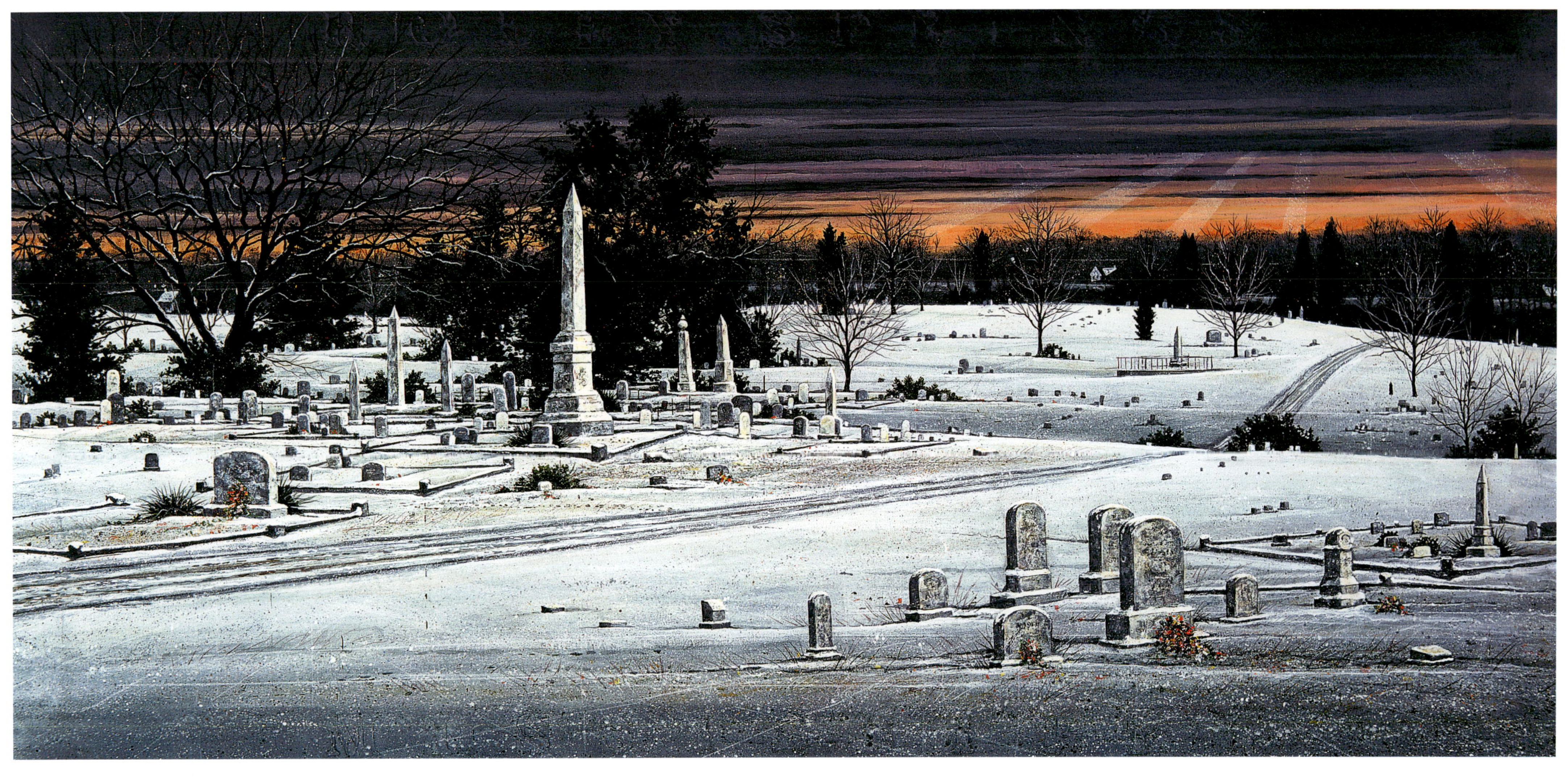

Holly Springs Necropolis, ca. 2004
Polymer paint on canvas, 48 x 91. Collection of Dr. Ben Martin, Holly Springs, Mississippi. Photograph by Jack Meyer.

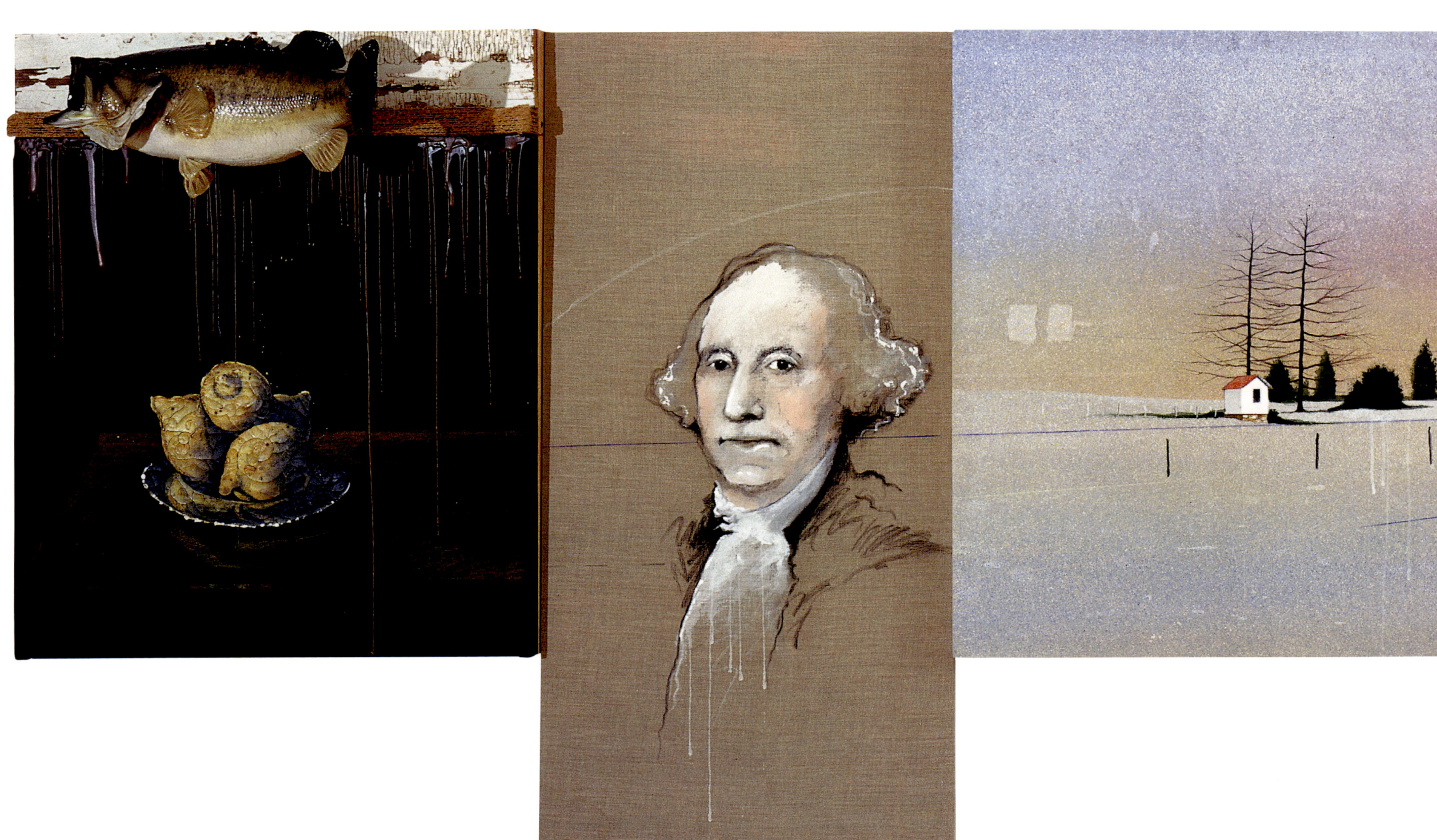

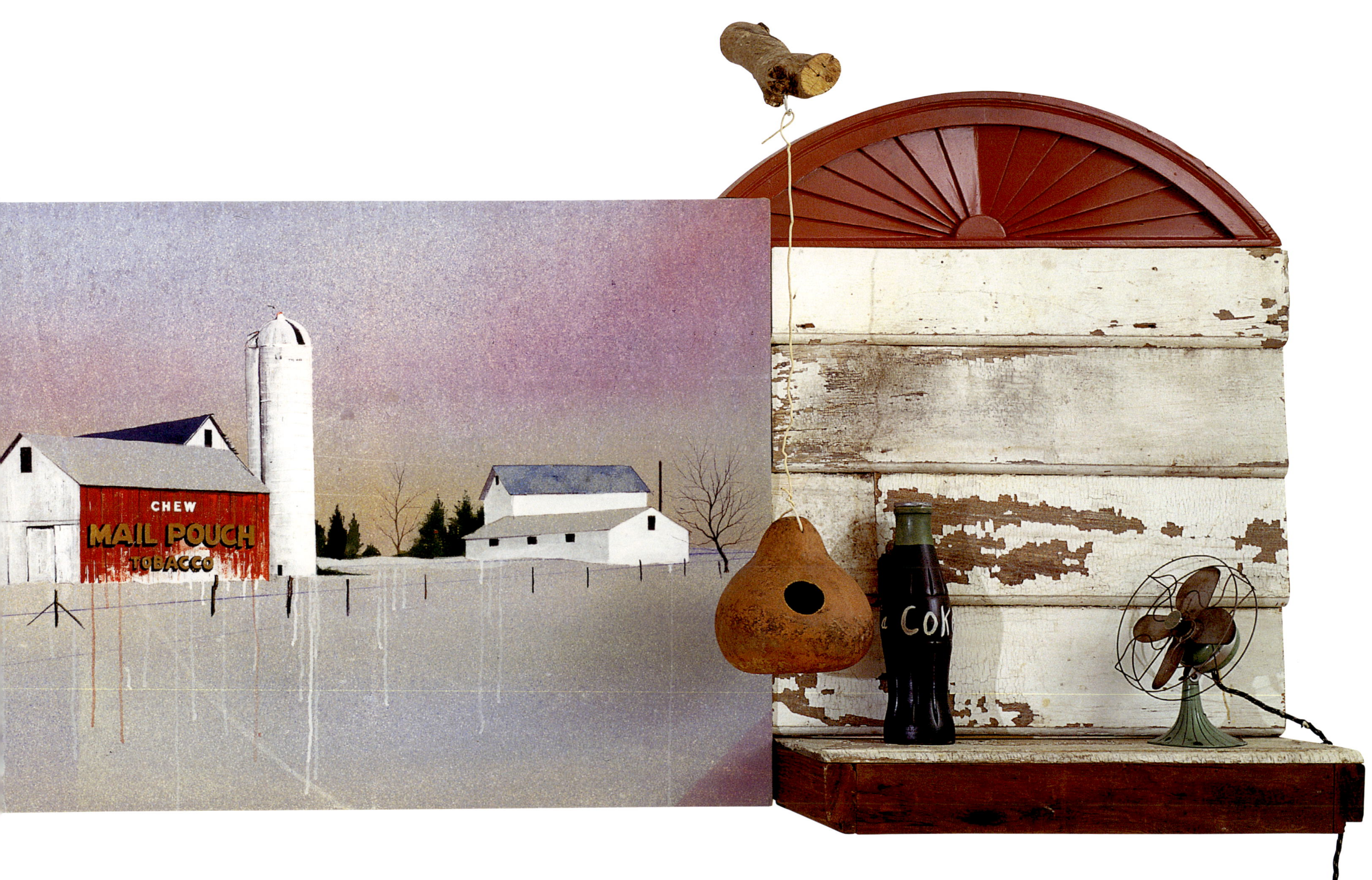

Large Mouth Founding Fatherland, 1989
Polymer paint on canvas, fish, wood, gourd, wax, fan, wire, 40 x 160 x 12. Collection of The Ogden Museum of Southern Art, New Orleans, Louisiana. Photograph by Jack Kotz.

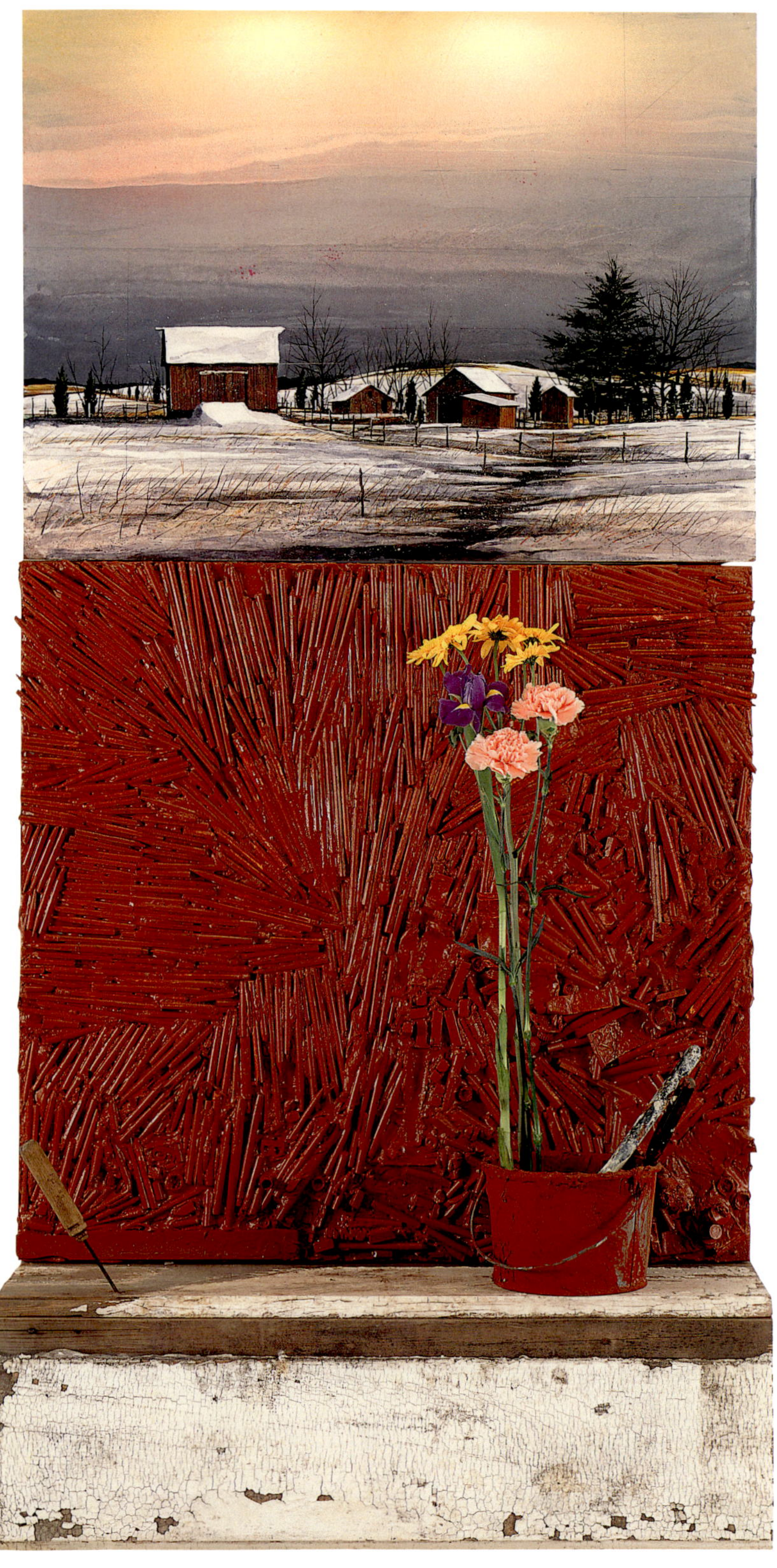

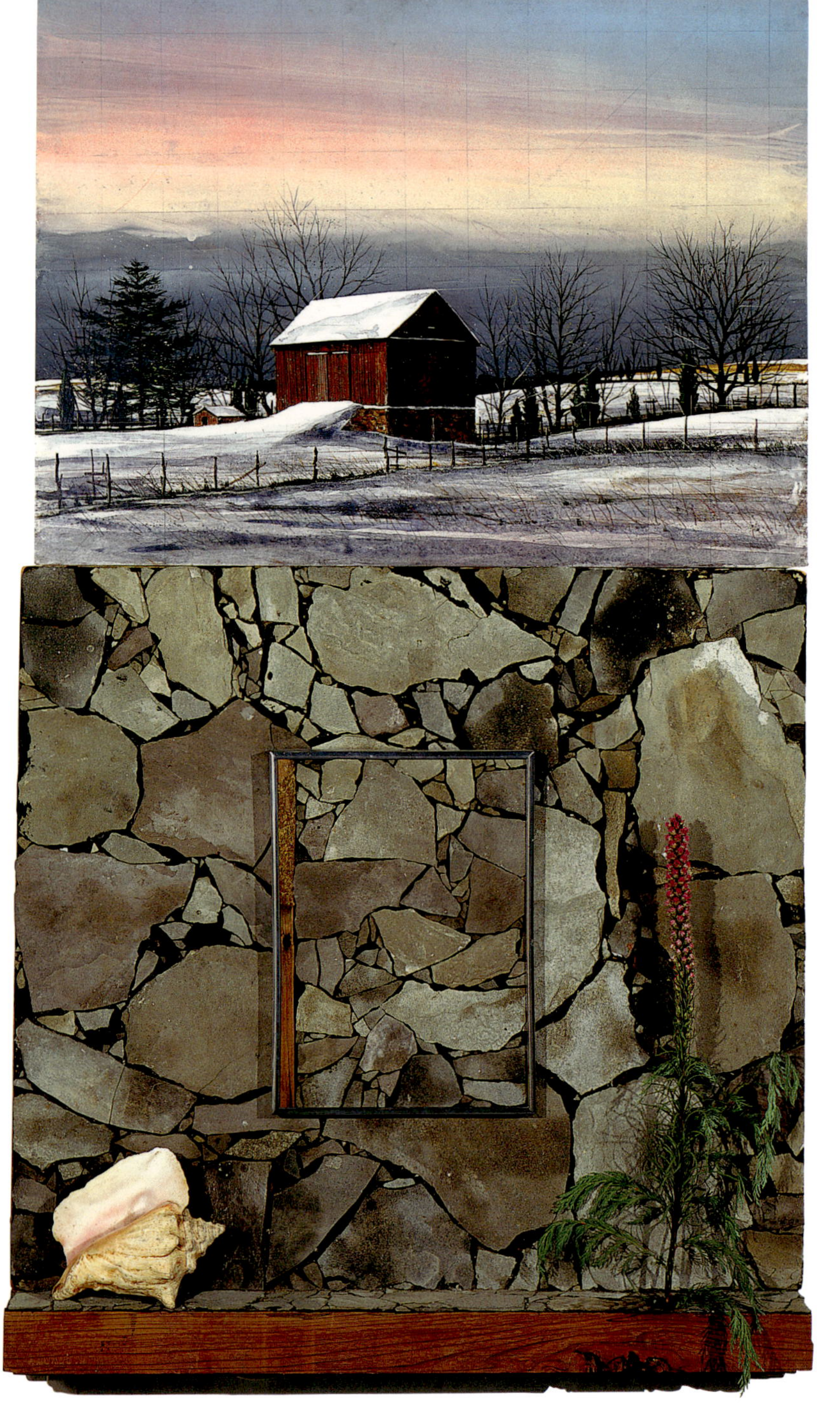

Rose Red Roof Rot Run, 1989
Polymer paint, wood, metal, ice pick, fresh flowers, 63 x 31 1/2 x 12. Private collection. Photograph by Jack Kotz.

Snow Sleet Slate Slough, 1989
Polymer paint, slate, shell, fresh flowers, wood, 68 x 31 x 8. Collection of Art Museum of Western Virginia, Roanoke. Photograph by Jack Kotz.

Probate—Rebate—Consecrate, 1990
Polymer paint, parchment, wood, gourd, book, flowers, 52 x 36 x 8. Collection of The Corcoran Gallery of Art, Washington, D.C. 1996.3 a-c. Photograph by Jack Kotz.

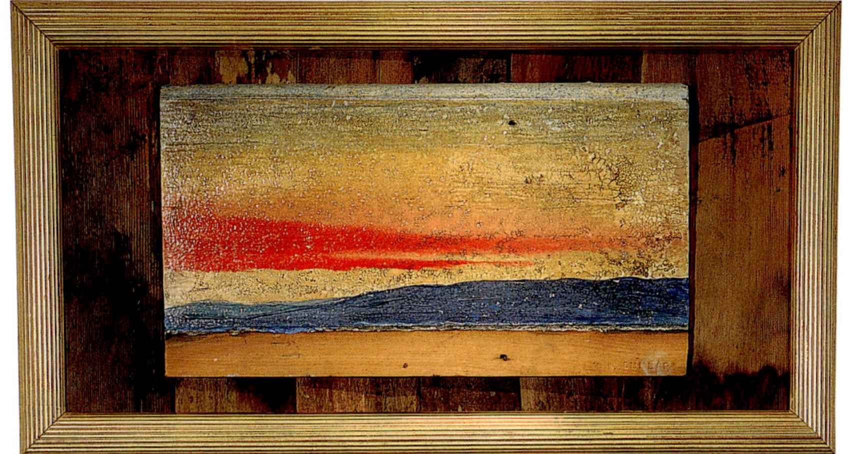

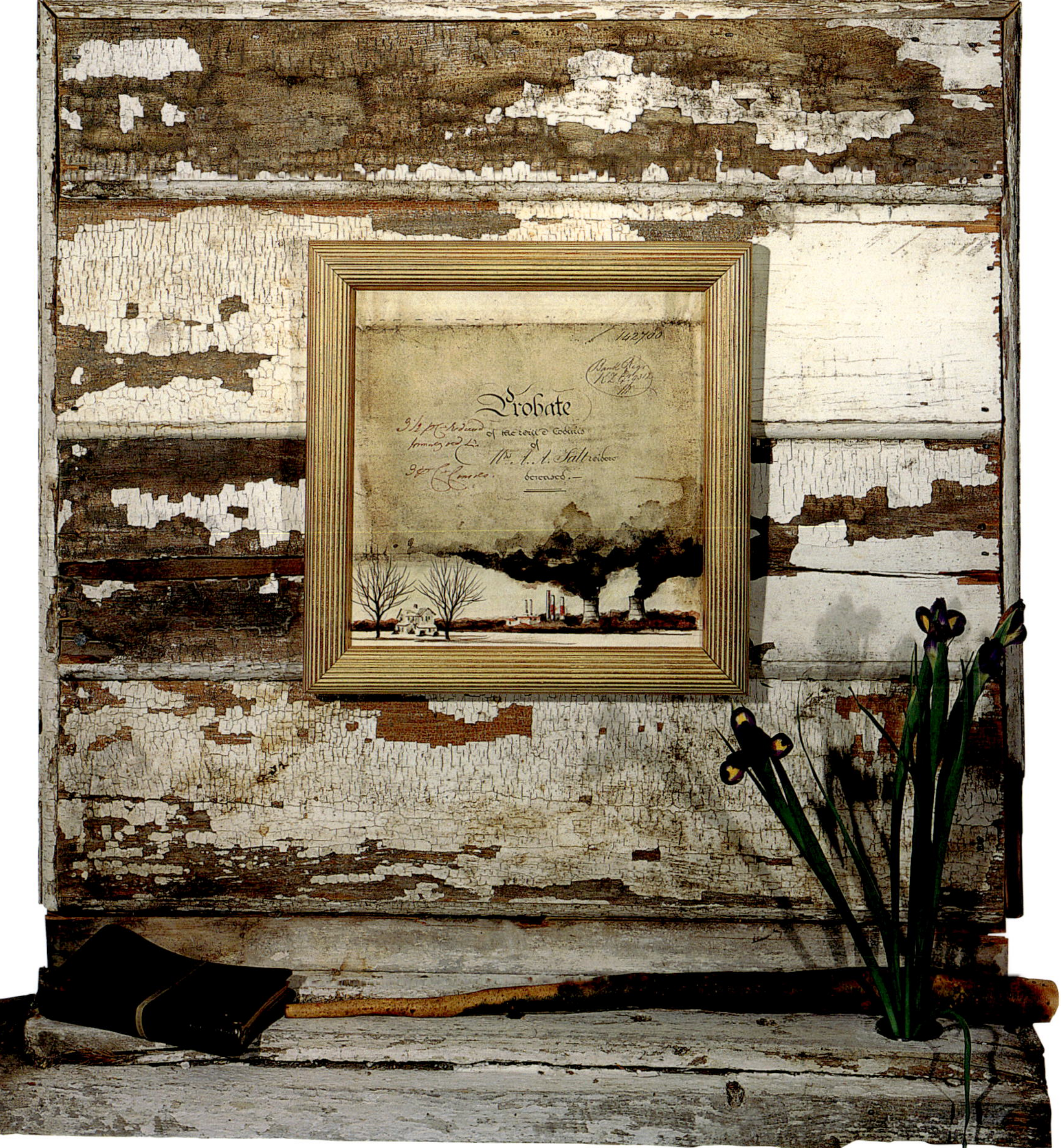

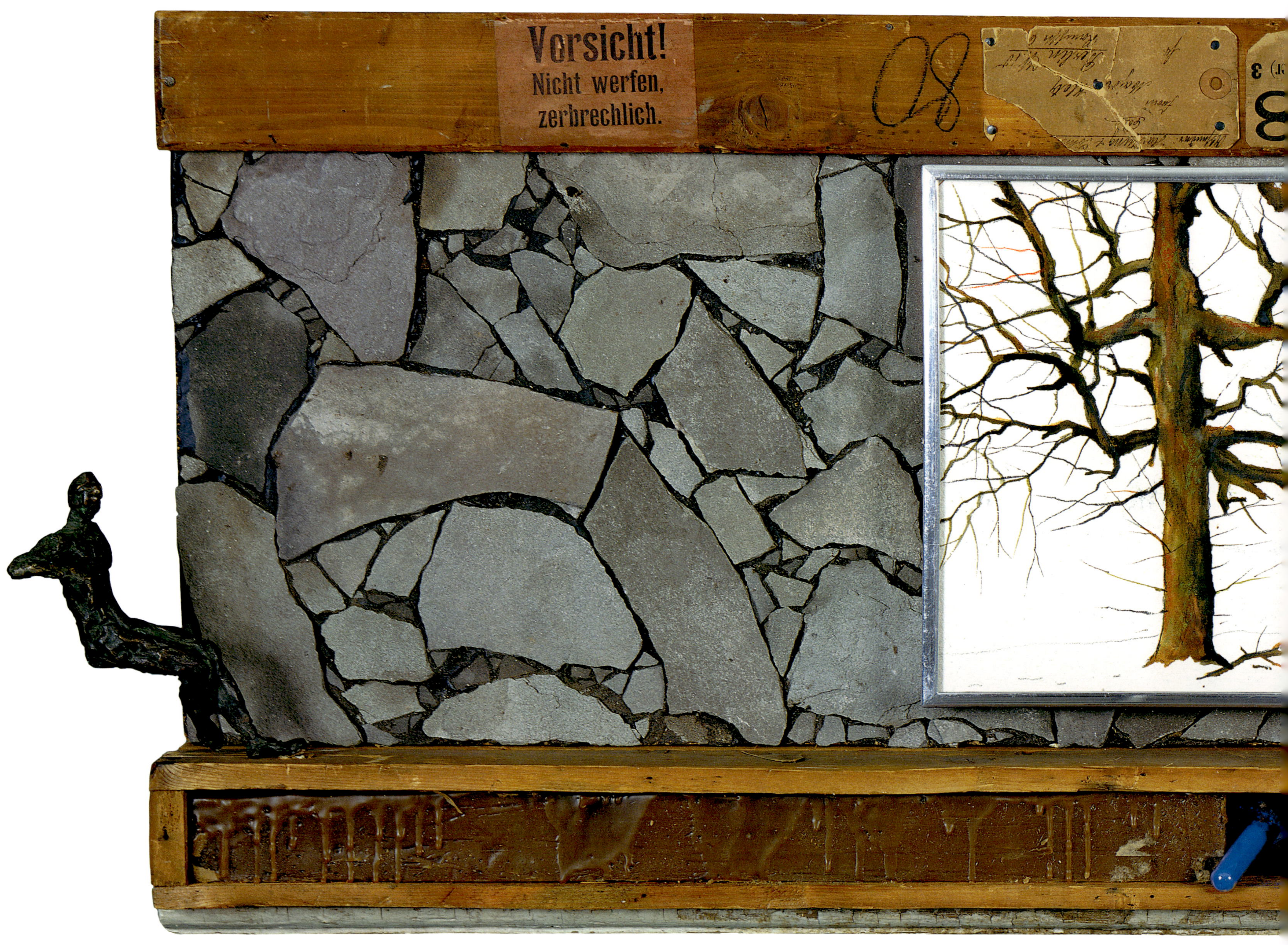
Vorsicht!
Nicht werfen,
zerbrechlich.
08

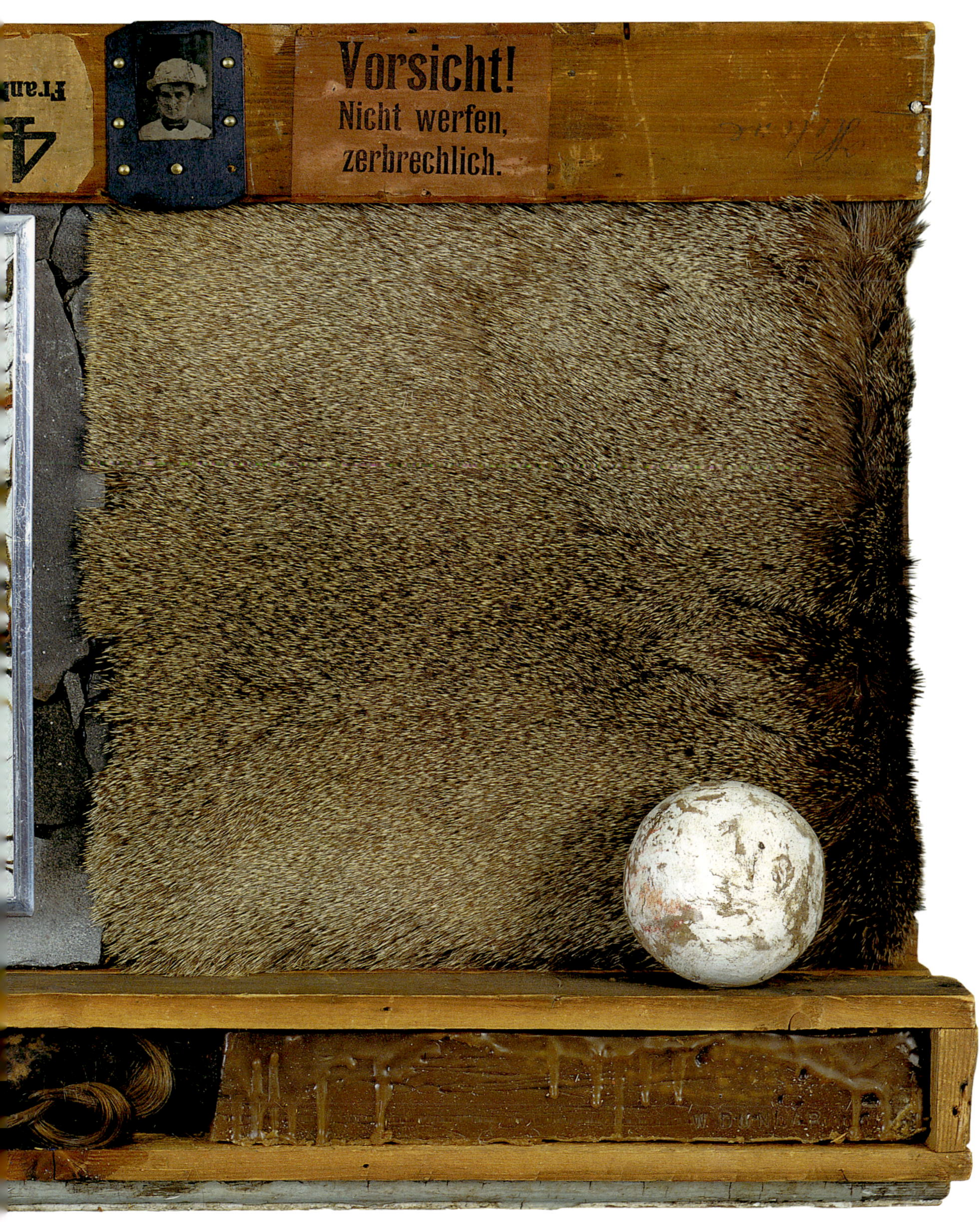

Slate Springs Eternal, 1989–90
Wood, slate, wax, bronze, willow ball, watercolor on paper, hair, dry pigment, deer hide, 17 1/2 x 37 x 4. Private collection. Photograph by Jack Kotz.

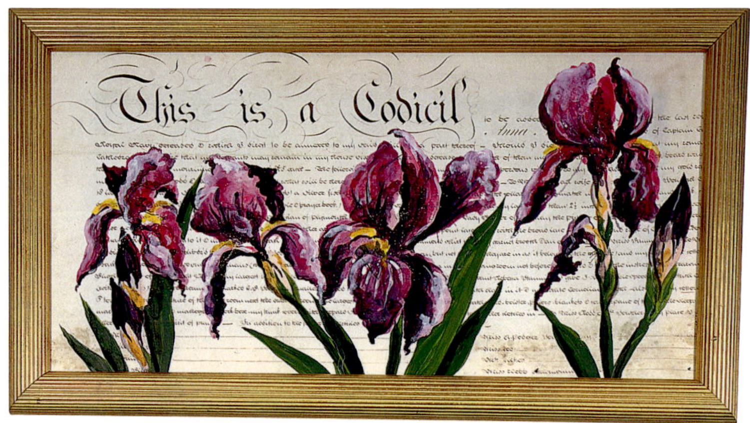

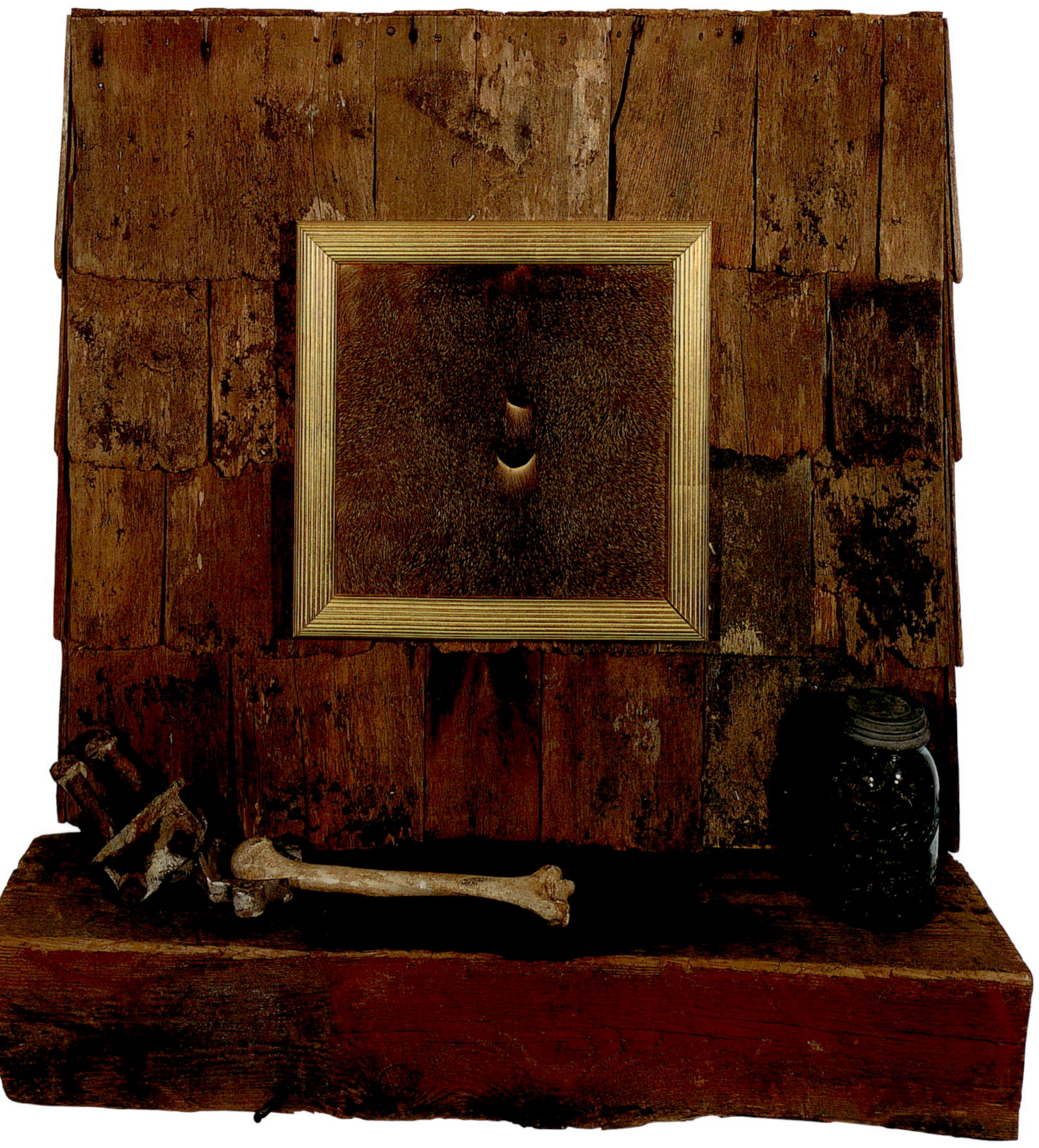

Funny Bone, Fruit Jar, Flower Fur, 1990
Oil paint on parchment, wood, bone, metal, glass, insect carcasses, 52 x 36 x 8. Private collection. Photograph by Jack Kotz.

Genesis of the Art Wars, 1990
Slate, oil paint on stretched paper, paint, snake, nest, arrows, palette, 48 x 24. Private collection. Photograph by Jack Kotz.

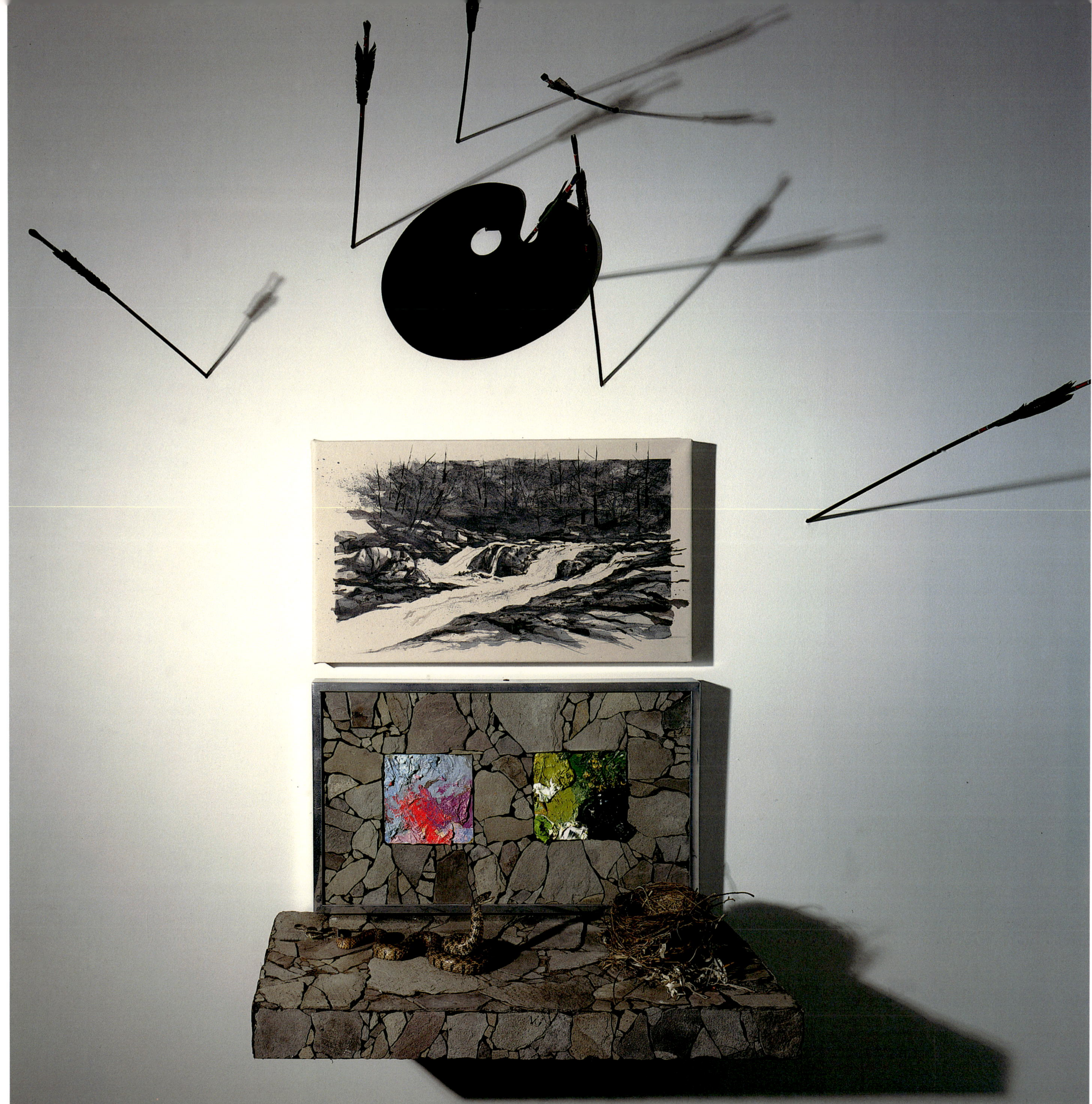

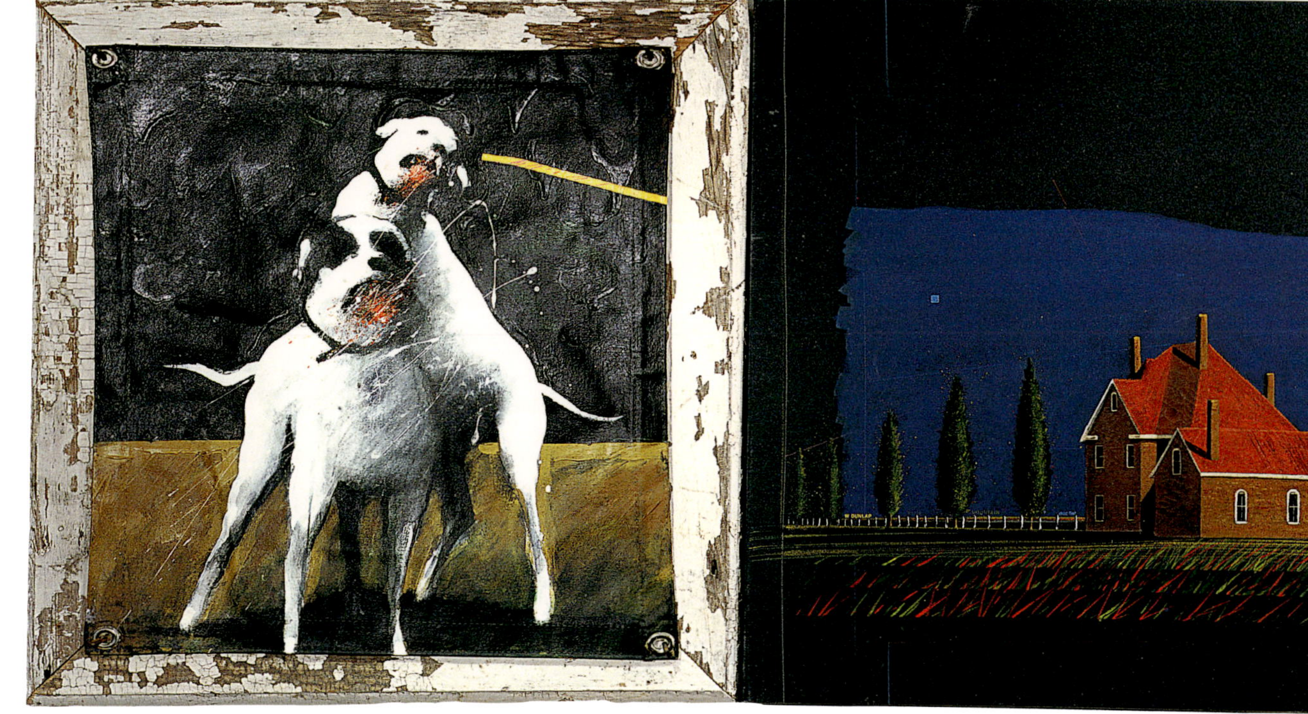

Bad Dog, 1990
Wood, canvas, polymer paint, metal, knife, 28 x 119. Private collection. Photograph by Adam Reich.

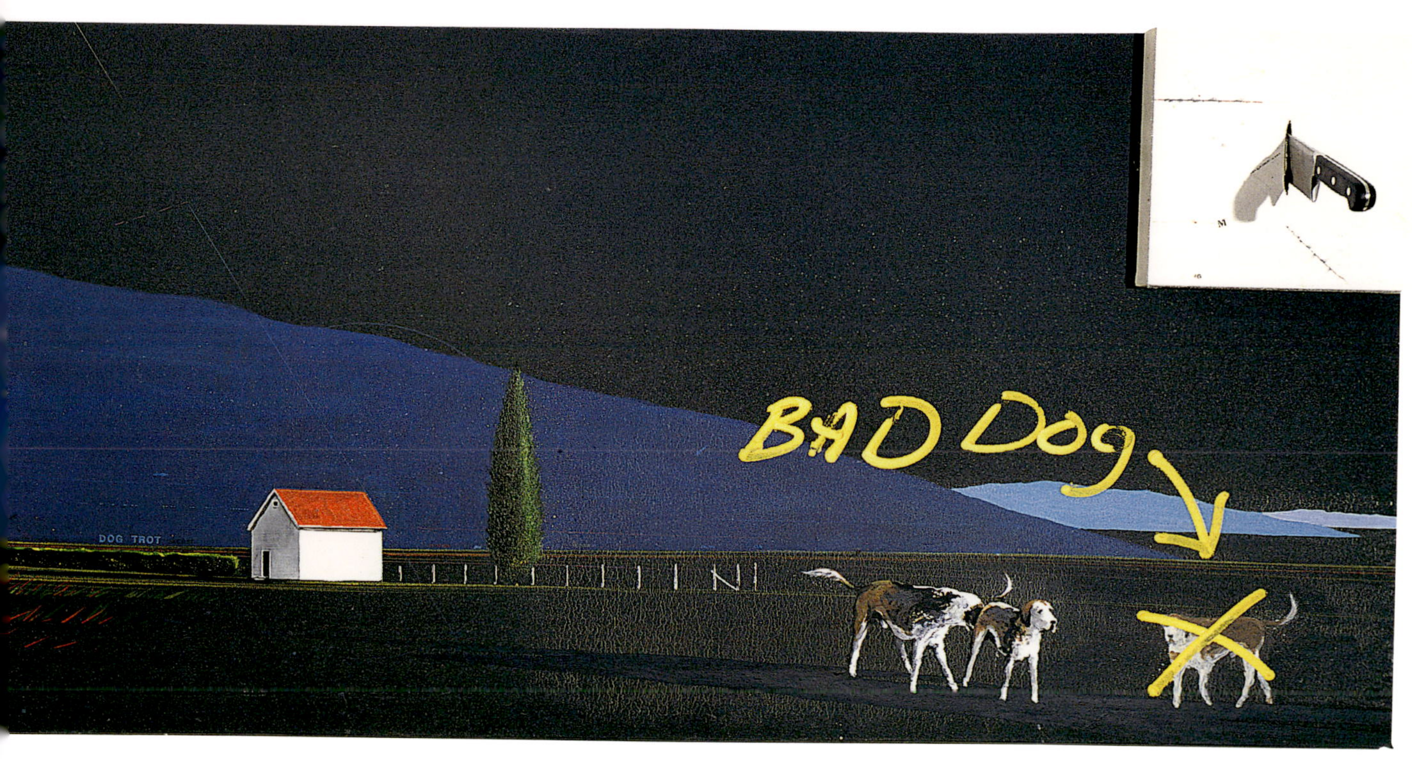

BAD Dog
DOG TROT

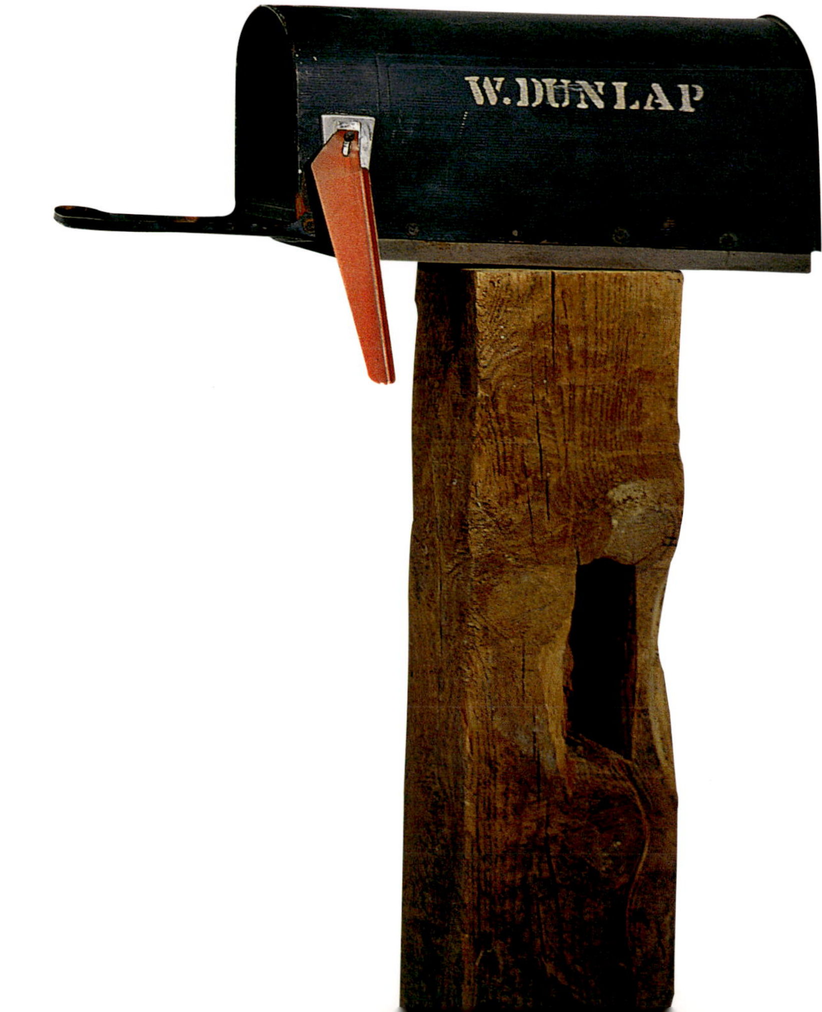

W.DUNLAP

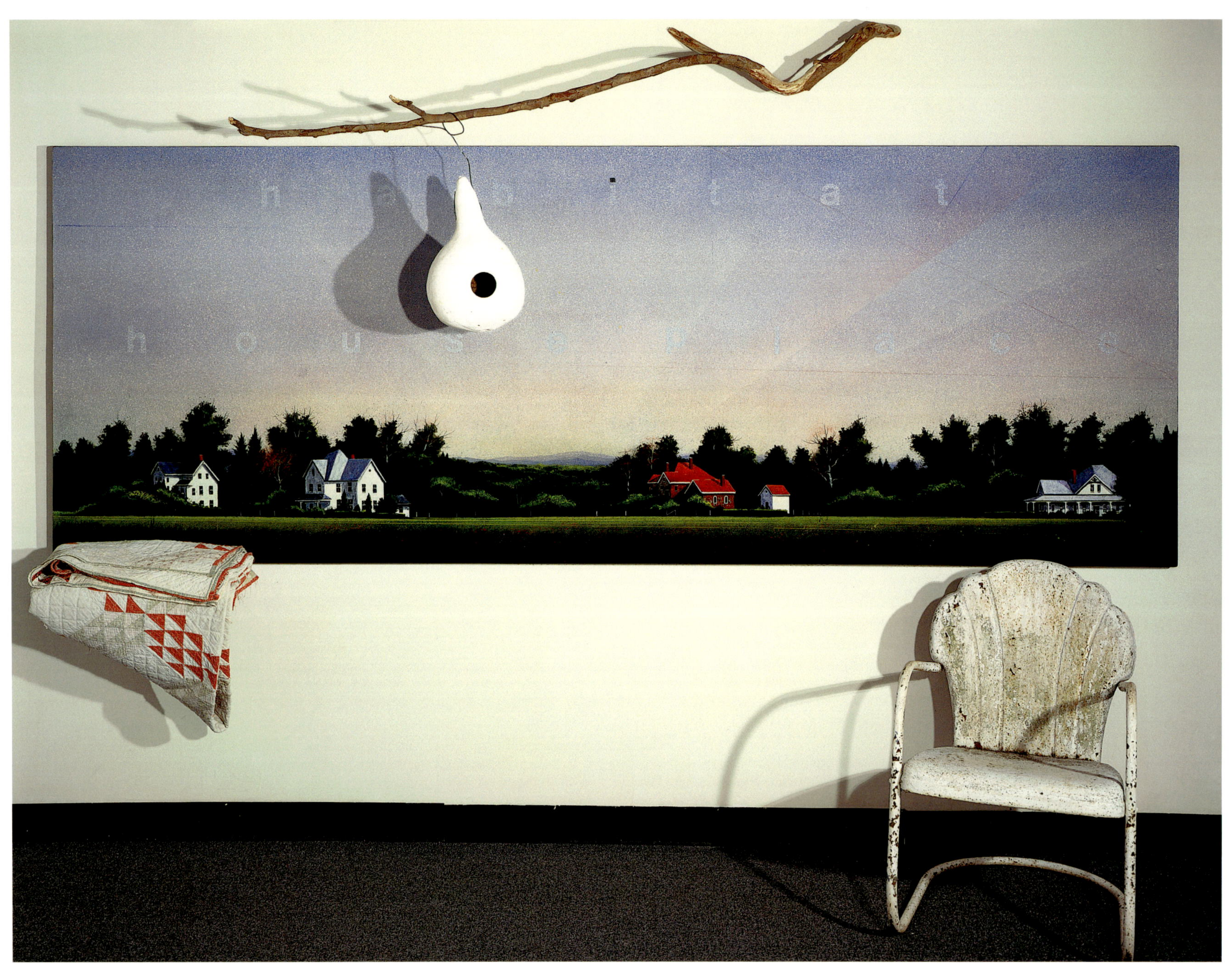

Habitat/House Place/Home Front, 1991
Polymer paint on canvas, wood, gourd, quilt, chair, 28 x 94 1/2 x 116. Collection of Exxon Mobil Corporation, Fairfax, Virginia. Photograph by Jack Meyer.

Object Lesson Series: Willing Spirit/Weak Flesh, 1991
Wood, polymer paint, feather, paper, steel, velvet, preserved komodo dragon, 38 x 39 x 18 1/2. Private collection. Photograph by Adam Reich.

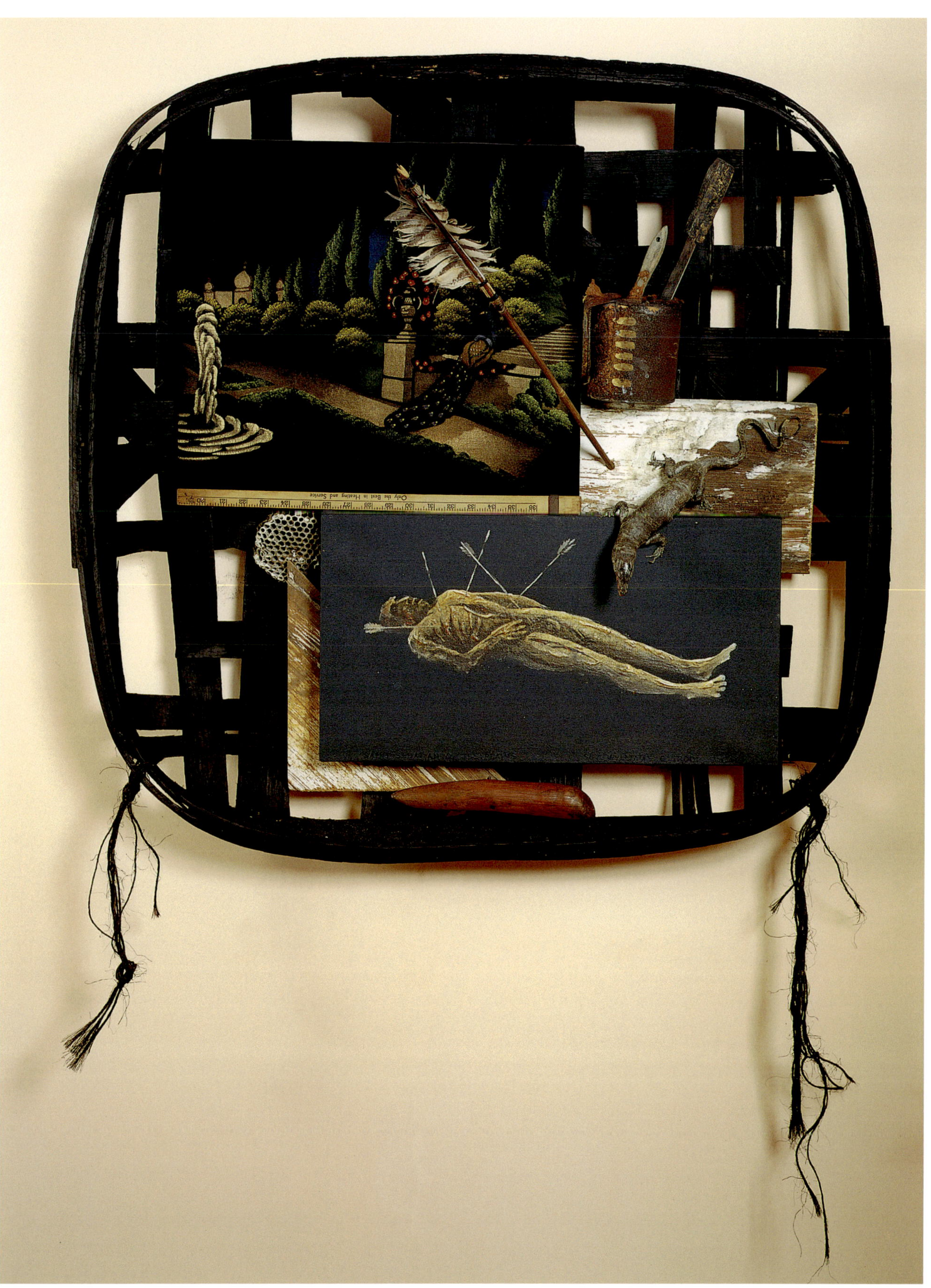

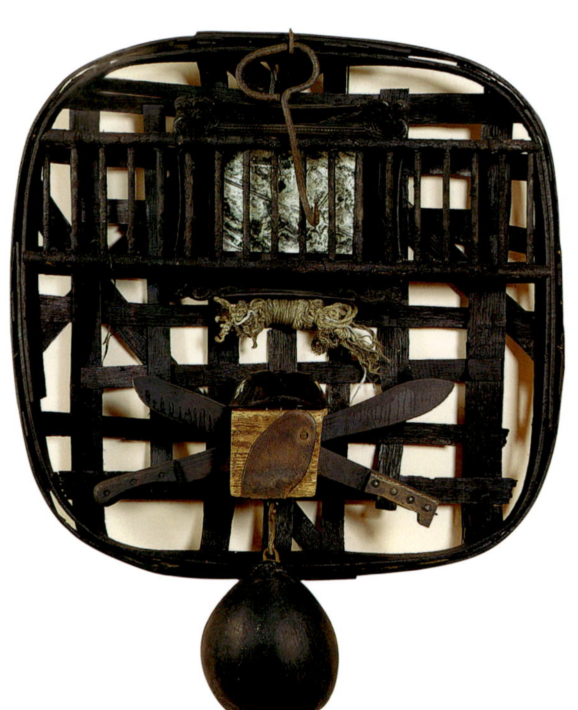

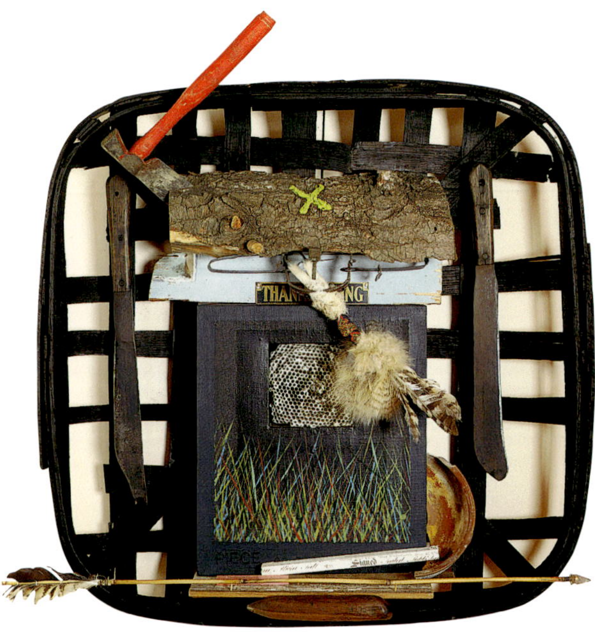

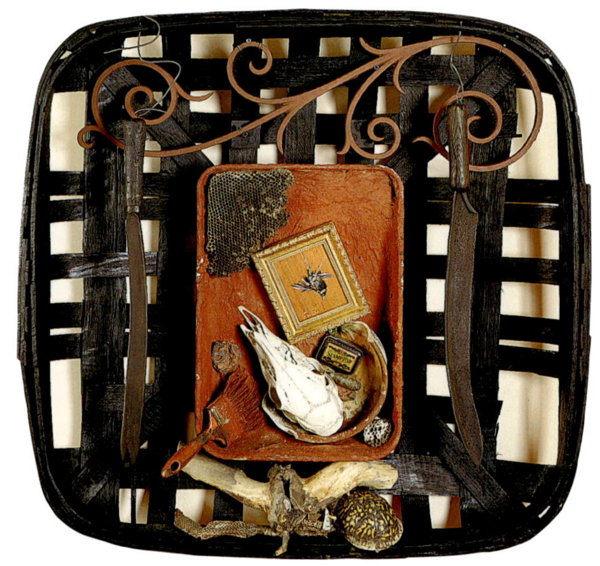

Object Lesson Series: Lights Out—1939–45, 1991
Wood, steel, rope, polymer paint, leather, gourd, snake skin, 35 x 36 x 9. Private collection. Photograph by Adam Reich.

Object Lesson Series: Hatchet Face/Go West, 1991
Wood, steel, polymer paint, fired clay, parchment, hawk's foot, beads, paper, knives, 35 x 36 x 8 1/2. Private collection. Photograph by Adam Reich.

Pro/Found/Object Lesson: Brush with Fates, 1991
Wood, iron, steel, beeswax, bone, shell, rock, polymer paint, fired clay, 36 x 36 x 7. Private collection. Photograph by Adam Reich.

Object Lesson Series: Hunt and Peck/Clarence Darrow's Arrow, 1991
Polymer paint, wire, wood, beeswax, fur, paper, canvas, 52 x 36 x 33. Private collection. Photograph by Jack Meyer.

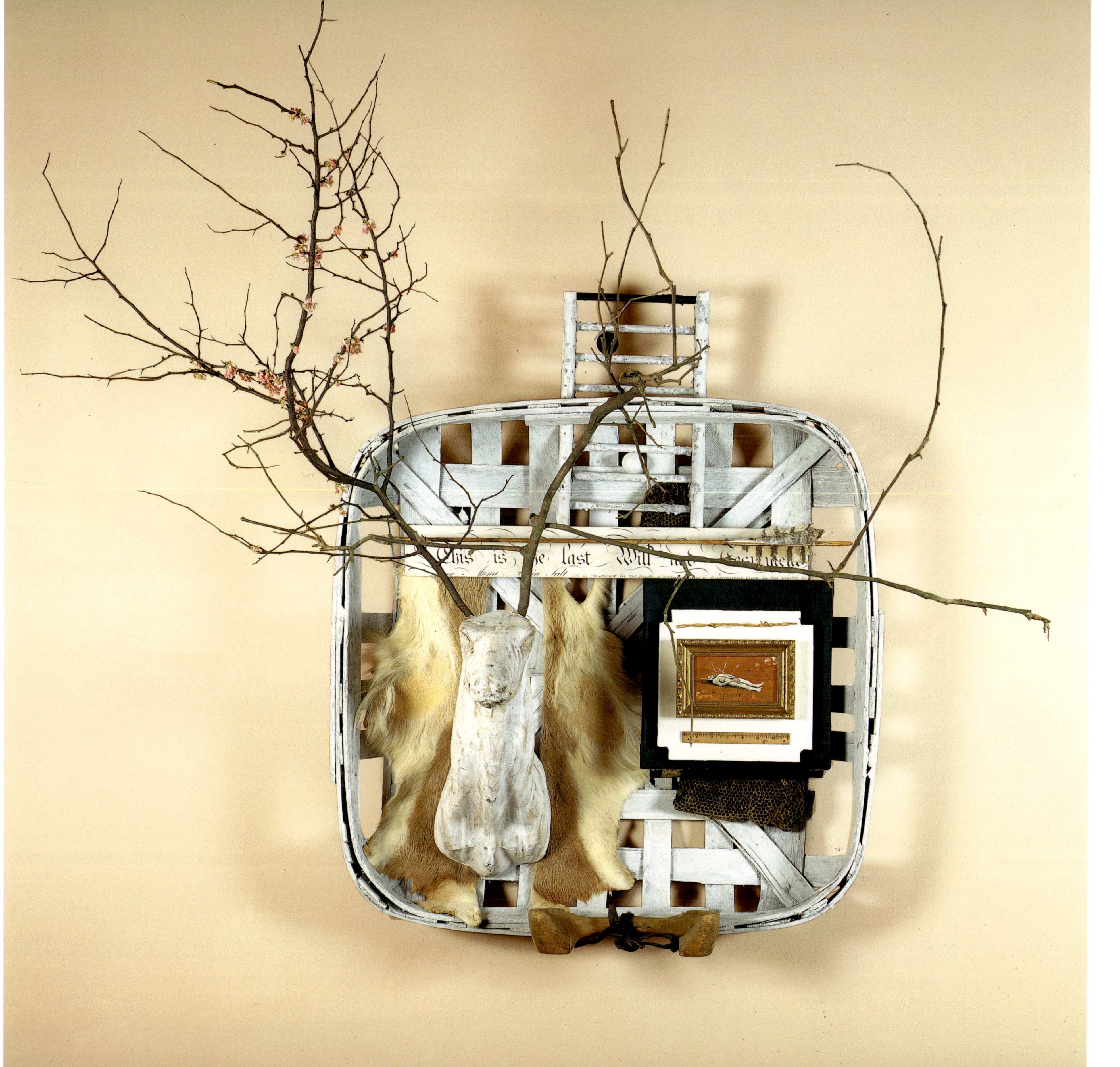
This is the last Will and Testament

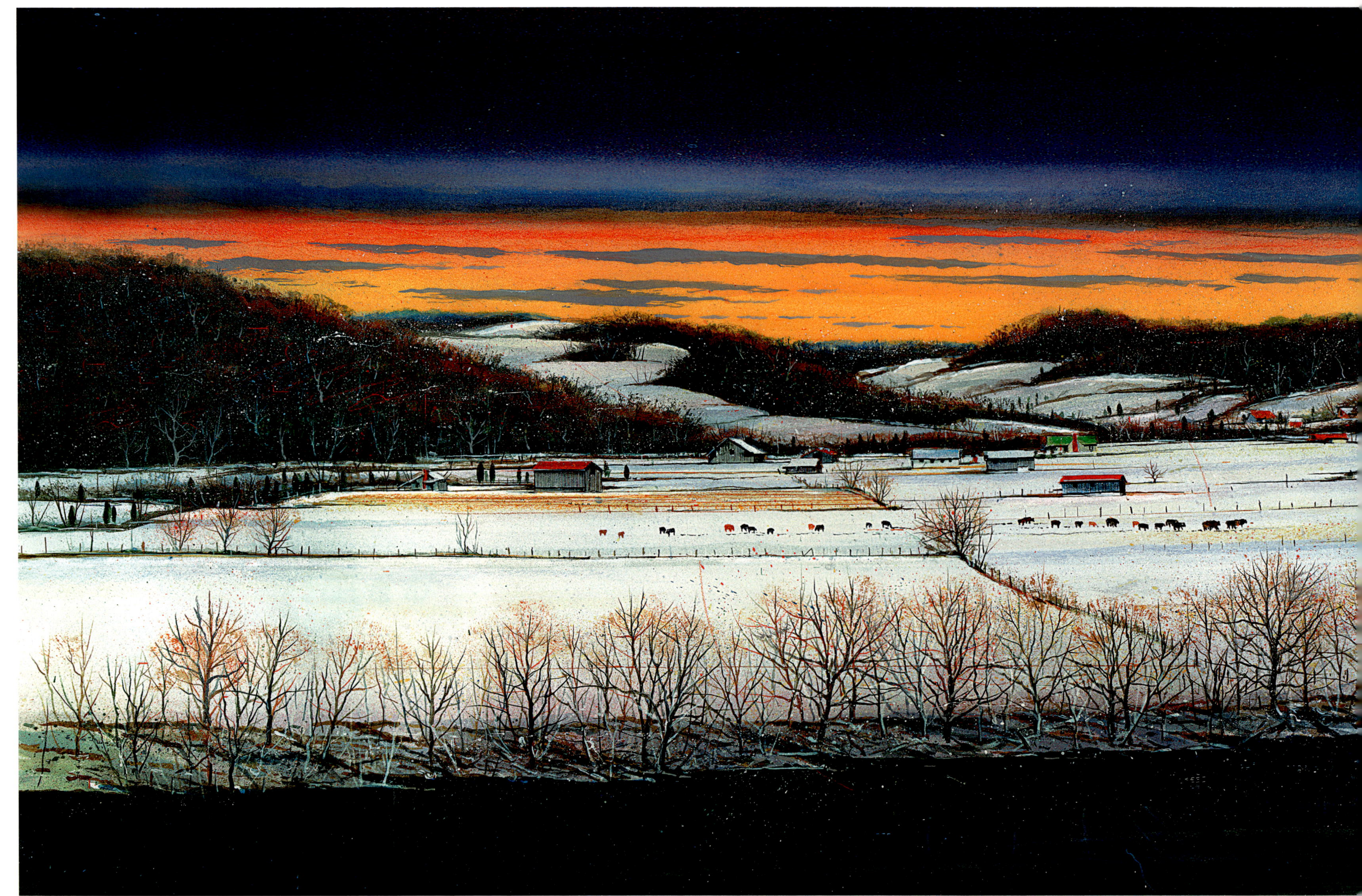

East Across the Caney Fork, 1995
Oil paint and dry pigment on rag paper,
28 x 72. Collection of Frank Hunger, Nashville,
Tennessee. Photograph by Jack Meyer.

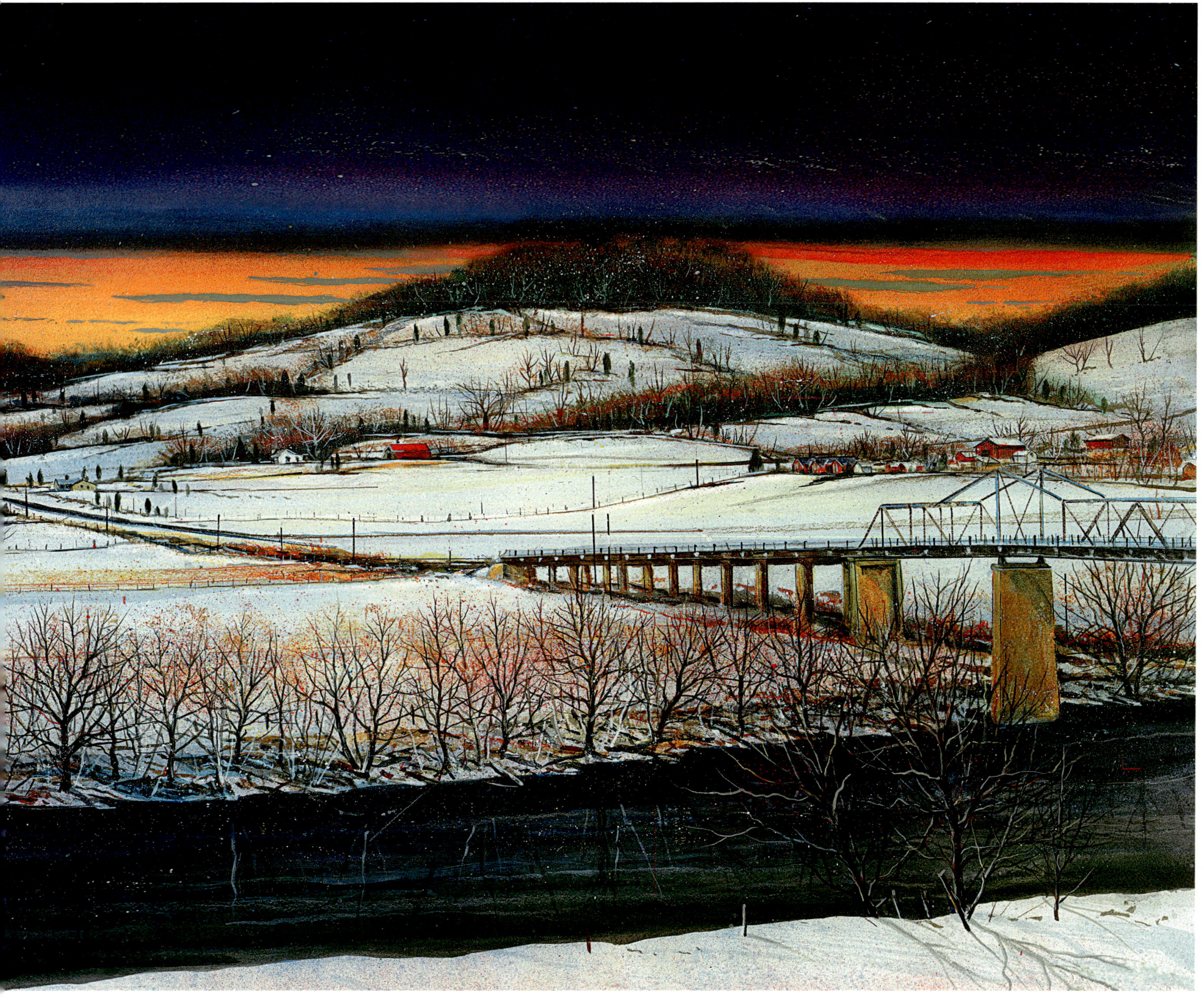

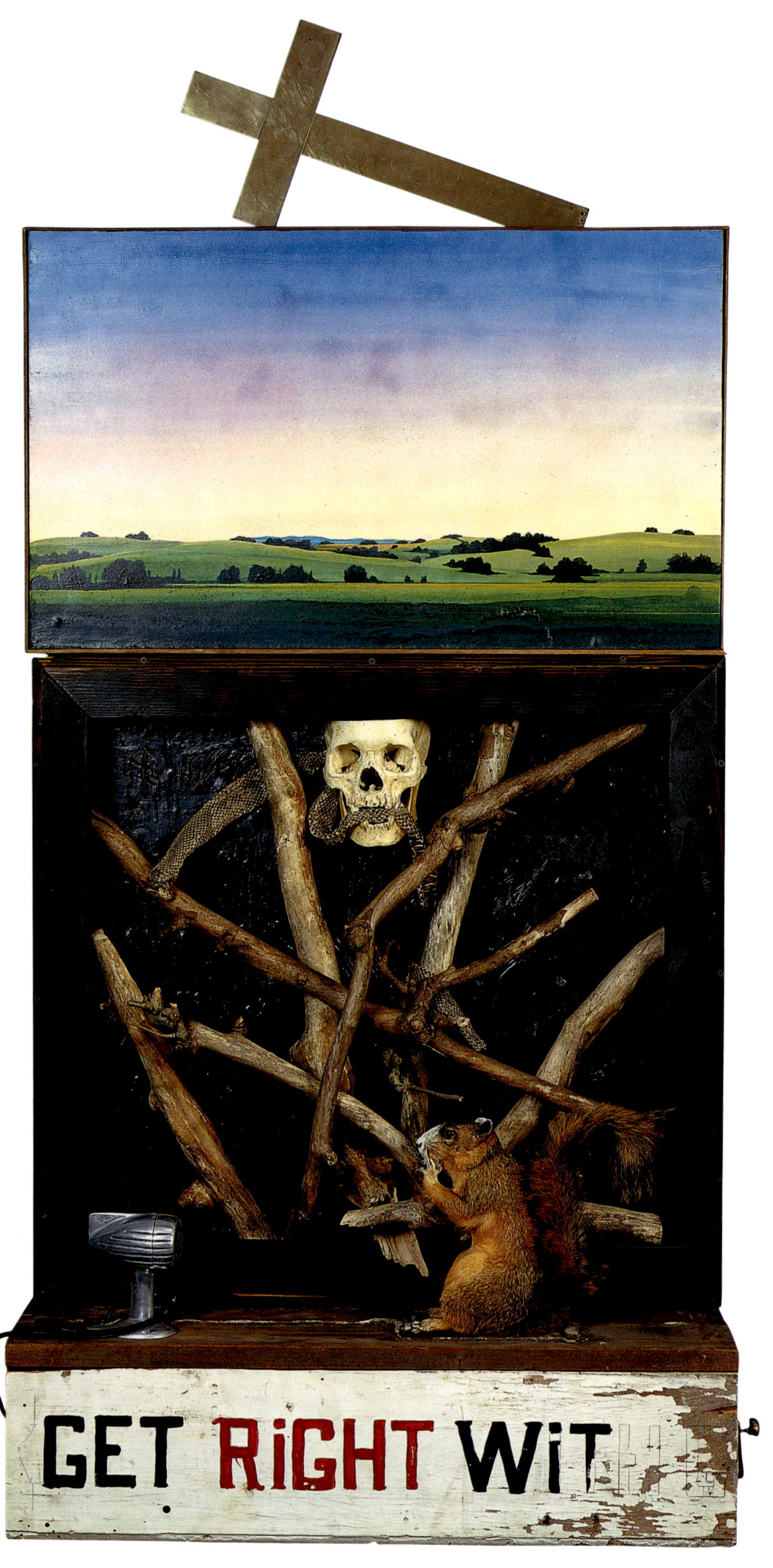

He'll Set Your Fields on Fire, 1995

Polymer paint, wood, brass, bone, aluminum, preserved squirrel, 58 x 34 x 12. Private collection. Photograph by Jack Kotz.

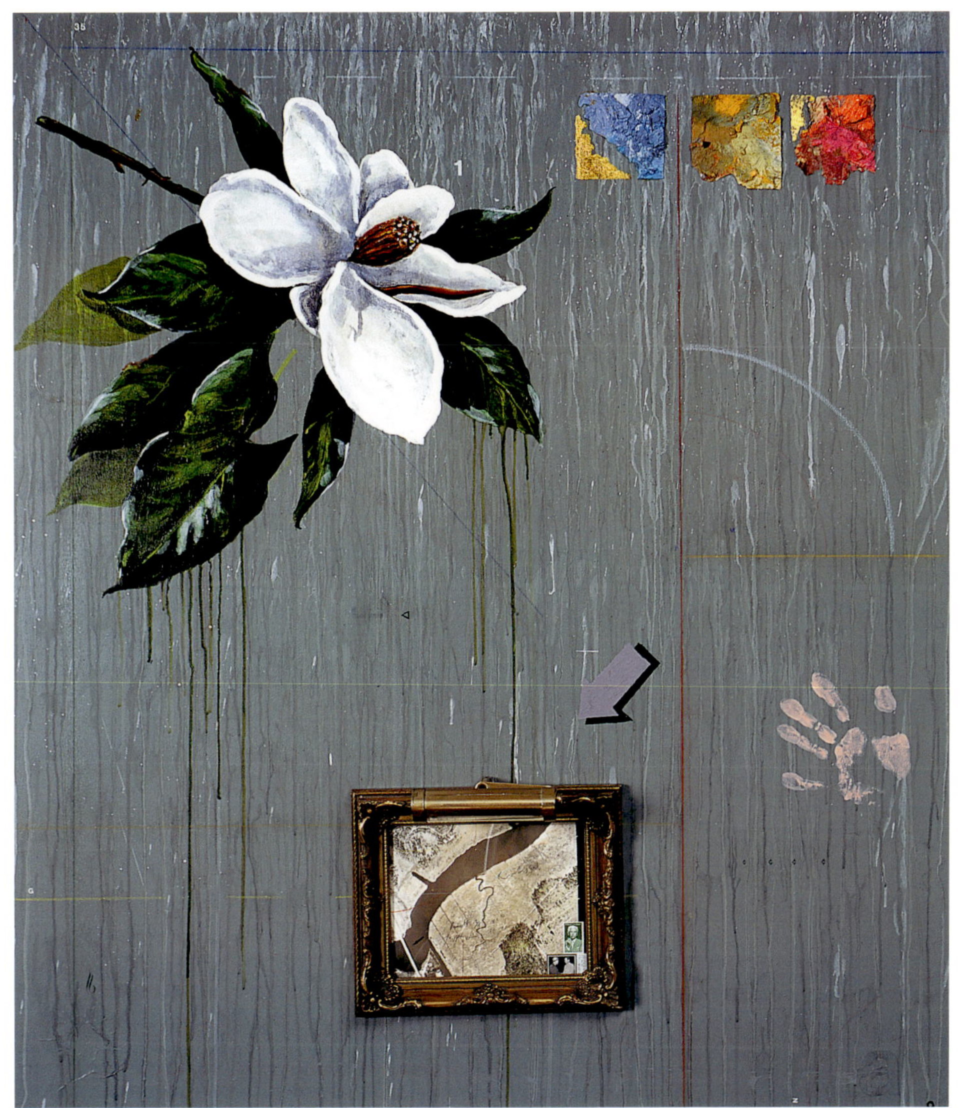

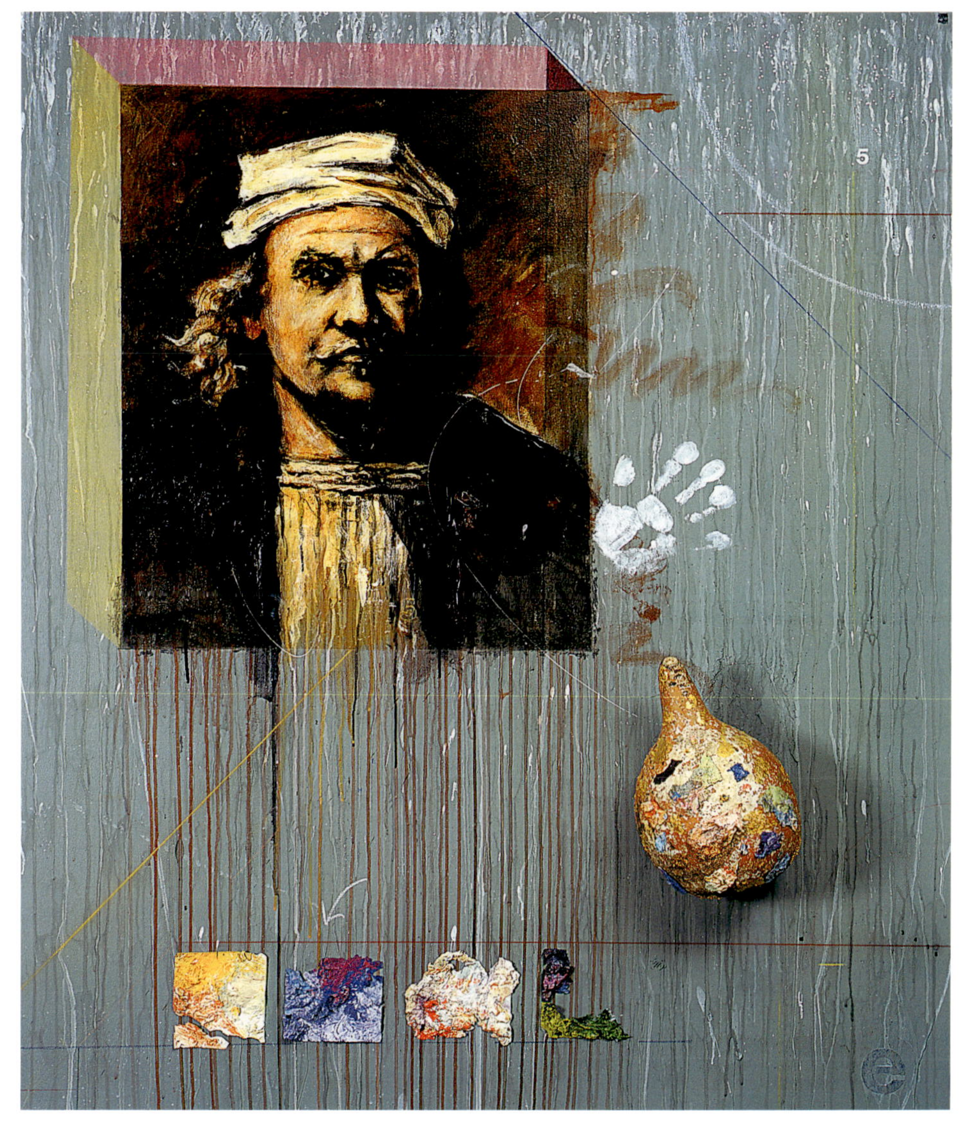

Art Hath an Enemy Called Ignorance,
1996
Polymer paint on canvas, gourd, gold leaf; diptych, 54 x 94. Collection of Jane and Wood Hiatt, Jackson, Mississippi. Photograph by Hubert Worley.

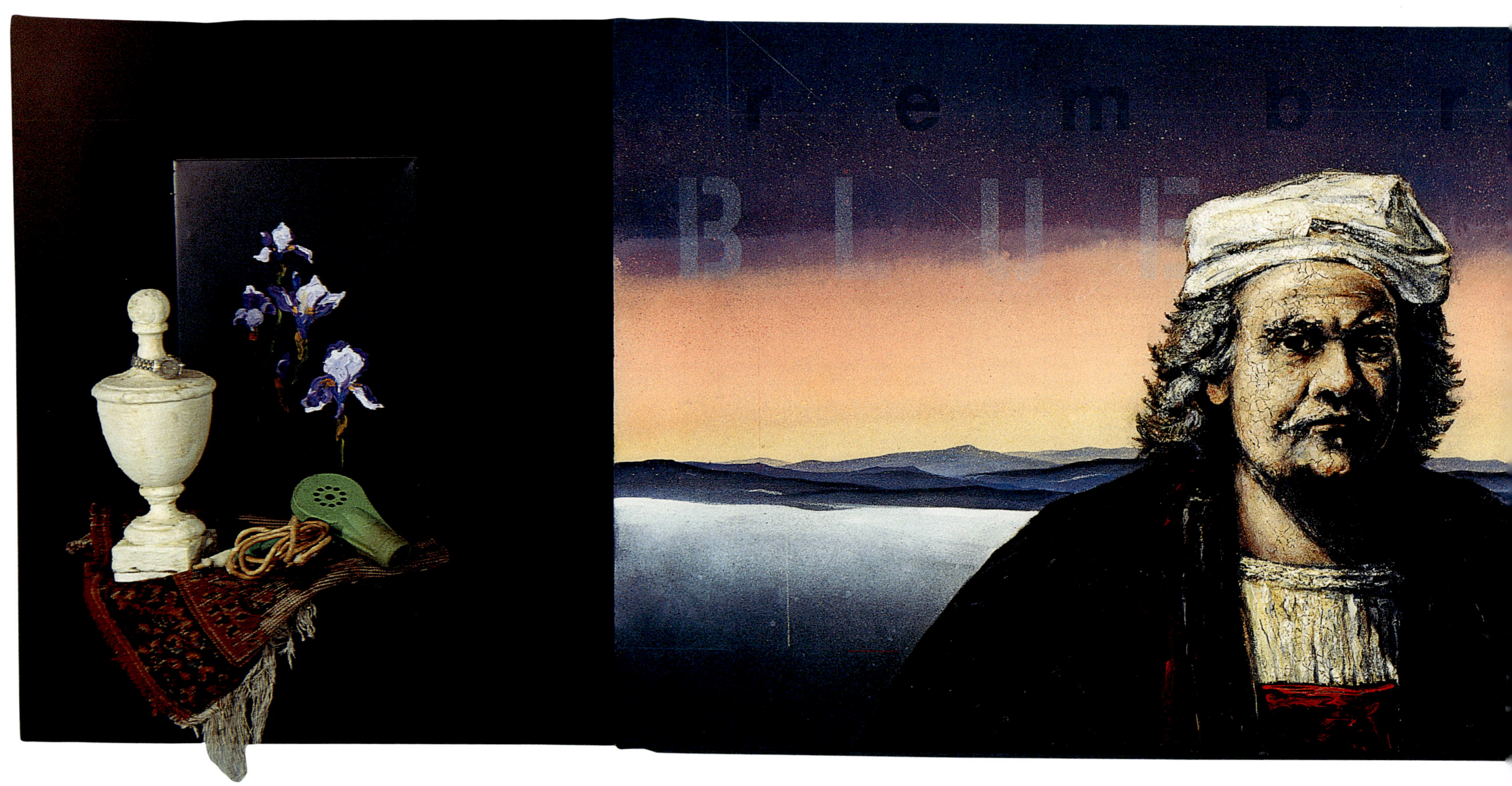
r e m b r

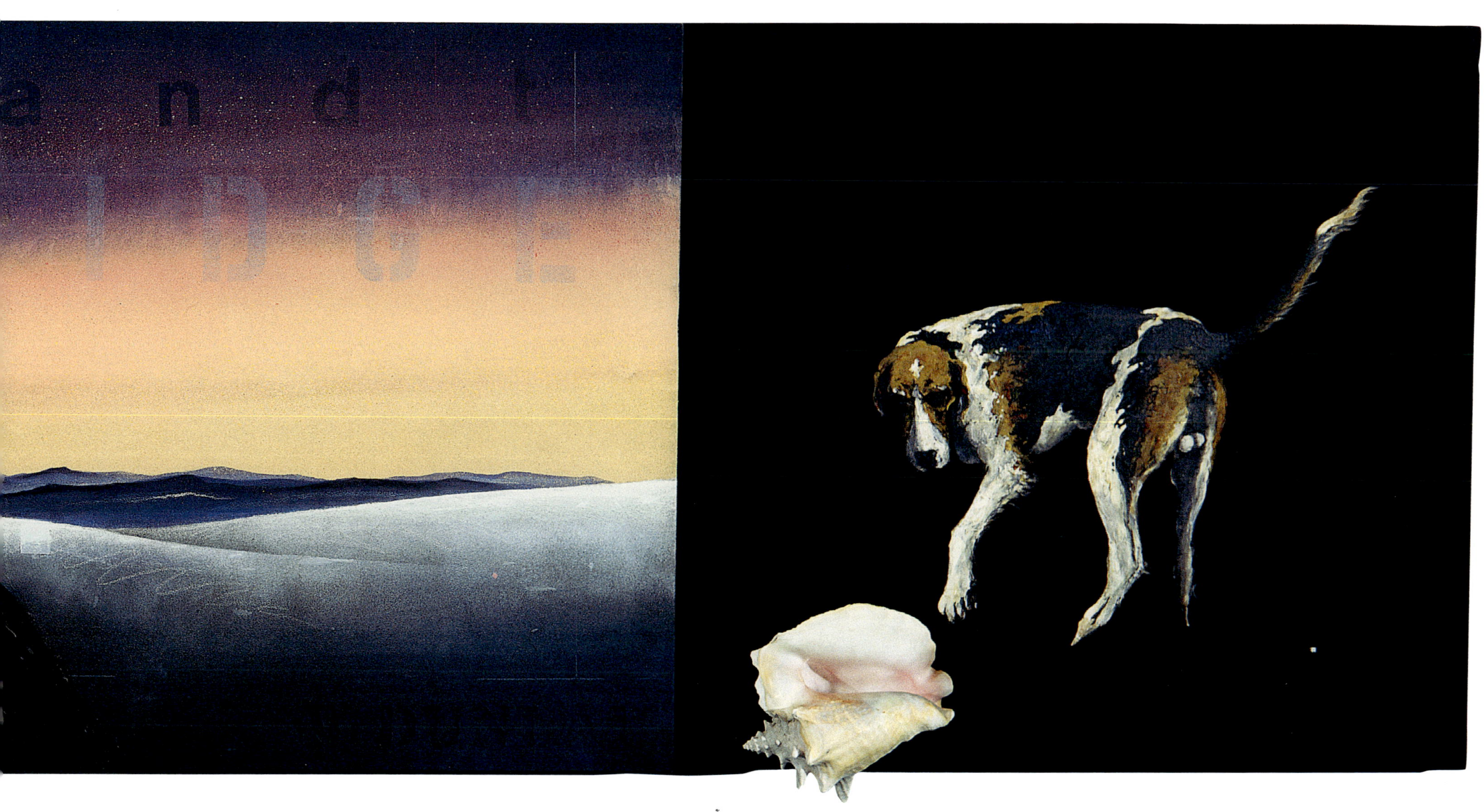

Rembrandt in the Blue Ridge, 1994–95
Polymer paint on canvas, wood, shell, fabric, metal, found materials; triptych, 36 x 146 x 8. Private collection of Jim and Liba Lambe, Roaring Gap, North Carolina. Photograph by Jack Meyer.

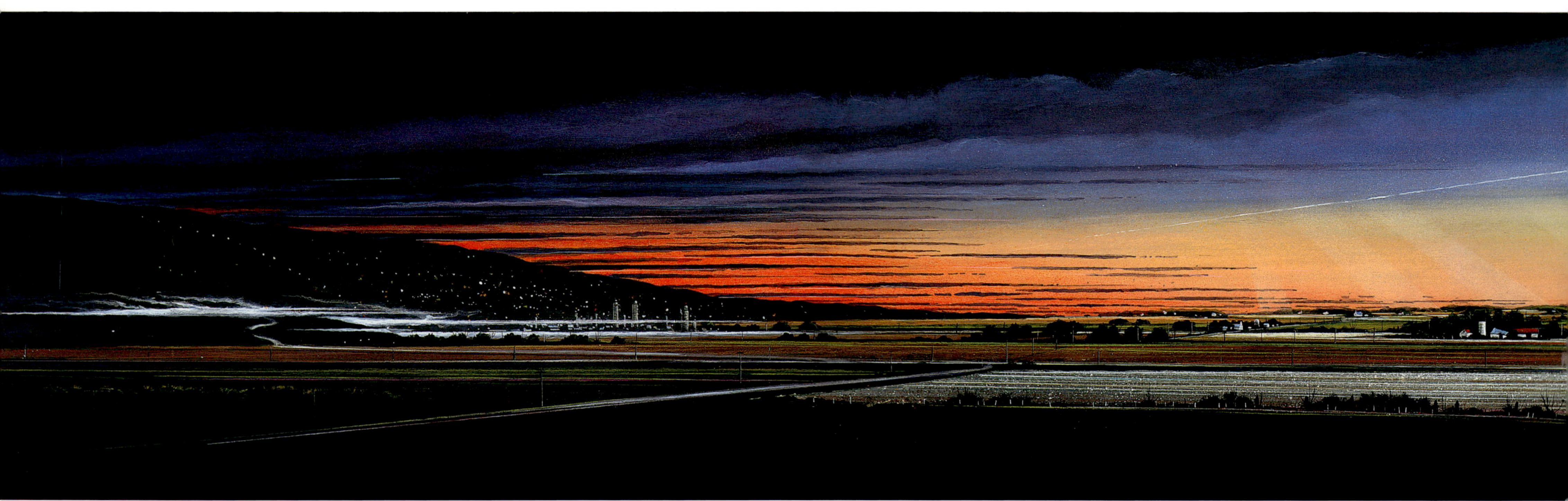

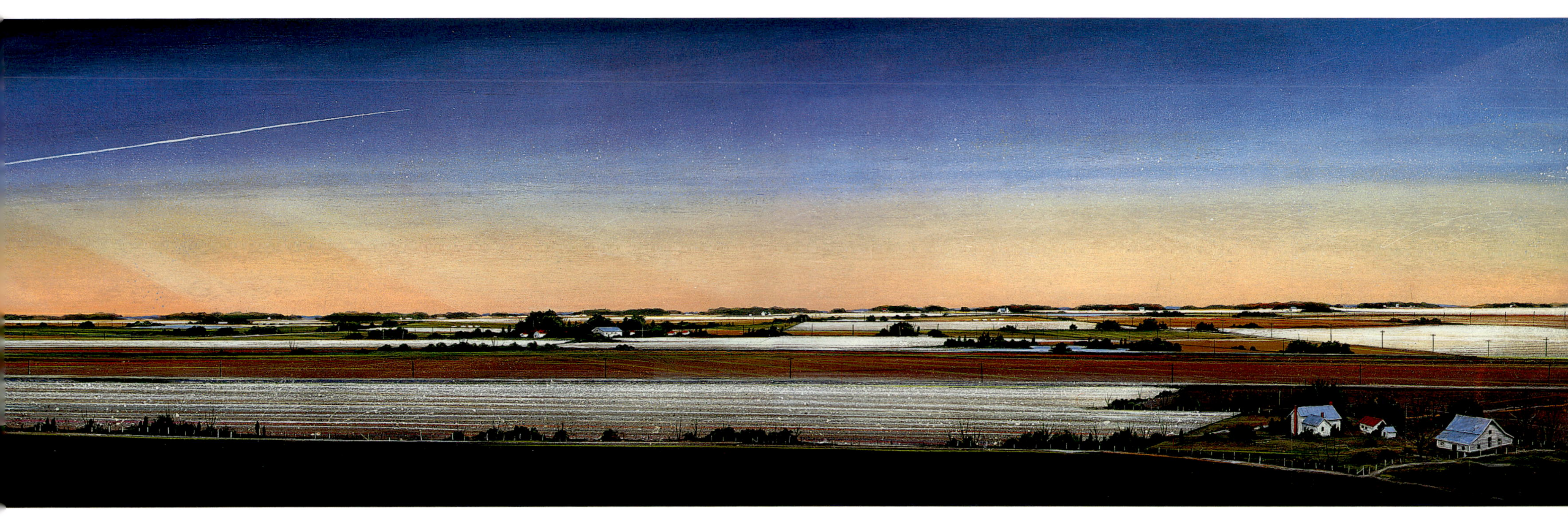

Flat Out, 1998
Polymer paint on wood panel, diptych,
24 x 192. Collection of Terra Industries, Yazoo City, Mississippi. Photograph by Jack Meyer.

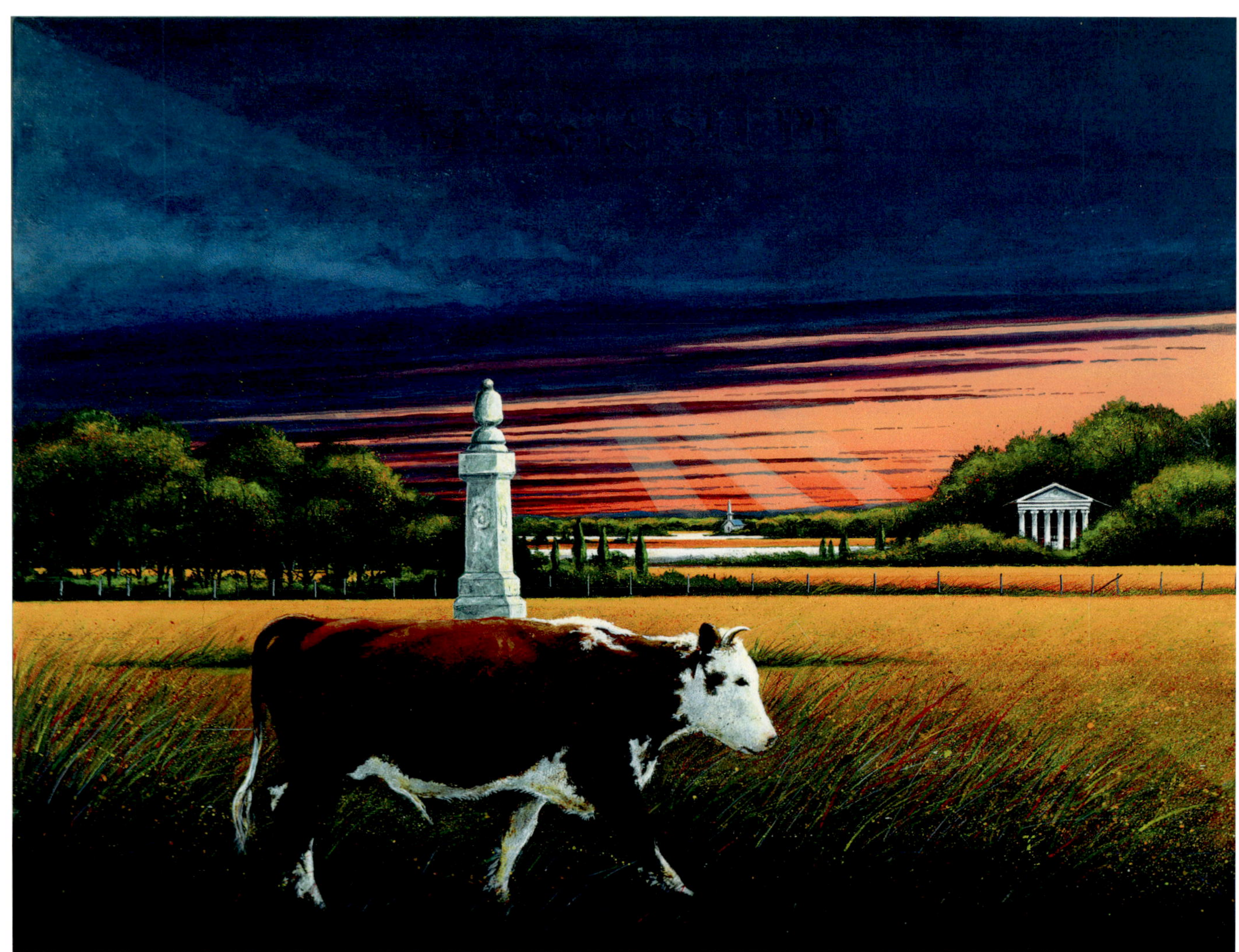

Young Bull and War Memorial, 1998
Polymer paint on linen canvas, 48 x 60. Collection of U.S. Court of Appeals for the Fifth Circuit, New Orleans, Louisiana. Photograph by Jack Meyer.

Down Stream, Deep Pool, 1999
Oil paint on paper, 36 x 78. Collection of Jan and Lawrence Farrington, Ridgeland, Mississippi. Photograph by Hubert Worley.

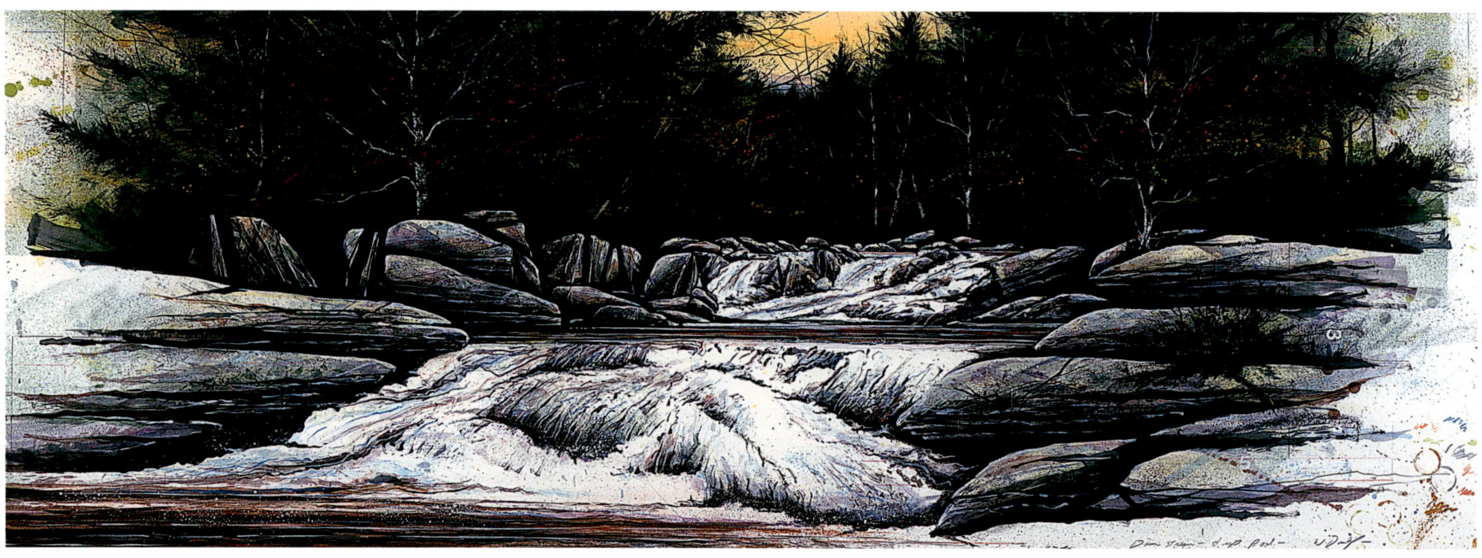

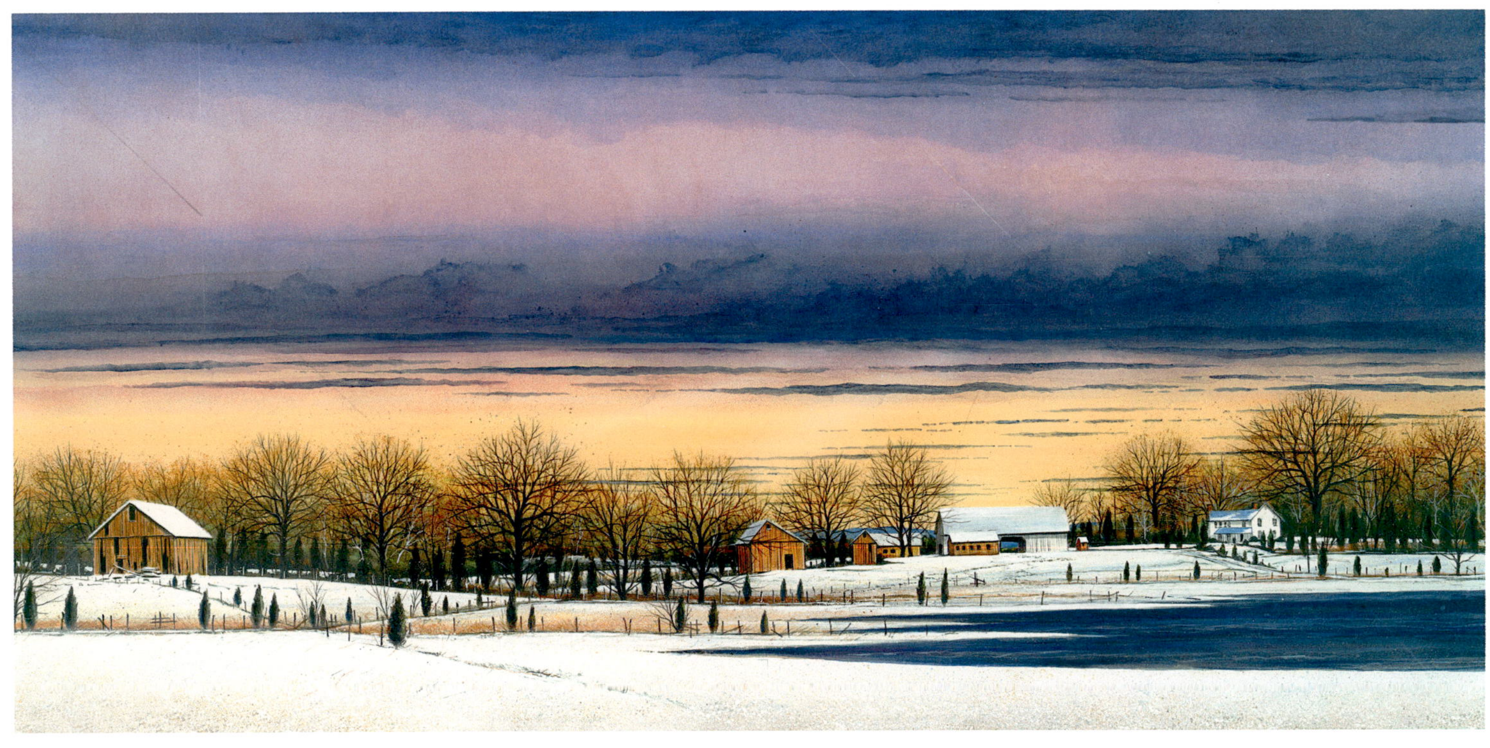

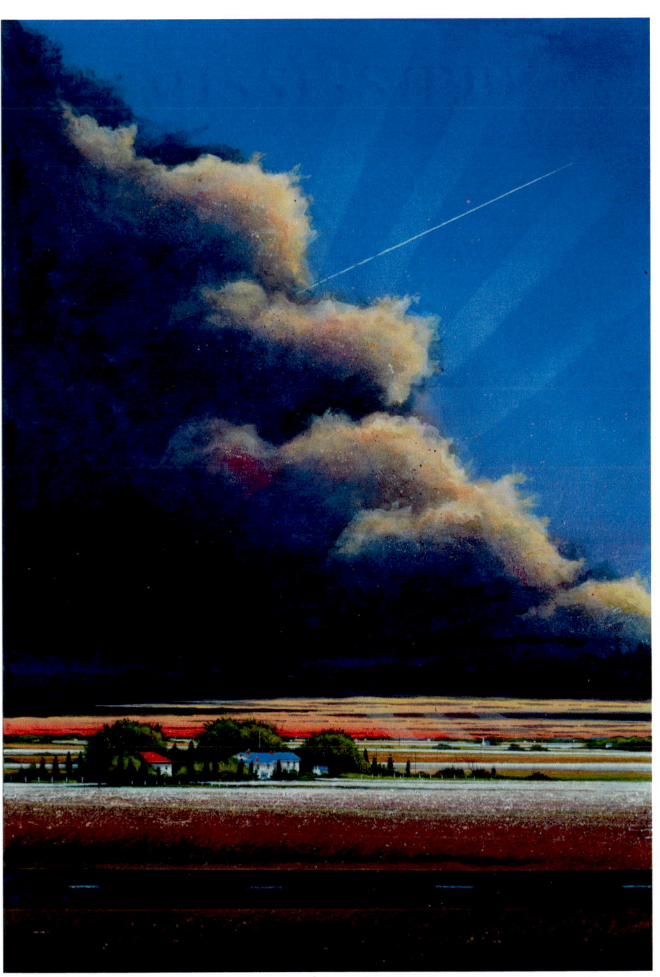

Winter Watch, 1999, 1999
Oil paint and dry pigment on rag paper, 25 x 52.
Collection of U.S. Department of State,
Washington, D.C. Photograph by Jack Meyer.

Flat Out for Bob Garrard, 1998
Polymer paint on canvas, 34 x 50. Collection of
Delta State University, Cleveland, Mississippi.
Commissioned by Mary Jane Whittington of
Greenwood, Mississippi, in honor of her brother,
December 13, 1919–November 13, 1950, a
WWII fighter pilot on the USS *Saratoga*.
Photograph by Jack Meyer.

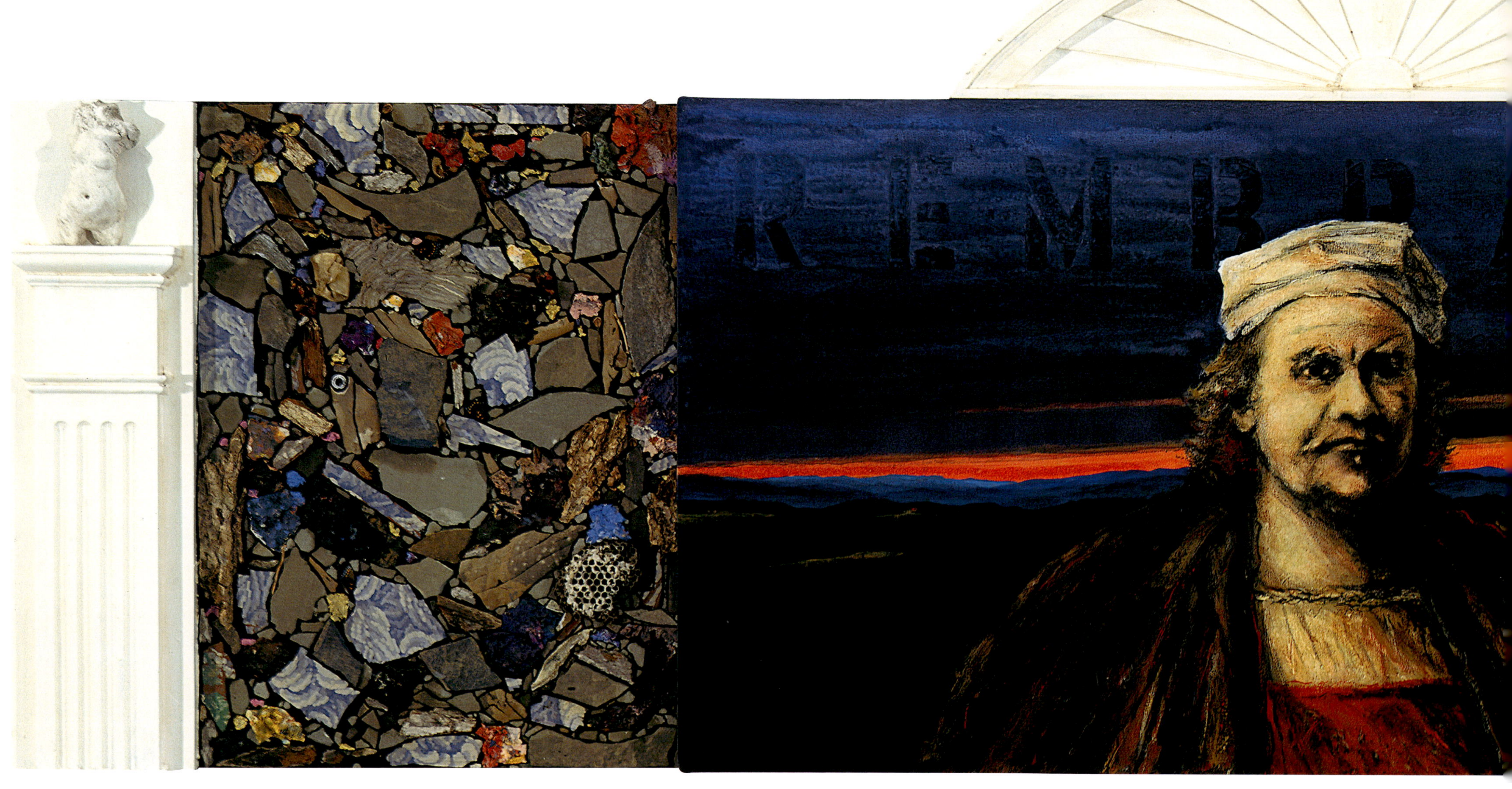
R E M B R

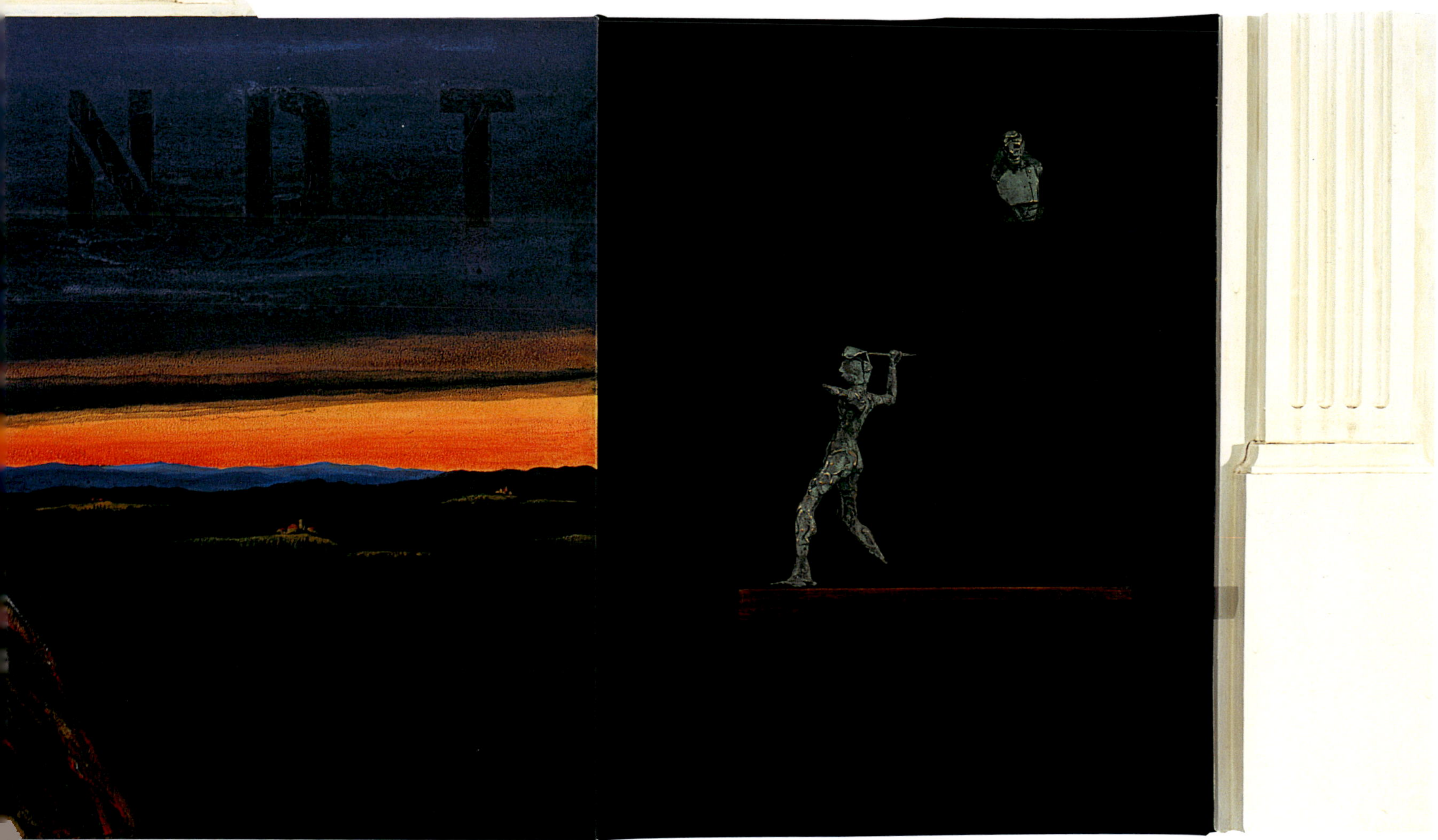

Rembrandt in Umbria with Etruscan Warrior, 2000

Polymer paint on canvas, slate, bronze, velvet, wood, 30 x 108 x 4. Collection of James V. Kimsey, McLean, Virginia. Photograph by Jack Meyer.

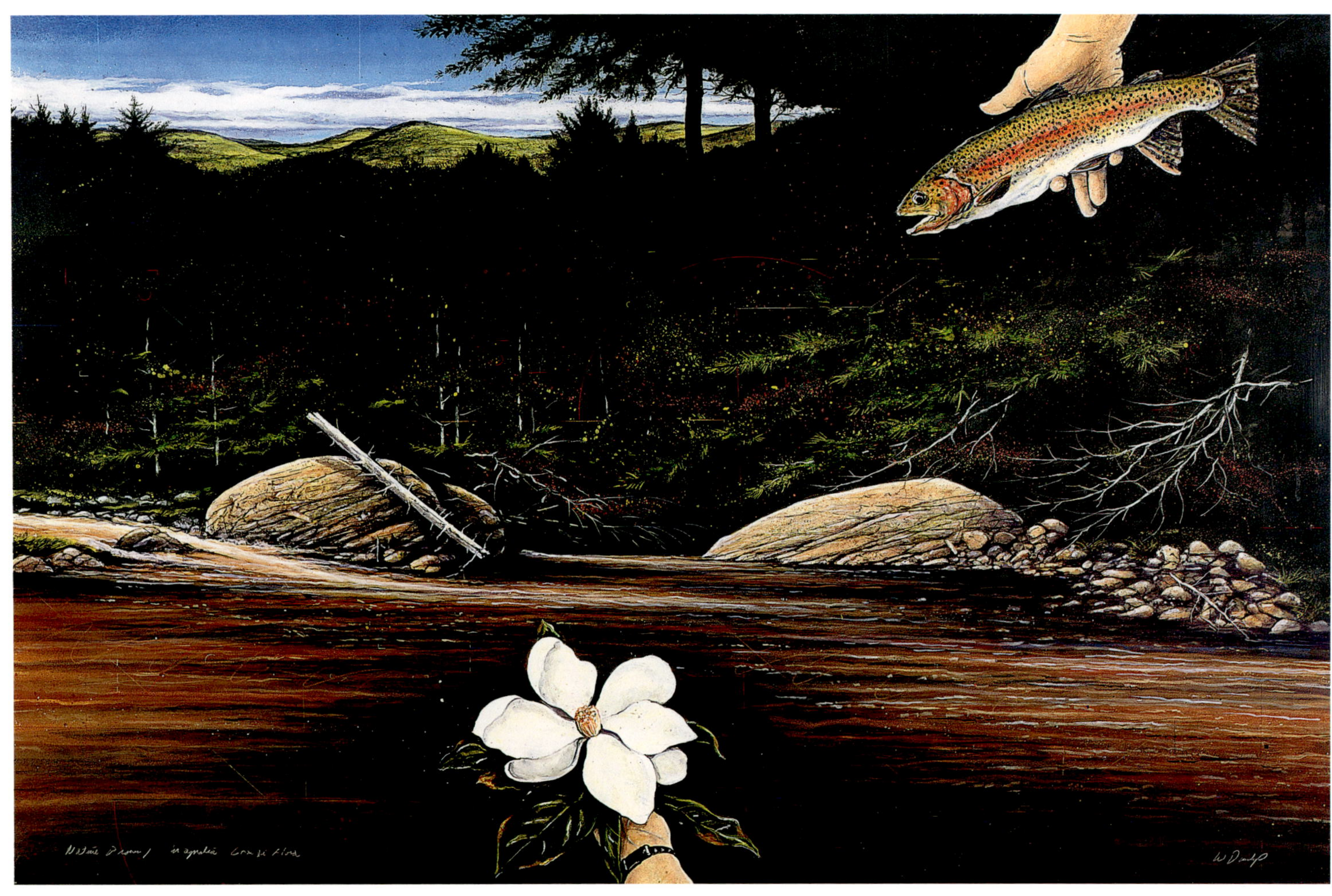

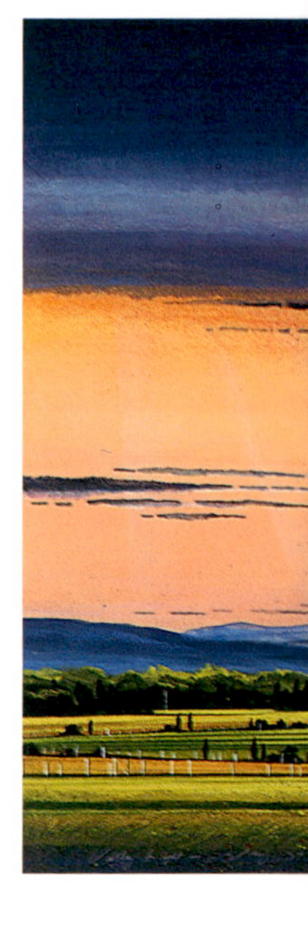

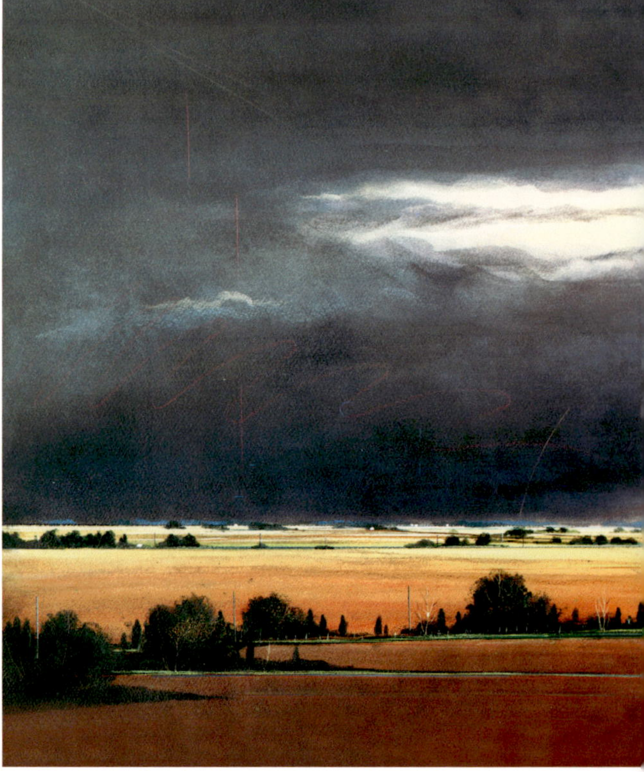

Native Brown—Granda Floria, 2000
Oil paint and dry pigment on rag paper, 42 x 63. Private collection. Photograph by Don Queralto.

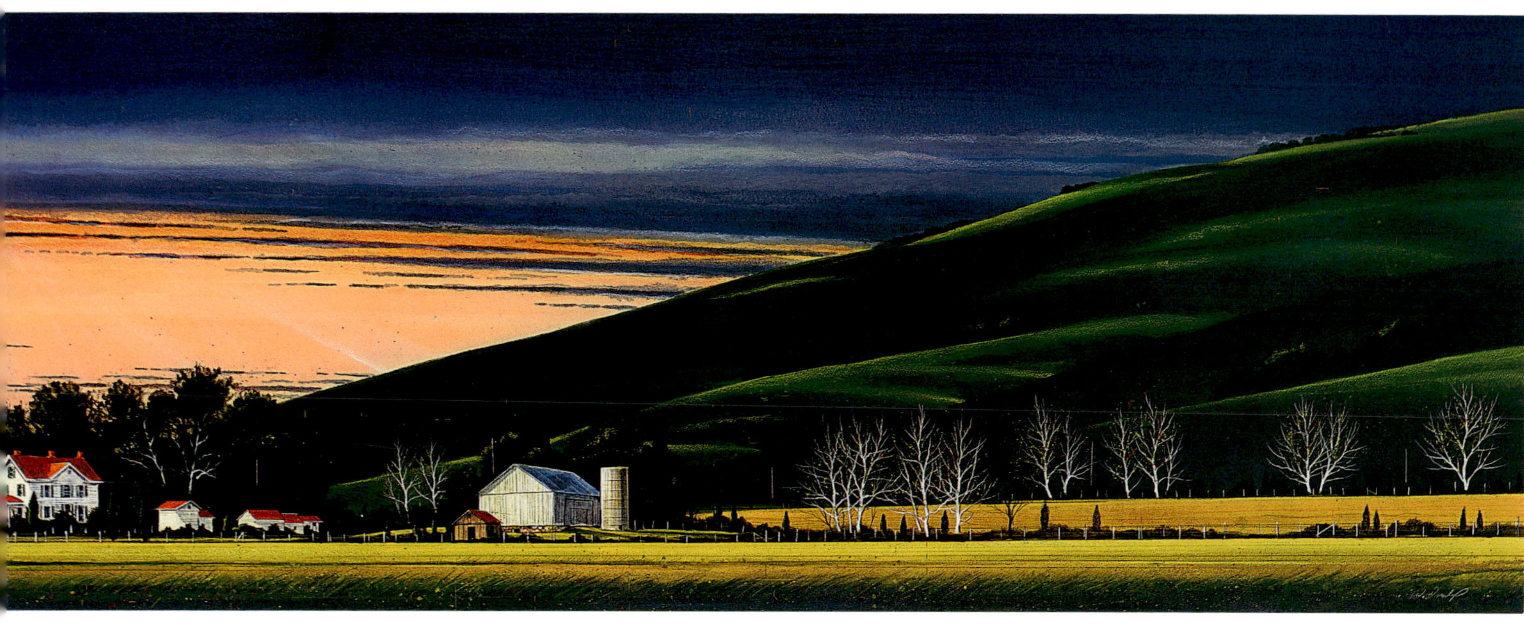

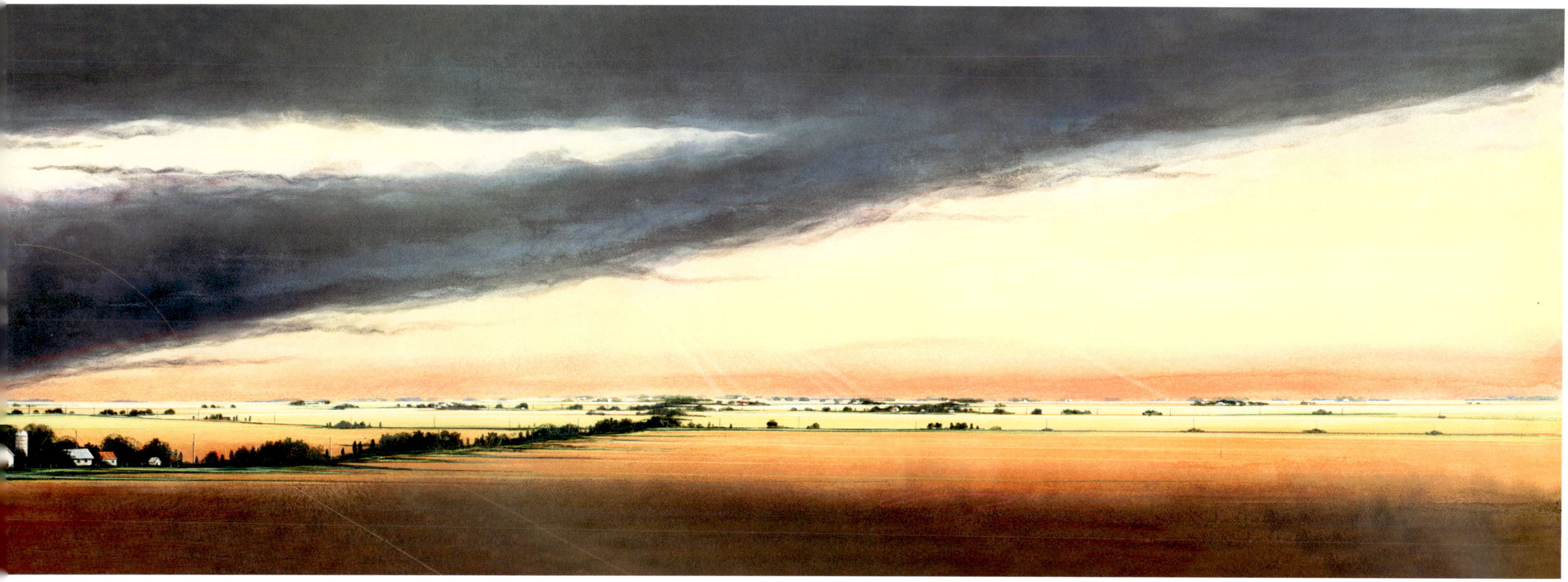

Valley Light—Spring Storm, 2001
Oil paint and dry pigment on rag paper, 24 x 70. Collection of U.S. State Department Embassy, Phnom Penh, Cambodia. Photograph by Jack Meyer.

Flat Out—Storm Front, 2001
Oil paint and dry pigment on rag paper, 24 x 72. Private collection. Photograph by Jack Meyer.

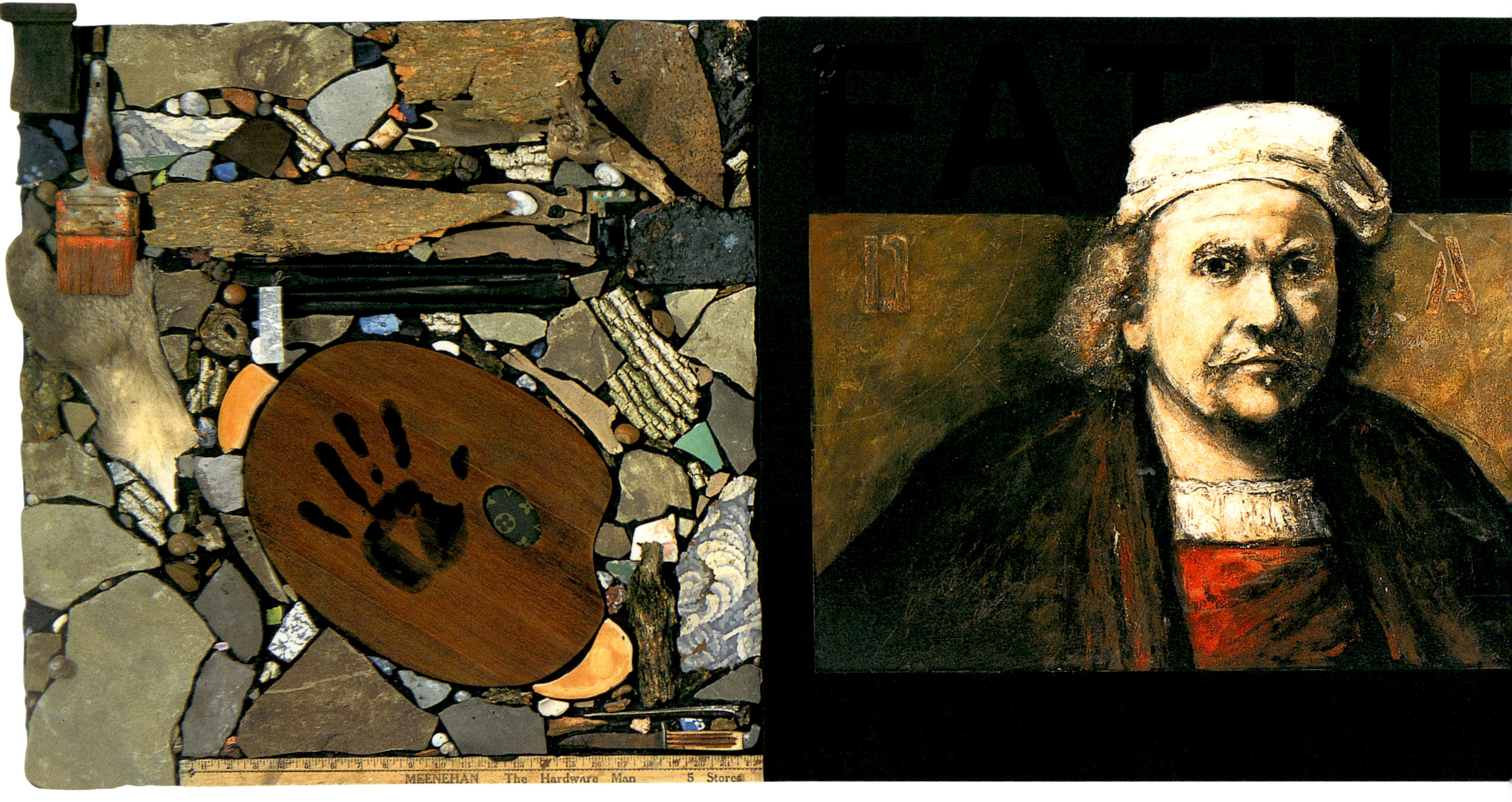
FATHE
MEENEHAN The Hardware Man 5 Stores

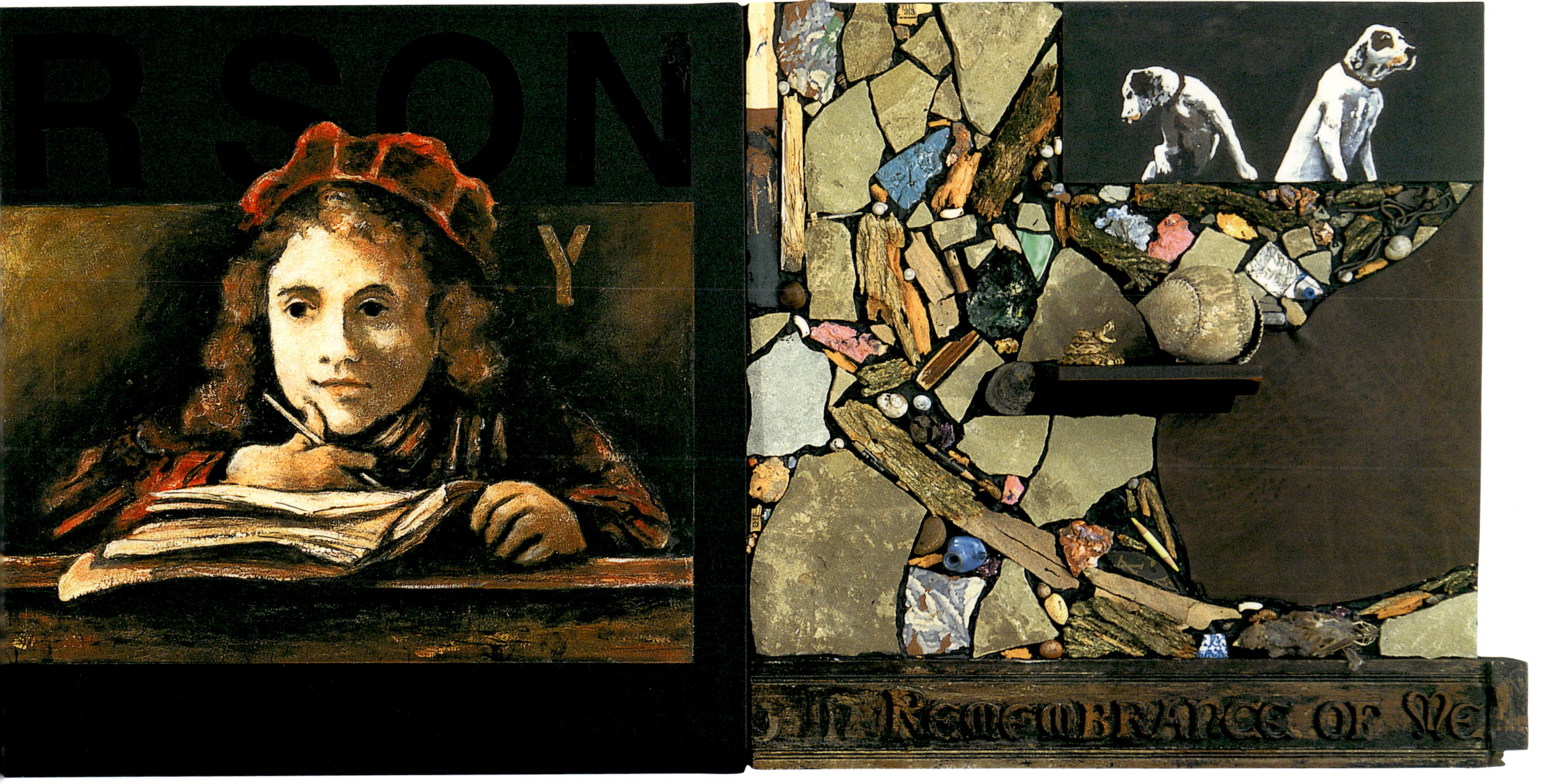

Rembrandt and Titus—Father and Son, 2002
Polymer paint on canvas, wood, slate, leather, metal, found objects; triptych, 30 x 120 x 11.
Collection of Lauren Rogers Museum of Art, Laurel, Mississippi. Photograph by Jack Meyer.

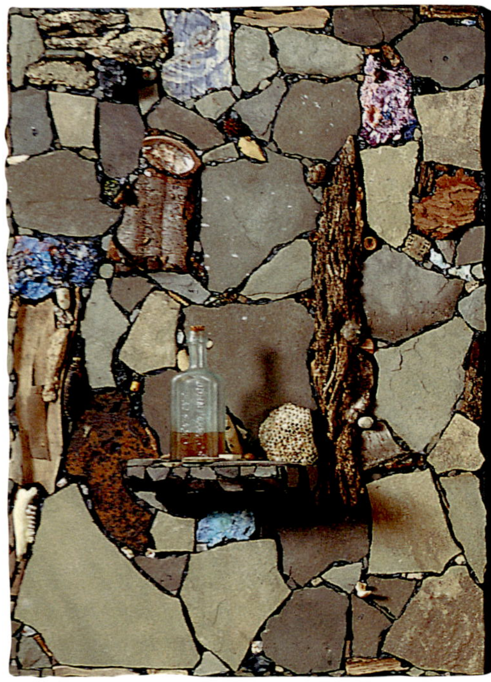

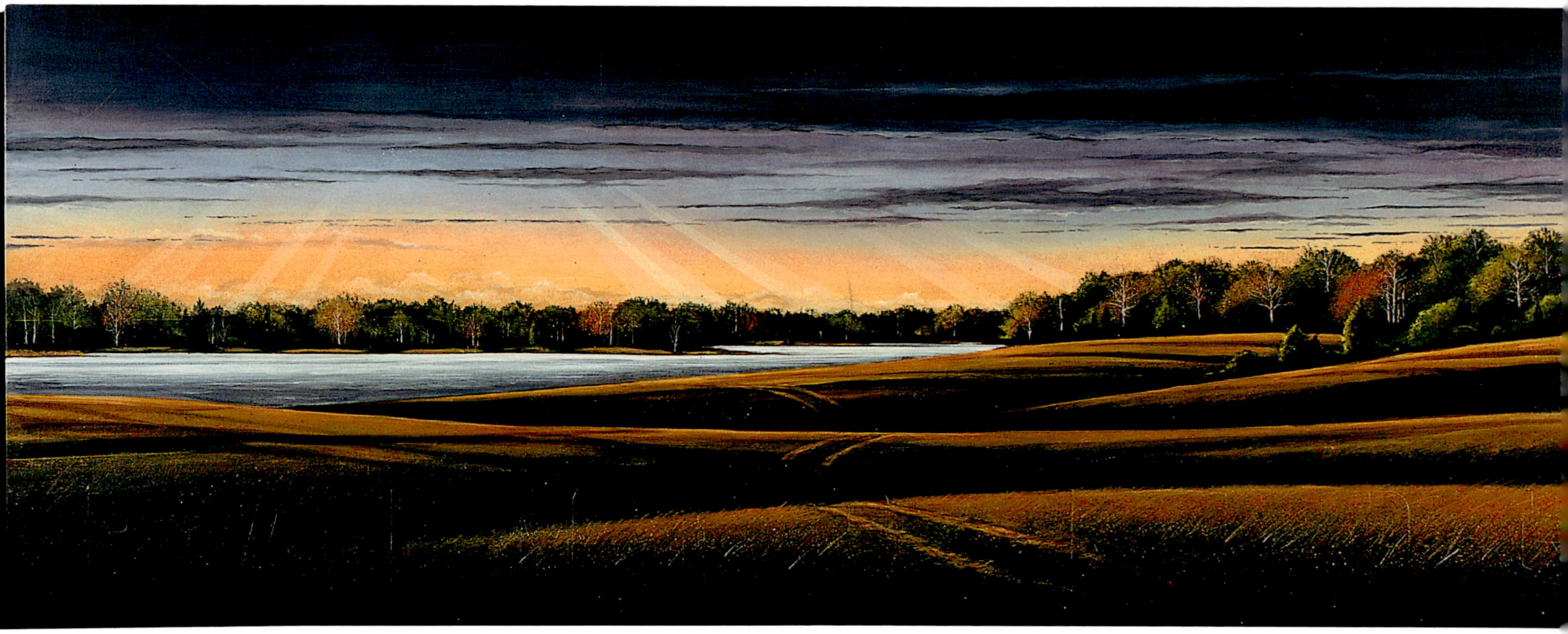

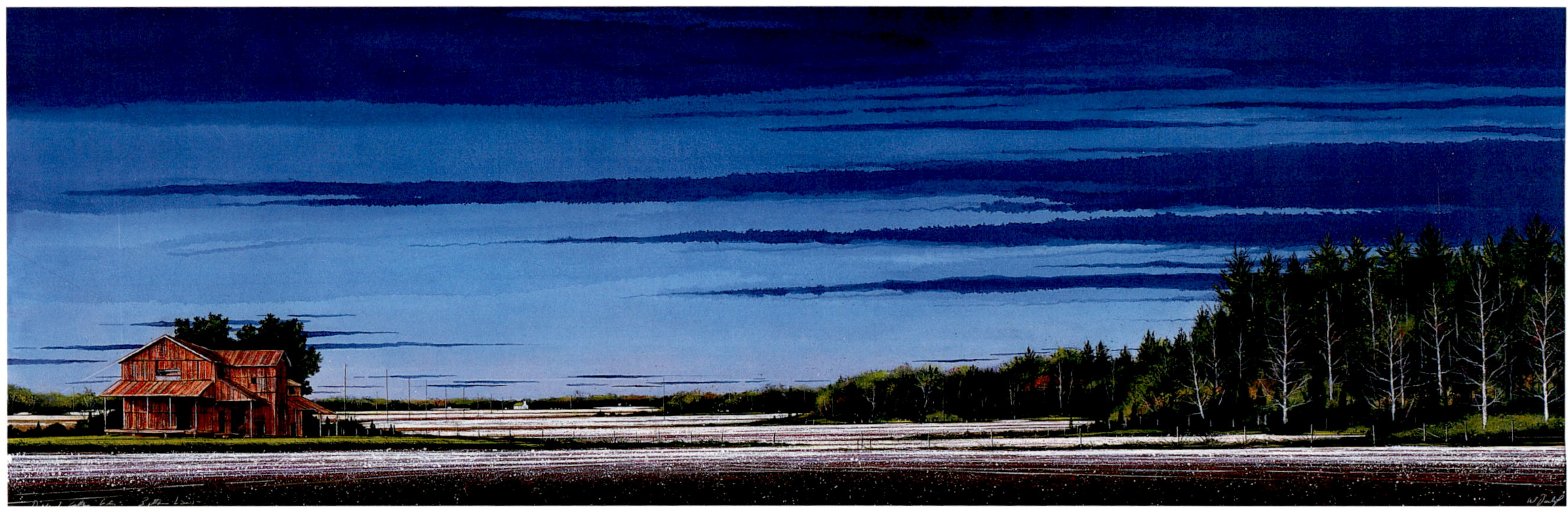

Defunct Cotton Gin, Bottom Land, 2003
Oil paint on paper, 24 x 72. Collection of Fred E. Carl Jr., Greenwood, Mississippi. Photograph by Jack Meyer.

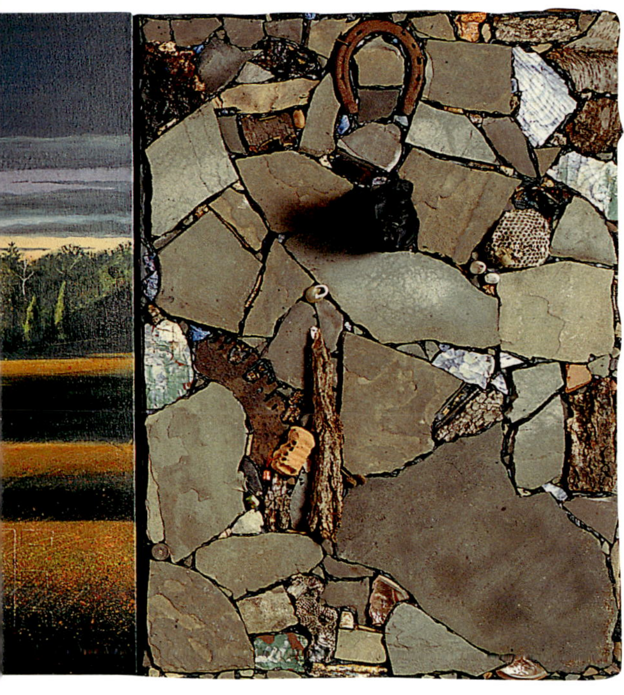

Palmer Ridge, 2002
Polymer paint on canvas, slate, wood, metal, bourbon; triptych, 34 x 96. Collection of Tine and John N. Palmer, Jackson, Mississippi. Photograph by Hubert Worley.

White Dog, 2003–4
Oil paint over ink on paper, triptych, 27 1/2 x 20 1/2. Collection of Luther H. Hodges Jr., Chapel Hill, North Carolina. Photograph by John E. Powell.

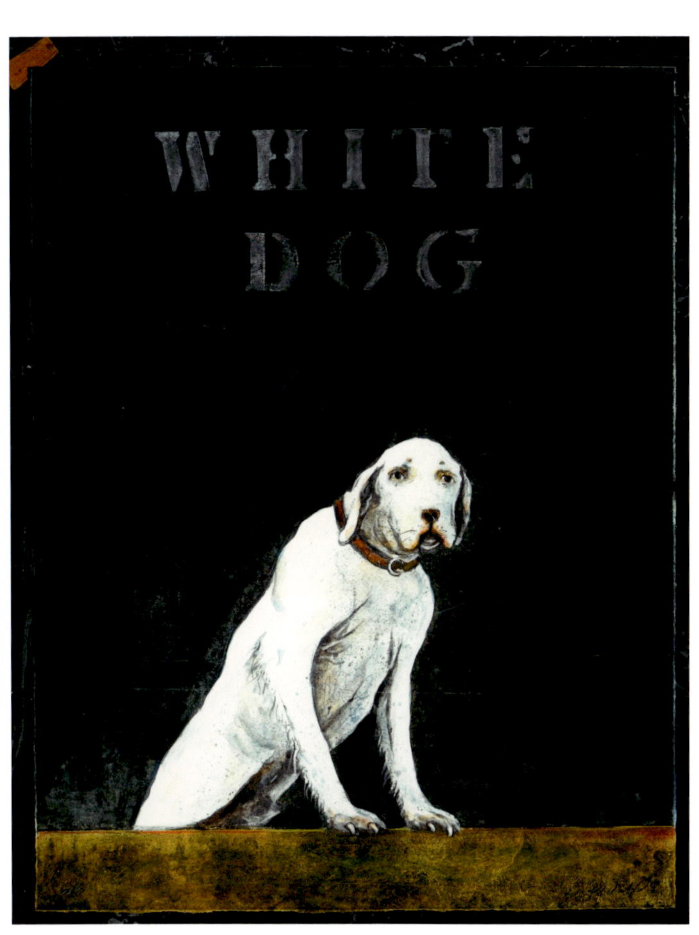

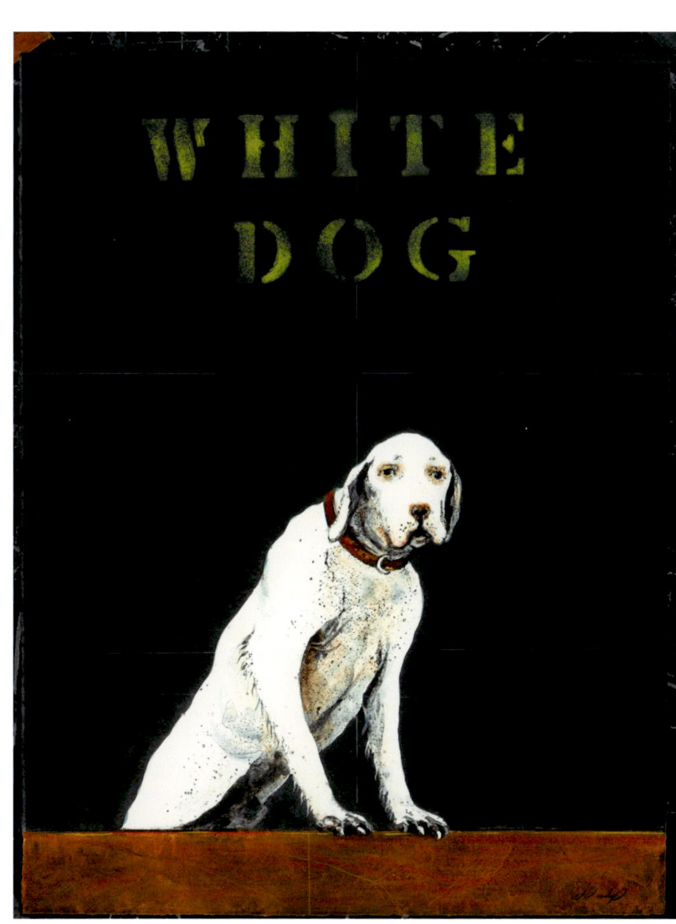

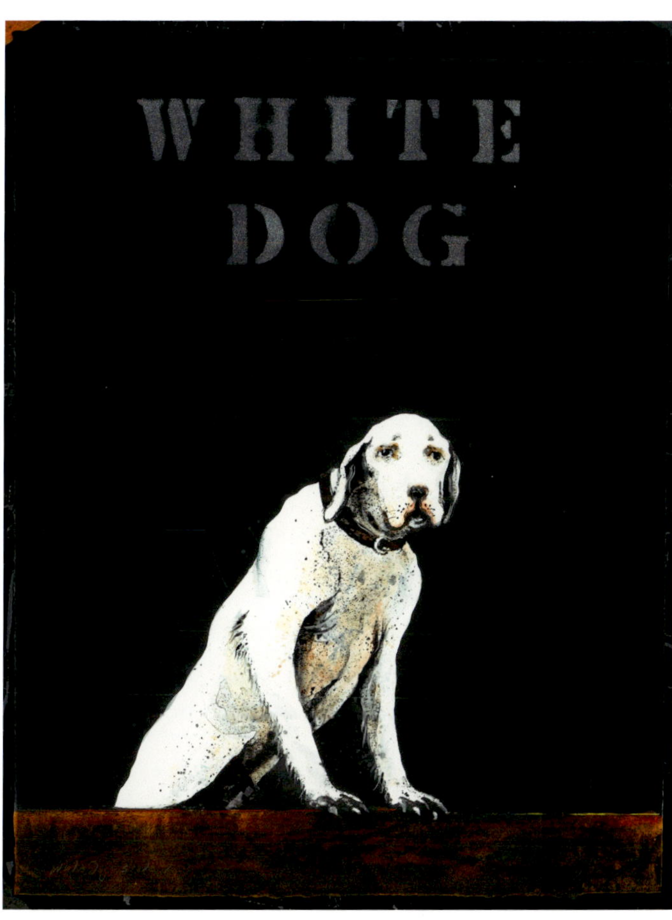

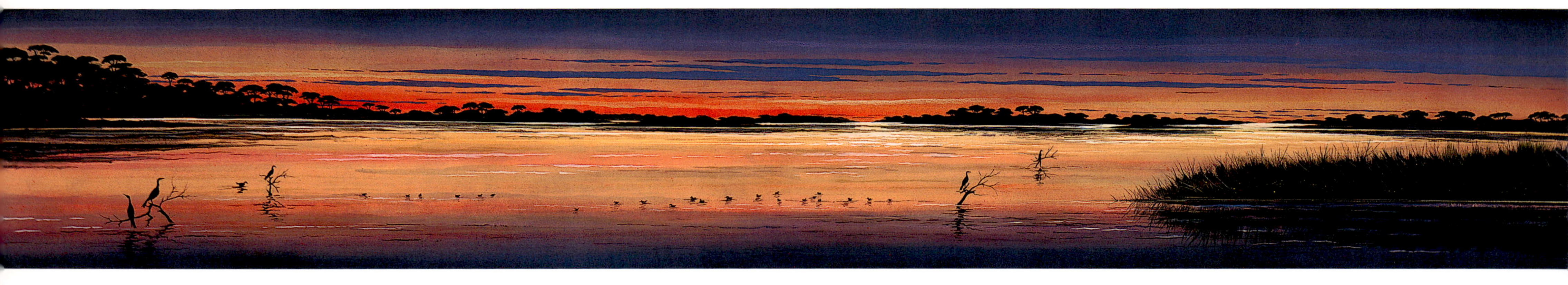

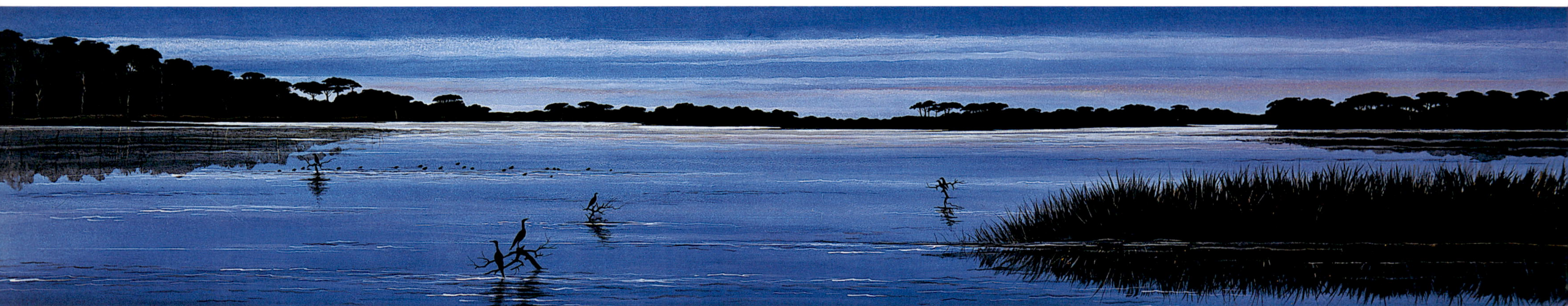

Barrier Light I, 2003
Oil paint and dry pigment on rag paper, 18 x 72. Courtesy of Søren Christensen Gallery, New Orleans, Louisiana. Photograph by Jack Meyer.

Barrier Light—Series II, 2004
Oil wash and dry pigment on rag paper, 24 x 72. Collection of Gina and David Collis, Winterpark, Florida. Photograph by Jack Meyer.

Fall Line Valley Watch, 1990
Oil paint and dry pigment on paper, 34 x 72. Collection of Jill and Robert St. John, Hattiesburg, Mississippi. Photograph by Hubert Worley.

House Place—Stock Tracks, 2004
Oil paint and dry pigment on rag paper, 28 x 72. Collection of Luther H. Hodges Jr., Chapel Hill, North Carolina. Photograph by Linda Burgess.

Bull Bison and Wounded Knee, 1995–96
Polymer paint, wood, bone, bronze, slate, linoleum, horn, 27 1/2 x 87 x 8. Collection of Martha Dale and Eddie Fritz, McLean, Virginia. Photograph by Jack Kotz.

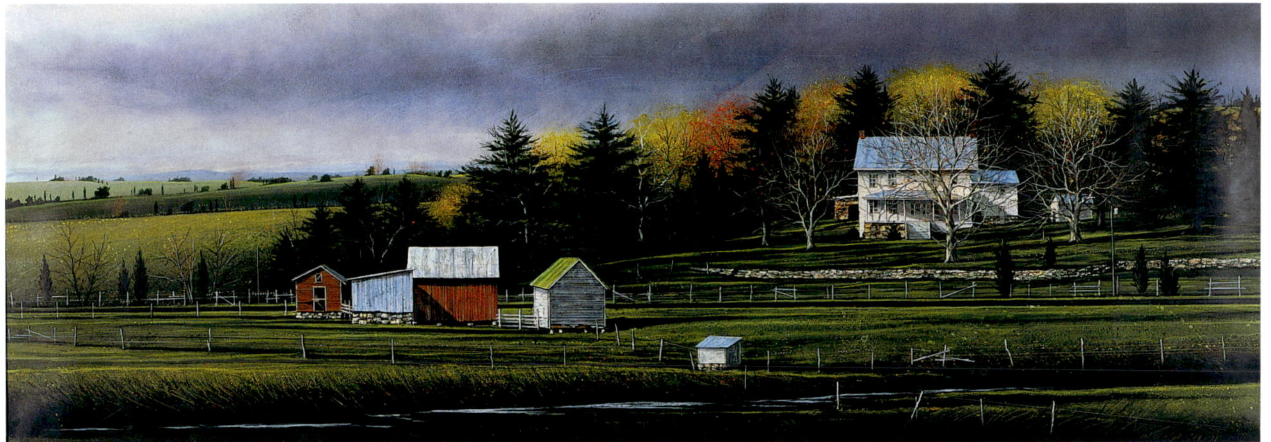

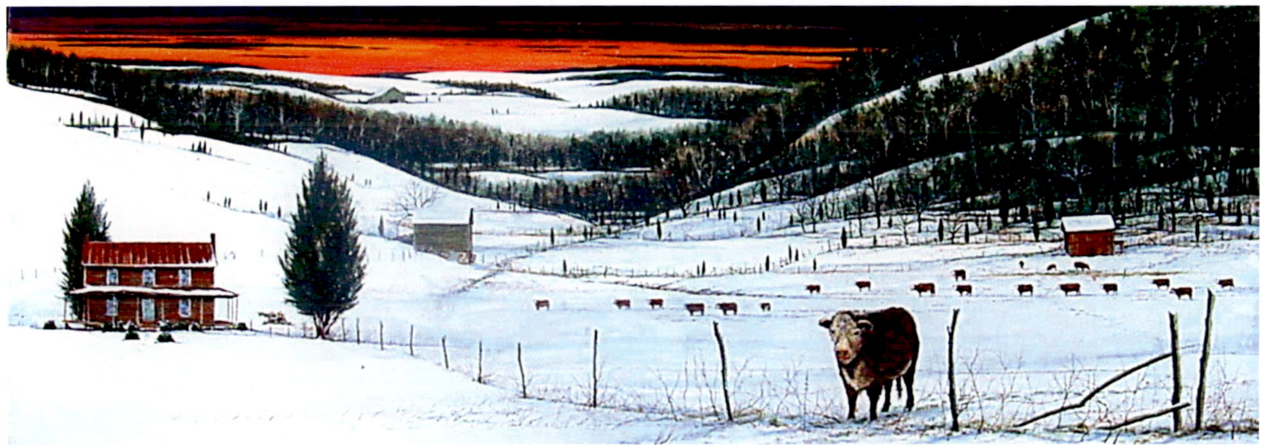

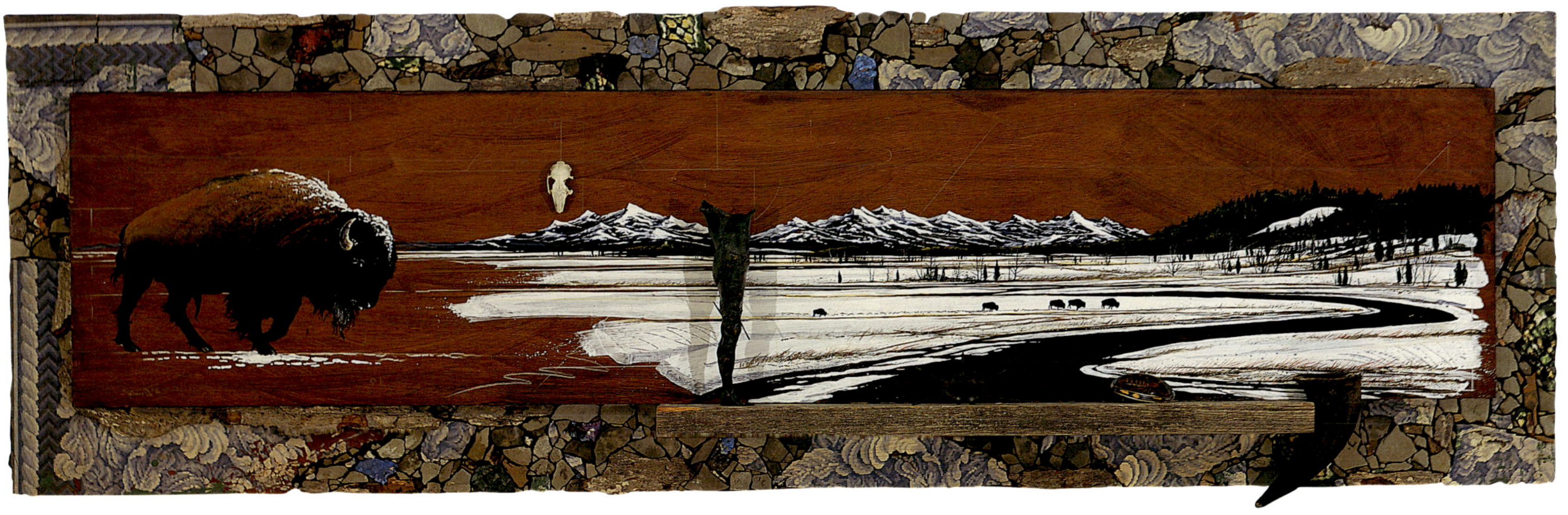

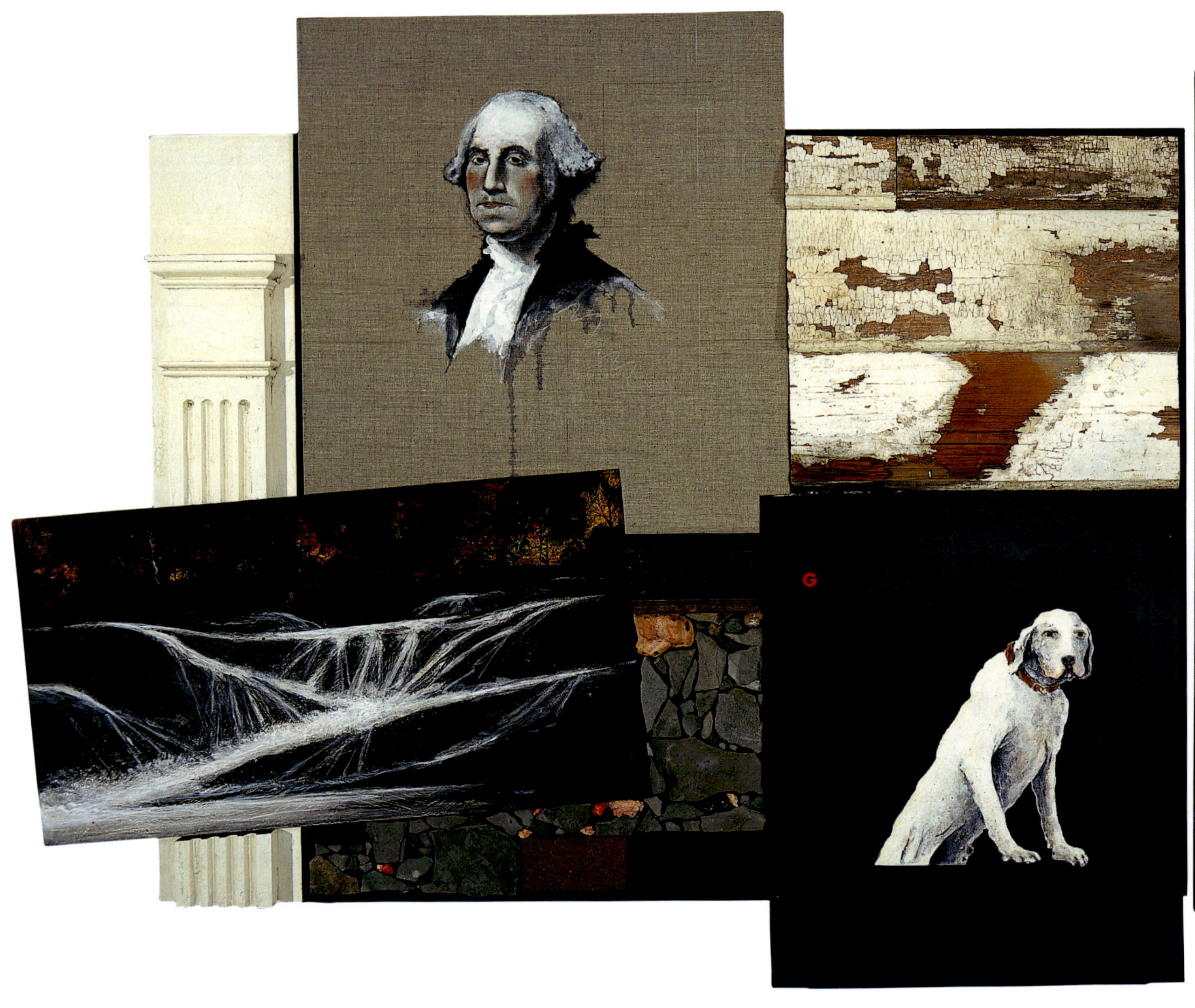

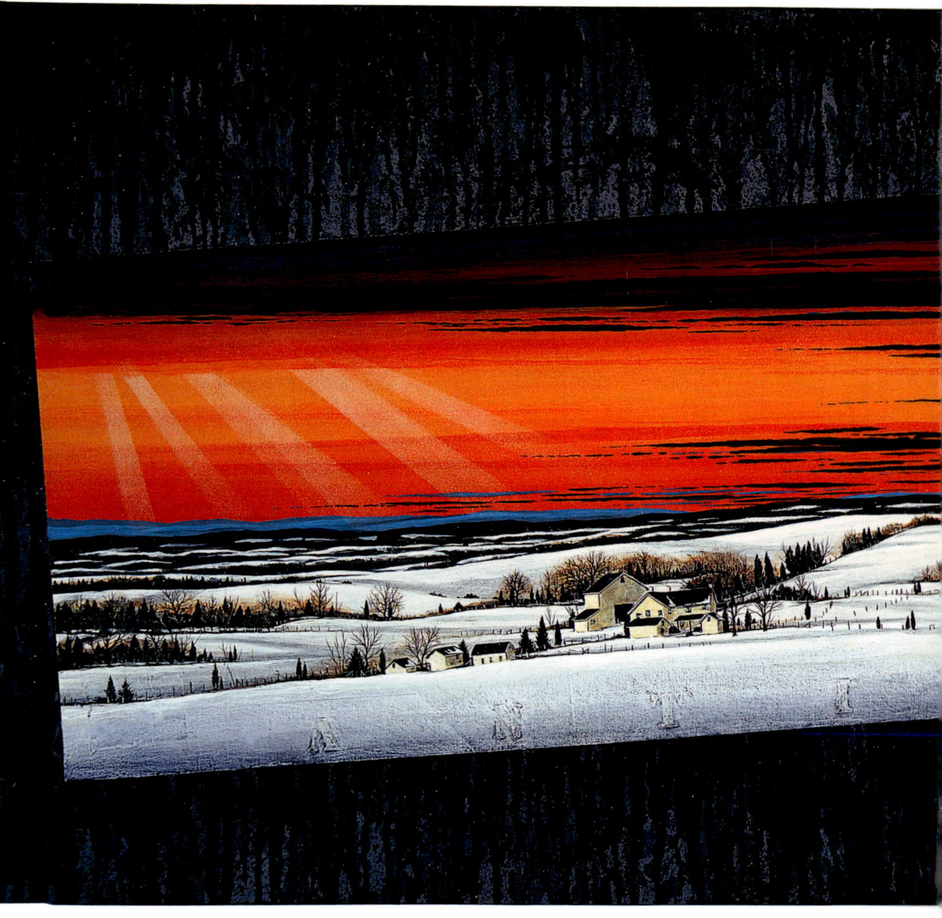

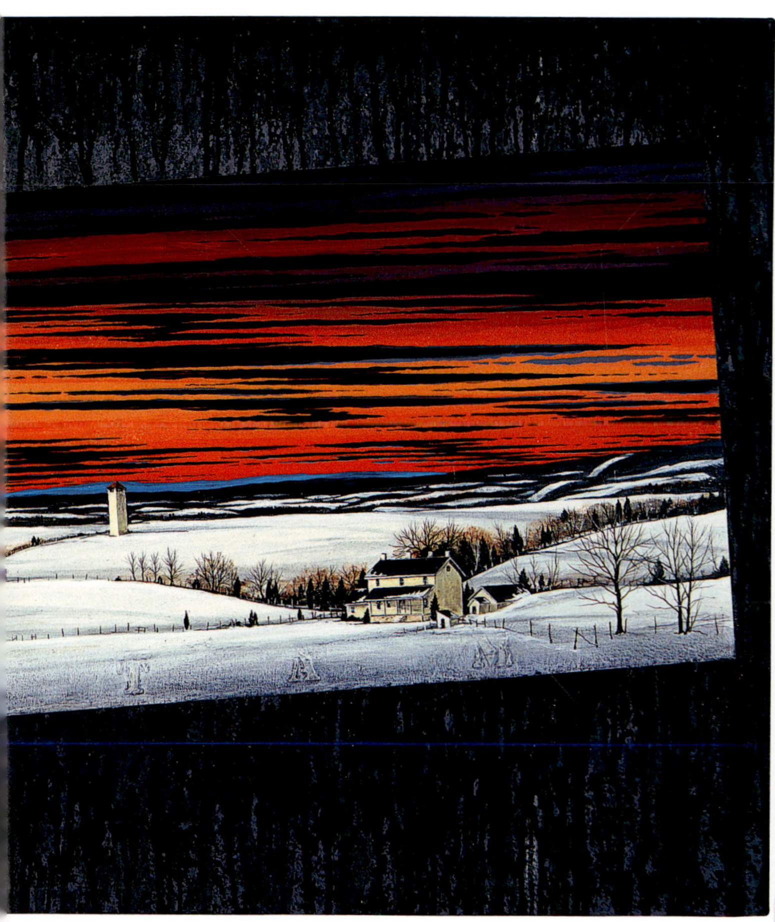

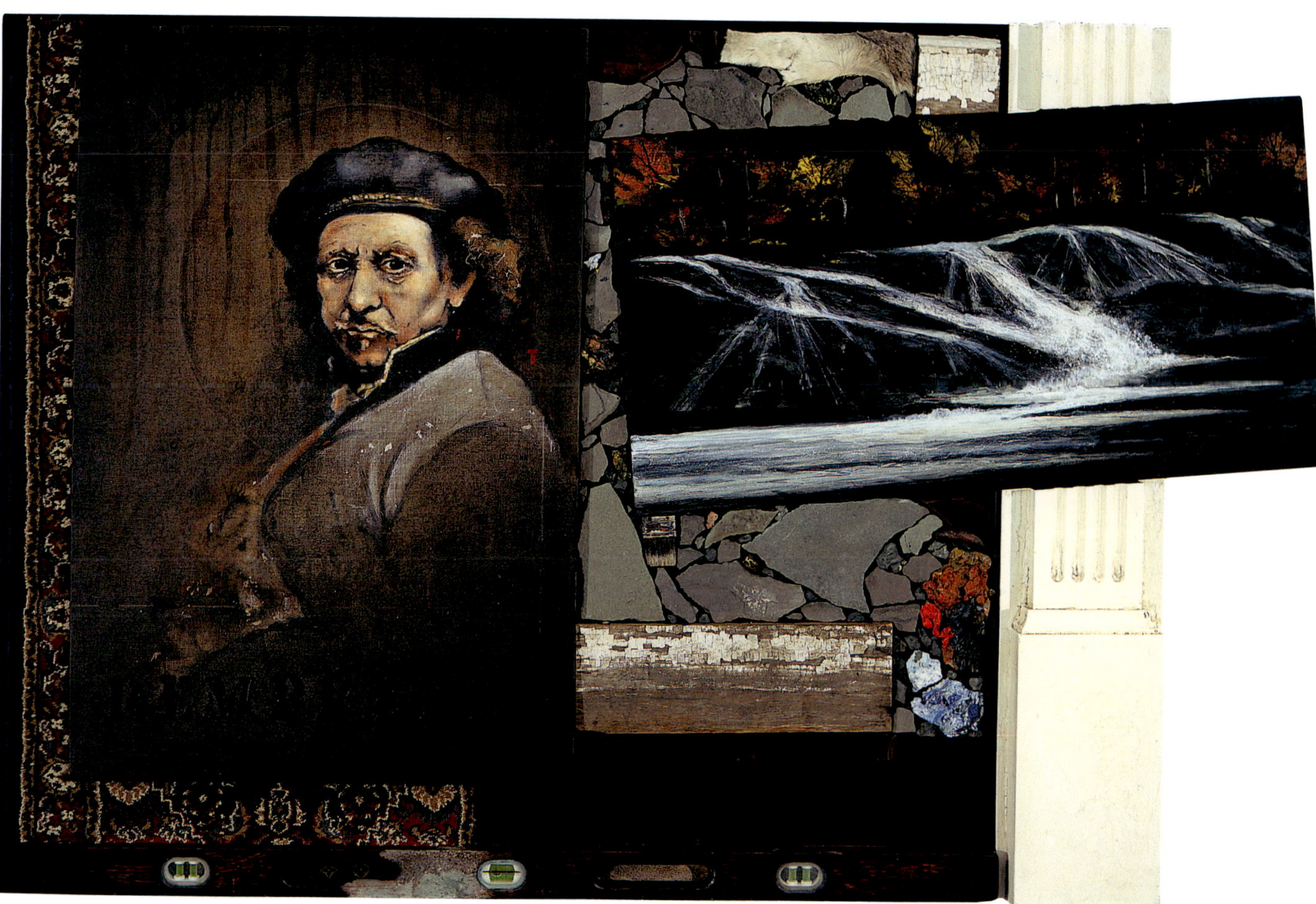

Landscape and Variable—Landscape Askew, 2003

Polymer paint on canvas, slate, wood, leather, 41 x 180. Collection of Washington, D.C., Convention Center. Photograph by Jack Meyer.

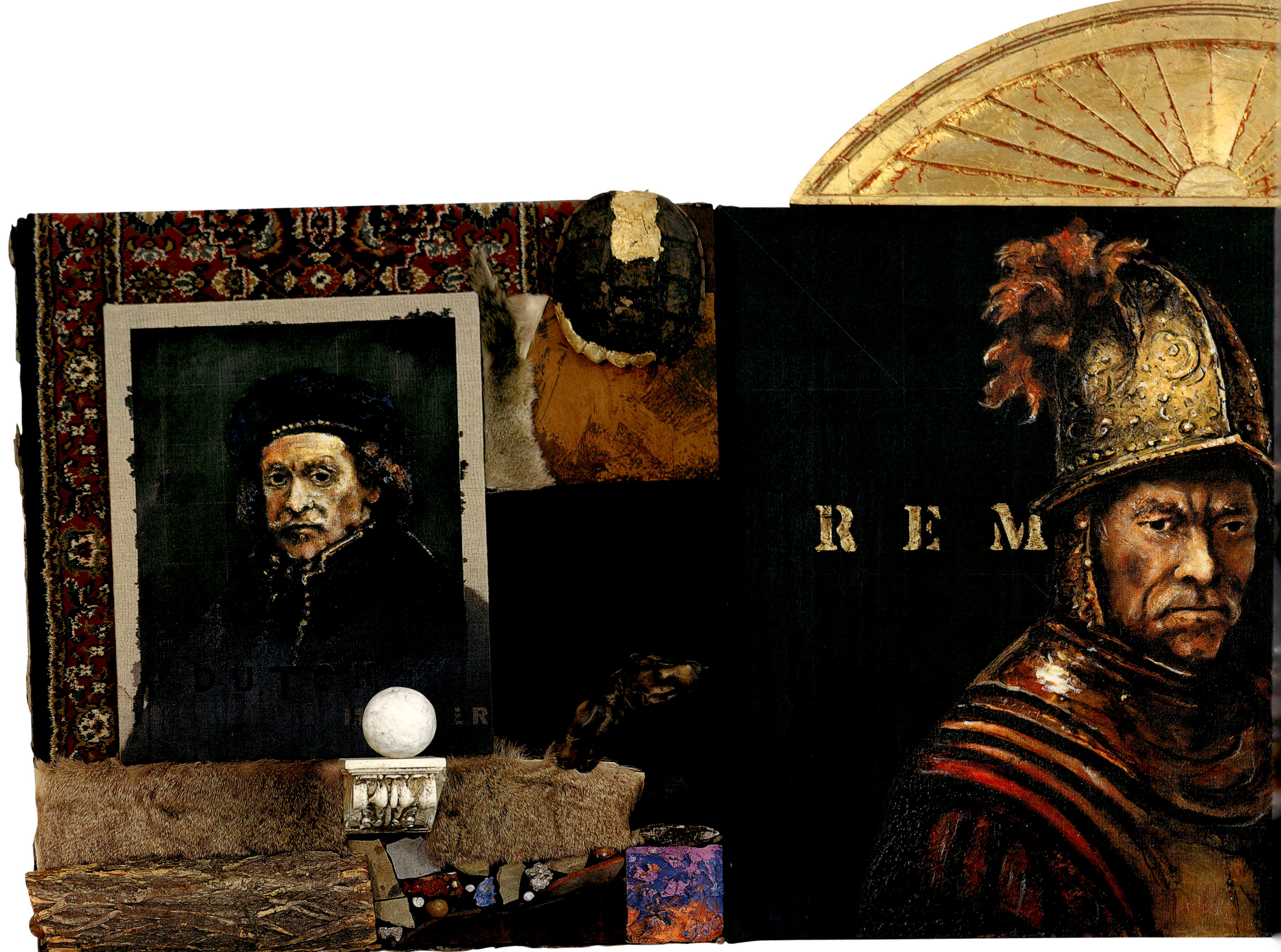
R E M

All That Glitters . . ., 2004

Wood, canvas, clay, slate, tortoise shell, velvet, leather, gold leaf, tintype, found objects; triptych, 32 1/2 x 102. Collection of Sharon and Bruce Bradley, Washington, D.C. Photograph by Jack Meyer.

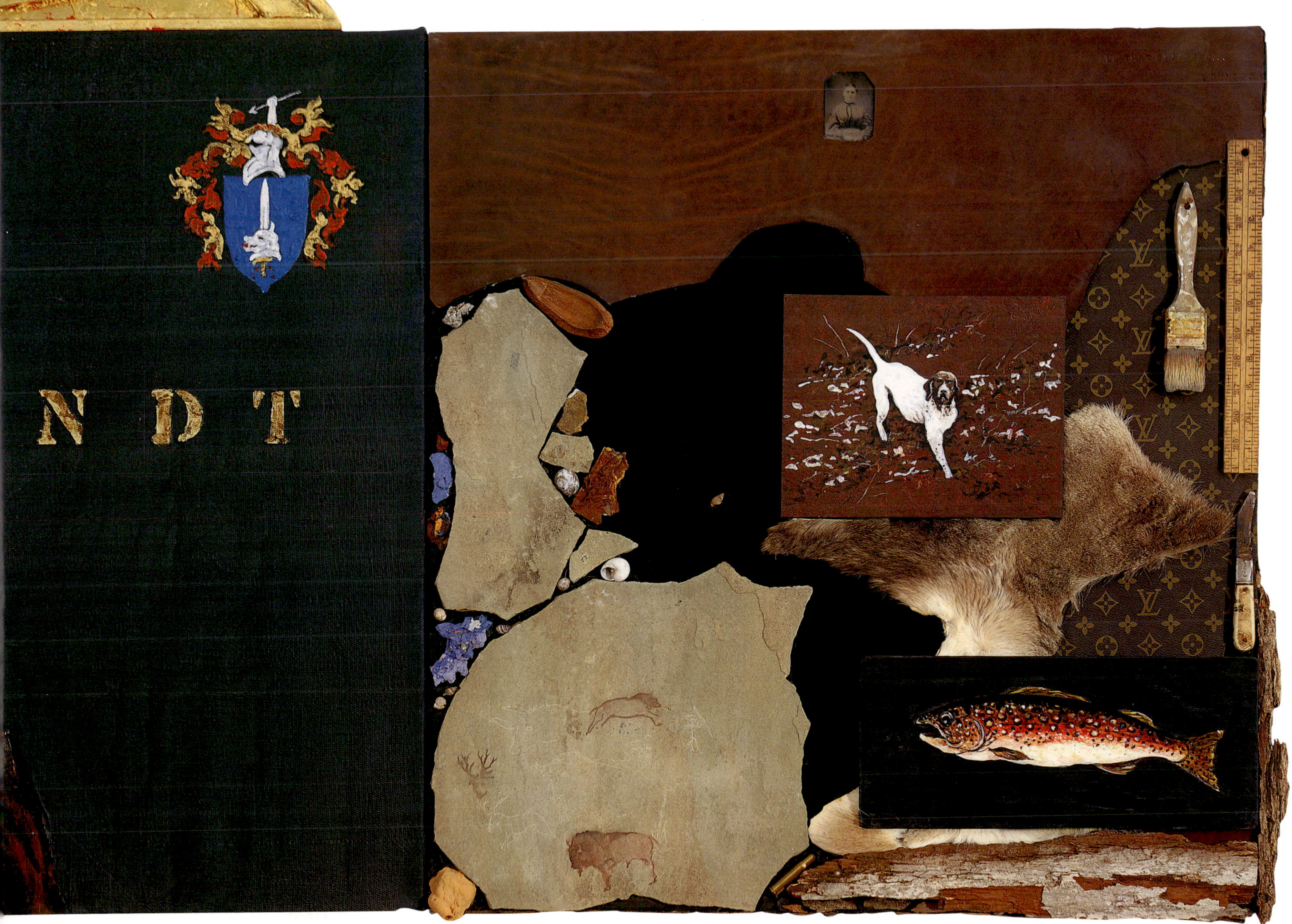

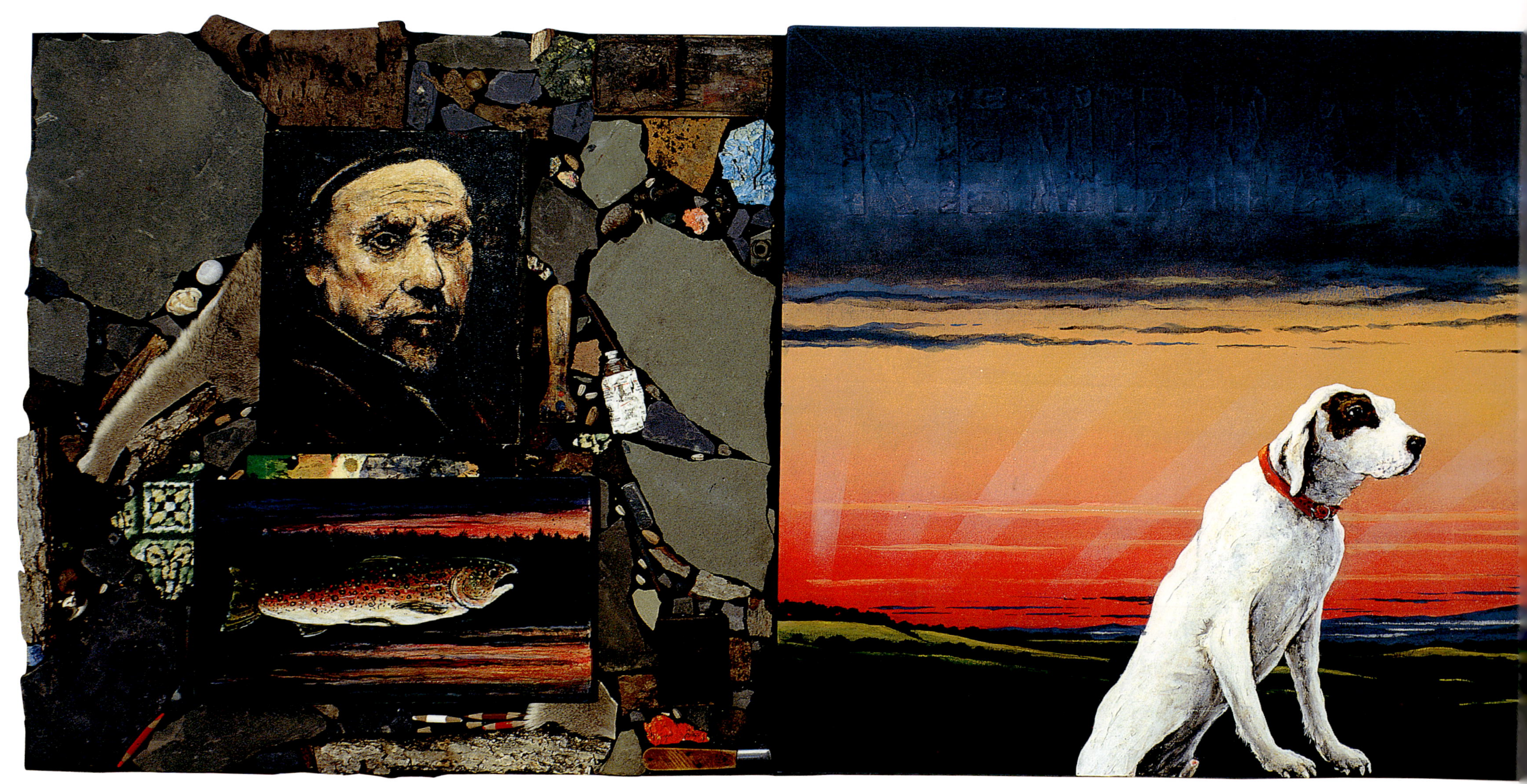

Rembrandt and Spook, 2005
Mixed media construction, triptych,
30 x 120. Private collection. Photograph by
Jack Meyer.

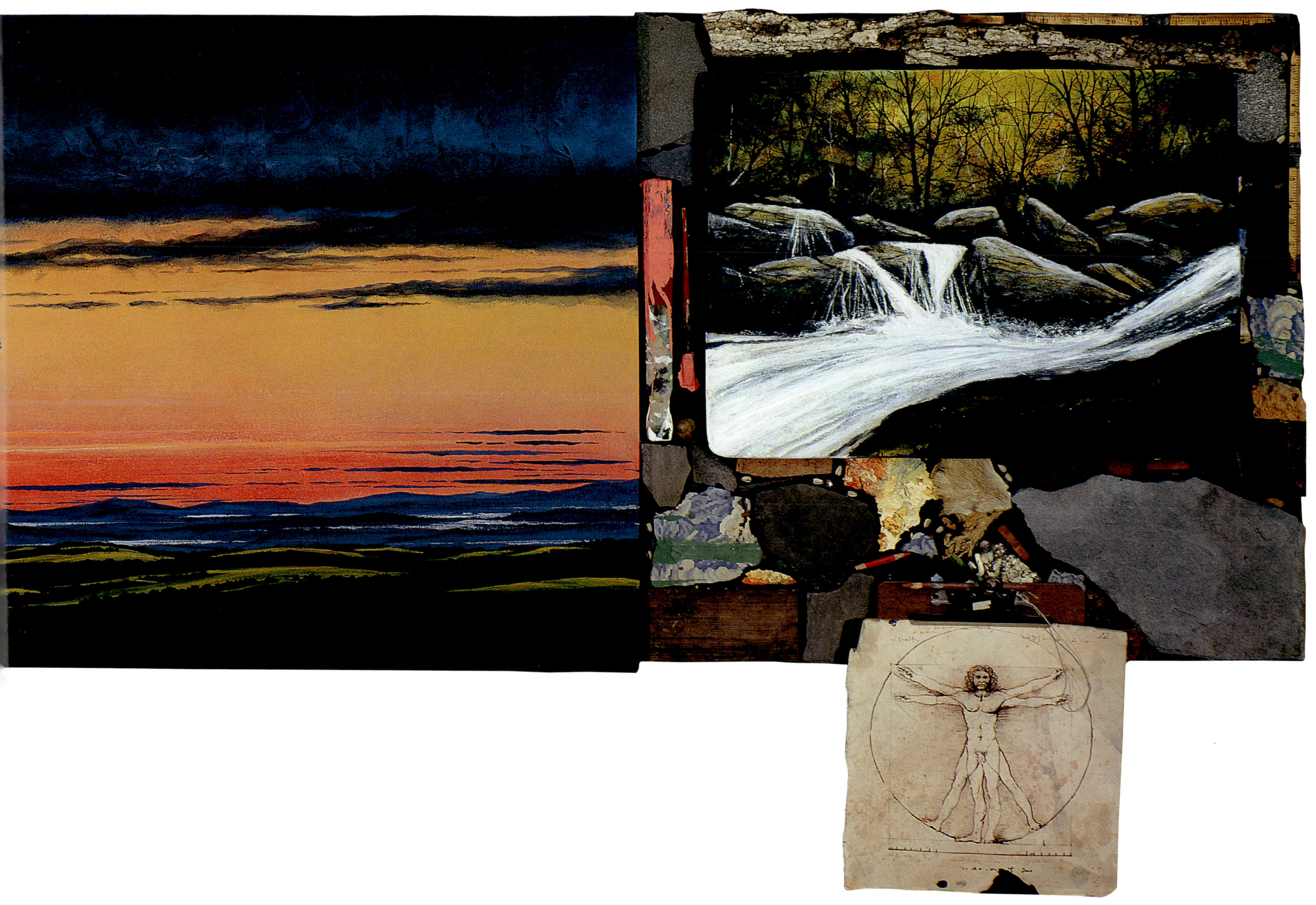

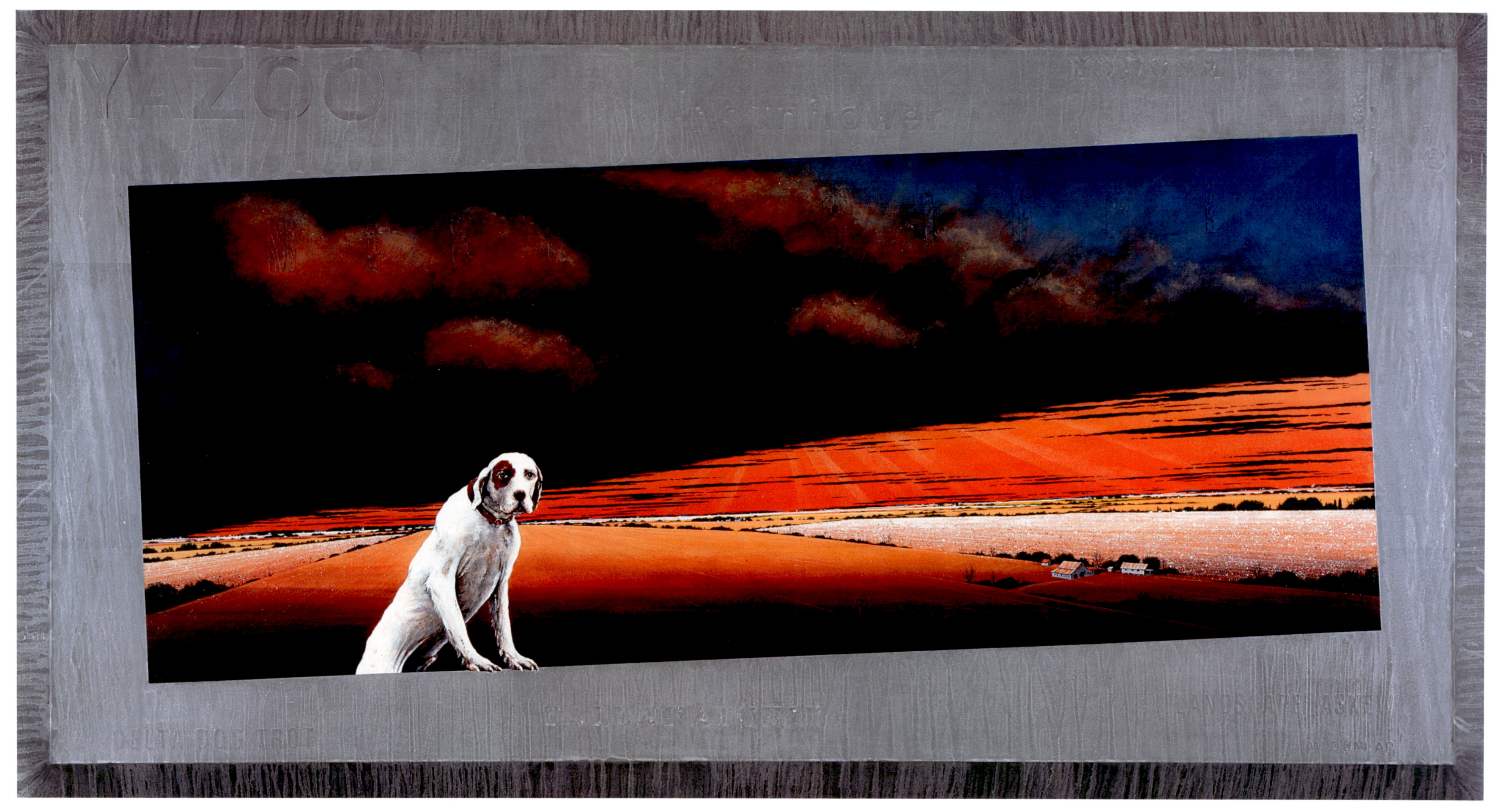

Delta Dog Trot, Landscape Askew, 2003
Polymer paint on canvas, 78 x 144. Collection of Viking Range Corporation, The Alluvian Hotel, Greenwood, Mississippi. Photograph by Tom Joynt.

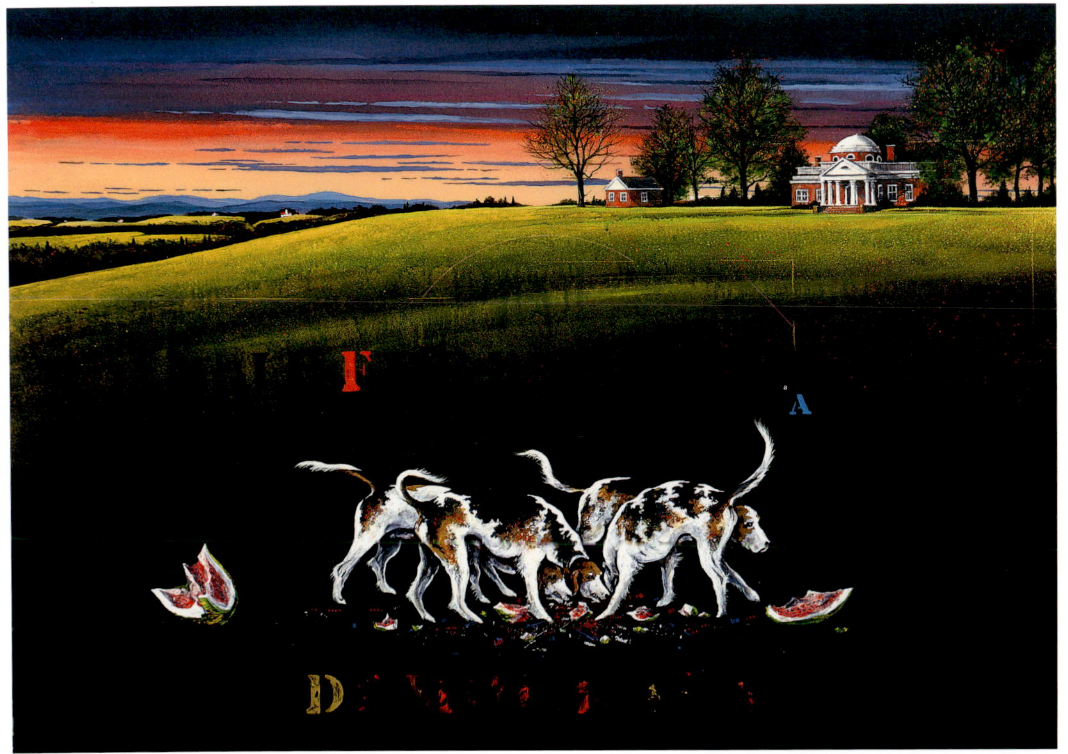

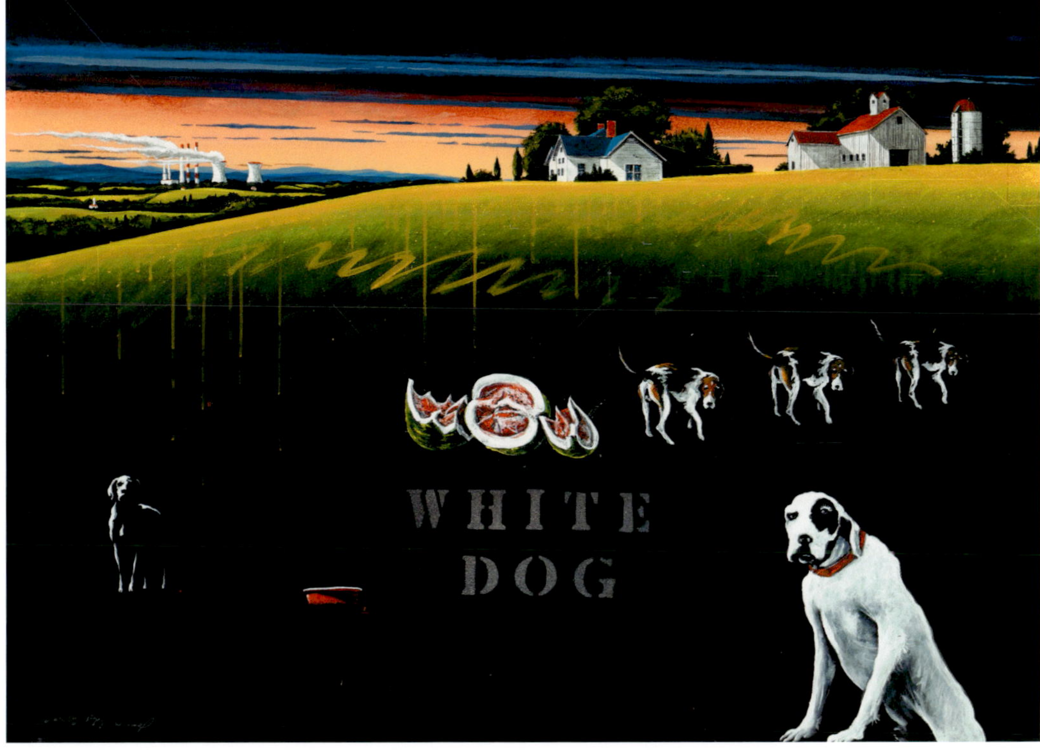

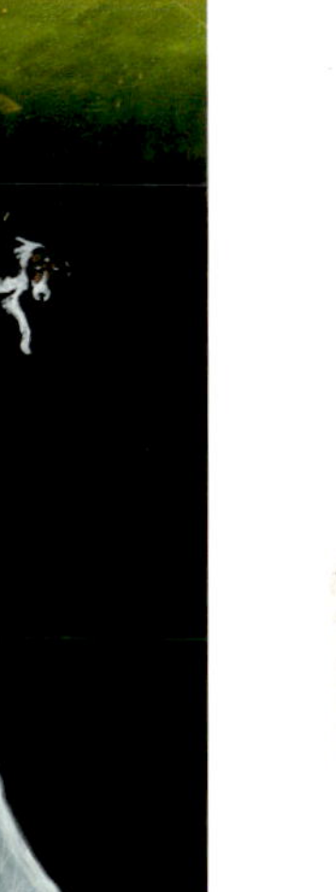

Jeffersonian Democracy—A Work in Progress, 2005
Polymer and oil paint on rag paper, 38 x 51. Collection of Julia Reed and John Pierce, New Orleans, Louisiana. Photograph by Jack Meyer.

White Dog Allegory, 2005
Oil and polymer paint on rag paper, 39 x 52. Private collection. Photograph by John E. Powell.

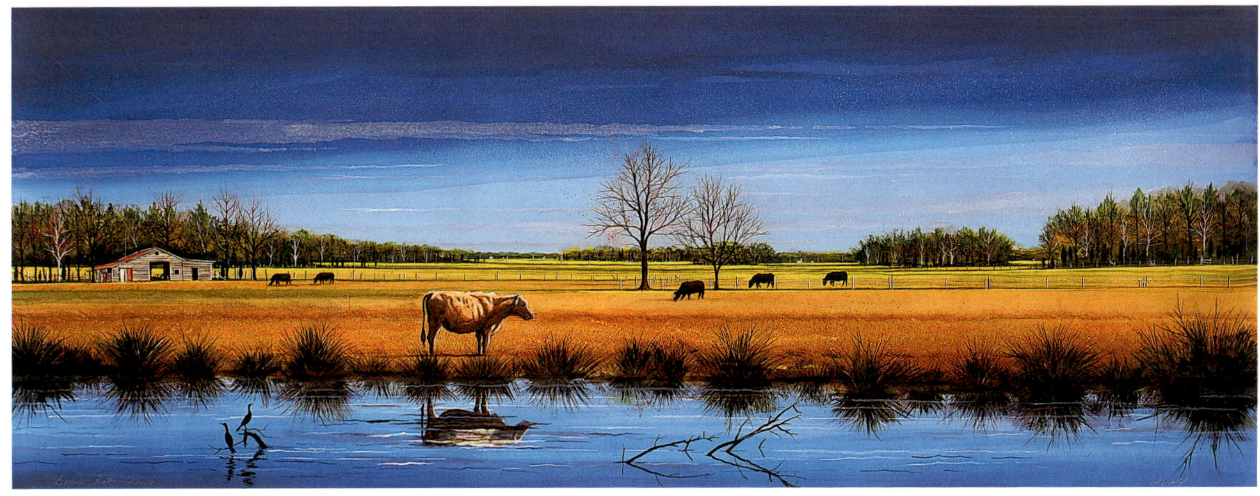

Bovine and Bottom Land, 2005
Oil wash and dry pigment on rag paper, 24 x 60. Collection of Mr. and Mrs. Tom Johnson, Atlanta, Georgia. Photograph by Jack Meyer.

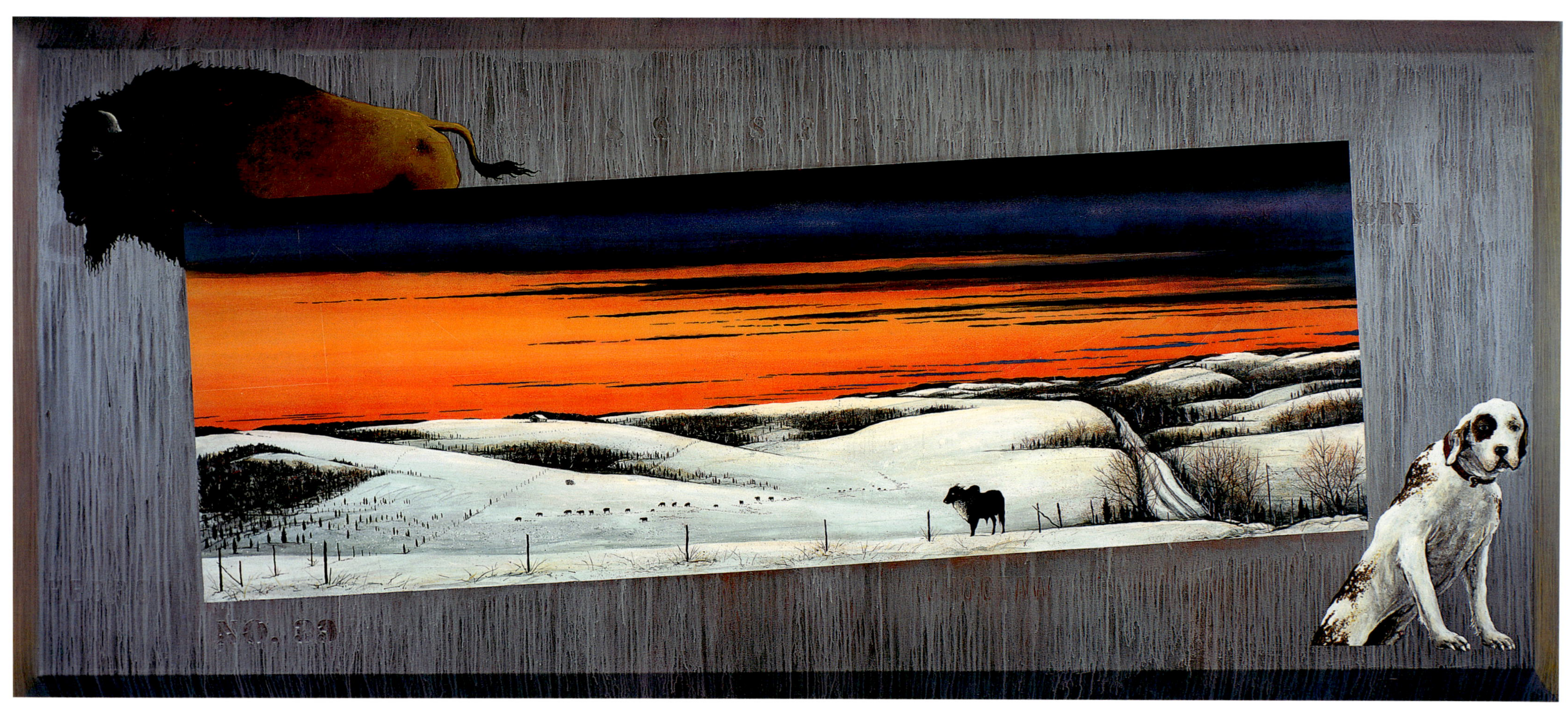

Landscape Askew/Timber Line, 2005
Polymer paint on canvas, 60 x 132. Collection of Governor Ray Mabus, Ridgeland, Mississippi. Photograph by Jack Meyer.

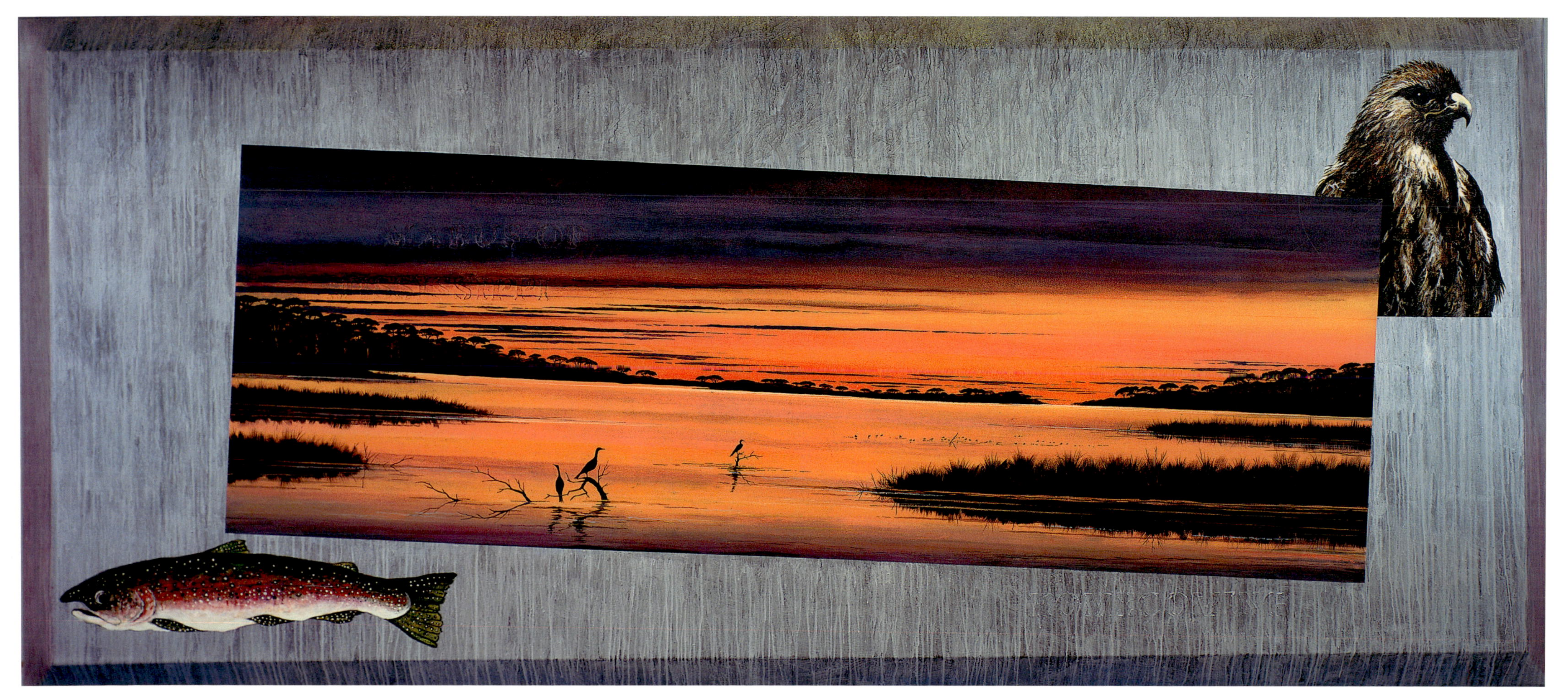

Landscape Askew/Barrier Light, 2005
Polymer paint on canvas, 60 x 132. Collection of Governor Ray Mabus, Ridgeland, Mississippi. Photograph by Jack Meyer.

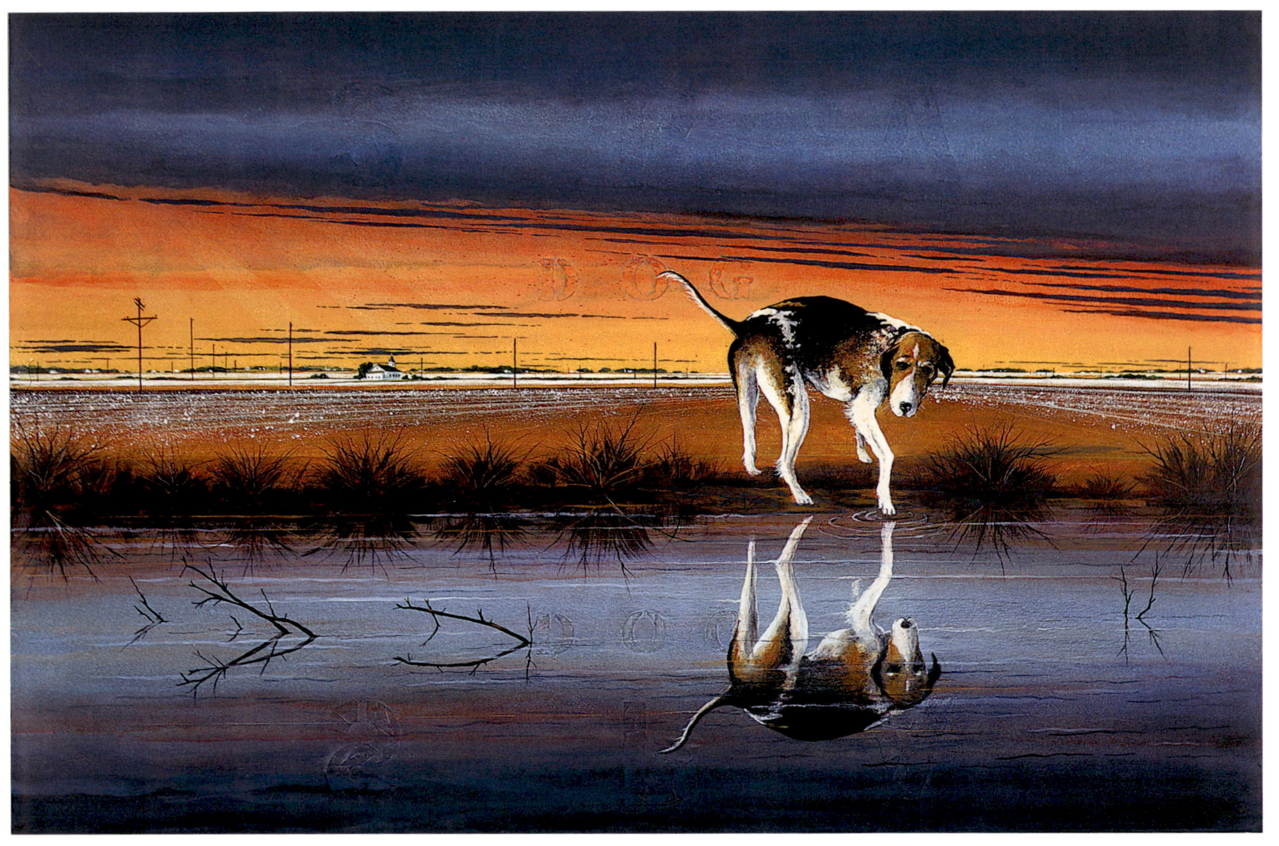

Narcissus—Spa Dog, 2005
Polymer paint on canvas, 40 x 66. Collection of Viking Range Corporation, The Alluvian Hotel, Greenwood, Mississippi. Photograph by Jack Meyer.

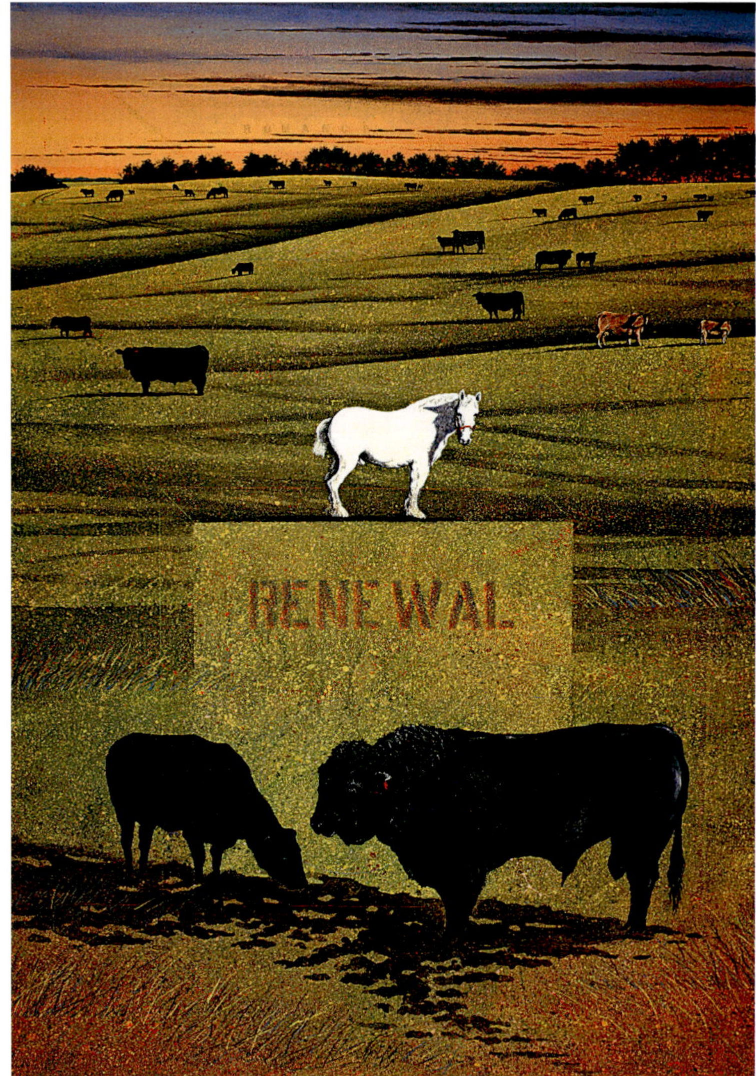

Riverdale Renewal, 2005
Polymer paint on canvas, 48 x 72. Collection of Donna and Jim Barksdale, Ridgeland, Mississippi. Photograph by Jack Meyer.

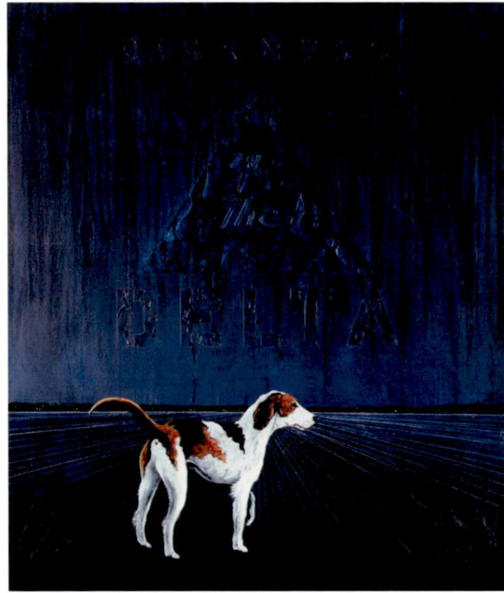

Darkness on the Delta, 2005
Polymer paint on canvas, 60 x 140. Collection of Viking Range Corporation, The Alluvian Hotel, Greenwood, Mississippi. Photograph by Jack Meyer.

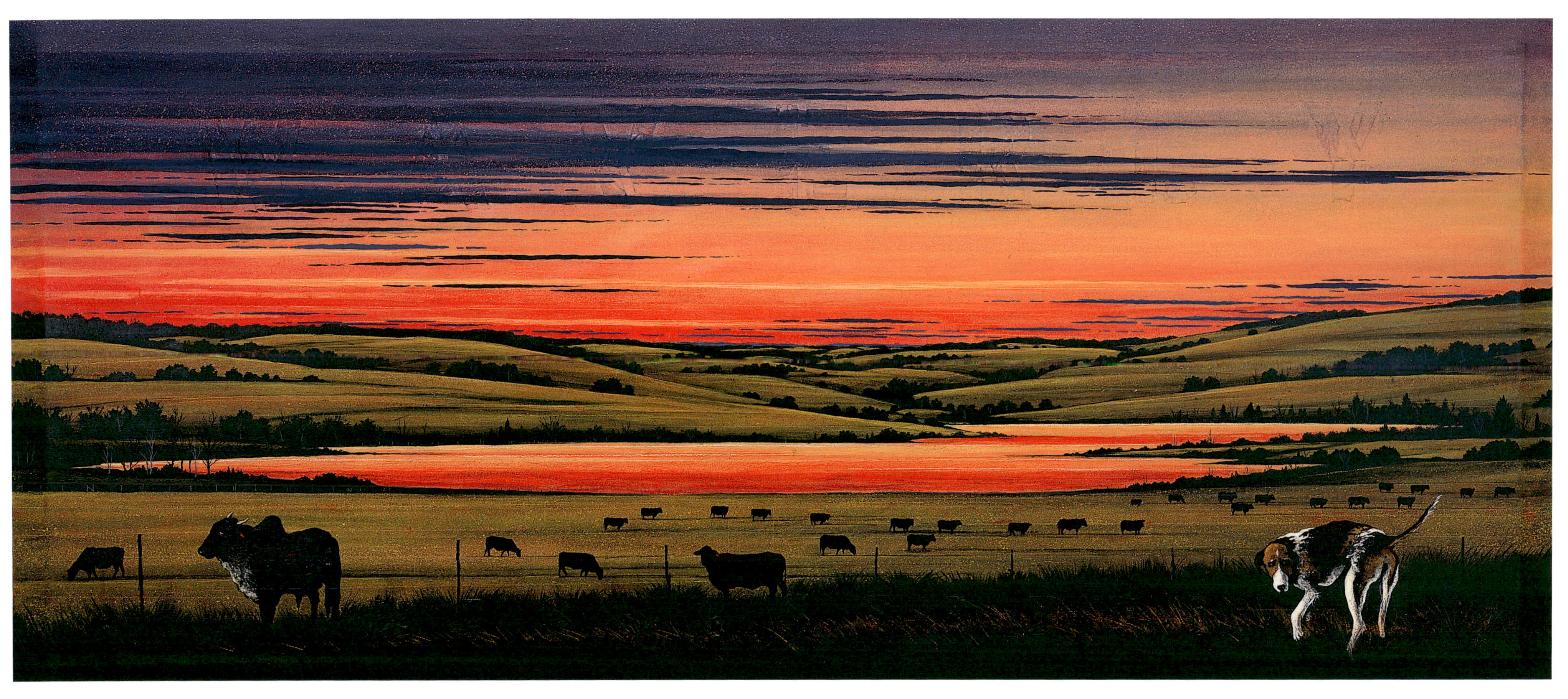

Early Light—Rolling Hills, 2006
Polymer paint on canvas, 35 x 77. Collection of Mr. and Mrs. George Bryan, Westpoint, Mississippi. Photograph by Jack Meyer.

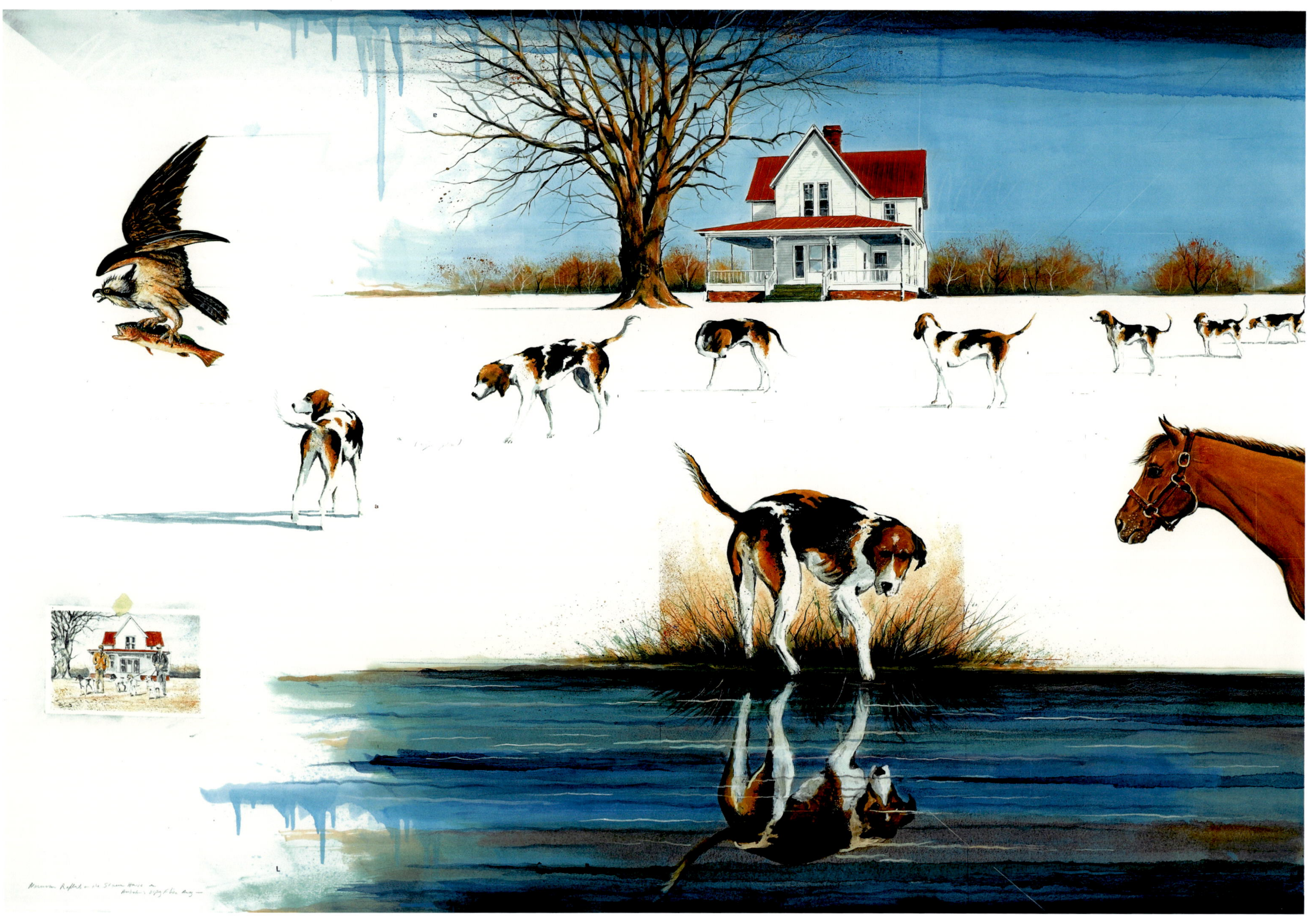

Narcissus Reflects on the Starnes House as Audubon's Osprey Flies Away, 2005
Oil paint and dry pigment on rag paper, 42 x 61. Private collection. Photograph by John E. Powell.

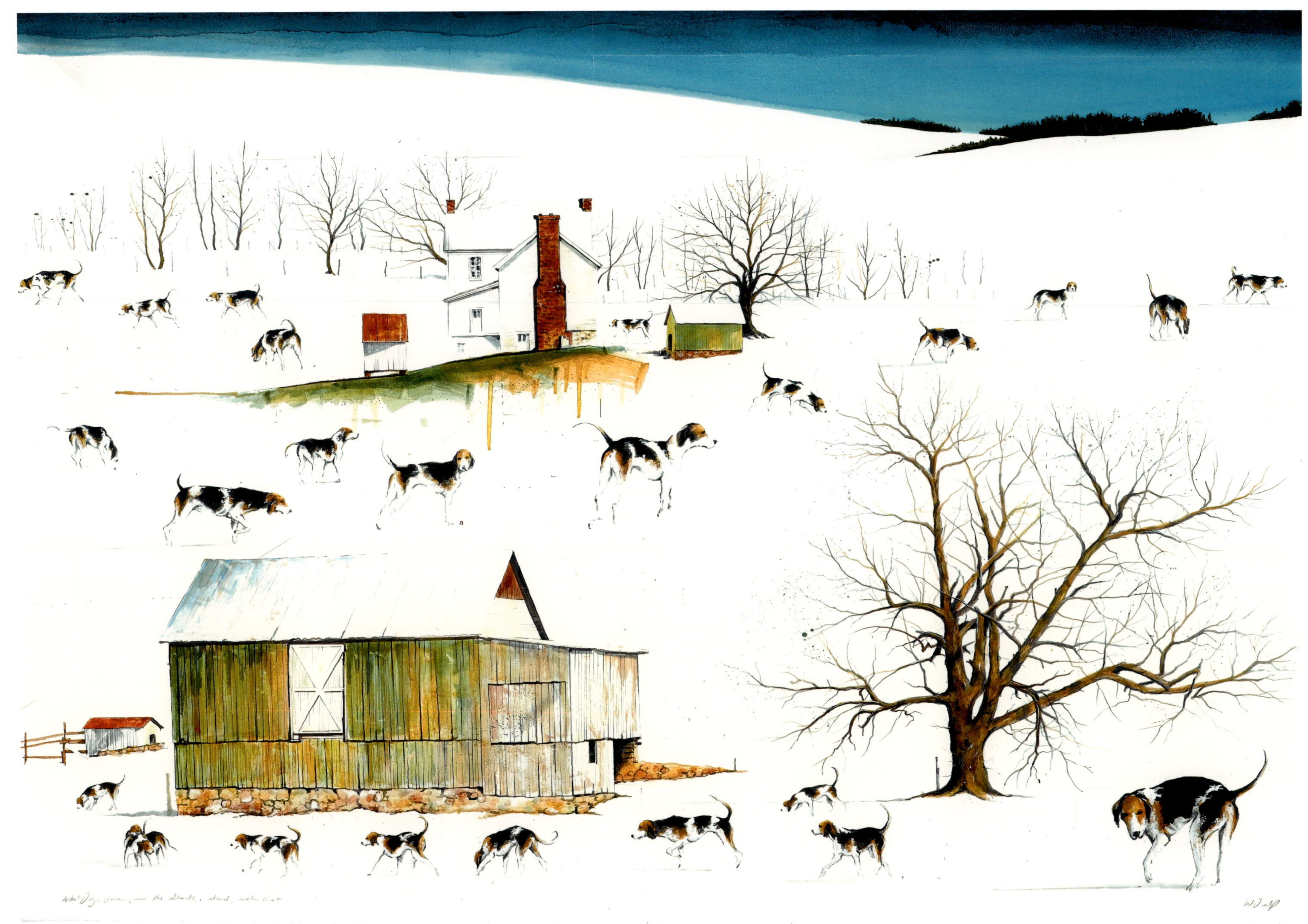

What Dogs Dream: The Ultimate, Eternal, Endless Hunt, 2005
Oil paint and dry pigment on rag paper, 42 x 61. Private collection. Photograph by John E. Powell.

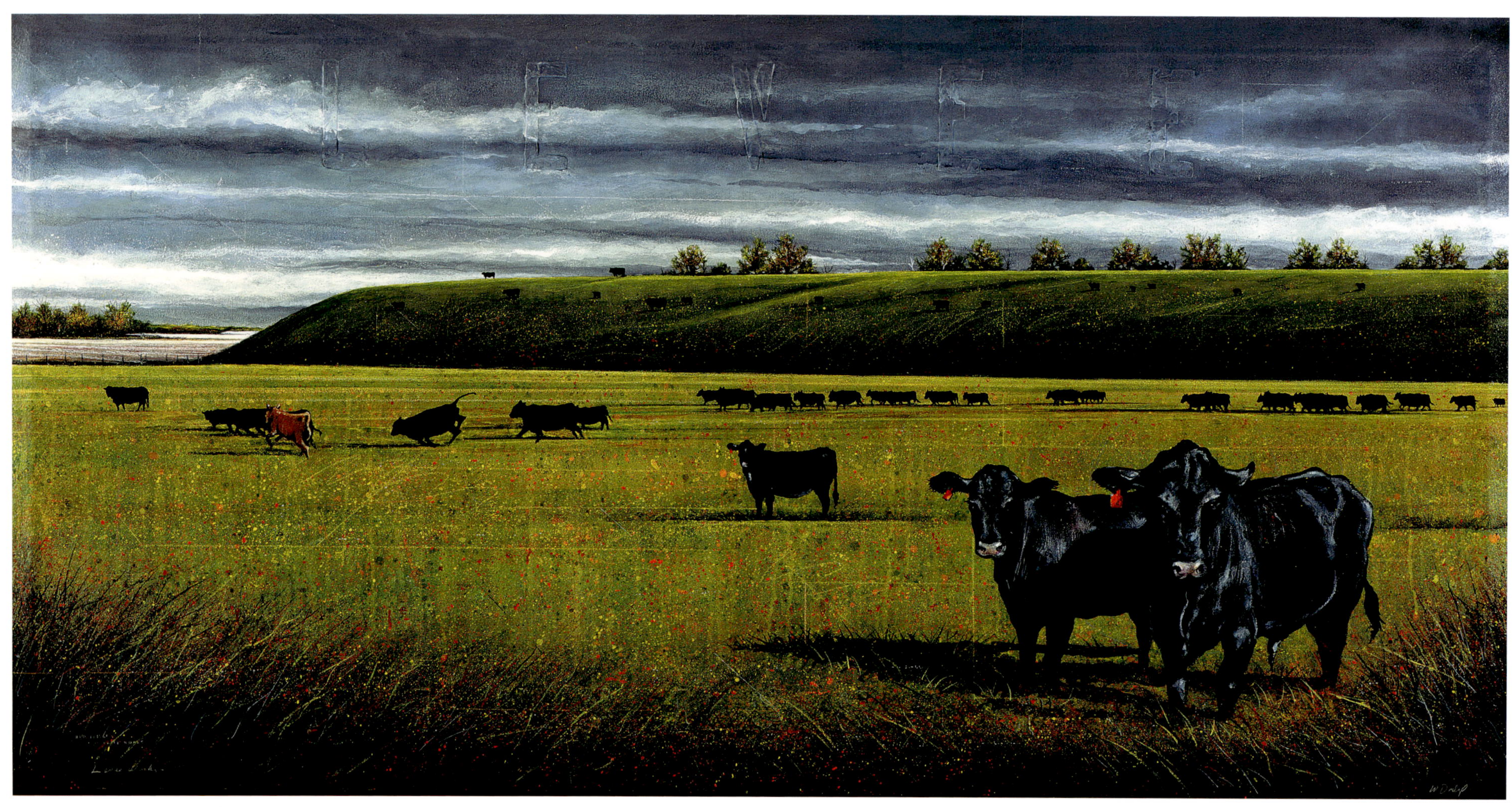

Bud Little's Levee Works, 2006

Polymer paint on canvas, 36 x 70.

Collection of Dr. and Mrs. Bud Little, Horn Lake, Mississippi. Photograph by Don Queralto.

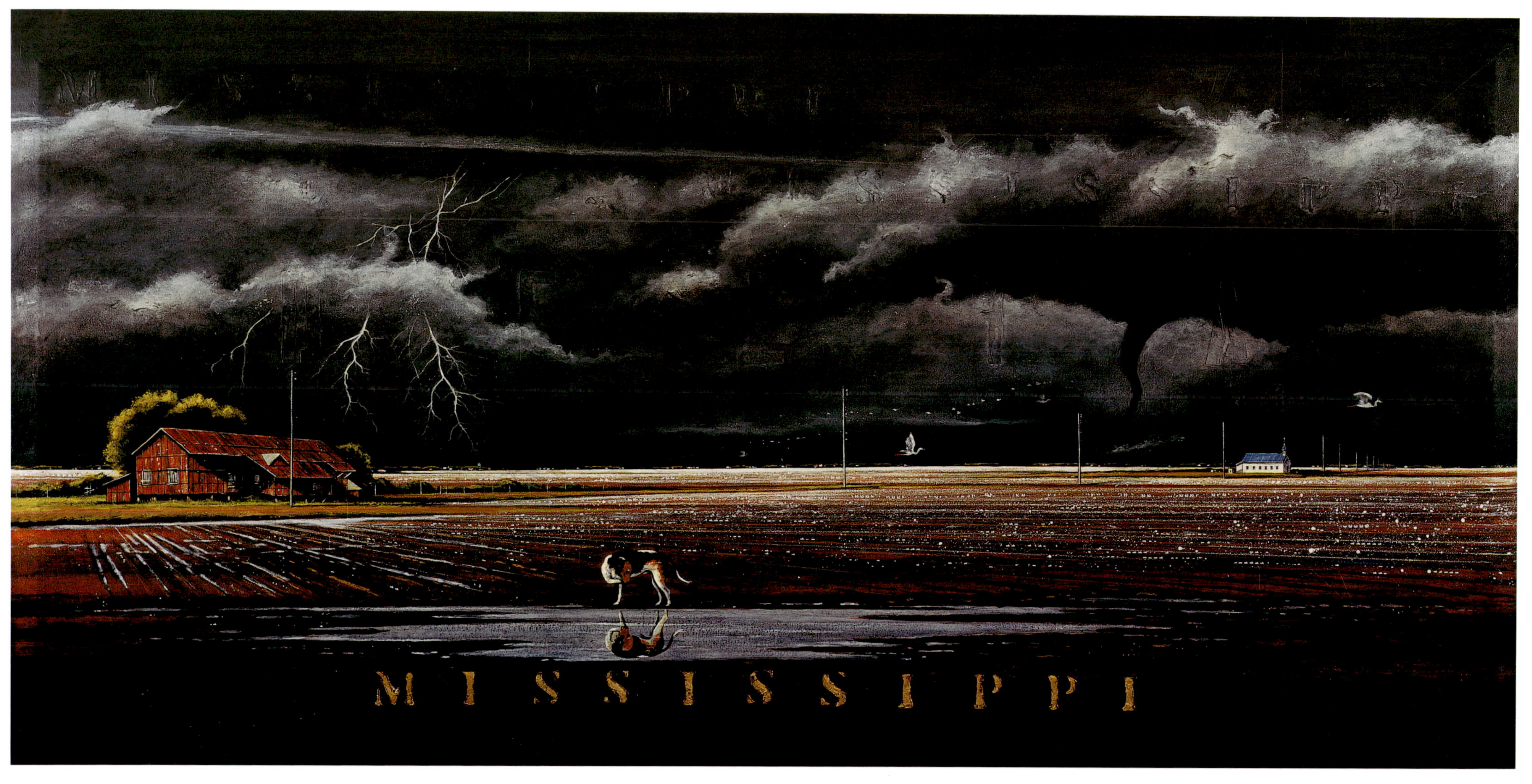

Father of Waters—History of Mud, 2006
Polymer paint, gold leaf, and silver leaf on canvas, 40 x 82. Collection of Julia Reed and John Pierce, New Orleans, Louisiana.
Photograph by Don Queralto.

Acknowledgments

Involuntary exclusion is the greatest fear of all acknowledgment writers. I am especially vulnerable given the hordes of people who have helped, coached, supported, prayed for, and otherwise buttressed my work and this book.

So where does one begin? Possibly with a family who had no particular stake in my becoming an artist—but never uttered a discouraging word. Or Roddy Simmons's mother Paula who organized an "Art club" in high school that gave me my first exposure to methods and materials. Then there was Coach Jack Taylor and his expletive-filled admonition to "keep your head down and your feet moving"—words I live by to this day.

I can't overemphasize the importance of people like the late Linda Berry—with whom I started and ended Art school. She was the most gifted of us all. And Bryant Allen, sculptor-cum-Art dealer who early on showed me the ropes.

They all mattered greatly, but no more or less than the host of friends, artists, mentors, collectors, curators, registrars, museum directors, Art dealers, airline pilots, auto mechanics, and bootleggers who have meant so much to me.

As to the particulars of this book, much thanks goes to Seetha Srinivasan whose idea this was, and who, with tenacity and patience, shepherded it to fruition. Under her stewardship the University Press of Mississippi has published some remarkable books, many of them about Art.

My old and dear friend John Langston, whose eye I envy and under whose cool, calm, and collected demeanor any problem (and there were multitudes) became an opportunity.

Valerie Jones could have brought a sense of order to the San Francisco earthquake. She made it all appear seamless.

Anne Stascavage did the same for tons of text. By weeding out errant adjectives and applying splints to my fractured compound sentences, she has added grace to this book's voice.

Pete Halverson, whose skill at scanning made the transmogrification of Art into Book possible (he must dream of Rembrandt at night).

There were many photographers involved, but a special note of appreciation to Hubert Worley, who tirelessly tracked down reclusive works of Art and brought their likeness back alive.

The sponsors of this book are listed elsewhere. However, a most heartfelt thank you is due those who put their money where their taste is.

The glorious Julia Reed is a one-woman Mardi Gras, as indefatigable as she is divine. Her penetrating vision and perfectly tuned ear allow her to see and hear all. With great good style and stinging wit, she passes it along.

The Grand Inquisitor, Jesuit-trained road warrior, and running buddy Rick Gruber, who, try as I might to throw off the track, kept his faith in the power of Art and place not only to coexist but also to transcend. Because of our time together, I see things differently.

And finally, a thousand thanks to Linda Burgess and our daughter Maggie, who make it all worthwhile.

Now whom have I missed? You know who you are—so write your name and my debt to you in the space provided below.

Chronology

1944 William Ralph Dunlap is born January 21 in Webster County, Mississippi, to Sam Coleman Dunlap and Margaret Cooper Dunlap.

1947 Father dies, September 17.

1950–51 Family lives with maternal grandparents in Mathiston, Mississippi. Major winter storm covers north Mississippi in snow and ice for weeks. Makes strong visual impression. Mother takes degree in English literature from Mississippi State University and teaches at Eupora High School.

1952–57 Mother remarries. Family lives in Port Arthur and Fort Worth, Texas, and Charleston, South Carolina, before returning to Mississippi in 1958. William and brother Sam spend summers with grandparents in Grady and Mathiston, Mississippi, where he attends church, runs wild in the woods, and occasionally goes foxhunting with grandfather, Cas Cooper. Pours over stacks of WWII vintage magazines. Listens closely as older women and men of substance talk.

1962 Graduates Morton High School. Senior class travels to New Orleans where he visits the New Orleans Museum of Art (formerly, the Delgado) and sees French Quarter art galleries. Works as lifeguard at Roosevelt State Park in the summer of William Faulkner's and Marilyn Monroe's deaths. In the fall James Meredith integrates Ole Miss. Willem de Kooning paints "Door to the River."

1963–64 Attends Hinds Community College on music and track scholarship. On trips to Washington and New York, Dunlap visits galleries and museums; he is taken by art at New York World's Fair including Michelangelo's *Pietà* from the Vatican, the paintings of Velázquez and Goya in the Spanish Pavilion, and an installation of Pop Art in the New York Pavilion.

1965 Attends Belhaven College in Jackson, Mississippi, where English professor William Derratt introduces him to Eudora Welty and Robert Penn Warren and their work. Wins collegiate art sculpture competition for *Sprinters*. Works with sculptor and gallery owner Bryant Allen in Jackson, Mississippi. Is involved with New Stage and Jackson's Little Theatre. Plays drums with pianist Bill Lamb's Trio.

1966 Studies with Dr. Sam Gore, and receives bachelor of science degree in art from Mississippi College. Works with sculptor Katherine Speed. *Sprinters*, included in the Southern Sculpture Traveling Exhibition, is purchased by Winthrop Rockefeller for the Arkansas Art Center. Remains active in music scene as percussionist playing and recording with various artists since 1964. Tours with R&B group, Tim Whitsett and the Imperial Show Band. Visits Montreal, Canada. Art in general and the U.S. Pavilion at the World's Fair make strong impression. On cross-country road trip via Route 66, sees the vastness of the American landscape. Sketches and makes photographs. In Los Angeles, visits Jackson Pollock retrospective and American sculpture of the 1960s exhibit at the L.A. County Museum. Is unable to gain admission to Art Center School of Design, Pasadena, California, because of residence requirements.

1967 Is accepted into graduate school at the University of Mississippi, where he operates the foundry and studies with Noyes Long and Dean Aydelott. Casts bronze and aluminum sculpture and makes first etchings and lithographs with Jack Lemon who later founds Landfall Press. Fellow artist/students Robert Marsh, Herschel George, John Davis, Dale Raeburn, Bill Lester, and George Alexander become lifelong friends. Initiates the Family Portrait Series working from a cache of old photos given to him at funeral of grandfather, Clough Dunlap.

1968 Marries Bobbye Jean Kitchens, daughter of future folk artist O. W. "Pappy" Kitchens. Plays touch football in the Grove at Ole Miss. Continues printmaking, sculpture, and music, playing with Joe Seawright's Oxford-based R&B band. Teaches art survey course at Mississippi Valley State University along with Dr. Louis Dollarhide.

1969 Receives MFA in sculpture and printmaking from the University of Mississippi and a Danforth Award in the Visual Arts. Arkansas Art Center in Little Rock acquires drawing for Permanent Collection.

1969–70 Accepts teaching position at Hinds Community College. Makes terracotta sculpture and initiates Old Masters Re-Considered Series, "teaching himself to paint" by appropriating images and emulating techniques from artists such as Rembrandt, Vermeer, and Velázquez.

1970 Former professor from Ole Miss, Noyes Long, calls from North Carolina with job offer. Moves to Blowing Rock, North Carolina, and begins teaching at Appalachian State University with fellow Mississippians Warren Dennis and Larry Edwards and former Ole Miss mentor Dean Aydelott. Father-in-law O. W. "Pappy" Kitchens visits and begins prolific decade that will produce a significant body of work in the folk art vein. Exhibits in Boone, North Carolina; at the Mississippi Arts Festival in Jackson; and at Averett College in Danville, where Ole Miss classmate Robert Marsh teaches. While there he meets Dr. John Harbert, co-owner of Adams Davidson Gallery in Washington, D.C., who invites them to exhibit.

1972 Begins to exhibit regularly.

1973 Meets Ted Potter and Chessie Dunn at Southeastern Center for Contemporary Art in Winston-Salem, North Carolina, then located in Old Salem.

1974 Establishes and serves as director of ASU-NY, 67 Vestry Street, an Appalachian State University extension campus in New York City. James Dickey visits and Dunlap makes life mask, which temporarily blinds the poet and lands them both on the cover of *Esquire* magazine. Visits Black Mountain poet Jonathan Williams and Tom Meyer in Cumbria, England. Travels to London, Paris, Rome, Amsterdam, and joins artists Claudia DeMonte and Ed McGowin in Paris and Germany for Cologne Art Fair. First New York show at the Italiander Gallery, 11 West 57th Street.

1975 Serves as director of the University Art Gallery and is active in the Artist/Lecture Series at Appalachian State University. Brings to campus Margaret Mead, John Cannaday, Tom Wolfe and James Dickey, Lyle Bonge, Jonathan Williams, Vito Acconci, John Barth, and Marcia Tucker. Guest artist/lecturer, Mississippi Arts Festival, Jackson, Mississippi, where he first exhibits site-specific installation/performance piece. Wearing a white suit, Dunlap makes faux stump speeches flanked by "Dunlap for Governor" and "Impeach Dunlap" posters. State officials are not amused.

1976 Takes sabbatical from Appalachian State University to work and exhibit. Wife returns to graduate school in Louisiana. Organizes Southern Rim Conference, Appalachian State University, a gathering of artists, critics, and curators who discuss recurring regionalism and the changing role of culture in the South. Participants include William Eggleston, Ed McGowin, Charmaine Locke, Jim Roche, John Alexander, James Surls, Terry Allen, Marcia Tucker, Paul Schimmel, Bill Christenberry, Jerry Noe, Bill Fagaly, and Jane Livingston. Guest artist/lecturer at George Washington University.

1977 Serves as director of the Appalachian House, 3rd Street S.E., an Appalachian State University extension campus in Washington, D.C. Guest artist/lecturer at Mississippi Museum of Art, Jackson, and Mint Museum of Art, Charlotte, North Carolina. Is featured artist at the Darlington Arts Festival, Darlington, South Carolina, where he exhibits a five-story-tall inflatable sculpture. Meets Darlington's legendary "Have Mercy," a mythical, larger-than-life figure in Darlington's black community.

1978 Takes Appalachian student/artists to work with Christo and Jeanne-Claude on their *Wrapped Walkways*, Kansas City, Missouri. Sees major Monet exhibit at St. Louis Museum and Asian art at the Nelson Atkins Museum in Kansas City. Conceives and organizes "The Artist as Performer," Appalachian State University, which brings Bill Murray, John Alexander, Dan Rizzi, and Van Schley to collaborate with performance artist Dana Atchley of Crested Butte, Colorado. Guest artist/lecturer at Corcoran School of Art, University of North Florida, and Pennsylvania State University. Organizes "The Business of Art," a panel discussion at Appalachian State University. Extended travel to Spain, Portugal, and North Africa.

1979 At the invitation of former Appalachian State University colleague Larry Edwards, Dunlap accepts position as Professor of Art and Director of Special Projects, Memphis State University, for one year. Serves as moderator for the controversial panel "Recurring Regionalism: The Southern Rim," College Art Association of America Conference, Washington, D.C. Is never invited back. Guest artist/lecturer at Rutgers University and Southeastern Center for Contemporary Art (SECCA), Winston-Salem, North Carolina. Archeological study and travel in Greece and the Cycladic Islands. Makes *Memphis: Home of the Blues*, a video with Linda Burgess and A. J. Jaeger. Spends time in Utah and Oregon on South Fork of the Salmon River and Hell's Canyon. Makes the triptych *Landscape with "Have Mercy."*

1980 Moves studio to McLean, Virginia. Makes driving trip from Cumbria, England, to London, Paris, and Rome with Dr. John Harbert. Presents "O. W. Pappy Kitchens: Folk Artist and Visionary," Southeastern College Arts Conference, Birmingham, Alabama. Spends extended time in Utah and Oregon on the South Fork of Salmon River. Researches American Civil War. Travels to battlefields in Virginia, Maryland, and Pennsylvania. Is taken with Philippoteaux's *Battle of Gettysburg* cyclorama.

1981 Guest artist/lecturer, University of Alabama in Birmingham. Goes on hunting trip to the Eastern Oregon Malheur National Forest, the source of deer head imagery in his work.

1982 Makes lithographs with Tamarind master printmaker Bill Lagattuta at Masters Editions, Denver, Colorado. Makes *Three Deer Head for Antietam* painting from hunting experience.

1983 Captain of Island #12 in Christo and Jeanne-Claude's *Surrounded Islands* project, Biscayne Bay, Miami, Florida, and keeps journal about the experience which is published in the *Washington Post*. Begins Antecedents Series incorporating family archival photographs in collaboration with John Reuter and Polaroid's 20 X 24 camera in Boston. Takes apartment with Linda Burgess in Maritime Alps in southeastern France and meets Fluxist artist Jean Dupuy and his wife, Olga. Serves as moderator for "Visual Language: The Southern Birthright," Birmingham Museum of Art.

1984 He and wife Bobbye Jean divorce. Is commissioned by the Corcoran Gallery of Art, Washington, D.C., to make *Panorama of the American Landscape*, a cyclorama for the Rotunda Gallery. Begins a decade-long collaboration of making lithographs and monotypes with Tamarind master printer David Salgado at Trillium Graphics in San Francisco. Guest artist/lecturer, "The Artist Today," Art Center College of Design, Pasadena, California.

1984–85 Works with photography curator Frances Fralin on exhibition and book, *The Indelible Image: Photographs of War—1846 to the Present*, Corcoran Gallery of Art, Washington, D.C. Does research in archives in London, Paris, New York City, and Washington, D.C. First encounters Dr. William Bell's 1876 carte de visite photograph of the mutilated corpse of Sergeant Wylliams, late of the 7th Cavalry, and begins to incorporate it into various works.

1985 Receives Visual Arts Award from Mississippi Institute of Arts and Letters. Painting appears on cover of *Harper's Magazine*, February issue. In April, *Panorama of the American Landscape*, a fourteen-panel cyclorama, opens at the Corcoran Gallery of Art, Washington, D.C. *The Painter's Landscape*, a video documentary about the Corcoran cyclorama, is directed by A. J. Jaeger and produced by Mississippi Authority for Educational Television. Guest artist/lecturer at "The Artist and the Marketplace," Southeastern Center for Contemporary Art (SECCA), Winston-Salem, North Carolina. Joins John Alexander, Paul Manes, Linda Burgess, Barbara Rose, Jane Livingston, and Connie Sullivan in Todi, Italy, for summer of painting and travel. He and Burgess visit Gore Vidal, Howard Auster, and Liz Carpenter in Ravello, Italy.

1986 Begins collaboration with Tamarind master printer Kappy Kuhn at Winstone Press in Mocksville, North Carolina. Receives SECCA/RJR Southeastern Artists Fellowship. *Panorama of the American Landscape* is shown at the Southeastern Center for Contemporary Art (SECCA), Winston-Salem, North Carolina, and begins an on-going exhibition tour. Works with Tamarind master printer Bill Lagattuta and Mike Hart at Peregrine Press, Dallas, Texas. Executes a limited edition of *Rembrandt Commemorative Print* for the Rembrandt Society, Mississippi Museum of Art, Jackson, Mississippi. Guest artist/lecturer for Barney House Lecture Series, Smithsonian Institute.

1987 Receives a grant for *Landscape and Light, Polaroid Spectrum Project*. Purchases Starnes House and Church of Christ in Mathiston, Mississippi. Travels to Indonesia, Bali, and Borobodur with art writer/critic and scholar, Dr. Jan Fontain. Is commissioned by Mississippi Chemical Company. Begins ongoing association with Art in Embassies Program loaning work to U.S. embassies around the world.

1988 Receives Rockefeller Foundation International Fellowship and serves as Resident Scholar, Bellagio Study Center, where he and artist/writer Linda Burgess marry. They buy loft at 548 Broadway, New York City, and paint and travel extensively in Italy. *Panorama of the American Landscape* is shown at the Philharmonic Hall Art Museum, Naples, Florida. Visits Robert Rauschenberg at Captiva Island studio. Begins tenure as arts commentator on PBS television show, *Around Town*, and *WETA Magazine* contributor, WETA-TV, Public Broadcasting System. *Panorama of the American Landscape* exhibits at Cheekwood Fine Art Center in Nashville, Tennessee.

1989 *Around Town*, WETA-TV, receives an Emmy and Helen Hayes/Washington Post Distinguished Community Service Award. Collaborates with Willie Morris on the book *Homecomings*, published by the University Press of Mississippi. Guest artist/lecturer for "Confessions of a Southern Artist," Virginia Beach Arts Center.

1990 Visual arts director and exhibition curator for *An Appalachian Summer*, Boone, North Carolina. Travels to Venice for the Biennale and to Istanbul, Athens, and the Black Sea. Serves as coordinator for Museum Project, Appalachian State University. Receives Painting Award from the Virginia Commission for the Arts. With Willie Morris is honored by Senator Thad Cochran, Senate Caucus Room, Washington, D.C., for *Homecomings*. Guest artist/lecturer for "Arts in Mississippi," panel discussion with Eudora Welty and Willie Morris, Jackson, Mississippi; "Art Criticism: Its Form and Function," The Arts Club of Washington, D.C.; "Religion and Art" episode, Richard Love's syndicated television show *American Art Forum*, Chicago, Illinois; "Manipulated Image: Manipulated Message," Society of Communicating Artists, Charlotte, North Carolina. Trunk Series, oil and graphite on paper, is acquired by the Metropolitan Museum in New York.

1991 Receives Mississippi Governor's Award for Excellence in the Arts. Guest artist/lecturer and curator of *Scale and Content: Painting in the Late 20th Century*, at Appalachian Summer Arts Festival,

Boone, North Carolina. Lectures on the making of *Panorama of the American Landscape* at the Aspen Museum of Art and the Sherry French Gallery in New York, during its installation at both locations.

1992 Receives Special Project Grant from Virginia Commission for the Arts. Guest artist/lecturer for "The Art of Collecting: Strategies for the 90s," Corcoran Gallery of Art, Washington, D.C.; "Art and Censorship," Sherry French Gallery, New York.

1993 Travels through Tuscany, Florence, and Rome, and makes painting at Lorenzo de' Medici Villa. Later, travels to Kenya and Tanzania with United Nations Development Program on Sustainable Development Project. Guest artist/lecturer for "Public Perspectives on the Media," *American Journalism Review*, University of Maryland, College Park, Maryland; "Censorship in the Arts," Millsaps College, Jackson, Mississippi; and "The Business of Local Arts," Knight Center for Specialized Journalism, University of Maryland. Gives commencement address for the Corcoran School of Art.

1994 Receives Lila Wallace Foundation International Arts Fellowship to research, compare, and contrast Cha Praya–Mekong River culture to that of the Yazoo–Mississippi Delta. Moves to Bangkok, Thailand. Serves as Resident Scholar at Silpakorn Fine Arts University. Meets writers William Warren and David Chandler. Travels extensively throughout Southeast Asia—Vietnam, Cambodia, and Burma. Meets photographer/archivists Doug Niven and Chris Riley, who are working on *Killing Field* project. Guest artist/lecturer for "Culture and Society: A Global View," Canadian Embassy, Washington, D.C. Cover for *Flyfishing through the Midlife Crisis*, a book by Howell Raines.

1995 Daughter Margaret Staeger Gore Dunlap is born in Washington, D.C. Guest artist/lecturer for "Folk Art Today: Passionate Visions," Corcoran Gallery of Art, Washington, D.C. Cover for the fall issue of the *Shenandoah Review*.

1996–97 Returns to Vietnam and co-curates *A Winding River: Contemporary Painting from Vietnam*, for the Meridian International Center, Washington, D.C. Cover for *A World Lost*, a novel by Wendell Berry. Commissioned by the State of Mississippi to make portrait of former governor Ray Mabus. Painting is installed in the Old Capitol Building, Jackson, Mississippi.

1998–99 Commission for U.S. Court of Appeals for the Fifth Circuit in New Orleans. Co-curates *Outward Bound: American Painting on the Brink of the 21st Century*, which travels to venues in Southeast Asia.

1999 Mother Margaret dies April 13 in Mississippi. Dunlap moves New York studio at 548 Broadway to Coral Gables, Florida. Visits American Academy in Berlin and Ravello, Italy, where he models and casts a bust of Gore Vidal.

2000 Travels to Kenya and Tanzania on photography, painting, and hunting trip. Performs *Dialogue, Monologue, Travelogue, Hollow Log (A Performance)* at the Corcoran Gallery of Art and New Orleans Museum of Art as part of Triennial Exhibition.

2001 On September 11, is in Madrid with writers from National Gallery of Art group when he learns of terrorist attack in U.S. Spends the next week either at the bullfights or at the Prado standing in front of works by Hieronymus Bosch, Velázquez, and Goya.

2002 In Spain and Portugal visits the Dali Museum and Miro studio on Majorca. Guest artist/lecturer at the Holland Hall School, Tulsa, Oklahoma; the Chautauqua Institution, Chautauqua, New York. Performs *Real Art in a Virtual World,* Florida Avenue Theatre, Washington, D.C. Co-curates traveling exhibition *True Colors: Meditations on the American Spirit* for the Meridian International Center.

2003 Visits artist Francis Bacon's birthplace and studio in Dublin, Ireland. In Scotland, visits Paul and Debra Richard in the Kyles of Bute. Locates ancient village of Dunlop whose kirkyard cemetery is full of ancestors. Cover and featured artist in the *Ontario Review*, fall issue. Makes commissions for the Alluvian Hotel, Greenwood, Mississippi; the Washington Convention Center in D.C.; and Nissan Corporation.

2004 Begins annual association with the Conference for the Book at the University of Mississippi hosting panel discussions.

2005 Paints portraits for *Faces of the Fallen*, soldiers killed in the wars with Iraq and Afghanistan, Arlington National Cemetery, Arlington, Virginia.

2006 Returns to Thailand and Cambodia with Linda Burgess and daughter, Maggie. Hosts "Writing About Art" panel for the Conference for the Book, Oxford, Mississippi.

Exhibition History

Solo Exhibitions

1969 Bryant Galleries, Jackson, Mississippi
Studio One, Jackson, Mississippi

1971 Bryant Galleries, Jackson, Mississippi
Mississippi Art Association Gallery, Jackson, Mississippi

1972 Averett College, Danville, Virginia
Bryant Galleries, Jackson, Mississippi
Mississippi Art Association Gallery, Jackson, Mississippi
Regional Gallery of Art, Boone, North Carolina

1973 Fielding L. Wright Art Center, Delta State University, Cleveland, Mississippi
Mint Museum of Art, Charlotte, North Carolina
New Morning Gallery, Asheville, North Carolina
Regional Gallery of Art, Boone, North Carolina

1974 Adams Davidson Galleries, Washington, D.C.
Gallery 2+2, New Orleans, Louisiana
Italiander Gallery, New York, New York
Lamar Advertising, Jackson, Mississippi
Roanoke Fine Arts Center, Roanoke, Virginia

1975 *Hybrid Series*, Adams Davidson Galleries, Washington, D.C.
Mint Museum of Art, Charlotte, North Carolina
New Morning Gallery, Asheville, North Carolina
Sycamore Gallery, Memphis, Tennessee

1976 Adams Davidson Galleries, Washington, D.C.
Averett College, Danville, Virginia
Greenwood Arts Festival, Greenwood, Mississippi
Lauren Rogers Museum of Art, Laurel, Mississippi
Quadrum Gallery, Marblehead, Massachusetts
Stone Gallery, Davidson, North Carolina
University of Mississippi, Oxford, Mississippi

1977 Adams Davidson Galleries, Washington, D.C.
Lauren Rogers Museum of Art, Laurel, Mississippi
Main Street, Houston, Texas
Quadrum Gallery, Boston, Massachusetts

1978 Adams Davidson Galleries, Washington, D.C.
Coffey Gallery, Boone, North Carolina
Gulf States AIA (American Institute of Architects) Convention, Gulfport, Mississippi
Quadrum Gallery, Boston, Massachusetts

1979 Adams Davidson Galleries, Washington, D.C.
Quadrum Gallery, Boston, Massachusetts
Sycamore Gallery, Memphis, Tennessee

1980 *Off the Interstate—Landscapes and Light*, Heath Gallery, Atlanta, Georgia
Quadrum Gallery, Boston, Massachusetts

1981 *Large Works on Paper*, Quadrum Gallery, Boston, Massachusetts
Trunk Series, Angus Whyte Gallery, Washington, D.C.

1982 Bryant Galleries, Jackson, Mississippi
Hodges Taylor Gallery, Charlotte, North Carolina
Quadrum Gallery, Chestnut Hill, Massachusetts

1983 Gallery 4, Alexandria, Virginia
Quadrum Gallery, Chestnut Hill, Massachusetts

1985 *Panorama of the American Landscape*, Corcoran Gallery of Art, Washington, D.C. (Traveled to Appalachian State University, Boone, North Carolina; The Art Gallery, Center for Financial Studies at Fairfield University, Fairfield, Connecticut; Asheville Art Museum, Asheville, North Carolina; Aspen Art Museum, Aspen, Colorado; Cheekwood Fine Arts Center, Nashville, Tennessee; Chrysler Museum, Norfolk, Virginia; Fielding L. Wright Art Center, Delta State University, Cleveland, Mississippi; General Electric World Headquarters, Stamford, Connecticut; Gibbes Museum of Art, Charleston, South Carolina; Memphis University Gallery and Museum, Memphis, Tennessee; Mississippi Museum of Art, Jackson, Mississippi; Naples Philharmonic Gallery of Art, Naples, Florida; Ogden Museum of Southern Art, New Orleans, Louisiana; Sherry French Gallery, New York, New York; Southeastern Center for Contemporary Art (SECCA), Winston-Salem, North Carolina)
Places and Things, Meredith Long & Company, Houston, Texas
Quadrum Gallery, Chestnut Hill, Massachusetts
Robert Brown Gallery, Washington, D.C.

1986 Hodges Taylor Gallery, Charlotte, North Carolina
Mississippi Museum of Art, Jackson, Mississippi

1987 Bryant Galleries, Jackson, Mississippi
Hattiesburg Civic Arts Council, Hattiesburg, Mississippi
National Academy of Science, Washington, D.C.
Neuhaus Gallery, Washington, D.C.
Sherry French Gallery, New York, New York

1988 *American Light and Landscape*, Sherry French Gallery, New York, New York (Traveled to Holland Hall, Tulsa, Oklahoma)
Cheekwood Fine Arts Center, Nashville, Tennessee
Maitland Art Center, Maitland, Florida
Marlborough Galleries, Boston, Massachusetts
Naples Philharmonic Gallery of Art, Naples, Florida
Somerhill Gallery, Durham, North Carolina

1989 Appalachian State University, Boone, North Carolina
Fielding L. Wright Art Center, Delta State University, Cleveland, Mississippi
Hodges Taylor Gallery, Charlotte, North Carolina
Marlborough Galleries, Boston, Massachusetts
Memphis State University, Memphis, Tennessee
Sherry French Gallery, New York, New York

1990 *Imaginary Landscape*, Jones Troyer Fitzpatrick Gallery, Washington, D.C.
Art Gallery, Center for Financial Studies, Fairfield University, Fairfield, Connecticut
Bryant Galleries, Birmingham, Alabama
Bryant Galleries, Jackson, Mississippi
General Electric World Headquarters, Stamford, Connecticut
Marlborough Galleries, Boston, Massachusetts
Neville-Sargent Gallery, Chicago, Illinois

1991 Aspen Art Museum, Aspen, Colorado
Bryant Galleries, Jackson, Mississippi
Jones Troyer Fitzpatrick Gallery, Washington, D.C.
Sherry French Gallery, New York, New York

1992 *Ridges and Wetlands*, Naples Philharmonic Gallery of Art, Naples, Florida
William Dunlap: Re-Constructed Re-Collections, Art Museum of Western Virginia, Roanoke, Virginia
Marita Gilliam Gallery, Raleigh, North Carolina

1993 Mississippi Museum of Art, Jackson, Tupelo, Biloxi, Mississippi
Sherry French Gallery, New York, New York
Sherry French Gallery, Palm Beach, Florida
Southside Gallery, Oxford, Mississippi
Taylor Contemporanea, Hot Springs, Arkansas
Vaughan-Goodman Fine Paintings, Jackson, Mississippi

1994 Hodges Taylor Gallery, Charlotte, North Carolina
Kurts Bingham Gallery, Memphis, Tennessee
Troyer Fitzpatrick Lassman Gallery, Washington, D.C.

1995 *In the Spirit of the Land*, Corcoran Gallery of Art, Washington, D.C. (Traveled to Albany Museum of Art, Albany, Georgia; Contemporary Arts Center, New Orleans, Louisiana; Mississippi Museum of Art, Jackson, Mississippi; Ogden Museum of Southern Art, New Orleans, Louisiana)

1996 Addison/Ripley Fine Art Gallery, Washington, D.C.
Anderson Gallery, Virginia Commonwealth University, Richmond, Virginia
Bryant Galleries, Jackson, Mississippi
Misia Broadhead Studio Gallery, Middleburg, Virginia
Naples Philharmonic Gallery of Art, Naples, Florida
Southeastern Center for Contemporary Art (SECCA), Winston-Salem, North Carolina

1997 *William Dunlap: Constructions*, Contemporary Art Center, New Orleans, Louisiana
Anderson Gallery, Virginia Commonwealth University, Richmond, Virginia

1998 Addison/Ripley Fine Art Gallery, Washington, D.C.
Albany Museum of Art, Albany, Georgia
Hodges Taylor Gallery, Charlotte, North Carolina
Southside Gallery, Oxford, Mississippi
Susan Conway Gallery, Santa Fe, New Mexico

1999 Southside Gallery, Oxford, Mississippi

2000 Bryant Galleries, Jackson, Mississippi
ERL Gallery, Winston-Salem, North Carolina

2001 *Objects Found and Fashioned*, Ogden Museum of Southern Art, New Orleans, Louisiana
Marsha Ralls Collection, Washington, D.C.
Sherry French Gallery, New York, New York

2002 *Miro, Miro on the Wall*, Contemporary Arts Center, New Orleans, Louisiana
That's What I Like about the South, Emerson Gallery, McLean, Virginia
Holland Hall, Tulsa, Oklahoma
Galerie Simonne Stern, New Orleans, Louisiana

2003 *Landscape & Variable*, Lauren Rogers Museum of Art, Laurel, Mississippi

2004 *Look at It, Think about It: Recent Work*, University of Mississippi Museum, Oxford, Mississippi
Recent Work, Søren Christensen Gallery, New Orleans, Louisiana
Size Matters: Panorama of the American Landscape, Gibbes Museum of Art, Charleston, South Carolina

2005 *Recent Work*, Norton Gallery of Art, West Palm Beach, Florida

2006 *What Dogs Dream*, Morris Museum of Art, Augusta, Georgia; Mississippi Museum of Art, Jackson, Mississippi; Ogden Museum of Southern Art, New Orleans, Louisiana

Group Exhibitions

1968 Mississippi Arts Association Traveling Exhibition, Manchester Institute of Arts and Sciences, Manchester, New Hampshire
National Watercolor Exhibition (Deposit Guaranty National Bank Purchase Award), Mississippi Arts Festival, Jackson, Mississippi
Ocala Art Exhibition (First Award in Watercolor, Merit Award in Mixed Media), Ocala, Florida
Second Annual Prints, Drawings and Crafts Exhibition, Arkansas Arts Center, Little Rock, Arkansas

1969 Eleventh Annual Exhibition of Prints and Drawings, Oklahoma Arts Center, Oklahoma City, Oklahoma
Fifth Dulin National Print and Drawing Competition, Dulin Gallery of Art, Knoxville, Tennessee
Mississippi Collection, Mississippi Art Association, Mississippi Arts Festival, Jackson, Mississippi
Ocala Art Exhibition (Best in Show, Print Award), Ocala, Florida

Winterpark Arts Festival (Painting, Graphics, and Sculpture Awards), Winterpark, Florida

1970 American Drawing Biennial XXII, Norfolk Museum of Arts and Sciences, Norfolk, Virginia

Arts and Crafts Exhibition (Best in Show, Painting), Mississippi Arts Festival, Jackson, Mississippi

First Annual Print and Drawing Show, Georgia State University, Atlanta, Georgia

Images on Paper, Mississippi Art Association, Jackson, Mississippi

National Drawing Exhibition, Gallery of Contemporary Art, Winston-Salem, North Carolina

North Carolina Juried Artists Exhibition, North Carolina Museum of Art, Raleigh, North Carolina

Virginia Beach Arts Festival (First Drawing Award), Virginia Beach, Virginia

1971 American Drawing Biennial XXIII, Norfolk Museum of Arts and Sciences, Norfolk, Virginia

Eighth Annual Piedmont Graphics Exhibition, North Carolina Museum of Art, Raleigh, North Carolina

North Carolina Artists Exhibition, North Carolina Museum of Art, Raleigh, North Carolina

Roanoke Festival in the Park, Fine Arts and Crafts Show, Roanoke, Virginia (First Award)

1972 *Art on Paper: Dillard Paper Company*, Weatherspoon Art Museum, Greensboro, North Carolina

National Painting Exhibition, Gallery of Contemporary Art, Winston-Salem, North Carolina

1973 *Edwards, Dennis, and Dunlap: Distinguished Alumni*, University of Mississippi, Oxford, Mississippi

Contemporary American Genre Show, Adams Davidson Galleries, Washington, D.C.

Juried Exhibition, Hickory Museum of Art, Hickory, North Carolina

Realist Invitational, Gallery of Contemporary Art, Winston-Salem, North Carolina

1974 *Realism in North Carolina*, Mint Museum of Art, Charlotte, North Carolina

Fortieth Semi-Annual Southeastern Juried Exhibition, Southeastern Center for Contemporary Art (SECCA), Winston-Salem, North Carolina

1975 *Southeastern Printmakers*, Western Carolina University, Cullowhee, North Carolina

1976 *Survey of Realist Paintings*, New Morning Gallery, Asheville, North Carolina

Bicentennial Invitational Exhibition, Dimock Gallery, George Washington University, Washington, D.C.

1977 Darlington Arts Festival, Darlington, South Carolina

1978 *After Images: Art about Art*, North Carolina Museum of Art, Raleigh, North Carolina

Artists Invitational Exhibition, Salisbury, North Carolina

Realist Invitational, Southeastern Center for Contemporary Art (SECCA), Winston-Salem, North Carolina

1979 *Art Patron Art*, Southeastern Center for Contemporary Art (SECCA), Winston-Salem, North Carolina

Southern Realism, Mississippi Museum of Art, Jackson, Mississippi

Southern Graphics Invitational: Drawings, Mint Museum of Art, Charlotte, North Carolina (regional tour)

1981 *Contemporary American Art*, National Academy of Design, New York, New York

More than Land or Sky: The Art of Appalachia, National Museum of American Art, Smithsonian Institution, Washington, D.C. (Traveled to Birmingham Museum of Art, Alabama; and Southeastern Center for Contemporary Art (SECCA), Winston-Salem, North Carolina)

1982 Birmingham-Southern College, Birmingham, Alabama Greenwood Arts Festival, Greenwood, Mississippi

New Acquisitions, Corcoran Gallery of Art, Washington, D.C.

Sawtooth Center for the Arts, Winston-Salem, North Carolina

Southeastern Center for Contemporary Art (SECCA), Winston-Salem, North Carolina

1983 *The American Landscape: Current Visions*, Bolen Gallery, Santa Monica, California

Contemporary American Art, National Academy of Design, New York, New York

1984 *Art Attack*, Olshonsky Gallery, Washington, D.C.

Contemporary Art Acquisitions: 1980–1983, Equitable Gallery, New York, New York

Drawing Invitational, Somerhill Gallery, Durham, North Carolina

In and Around Washington, Times Journal Building, Springfield, Massachusetts

1985 *Reveries and Mississippi Memories*, Lauren Rogers Museum of Art, Laurel, Mississippi

Blount Invitational Art Show, Montgomery, Alabama

W. C. Bradley Company Museum, Columbus, Georgia

1986 *American Landscape Painting*, Meredith Long & Company, Houston, Texas

Masterworks on Paper from the Corcoran Collection, Corcoran Gallery of Art, Washington, D.C. (Traveled to Burling Library, Grinnell, Iowa; Cincinnati Art Museum, Cincinnati, Ohio; and Midland Art Council, Midland, Michigan)

1987 Eighth Annual Art Auction: WPA, Duke Ellington School of the Arts, Washington, D.C.

Elvis, Southeastern Center for Contemporary Art (SECCA), Winston-Salem, North Carolina

Oxford Influence, University of Mississippi, Oxford, Mississippi

Ten Years of Southeast Seven, Southeastern Center for Contemporary Art (SECCA), Winston-Salem, North Carolina (Traveled to Tennessee Fine Arts Center at Cheekwood, Nashville, Tennessee)

1987– Works on Loan: Art in Embassies Program, U.S. Mission, West Berlin, Germany; U.S. Embassies in Bandar Seri Begawan, Brunei; Roumania; Port Louis, Mauritius

1988 *The Boys of Mississippi*, University of Mississippi, Oxford, Mississippi

Changing Selections: Prints from the Winstone Press, North Carolina Museum of Art, Raleigh, North Carolina

Charged! Places and Things, Sherry French Gallery, New York, New York (Traveled to Chicago International Art Exposition, Chicago, Illinois; and Wichita Art Museum, Kansas)

Coming Home, Hinds Community College, Raymond, Mississippi

Focus on Art: 1988, National Council of Jewish Women, Essex County, New Jersey

Landscape Transformed, Dimock Gallery, George Washington University, Washington, D.C.

Looking South: A Different Dixie (Ruth Appelhof, curator), Birmingham Museum of Art, Alabama (Traveled to Brooks Museum of Art, Memphis, Tennessee; Columbus Museum of Art, Columbus, Georgia; Contemporary Art Center, New Orleans, Louisiana; Museum of Fine Arts, St. Petersburg, Florida; and Sheldon Swope Art Museum, Terre Haute, Indiana)

Prints: Washington, The Phillips Collection, Washington, D.C.

Collector's Show, Arkansas Art Center, Little Rock, Arkansas

Landscape Show, Cumberland Gallery, Nashville, Tennessee

1989 *By Land or By Sea*, Island Gallery, Vero Beach, Florida

Contemporary Environments (curated by the Art Advisory Service, Museum of Modern Art, New York City), General Electric, Fairfield, Connecticut; Pfizer Company, New York City

From the Potomac to the Anacostia, Washington Project for the Arts, Washington, D.C.

Landscape Is Real Estate, Robert Brown Gallery, Washington, D.C.

Landscape: Three Perspectives, Maryland Art Place, Baltimore, Maryland (Traveled to Albright-Knox Art Gallery, Buffalo, New York; Chicago International Art Exposition, Chicago, Illinois; Cudahy's Gallery, Richmond, Virginia; Dennis Morgan Gallery, Kansas City, Missouri; Los Angeles International Art Fair, Los Angeles, California; New York Women's Foundation Benefit Auction, New York, New York; Philadelphia Museum of Art, Art Sales and Rental Gallery, Philadelphia, Pennsylvania; Robert Kidd Gallery, Birmingham, Michigan; and Somerville Manning Gallery, Greenville, Delaware)

Landscape: Travelogue Painted from Memory, Imagination, or Reality, Ruth Siegel Gallery, New York, New York

Landscapes: Rural and Urban, Neville-Sargent Gallery, Chicago, Illinois

Love and Charity: Contemporary Tradition of Caritas, Sherry French Gallery,

New York, New York (Traveled to Dowd Fine Arts Gallery, SUNY at Cortland, New York; Noyes Museum of Art, Oceanville, New Jersey; Roanoke Museum of Fine Arts, Roanoke, Virginia; and Roland Gibson Gallery, SUNY at Potsdam, New York)

Made in America, Virginia Beach Center for the Arts, Virginia Beach, Virginia

Religion: The Spiritual in Art, Sherry French Gallery, New York, New York

Trains and Planes: The Influence of Locomotion, Sherry French Gallery, New York, New York (Traveled to Evansville Museum of Arts, History, and Science, Evansville, Indiana; National Academy of Science, Washington, D.C.; Noyes Museum of Art, Oceanville, New Jersey; and Roberson Center for the Arts and Sciences, Binghamton, New York)

1990 *Available for Commission*, Sherry French Gallery, New York, New York

A Meeting Place: Imagery and Abstraction in Contemporary Art, Roanoke Museum of Fine Arts, Roanoke, Virginia

Waiting for Cadmium, Sherry French Gallery, New York, New York

Chicago International Art Exposition, Chicago, Illinois

Virginia Commission for the Arts Award Winners, Peninsula Fine Arts Center, Newport News, Virginia

1991 *The Eternal Landscape*, Southeastern Center for Contemporary Art (SECCA), Winston-Salem, North Carolina

The Eternal Male, Sherry French Gallery, New York, New York

Expedition: Estes Park, Sherry French Gallery, New York, New York

A Mississippi Mixture, Greenville Arts Council, Greenville, Mississippi

Re-collecting the Remembered Landscape, Jones Troyer Fitzpatrick Gallery, Washington, D.C.

Scale and Content: Painting in the Late 20th Century, Appalachian State University, Boone, North Carolina

To Grant or Not To Grant, Sherry French Gallery, New York, New York (Traveled to Knoxville Museum of Art, Knoxville, Tennessee)

Sherry French Gallery, Palm Beach, Florida

1992 *The New Whitney Dissenters*, Fitchburg Art Museum, Fitchburg, Massachusetts

Southern Genre, Kurts Bingham Gallery, Memphis, Tennessee

The Southern Way, Vaughan-Goodman Fine Paintings, Jackson, Mississippi

1993 *Flowers in February*, Sherry French Gallery, New York, New York

Legend, Emerson Gallery, McLean, Virginia

The Maine Show, Sherry French Gallery, New York, New York

1994 *El Espiritu de la Tierra: Permanent Collection from the U.S. Chancellory in La Paz, Bolivia*, Lee Kimche and Associates, Washington, D.C.

Vividly Told, Morris Museum of Art, Augusta, Georgia

1995 *G. W., B.M.O.C.: Images of George Washington, Past and Present*, Dimock Gallery, Washington, D.C. (Traveled to Southside Gallery, Oxford, Mississippi)

1997 *Black and White*, Byrne Gallery, Middleburg, Virginia (Traveled to Addison/Ripley Fine Art Gallery, Washington, D.C.; and Washington Design Center, Washington, D.C.)

Body and Soul: Contemporary Figures, Columbus Museum of Art, Columbus, Georgia

1998 *Sacred Sites: The American Civil War, Then and Now*, Chrysler Museum of Art, Norfolk, Virginia

Survey of the American Landscape, Blue Spiral Gallery, Asheville, North Carolina

1999 *Outward Bound: American Art on the Brink of the Twenty-first Century*, Meridian International Center, Washington, D.C. (Traveled to Southeast Asia)

2001 *William Dunlap and David Rae Morris*, Southside Gallery, Oxford, Mississippi

New Orleans Museum of Art Triennial, New Orleans, Louisiana

2002 *The Fantastic Four*, Catherine Smith Gallery, Appalachian State University, Boone, North Carolina

True Colors: Meditations on the American Spirit, Meridian International Center, Washington, D.C. (Traveled to National Arts Club, New York, New York; and international venues)

Uncommon Ground, Stifel Fine Arts Center, Oglebay Institute, Wheeling, West Virginia

2003 *My South*, Splashlight Studios, New York, New York

Galerie Simonne Stern, New Orleans, Louisiana

2004 *Contemporary Painting*, McLean Project for the Arts, McLean, Virginia

2005 *Common Ground*, Corcoran Gallery of Art, Washington, D.C.

Southern Trace, Brenau University Galleries, Gainesville, Georgia

Public and Corporate Collections

Agip Petroleum, Washington, D.C.
Alabama Power, Birmingham, Alabama
American Bar Association, Washington, D.C.
Applied Data Research, Washington, D.C.
Arkansas Art Center, Little Rock, Arkansas
Art Museum of Western Virginia, Roanoke, Virginia
Asheville Art Museum, North Carolina
Bank of Virginia, Richmond, Virginia
Bell South, Washington, D.C.
Blount Collection of American Paintings, Montgomery Museum of Fine Arts, Montgomery, Alabama
Booze, Allen and Hamilton, Washington, D.C.
Branch Bank and Trust, Charlotte, North Carolina
Cassidy and Pinkard, Washington, D.C.
Cato Corporation, Charlotte, North Carolina
Charlotte International Airport, Charlotte, North Carolina
Charlotte Observer, Charlotte, North Carolina
Chevy Chase Savings and Loan, Chevy Chase, Maryland
Commerce Bancshares, Inc., Kansas City, Missouri
Corcoran Gallery of Art, Washington, D.C.
Cullen and Nordstrom, Washington, D.C.
Dillard Paper Company, Greensboro, North Carolina
Durham Research Properties, Durham, North Carolina
Equitable Collection, New York, New York
Exxon-Mobil, Fairfax, Virginia
Farm Credit Administration, McLean, Virginia
Federal Express, Memphis, Tennessee
Fielding L. Wright Art Center, Delta State University, Cleveland, Mississippi
Fine Art Associates, Palm Beach, Florida
First Boston Corporation, New York, New York
First Union National Bank, Charlotte, North Carolina
Fisher Brothers, New York, New York
Frito-Lay Company, Dallas, Texas
Gannett Corporation, Washington, D.C.
Gibbes Museum of Art, Charleston, South Carolina
Hanes Corporation, Winston-Salem, North Carolina
Hattiesburg Civic Arts Council, Hattiesburg, Mississippi
Hunton Williams, Washington, D.C.
IBM Corporation, New York, New York
Judy Norell Corporation, Washington, D.C.
Kaiser Permanente, Durham, North Carolina
Kidder Peabody Company, New York, New York
Kirkpatrick and Coty, Washington, D.C.
Knight-Ridder Foundation, Miami, Florida
Lane and Edson, Washington, D.C.
Lauren Rogers Museum of Art, Laurel, Mississippi
Main Hurdman, Inc.,Washington, D.C.
Massachusetts Financial Services, Boston, Massachusetts
McDonald's Corporation, Chicago, Illinois
McGuire, Woods, Battle and Boothe, McLean, Virginia
McKenna, Conner and Cuneo, Washington, D.C.
Meredith Long and Company, Houston, Texas
Metropolitan Museum of Art, New York, New York
Miles and Stockbridge, Fairfax, Virginia
Mint Museum of Art, Charlotte, North Carolina
Mississippi Museum of Art, Jackson, Mississippi
Mobile Communication Corporation of America, Jackson, Mississippii
Morris Museum of Southern Art, Augusta, Georgia
Museum of Mississippi History, Jackson, MIssissippi
National Bank of Washington, Washington, D.C.
National Council of Jewish Women, New York, New York
Nations Bank, Charlotte, North Carolina
Nissan Corporation, Canton, Mississippi
Norfolk Museum of Art, Norfolk, Virginia
North Carolina National Bank, Charlotte, North Carolina
Ogden Museum of Southern Art, New Orleans, Louisiana
Oliver Carr Company, Washington, D.C.
Pepsi-Cola Company of America, Washington, D.C.
Planters Bank and Trust Company, Greenville, Mississippi
Prudential Insurance Company of America, Newark, New Jersey
R. J. Reynolds Corporation, Winston-Salem, North Carolina
Radisson Hotel, Charlotte, North Carolina
Riggs Bank, Washington, D.C.
Robinson, Bradshaw and Hinson, Charlotte, North Carolina
Rockdale County Hospital, Atlanta, Georgia
Sara Lee Corporation, Winston-Salem, North Carolina
Shearson Lehman Company, McLean, Virginia
Signet Bank, Washington, D.C.
Smith, Pachter, McWhorter, D'Ambrosio, Washington, D.C.
Spengler, Carlson, Gubar, Brodsky and Frischling, New York, New York
Sterling Capital Management, Charlotte, North Carolina
Sutherland, Asbill and Brennan, Washington, D.C.
Thurston Aviation, Charlotte, North Carolina
Times Journal Company, Springfield, Virginia
Travelstead Group, New York, New York
United States Embassy, Helsinki, Finland
United States Embassy, Lisbon, Portugal
United States Embassy, Berlin, Germany
United States Embassy, Port Louis, Mauritius
United States Embassy, Phnom Penh, Cambodia
United States Mission, Bandar Seri Begawan, Brunei
United States State Department, Washington, D.C.
University of Mississippi, Oxford, Mississippi
Viking Range Corporation, Greenwood, Mississippi
Vinnell Corporation, Washington, D.C.
Wandel and Goltermann, Inc., Research Triangle, North Carolina
Washington Convention Center, Washington, D.C.
Washington Post, Washington, D.C.
W. C. Bradley Collection, Columbus, Georgia
Winthrop Rockefeller Foundation, Little Rock, Arkansas
Woodward and Lothrop, Washington, D.C.

Bibliography

1971 "One-Man Show by Bill Dunlap Opens Season at Municipal Art Gallery," *Clarion-Ledger/Jackson Daily News*, 5 September 1971.

"Words and Images by Knecht and Dunlap," *Verve* 3 (Spring 1971).

1973 Coleman, J. P. *Choctaw County Chronicles: A History of Choctaw County, Mississippi, 1830–1973*. Ackerman, Mississippi, 1973. Illustration page 284.

Dollarhide, Louis. "Keeping Up with Bills—Anderson and Dunlap," *Jackson Daily News*, 30 December 1973.

Van Kleeck, Richard. "Dunlap's an Example of 'Brandywine Tradition,'" *Asheville Citizen-Times*, 12 August 1973.

1975 Forgey, Ben. "Review of Art," *ARTnews* 74 (Summer 1975).

McLendon, James. "ASU Art Students Have NY 'Campus,'" *Winston-Salem Journal*, 7 September 1975.

1976 Ayres, B. Drummond. "Cultural Activities in South Grow with Its Economy," *New York Times*, 1 November 1976.

Esquire Magazine 85.2 (February 1976). Cover.

Krebs, Patricia. "Dunlap: An Inspired Eclectic," *Charlotte Observer*, 29 November 1976.

"Personalities—Dunlap and Dickey," *Washington Post*, February 1976.

Richard, Paul. "Review of Adams Davidson Exhibition," *Washington Post*, 3 May 1976.

1977 Krebs, Patricia. "Artist for Hire: The 70s Became the Age of Commission," *Charlotte Observer*, 6 March 1977.

Northrop, Guy. "Bill Dunlap and the Mississippi Connection," *Commercial Appeal* (Memphis), 6 February 1977.

1978 Chapin, Catherine. "Bank Shows High Interest in Local Art," *Charlotte Observer*, 16 August 1978.

Forgey, Ben. "Review of Interstate Exhibit," *Washington Post*, 24 April 1978.

Hodges, Dorothy D., and Theo Inman. "16 Featured Artists," *Contemporary Art/Southeast* 11.1 (1978).

Richard, Paul. "Review of Adams Davidson Exhibit," *Washington Post*, 24 April 1978.

1979 *Art Patron Art*. Catalogue. Winston-Salem, North Carolina: Southeastern Center for Contemporary Art, 1979.

Davignon, Arsene. "Dunlap Show: An Embarrassment of Riches," *Boston Herald-American*, 28 May 1979.

Pendergraft, Norma. "Review and Reproduction:

Art Patron Art," *Art Voices South*, March 1979.
Southern Realism. Catalogue. With essays by John B. Henry III, Tom Dewey, and Michael E. Kampen. Jackson: Mississippi Museum of Art, 1979.

1981 Burton, Marda Kaiser. "William Dunlap: Man on the Move," *American Artist*, October 1981.
The Bernhardt Collection. Catalogue. Lenoir, North Carolina: Bernhardt Furniture Industries,1981.
Franklin, Ben A. "Museum Exhibits Appalachian Art," *New York Times*, 1 November 1981.
Hertzog, Joan. "Art of Mississippi Shows Off Folks from Home," *Capital Reporter*, 18 June 1981.
Nosanow, Barbara Shissler. *More than Land or Sky: Art from Appalachia*. Catalogue. Washington, D.C.: Smithsonian Institution Press, 1981.
Richard, Paul. "Stripes and More Stripes," *Washington Post*, 2 May 1981.

1982 Howell, Camille. "Appalachia Reflected in Art," *Charlotte Observer*, 25 July 1982.

1983 Dunlap, William. "The Surrounding of Island #12," *Washington Post*, 15 May 1983.
Howell, Camille. "Dunlap's Works Speak to the South," *Charlotte Observer*, 15 May 1983.
Kotz, Mary Lynn. "The Southern Muse," *ARTnews* 82 (February 1983).
Richard, Paul. "Summoning Spirits from the Land: William Dunlap at Gallery 4," *Washington Post*, 4 March 1983.

1984 *Contemporary Art, Acquisitions: 1980–1983*. Catalogue. New York: Equitable
Life Assurance Society of the United States, 1984. Library of Congress #84-080953.
Leonard, E. *Painting the Landscape*. New York: Watson-Guptil Publications, 1984.

1985 Clarity, James F., and Warren Weaver, Jr. "Under the Corcoran Dome," *New York Times*, 26 April 1985.
Jaeger, A. J. *William Dunlap: The Painter's Landscape*. Thirty-minute video documentary, Yellow Cat Productions, premiered Public Broad casting Network, 1985.
Kessler, Pamela. "Well-Rounded William Dunlap," *Washington Post*, 26 April 1985.
Kotz, Mary Lynn. "William Dunlap, Corcoran Gallery of Art," *ARTnews* 84 (September 1985).
Livingston, Jane. *William Dunlap: The Corcoran Panorama*. Essay for exhibition. Washington, D.C.: Corcoran Gallery of Art, 1985.
Luter, Nell. "Dunlap's Work Lets People Move through an Invented Nation," *Clarion-Ledger/Jackson Daily News*, 10 November 1985.
McCoy, Mary. "William Dunlap: Corcoran Gallery of Art," *New Art Examiner* 12 (Summer 1985).
Richard, Paul. "William Dunlap," *Washington Post*, 13 June 1985.
The W. C. Bradley Company Centennial Art Collection 1985. Columbus, Georgia: W. C. Bradley Company, 1985. Library of Congress #85-71547.
Welzenbach, Michael. "Bucolic Battlefields," *Washington Post*, 21 April 1985.

1986 Livingston, Jane. "William Dunlap," *William Dunlap: Places and Things*. Catalogue. Houston, Texas: Meredith Long & Company, 1986.
Luter, Nell. "Bill Dunlap Etching Finds a Home with Rembrandt Group," *Clarion-Ledger/Jackson Daily News*, 20 July 1986.
Myers, Leslie R. "Mississippi Artist to Share Self," *Clarion-Ledger* (Jackson, Mississippi) April 1986.
Reveries and Mississippi Memories. Catalogue. Laurel, Mississippi: Lauren Rogers Museum of Art, 1986.

1987 Aiken, Edward. *Mississippi: An Illustrated History*. Jackson: University Press of Mississippi, 1987.
Bumgardner, Ed. "Portrayals of Elvis," *Winston-Salem Journal*, August 1987.
Carr, Genie. "His Massive Panorama Depicts Real Places That Don't Exist,"
Clarion-Ledger/Jackson Daily News, 1 April 1987.
Carr, Genie. "Southern Artistry," *Winston-Salem Journal*, 1 May 1987.
Chadwick, Susan. "Critic's Choice," *Houston Post*, 16 May 1987.
Heller, Faith. "Powerful, Personal Art at SECCA Shows Influence of Past," *Winston-Salem Journal*, 5 April 1987.
Hieronymus, Clara. "Mississippi Artist Touches Brush with His Heritage," *Sunday Tennessean*, 13 September 1987.
Kotz, Mary Lynn. "Man about Town: Bill Dunlap Makes His Move," *Museum & Arts, Washington* (March/April 1987).
Luter, Nell. "Dunlap's Touches Set Landscapes Apart," *Clarion-Ledger/Jackson Daily News*, 1 April 1987.
McIntyre, Mike. "The Phillips Fan Club," *Washington Post*, 16 May 1987.
Meyer, Jon. *Southeast Seven X*. Catalogue. Winston-Salem, North Carolina: Southeastern Center for Contemporary Art, 1987. Library of Congress #87-63093.
Richard, Paul. "Galleries: Work by William Dunlap," *Washington Post*, 9 May 1987.
"William Dunlap Exhibit Continues," *Footnotes, Arts in the Academy* 15.3 (April 1987).

1988 Baronoff, Susan Marya. "Culture Klatch," *Dossier* (June 1988).
Baronoff, Susan Marya. "State of the Arts: The Fine Print," *Dossier* (September 1988).
Heller, Faith. "Ten Years of 'Southeast Seven': An Abundance of Individual Visions," *The Arts Journal* (January 1988).
"Landscape Artist Dunlap to Give Lecture at Depot," *Naples Daily News*, 1 March 1988.
Lieberman, Laura C. "'Looking South: A Different Dixie' Is But Successful,"
Atlanta Journal/Atlanta Constitution, 24 November 1988.
Marin, Ray. "Southern Look," *Impressions* (November 1988).
Nelson, James R. "In 'Looking South' Exhibit Size Is Impressive Factor," *Birmingham News*, 6 November 1988.
Porcelli, Karina. "The Artists Are Coming, The Artists Are Coming," *Washington Post Magazine*, 10 January 1988.
"What's On . . . , Maitland Show Has Shades of the Season," *Orlando Sentinel*, 29 October 1988.
"William Dunlap: Recent Works," *Durham Morning Herald,* 15 May 1988.

1989 Carr, Genie. "Artists' Auction Will Help SECCA Raise Money for New Auditorium," *Winston-Salem Journal*, 22 January 1989.
"Doers Profile: William Dunlap," *Washington Times*, November 1989.
Kiss, Tony. "Asheville Art Museum Exhibits 124-foot Panorama," *Asheville Citizen-Times*, 21 May 1989.
Kotz, Mary Lynn. "William Dunlap's Northern Offensive," *Museum & Arts, Washington*, (March/April 1989).
Lucas, Sherry. "Essays and Art," *Clarion-Ledger* (Jackson, Mississippi), 16 November 1989.
Meyer, Jon. "William Dunlap at Sherry French," *ARTnews* 88 (February 1989).
Morris, Willie. *Homecomings*. With the art of William Dunlap. Jackson: University Press of Mississippi, 1989.
"Up Against the Wall," *Asheville Citizen-Times*, 28 May 1989.
Welzenbach, Michael. "Landscapes at Robert Brown," *Washington Post*, 20 May 1989.

1990 "Dunlap Panorama Is a Corporate Favorite," *Corporate Art Newsletter*, May 1990.
Duvall, Lynn. "Dunlap Says What Counts Is His Art," *Birmingham News*, 17 June 1990.
Hatch, George. "Cadmium Fight Just Won't Fade," *Los Angeles Times*, 28 May 1990.
McDavid, O. C. "Dunlap Comes Home with Exhibit

of New Works," *Clarion-Ledger* (Jackson, Mississippi), May 1990.
Nelson, James. "Dunlap's Art Compels Viewer to Think about View," *Birmingham News*, June 1990.
Tully, Judd. "Primary Colors," *Art & Auction* (September 1990).
"William Dunlap, Paintings," *Eye Wash: The Washington Artist's Tabloid* 2.3 (April 1990).
Welzenbach, Michael. "Dunlap: Mississippi Native," *Washington Post*, 14 April 1990.
1991 McCoy, Mary. "Landscapes Made from Memory," *Washington Post*, 30 November 1991.
Nordheimer, Jon. "Couples Who Thread 225-Mile Tightrope," *New York Times*, 22 August 1991.
1992 McKenzie, Danny. "Successful Artist Renews His Roots in College Return," *Clarion-Ledger* (Jackson, Mississippi), 26 October 1992.
Pardee, Hearne. "William Dunlap at Sherry French," *ARTnews* 91 (March 1992).
Schwan, Gary. "Paintings of the Land We Love: French Gallery Offers Landscape Exhibition," *Palm Beach Post*, 17 April 1992.
Twardy, Chuck. "Living off the Landscape: Southern Artists Take a Scenic Route," *News & Observer* (Raleigh, North Carolina), 25 September 1992.
1993 Crawford, Bob. "William Dunlap Exhibit Is Lively and Challenging," *Roanoke Times & World-News*, 10 January 1993.
Donner, Rebecca. "Artist Captures America's Contemporary Landscape," *Sentinel-Record* (Hot Springs, Arkansas), 6 August 1993.
Morris, Willie. "Re-collections Captures Breadth of Dunlap's Work," *Clarion-Ledger* (Jackson, Mississippi), 22 July 1993.
1994 Richard, Paul. "A Cornerstone of Beauty," *Washington Post*, 11 May 1994.
1995 Dunlap, William. "Don't Label Us as 'Local,'" *Washington Post*, 17 April 1995.
Dunlap, Bill, and Linda Burgess. "Protecting Asia's Heritage," *ARTnews* 94 (April 1995).
1996 Downs, Buck. "William Dunlap," *Washington Review* (April/May 1996).
Patterson, Tom. "A Sense of Place," *Winston-Salem Journal*, 15 December 1996.
1997 Dunlap, William, and Linda Burgess. "Picturing the Past. Cambodia," *Washington Review* 23.1 (June/July 1997).
"The Museum Is Their Muse," *Washington Post*, 9 November 1997.
1999 Dunlap, William. "Bring Me the Head of Gore Vidal," *Washingtonian Magazine* (November 1999).
2000 Dunlap, William. "John Singer Sargent: Outside the Frame," *WETA Magazine* (April 2000).
"Galleries: Ferdinand Protzman Gallery," *Washington Post*, 13 April 2000.
2001 Conaway, Jim. "Suddenly a Capital Back in Focus," *Washington Post*, 14 October 2001.
Dunlap, William. "Art in Cuba: The Island of Reflected Images," *Washington Post*, 18 February 2001.
Gerhardt, Ann, and Dana Montgomery. "Cipro Nation," *Washington Post*, 24 October 2001.
2002 "The Reliable Source," *Washington Post*, 22 April 2002.
"Uncommon Ground," *News and Register* (Wheeling, West Virginia), 23 June 2002.
2003 Dunlap, William, and Linda Burgess. "The Art of Philosophy," *Art & Antiques* (January 2003).
Patton, Phil. "Driving: The Changing South Finds Its Way on I-85," *New York Times*, 11 July 2003.
Roberts, Roxanne. "Out and About," *Washington Post*, 15 December 2003.
2004 Forster, Steven. "Big Easy," *Times-Picayune* (New Orleans), 9 May 2004.
Reed, Julia. "A Fan's Notes," *New York Times Magazine*, 1 February 2004.
Reed, Julia. "Worlds Apart," *Vanity Fair* (April 2004).
Roberts, Roxanne. "Reliable Source," *Washington Post*, 30 November 2004.
2005 Heleander, Bruce. "Hypothetical Realism," *South Florida Times*, February 2005.
Roberts, Roxanne. "Reliable Source," *Washington Post*, 16 October 2005.
2006 Bostick, Kamille. "Morris Museum of Art: Major Acquisition Celebrated," *Augusta Chronicle*, 4 March 2006.
Uhles, Steven. "Dogs Dream at the Morris," *Augusta Chronicle*, 2–8 March 2006.

Title Index

www.upress.state.ms.us
The University Press of Mississippi is a member
of the Association of American University Presses.

Designed by John A. Langston

Manufactured in China

First edition 2006

Page 1: Details: Top, left and right: *Rembrandt and Titus—Father and Son,* 2002. Polymer paint on canvas, wood, slate, leather, metal, found objects; triptych, 30 x 120 x 11. Collection of Lauren Rogers Museum of Art, Laurel, Mississippi. Photograph by Jack Meyer. Bottom, left and right: *All That Glitters . . .*, 2004. Wood, canvas, clay, slate, tortoise shell, velvet, leather, gold leaf, tin-type, found objects; triptych, 32 1/2 x 102. Collection of Sharon and Bruce Bradley, Washington, D.C. Photograph by Jack Meyer.
Page 2–3: *Valley View Fog Lift,* 1994. Polymer paint on canvas, diptych, 48 x 192. Private collection. Photograph by Lisa Berg.
Page 4: Detail from *Panorama of the American Landscape,* 1985. Photograph by Jack Kotz.

Library of Congress Cataloging-in-Publication Data
Dunlap, William, 1944–
Dunlap / William Dunlap ; with a foreword by Julia Reed and an introduction by J. Richard Gruber. — 1st ed.
p. cm.
Includes bibliographical references and index.
ISBN-13: 978-1-57806-904-0 (cloth : alk. paper)
ISBN-10: 1-57806-904-1 (cloth : alk. paper) 1. Dunlap, William, 1944—Catalogs. I. Gruber, J. Richard. II. Title.
N6537.D85A4 2006
759'.13—dc22 2006013155
British Library Cataloging-in-Publication Data available

Gladiolus
in Tropical Africa